Business Model Innovation

Business Model Innovation

The Organizational Dimension

Edited by

Nicolai J. Foss and Tina Saebi

OXFORD
UNIVERSITY PRESS

Great Clarendon Street, Oxford, OX2 6DP,
United Kingdom

Oxford University Press is a department of the University of Oxford.
It furthers the University's objective of excellence in research, scholarship,
and education by publishing worldwide. Oxford is a registered trade mark of
Oxford University Press in the UK and in certain other countries

© Oxford University Press 2015

The moral rights of the authors have been asserted

First Edition published in 2015

Impression: 3

Published in the United States of America by Oxford University Press
198 Madison Avenue, New York, NY 10016, United States of America

British Library Cataloguing in Publication Data
Data available

Library of Congress Control Number: 2014953300

ISBN 978-0-19-870187-3

Printed and bound by
CPI Group (UK) Ltd, Croydon, CR0 4YY

CONTENTS

▨ LIST OF ILLUSTRATIONS

LIST OF TABLES

LIST OF CONTRIBUTORS

Shaz Ansari is a Reader (Associate Professor) at Judge Business School, University of Cambridge and Visiting Faculty at Rotterdam School of Management, Erasmus University. He holds a Ph.D. from the University of Cambridge. He serves on the Editorial Boards of Academy of Management Review, Organization Science, Journal of Management Studies and Organization Studies, and is a member of Erasmus Research Institute of Management (ERIM). His research interests include institutional processes and diffusion of practices; social movements, social and environmental issues in management, technological and management innovations; value creation and new markets; reputation management and bottom-of-the-pyramid strategies.

Julian Birkinshaw is Professor of Strategy & Entrepreneurship at the London Business School. His research focuses on strategy, innovation, and management in large, multinational corporations. He is a Fellow of the British Academy and a Fellow of the Academy of International Business.

Marcel Bogers is Associate Professor of Innovation and Entrepreneurship at the Mads Clausen Institute at the University of Southern Denmark. He obtained a combined B.Sc. and M.Sc. in Technology and Society (Innovation Sciences) from Eindhoven University of Technology and a Ph.D. in Management of Technology from Ecole Polytechnique Fédérale de Lausanne (Swiss Federal Institute of Technology). His main interests center around the design, organization, and management of technology, innovation, and entrepreneurship in general, and on openness and participation in innovation and entrepreneurial processes in particular. More specifically, he has studied areas such as business models, open innovation, users as innovators, collaborative prototyping, improvization, and learning-by-doing.

Ramon Casadesus-Masanell is the Herman C. Krannert Professor of Business Administration at Harvard Business School. He received his Ph.D. in Managerial Economics and Strategy from the Kellogg Graduate School of Management, Northwestern University. Casadesus-Masanell's fields of specialization are management strategy, managerial economics, and industrial organization. He studies strategic interaction between organizations that operate different business models. He is also interested in the limits to contracting and the role of trust for management strategy. He has published in *Management Science*, the *Journal of Economics & Management Strategy*, the *Strategic Management Journal*, the *Academy of Management Review*, *Long Range Planning*, the *Journal of Law & Economics*, the *Journal of Economic Theory*, the *USC Interdisciplinary Law Journal*, and the *Harvard Business Review*, among others.

Massimo G. Colombo is Full Professor of Innovation Economics, Entrepreneurship, and Entrepreneurial Finance at Politecnico di Milano. His areas of research include the organization, financing, and growth of high-tech entrepreneurial ventures, strategic alliances, acquisitions and open innovation, and innovation and entrepreneurship policy. Professor Colombo is Associate Editor of the *Journal of Small Business Management*. He is the author of numerous books, including *The Economics of Organizational Design* (Palgrave Macmillan, 2008), and has published more than 70 articles in international journals such as the *Strategic Management Journal*, the *Journal of Industrial Economics, Research Policy*, the *Journal of Business Venturing, Entrepreneurship Theory & Practice*, and many others.

Nicolai J. Foss is Professor and Department Head at the Copenhagen Business School. He also holds professorial positions at the Warwick Business School and the Norwegian School of Economics. His work mainly addresses the role of resources and organizational design in a strategy context, and has been published in the major management journals.

Daniel Kindström is Associate Professor of Industrial Marketing at Linköping University in Sweden. He is currently conducting research on service infusion, proactive market strategies, and dynamic business models. His research appears in journals such as *Journal of Business Research, European Management Journal, Journal of Service Management*, and *Journal of Business & Industrial Marketing*, as well as in several books and contributed chapters.

Christian Kowalkowski is Assistant Professor of Marketing in the Centre for Relationship Marketing and Service Management at Hanken School of Economics, Finland. He also holds a part-time position as Associate Professor of Industrial Marketing at Linköping University, Sweden. His current research activities concern service infusion, relationship dynamics, service innovation, and solutions marketing. He serves as an Associate Editor of the *Journal of Services Marketing* and has published articles in journals such as *European Journal of Marketing, Industrial Marketing Management, Journal of Business Research*, and *Journal of Business & Industrial Marketing*.

Sunyoung Leih is a postdoctoral scholar at the University of California, Berkeley. She received her Ph.D. in Management Studies from the University of Oxford and has (co-) authored articles and book chapters on strategic management, particularly the role of dynamic capabilities in the competitive performance of business enterprise. Her research on strategic management includes work on the cross-border transfer of organizational practices and on the management of intangibles such as knowledge and reputation. Prior to receiving her doctorate, she worked at the World Bank in Washington DC on poverty reduction for low-income countries.

Greg Linden is a post-doctoral Research Associate at the Institute for Business Innovation, a research unit at the Haas School of Business, UC Berkeley. He has authored numerous articles about the globalization of value creation and capture in high-tech sectors and co-authored *Chips and Change* (MIT Press, 2009) about the semiconductor industry. He holds a Master's Degree in Public Policy and a Ph.D. in Economics and has worked as a consultant on industrial policy projects in Asia.

Costas Markides is Professor of Strategy and Entrepreneurship and holds the Robert P. Bauman Chair of Strategic Leadership at the London Business School. A native of Cyprus, he received his BA (Distinction, 1983) and MA (1984) in Economics from Boston University, and his MBA (1985) and DBA (1990) from the Harvard Business School. He serves on the Editorial Boards of several academic journals and is on the Board of Directors of the Strategic Management Society. He has published several books on the topics of strategy and innovation. His current research explores business model innovation and the diffusion of social innovations.

Ali Mohammadi is a postdoctoral Research Fellow at the Center of Excellence for Science and Innovation Studies and Department of Industrial Economics and Management, Royal Institute of Technology, Sweden. His research focuses on entrepreneurship and innovation specializing in venture capital, business model innovation, and technology commercialization strategies. His research has been published in the *Journal of Industry and Innovation* and has been presented in several international conferences. His research has been awarded Pagliarani Best Paper Award, XXIV Scientific Meeting of the Italian Association of Management Engineering and has been selected as semi-finalist for best paper award, 2014 Financial Management Association annual meeting.

Torben Pedersen is a Professor in Global Strategy at Bocconi University, Italy. He received his Ph.D. from the Copenhagen Business School. His research interests are located at the interface between strategy and international business, and the focus is mainly on globalization, organizational design, off-shoring/outsourcing, knowledge management, and subsidiary strategies. He has published more than 100 journal articles and books on these topics, including in top journals such as the *Academy of Management Journal, Strategic Management Journal*, the *Journal of International Business Studies*, and the *Journal of Management*, among others. He is co-editor of the *Global Strategy Journal* and serves on several editorial boards. In addition, he is a Fellow of the Academy of International Business.

Klement A. Rasmussen is a Ph.D. Fellow at the Department of Strategic Management and Globalization at Copenhagen Business School. His main areas of research is in strategic management, notably business models and business model innovation and organizational design.

Joan E. Ricart, Fellow of the SMS and EURAM, is the Carl Schrøder Professor of Strategic Management and Chairman of the Strategic Management Department at the IESE Business School, University of Navarra. He was Director of the Doctoral Program (1995–2006), Associate Dean for Research (2001–2006), and Associate

Director for Faculty and Research (2006–2014). He is also Vice-president of the Iberoamerican Academy of Management. He was the Founding President of the European Academy of Management (EURAM) and President of the Strategic Management Society (SMS). He has published several books and articles in leading journals such as *Strategic Management Journal, Harvard Business Review, Journal of International Business Studies, Econometrica* and the *Quarterly Journal of Economics.*

Cristina Rossi-Lamastra is Associate Professor at the Politecnico di Milano School of Management. Her research interests are in the area of entrepreneurship, innovation, and organizational economics. Her studies in Open Source Software (OSS) deal mainly with firms' involvement in the OSS movement (business models, incentives, project participation, innovation processes). Cristina has published on these topics in *Management Science, Entrepreneurship Theory and Practice, Research Policy, Economic Letters, Industry & Innovation, Long Range Planning, Small Business Economics,* and others. She is Associate Editor of the *Journal of Small Business Management* and of the *Journal of Industrial and Business Economics.*

Tina Saebi works as a postdoctoral research fellow at the Center for Service Innovation (CSI) at the Norwegian School of Economics since January 2012. Her research focuses on business model innovation, strategic management, and dynamic capabilities. She obtained her M. Sc. degree in International Business Studies in 2005 and her Ph.D. from Maastricht University, School of Business and Economics in 2011.

José F. P. dos (Joe) Santos is Affiliated Professor of Practice in Global Management at INSEAD, Fontainebleau, and "Professor Catedrático Convidado" at the Universidade Católica Portuguesa, Porto. His career spans managerial work and scholarly work in different countries and continents. His research, teaching, and consulting are devoted to the general management of the multinational enterprise, with particular focus on the management of global integration and global innovation.

Henrik Sornn-Friese is Associate Professor at Copenhagen Business School, where he is Academic Director of *CBS Maritime*, as well as Director of CBS' flagship MSc program in *Economics and Business Administration*. He is author or co-author of several books and contributed chapters about shipping, as well as numerous articles in leading international journals such as *Transportation Journal, Industry and Innovation, Research Policy, International Journal of Maritime History,* and *Business History*. His works on the Danish maritime cluster have impacted directly on recent Danish maritime policy.

Bert Spector is Associate Professor of International Business and Management at Northeastern University's D'Amore-McKim School of Business. His research interests include organizational change, leadership, business model innovation, and management history. His articles have appeared in *Leadership, Management & Organizational History*, and the *Harvard Business Review*. His co-authored *The Critical Path to Corporate Renewal* (Harvard Business School Press, 1990, with

Michael Beer and Russell Eisenstadt), received the Johnson, Smith and Knisely Award for New Perspectives on Executive Leadership. He is currently completing *Leadership Discourse and Meaning*, scheduled to be published by Cambridge University Press in 2015.

Nils Stieglitz is Professor of Strategy at the Frankfurt School of Finance & Management. His research interests include organizational adaptation, strategic decision making, and organization design and he has been published in leading management journals such as *Management Science, Organization Science*, and the *Strategic Management Journal*.

Kristian J. Sund is Associate Professor of Strategy and Organization at Roskilde University in Denmark, where he heads the research group Management in Transition. Kristian holds an M.Sc. in Economics and Doctorate in Management from the University of Lausanne (HEC Lausanne) and an M.A. in Society, Science, and Technology from the Swiss Federal Institute of Technology (EPFL), where he also completed his post-doctoral research. His research currently focuses on business model innovation, organizational cognition, and perceived environmental uncertainty. He has authored and edited several books, including the acclaimed book series "The Future is in the Post" (Libri, 2010).

Jorge Tarziján is a Full Professor of Strategy at the School of Management, Pontificia Universidad Catolica de Chile and has been a Visiting Scholar at Harvard University. He received his Ph.D. in Managerial Economics and Strategy from the Kellogg G.S.M. Northwestern University and an M.Sc. from Katholieke Universiteit Leuven. He does research on corporate strategy, with particular emphasis on firms' boundaries, relational contracts, and the determinants of the firm's internal organization. He has published in *Strategic Management Journal*, the *Journal of Economic Behavior and Organization, Industrial and Corporate Change*, the *Journal of Business Research, B.E. Journal of Economic Analysis and Policy*, and *Harvard Business Review*, among others.

David J. Teece is the Tusher Professor in Global Business and the Director of the Tusher Center on Intellectual Capital at the Haas School of Business at the University of California, Berkeley. He has published six books and over 200 articles in which he has analyzed the role of product, process development, and intellectual property in the competitive performance of the enterprise. He is also Founder and Chairman of Berkeley Research Group, LLC ('BRG'), for which he also consults.

Ludo Van der Heyden is Professor of Technology and Operations Management and the Chaired Professor of Corporate Governance at INSEAD and the Academic Director of INSEAD's Corporate Governance Initiative. He has published in many journals, such as the *Journal of Economic Theory, Mathematics of Operations Research, Mathematical Programming*, the *International Journal of Game Theory*, and the *Harvard Business Review*, the *International Commerce Review*, and the *Family*

Business Review. Ludo Van der Heyden was co-Dean of INSEAD and was appointed as the first Honorary Professor of the recreated Handelshochschüle Leipzig. Before joining INSEAD, he taught at Harvard and Yale Universities.

Juan Andrei Villarroel holds a Ph.D. in Management of Technology from Ecole Polytechnique Fédérale de Lausanne, and an M.Sc. from Carnegie Mellon University. He has been on the faculty at Católica-Lisbon School of Business and Economics, visiting scholar at the University of Pennsylvania, visiting scholar at MIT Center for Collective Intelligence, and international Faculty Fellow at MIT Sloan School of Management. Dr Villarroel led several symposia on crowdsourcing at the Academy of Management (since 2007), co-authored the book *Leading Open Innovation* (MIT Press, 2013), and was invited as keynote speaker for the Deans and Directors annual meetings of EFMD and CEEMAN.

1 Business Models and Business Model Innovation

Bringing Organization into the Discussion

NICOLAI J. FOSS AND TINA SAEBI[*]

Introduction

The notion that companies have "business models" has become extremely influential, although perhaps still more so in the communication of business people and in the business press than in the management research literature. And yet, the latter literature has most definitely taken off within the last decade. With over 1,200 articles published in peer-reviewed academic journals between 1995 and 2010 addressing the notion of business models since (Zott, Amit, and Massa, 2011), the business model construct has gained substantial currency across strategy, entrepreneurship, and innovation literatures. There is little doubt that the construct resonates within several, overlapping communities, both practice-oriented and scholarly.

Much of the attraction of the business model construct arguably lies in its holistic approach. Thus, business models are sometimes characterized as mental constructs—presumably mainly residing in the upper managerial echelons of a company—that define the structure of the interlocking activities associated with key strategic choices. The relevant strategic choices relate to the firm's fundamental value proposition(s), the markets and market segments it addresses, the structure of the value chain which is required for realizing the relevant value proposition, and the mechanisms of value capture that the firm deploys, including its competitive strategy. Teece (2010: 172) summarizes this by stating that the "... essence of a business model is in defining the manner by which the enterprise delivers value to customers, entices customers to pay for value, and converts those payments to profit."

* We gratefully acknowledge support from the Center for Service Innovation at the Norwegian School of Economics, where Tina Saebi has been employed as a Post-doctoral Research Fellow. We also thank Anders Pico for efficient editorial work.

It is intuitive that this "manner" can be highly firm-specific and may thus serve to differentiate the firm in the marketplace. It is similarly intuitive that because of this firm-specificity and the underlying complexity that a business model contains, advantages associated with such differentiation may be hard to eliminate (e.g., by imitation) by the competition. Along similar lines, the firm that possesses a successful model may also be in a privileged position to change, renew, and even innovate that model. Such thinking has not been lost on the business community: Surveying more than 4,000 senior managers, a global survey conducted by the Economist Intelligence Unit (2005) found that the majority of managers preferred new business models over new products and services as a source of future competitive advantage. Similarly, an IBM survey (IBM Global Business Services, 2006) confirmed that managers increasingly perceive innovative business models as the key to sustained competitive advantage (Amit and Zott, 2012).

However, in spite of such massive resonance, in the academic as well as the practitioner community, much, and perhaps most, of the extant literature on business models and the innovation thereof suffers from deep-seated conceptual problems, little cumulative theorizing, and a lack of a sustained data collection and analysis. Thus, definitions of the core construct proliferate (in fact, there is some definitional variation across the chapters in this book), scholars do not scrupulously cite each other, and single-firm cases dominate empirical inquiry. By most standards, this seems problematic. However, these are typical characteristics of an emerging field rather than characteristics of bad research, and there are reasons to optimistically expect that these characteristics will gradually disappear as research in business models becomes increasingly cumulative.

In any case, it may seem to be something of a stretch to add more complexity to an influential, yet emerging and complex discourse, as we do in this volume, pressing the argument that the literatures on business models and business model innovation need to embrace organizational theory (in a broad sense). And yet, we argue that bringing organizational considerations into the discourse has the potential to clarify and align rather than confuse. Consider again the notion of a "model." On one understanding of this notion, namely the one that engineers and social scientists (notably economists) ascribe to, a model is fundamentally a set of relations between variables designed to capture reality in an essential way. Note that those who think of a business model in terms of managerial cognition hold a similar view: The mental model represents the key relations between the key elements of the firm's business. The point here, however, is that a model goes beyond the mere elements or variables; it also includes the *relations* between those elements or variables. In a nutshell, *our key argument is that in the context of a company, these relations are fundamentally organizational.*

Relations are organizational in a trivial sense—namely, these relations are embedded in the firm. However, more substantively they are organizational in the sense that they involve decision processes and outcomes, communication, interdependencies, decision authority, performance assessment and key performance indicators (KPIs), rewards, job descriptions, implicit and explicit contracts, and so on. This is the stuff from which organizational structure and control are made. Indeed, some notions of business models (and, per implication, business model innovation) make this point implicitly. For example, Zott and Amit (2010) place organization centrally, namely as part of the very definition of a business model. Thus, they argue that business models can be understood in terms of transaction content (i.e., value propositions), transaction structure—and transaction *governance*. Of course, the governance part directly links to the organizational dimension (Williamson, 1996).

Teece (2010) argues that the "architecture" of the firm's value creation and appropriation mechanisms is the hallmark of a business model. Although Teece does not specify this, an important part of an architecture is the organizational structure and control that supports the activities that allow the company to make its value proposition to the marketplace and embed the human and social capital that, with other resources, add value in those activities. In this volume, Santos, Spector, and Van der Heyden (chapter 3) argue that business models are all about "How is it being done?" rather than "What is being done?," "What is the segment being addressed?," and "How is revenue being captured?" The underlying argument is that business models uniquely address "how" issues, whereas the other issues are treated in the extant body of literature on marketing and competitive strategy. In such an interpretation, business models are fundamentally about the activities under the control of the firm that allow it to exploit an identified opportunity in the marketplace, and therefore also the structures and relations between the firm and its multiple stakeholders that support the value creation and value-capturing processes of the firm. Similarly, George and Bock (2011: 99) note that a "business model is the design of organizational structures to enact a commercial opportunity." In this volume, Birkinshaw and Ansari (chapter 5) even coin a new term for this organizational dimension of the business model, namely the "management model": "A firm's management model is the choices it makes about *how* work gets done—how activities are coordinated, how decisions are made, how objectives are set, and how employees are motivated."

Another fundamental organizational issue relates to the question at what level in the organization a business model exists. The literature does not provide any clear-cut answer to this. In this volume, Casadesus-Masanell, Ricart, and Tarziján (chapter 4) argue that business models exist at the level of business units. They may, however, reflect overarching corporate models.

In sum, scratching the surface of the business model construct immediately raises all sorts of fundamentally organizational concerns. In the remainder of this introductory chapter we discuss why it is important to link business models and business model innovation to the "organizational dimension," and we discuss the role of organization as an antecedent and moderator of business model innovation. We end by surveying the various ways in which the chapters in this volume meet the imperative of adding organizational content to our understanding of business model innovation.

Business Models and the Innovation Thereof

A BURGEONING LITERATURE

The notion of a "business model" has emerged as one of the most used pieces of management lingo over the last two decades, and is used constantly in the business press, in conversations between venture capitalists and those who seek their financial support, in the assessments firms make of competitors, and so on. It has entered the realm of political discourse, as when President Obama called for changes in the auto industry's business model as a crucial step in the recovery of that industry (Levi, 2009). There is clearly a very strong communicative appeal to the concept, arguably because of its holistic nature. For example, business models include more than the firm's current (business and marketing) strategy, and direct attention to the activities and the underlying organization that enable this strategy.

Moreover, the notion of a "model" has inherent attractions: A "model" is something that can be inspected, measured, and ascertained. Moreover, models can be replicated. Thus, entrepreneurs stand a better chance of getting funding from venture capitalists and other financiers when they can make convincing claims that they are not just pitching a value proposition, but a value proposition that is supported by value-chain activities, an identification of distinct segments and value appropriation mechanisms, and can perhaps also argue that all this is replicable.

In academic research, the business model construct has served multiple purposes, amongst others (1) as a basis for classification of firms (e.g., Timmers, 1998; Rappa, 2001; Amit and Zott, 2001; Osterwalder, Pigneur, and Tucci, 2005); (2) as an antecedent of heterogeneity in firm performances (e.g., Zott and Amit, 2010; Weill et al., 2005); and (3) as a new form of innovation (e.g., Teece, 2010; Markides, 2006).

As a classification device, the business model construct gained particular popularity in the early 2000s. As a response to the emergence of new e-business ventures, the business model construct was employed to understand and classify value drivers of (e-commerce) business models (cf. Amit and Zott, 2001; Rappa, 2001; Margretta, 2002; etc). Business models, with their simultaneous focus on value creation and value capture mechanisms were found more suitable to explain these "new forms of doing business" as compared to more traditional concepts in strategy. Research feeding into this discipline centered mostly on the definition of the construct, putting forward numerous definitions (Morris, Schindehutte, and Allen, 2005), typologies (e.g., Timmers, 1998), ontologies (Osterwalder, Pigneur, and Tucci, 2005), and taxonomies of business model (Weill et al., 2005) in an effort to categorize firms, especially in an e-business context.

A second wave of research brought forward an increased interest in the performance implications of business models. Largely rooted in strategic management research, business models are argued to be an important factor contributing to firm performance (cf. Dunford, Palmer, and Benveniste, 2010). As some types of business models are found to outperform others (cf. Zott and Amit, 2007, 2010; Weill et al., 2005), successful business models are seen as examples to be imitated (cf. Baden-Fuller and Morgan, 2010; Teece, 2010; Chesbrough, 2010) or replicated (Winter and Szulanski, 2001; Doz and Kosonen, 2010).

Finally, a research stream has considered business models as both a vehicle *and* a source of innovation. Research focusing on business models as enablers of innovation has described the business model as a "focusing device that mediates between technology development and economic value creation" (Chesbrough and Rosenbloom, 2002: 532). Relatedly, business models are increasingly perceived as a promising new unit of analysis and starting point for innovation strategies. Research in this field is often centered on identifying different types and dimensions of business model innovation (cf. Giesen et al., 2010). In this volume, Stieglitz and Foss (chapter 6) build on the economics of complementarity as well as the innovation literature to conceptualize and dimensionalize business model innovation. This research stream also highlights the potential of innovative business models to disrupt the "rules of the game" and transform industries or markets (cf. Voelpel, Leibold, and Tekie, 2004; Markides, 2006; Casadesus-Masanell and Ricart, 2011).

Notably, these streams within the overall business model literature have largely evolved in relatively isolated silos across various disciplines such as innovation management, strategic management, and entrepreneurship literatures without much interaction. Because the field is a new one and because it reaches across a number of heterogeneous management research streams, the business model field exhibits many "pre-paradigmatic" (cf. Kuhn, 1970) characteristics such as unclear core constructs, lack of theoretical foundations, and a lack of evidence based on empirics that goes beyond small-N samples with their characteristic problem of sometimes getting dangerously close to sampling on the dependent variable. Perhaps the core problem is that of lack of construct clarity. Such clarity matters much to the coordination of research efforts and hence the progress of knowledge.

UNCLEAR CORE CONSTRUCTS I: BUSINESS MODELS

In spite of their widespread use, the terms "business model" and "business model innovation" are not at all unambiguous. The term "business model" was introduced in the late 1950s but hardly used in popular or research publications until the 1990s, and only with the hype of the Internet did it reach a first peak in 2000 (Osterwalder et al., 2005; Zott, Amit, and Massa, 2011). To date, the concepts remain ambiguous as there is no commonly accepted or dominant theory or definition of business models. Thus, as Zott, Amit, and Massa (2011: 4) note in their impressive overview of the field:

> At a general level, the business model has been referred to as a statement (Stewart and Zhao, 2000), a description (Applegate, 2000; Weill and Vitale, 2001), a representation (Morris, Schindehutte, and Allen, 2005; Shafer, Smith, and Linder, 2005), an architecture (Dubosson-Torbay, Osterwalder, and Pigneur, 2002; Timmers, 1998), a conceptual tool or model (George and Bock, 2009; Osterwalder, 2004; Osterwalder, Pigneur, and Tucci, 2005), a structural template (Amit and Zott, 2001), a method (Afuah and Tucci, 2001), a framework (Afuah, 2004), a pattern (Brousseau and Penard, 2006), and a set (Seelos and Mair, 2007). Surprisingly, however, the business model is often studied without an explicit definition of the concept.

George and Bock (2011: 83) similarly point out that "definitions for business models vary widely, incorporating organizational narrative (Magretta, 2002), processes that convert innovation into value (Chesbrough and Rosenbloom, 2002), recipes for firm activities that incorporate organizational design and strategy (Slywotzky and Wise, 2003), 'flows' of information and resources (Timmers, 1998), and designed structures such as the firm's set of boundary-spanning transactions (Amit and Zott, 2001)."

Scholars often insist on the importance of construct clarity (e.g., Suddaby, 2010). Indeed, having core constructs that are clearly defined assists the coordination of research efforts and thus promotes the growth of knowledge. On the other hand, the history of social science is replete with core constructs that, while being ambiguous for a long time (or even permanently), have nevertheless been central in massive and often fruitful research efforts (e.g., in economics, the "utility" and "aggregate demand" constructs may serve as illustrations; in management, notions of "competence" or "capability" may be illustrations). The literatures on business models and the innovation thereof are no exception to this. Much research has been done and continues to be done in spite of continuing conceptual confusion.[1] Thus, the business model construct is used to denote rather different things, "... such as parts of a business model (e.g. auction model), types of business models (e.g. direct-to-customer model), concrete real world instances of business models

---

[1] There are, however, indications that we are now moving toward a "theorization stage" of the business model literature. As Lecocq, Demil, and Ventura (2010) observe, there has been an increase in studies that seek to anchor the construct in existing theories such as transaction-cost theory, entrepreneurship theories, RBV, or the Penrosian view of the firm, linking it to phenomena such as strategic change (e.g., Sosna, Trevinyo-Rodriguez, and Velamuri, 2010), performance (Amit and Zott, 2001), innovation (Chesbrough and Rosenbloom, 2002), replication (Winter and Szuanski, 2001), and competition (Casadesus-Masanell and Zhu, 2013). This development also gradually entails more explicit definitions, more theoretical foundations, some empirical evidence, and more and more relations with established research in, mainly, strategic management.

(e.g. the Dell model) or concepts (elements and relationships of a model)" (Osterwalder, Pigneur, and Tucci, 2005: 8).

Given this ambiguity in definitions and components, it is not surprising that there is no unified typology of business models or business model archetypes. For example, Afuah and Tucci (2001) propose three "generic strategies" of business models, including "run," "block," and "team-up" strategy. Zott and Amit (2010: 7) identify four "dominant value drivers": (i) novelty (adopt innovative content, structure, or governance), (ii) lock-in (build in elements to retain business model stakeholders such as customers), (iii) complementarities (bundle activities to generate more value), and (iv) efficiency (reorganize activities to reduce transaction cost). Similarly, Osterwalder and Pigneur (2010) characterize business models in terms of "patterns" such as "long tail," "multi-sided platforms," "freemium," and "open business models." Yet in another approach, business models are characterized based on the questions of "what rights are being sold" and "what type of asset are involved," resulting in fourteen different types of business models (Weill et al., 2005).

UNCLEAR CORE CONSTRUCTS II: BUSINESS MODEL INNOVATION

The disagreement among scholars about what a business model is complicates conceptualizing business model *innovation*. While practitioners and many researchers alike seem to agree on the strategic importance of business model innovation as a new source of competitive advantage (cf. Chesbrough, 2010; Teece, 2010; Ho, Fang, and Hsieh, 2011; Zott and Amit, 2007), the definitions used of business model innovation vary greatly across research studies. Definitions differ considerably with regard to what it is that constitutes such an innovation, such as in terms of novelty or radicalness or the role business model innovation plays in enhancing a firm's performance. For example, while some suggest that business model innovation needs to be new to the firm (cf. Johnson, Christensen, and Kagermann, 2008; Osterwalder, Pigneur, and Tucci, 2005), others, including most of the contributors to this volume, argue that it has to be new to the industry as well.

Not surprisingly, there is no dominant approach to conceptualizing and classifying business model innovation. For example, while Koen, Bertels, and Elsum (2011) classify business model innovation along the three dimensions of innovation in technology, value network, and financial hurdle rate, Giesen et al. (2007) and Lindgart et al. (2009) conceptualize business model innovation as innovations in value proposition, revenue model, and operating model. Others have typified business model innovation either by origin of innovation (i.e., the firm innovates its business model as a response to a threat or an opportunity) or by degree of innovativeness (i.e., market breakthrough vs. industry breakthrough, incremental vs. comprehensive innovation) (cf. Bucherer, Eisert, and Gassman, 2012).

EMERGING SHARED MEANINGS?

In spite of the extant differences in the definition and conceptualization of business models and the innovation thereof, a gradual convergence in meaning is becoming apparent in extant literature. Researchers seem to converge on the basic understanding that business models denote the firm's core logic for creating and capturing value by specifying the firm's fundamental value proposition(s), the markets and market segments it addresses, the structure of the value chain which is required for realizing the relevant value proposition, and the mechanisms of value capture that the firm deploys, including its competitive strategy (e.g., Teece, 2010). More specifically, business models refer to the system of activities underlying these value propositions, segments, value-chain structures, and revenue models, that is, the activities themselves and how they are linked in an architecture.

Indeed, if notions such as "model," "system," and "architecture" are seen as essential, these linkages become a key aspect of the business model. This directs attention to relations, communication, contracts, etc. Thus, a key aspect of business models is the structures and relations between the firm and its multiple stakeholders that support the value creation and value-capturing processes of the firm. In turn, a firm's organizational design is an inherent part of a firm's business model so as to support the firm's chosen strategy. Given this understanding, business model innovation may be defined as a realignment of activities, relations, routines, and contracts which results in a new configuration of how the firm creates and captures value that is the new to the product/service market in which the firm competes. Adopting this perspective brings us in close contact with extant theorizing on organizations and allows us to generate conceptual and empirical work that contributes to developing a cumulative, rigorous, and testable theory of business model innovation.

Why Organization Matters to Business Model Innovation: Antecedent, Moderator, and Configurational Elements

DEFINING "ORGANIZATION"

Pragmatically, we can think of "organization" as "that which is addressed by the rich body of organizational theory." In particular, we are interested in those parts of organizational theory that deal with the designable parts of organizations, that is, the boundaries and internal structuring of organizations. While organizational belief systems, culture, and psychological contracts surely matter to organizational performance, they are also dimensions of organizations that are arguably less given to direct design. They can be influenced by managerial and leadership actions as well as by the formal organizational design in place, but only indirectly. Moreover, the links between the levers that managers can pull and the outcomes in terms of consequences for, for example, organizational culture, are many, complex, and uncertain. Perhaps for this reason most of the contributions to this volume establish a link between business model innovation and organization in terms of organizational design. However, the chapters by Birkinshaw and Ansari (chapter 5) and Stieglitz and Foss (chapter 6) do touch on these softer aspects of organizations.

A large body of work on organizational design has identified a set of key variables along which organizational structure—that is, the "relatively enduring allocation of work roles and administrative mechanisms that creates a pattern of interrelated work activities" (Jackson and Morgan, 1982: 81)—can be characterized (e.g., Burton and Obel, 2004; Burns and Stalker, 1961; Galbraith, 1974; Miller and Dröge, 1986), such as (job and unit) specialization (with an implied allocation of decision rights, i.e., authority), and coordination by means of (workflow) formalization,[2] rules and targets, and other elements of planning. New business models typically involve changes in the organization's formal structure. In this volume, the chapter by Santos, Spector and Van der Heyden (chapter 3) is particularly taken up with these structural dimensions of business model innovation. Thus, they offer a rich and highly useful terminology for classifying various kinds of business model changes that is organized around what exactly happens to the activity set of the firm. Specifically, Santos et al. distinguish between "reactivating" (i.e., altering the set of activities performed by the company), "relinking" (altering the linkages between activities), "repartitioning" (i.e., altering the boundaries of the focal company by moving an organizational unit across business boundaries), and "relocating" (i.e., altering the (physical, cultural, and institutional) location between organizational units performing activities)—all of which are processes that are intimately connected to changes in organizational structure. Structural changes can also be observed in the pharma companies discussed by Rasmussen and Foss (chapter 12). These companies increasingly seek to engage in servitization efforts, which involve changed job descriptions for sales reps, new dedicated units, and new alliances with external service providers. Similarly, entrepreneurial ventures adopting innovative business models in high-tech industries need to readjust the organizational structure, decision rights, and human resource management practices to adapt to the need of absorbing knowledge from the external environments (Colombo, Mohammadi, and Rossi-Lamastra, chapter 9). Other companies expand their top management teams to better deal with the coordination challenges of major changes in business models (Stieglitz and Foss, chapter 6).

---

[2] Formalization refers to the degree to which communications and procedures in an organization are written (Daft, 1986).

However, as Ouchi (1977) clarified, organizational structure does not automatically translate into organizational control. Organizational control can broadly be defined as processes and administrative apparatus by which managers motivate and encourage organizational members to act in ways that further organizational goals and objectives and monitor whether the right behaviors are adopted. Organizational design therefore also encompasses governance mechanisms for monitoring and evaluating inputs and outputs and rewarding behaviors. As Birkinshaw and Ansari (chapter 5) note, many organizational theories "characterize the organization in structural terms (indeed, this field is often referred to as *structural* contingency theory), and with little regard for the underlying processes and sometimes informal systems through which work actually gets done." To capture these dimensions they coin the notion of a "management model" which they see as complementary to the business model. Innovating the business model may have to be complemented by innovating the management model, in their view.

There is little doubt that it is entirely warranted to draw attention to the non-structural organizational dimensions of business models and the innovation thereof. Thus, those firms in the pharma industry that seek to change their business models toward more service-oriented models typically also find that they need to change KPIs, reward systems, and management information systems to complement changes in the value proposition, value-chain organization, and so on. However, one may question whether it is necessary to coin a new construct, that of the "management model," to bring the organization more into contact with the business model construct. While this can be seen as a reaction to the relative neglect of organizational issues in the business model literature, an alternative route is to think of organization, in the structural sense as well as in the "management model" sense, as an integral part of a business model innovation. And yet, organization is not always best thought of as a complementary part of a business model innovation. Thus, certain organizations may, because of their structural features and other aspects of organizational design, be more capable when it come to business model innovation. This suggests that organization can be an *antecedent* of business model innovation.

However, even though all firms in an industry may recognize the need for engaging in business model innovation simultaneously, they may not be equally good at implementing business model innovation, for example, because organizational structures represent organizational power structures that are hard to change. Such contextual features suggest that organization can be a moderator in a relation that specifies business model innovation as the dependent variable. Finally, part of a business model innovation may be that the organizational design changes along with other components of the business model. In this situation, organization is really part of the business model innovation itself. In the following, we discuss these three possibilities.

ORGANIZATION AS AN ANTECEDENT
TO BUSINESS MODEL INNOVATION

Organizations may cultivate a preparedness for organizational change that facilitates business model innovations. Some organizations may develop dynamic capabilities that enable them to innovate their business models in a systematic manner. In chapter 2, David Teece and his co-authors draw attention to how the microfoundations of dynamic capabilities speak to this issue. For example, firms need to have mechanisms in place for sensing the need for business model innovation. Dynamic capabilities assist the firm in creating and capturing value by encompassing the "activities, processes, and leadership skills by which (1) the need for changing/innovating existing business models is recognized, and (2) the necessary assets are (a) accessed and (b) orchestrated in the pursuit of new value creation." They further determine the "… firm's agility and flexibility in implementing the new organizational design, including the alignment of new and existing activities and responses to the unforeseen internal and external contingencies that unavoidably accompany deploying a new business model" (Leih, Linden, and Teece, chapter 2).

Relatedly, a number of scholars have linked business model innovation to the need for learning and experimentation (cf. Sosna, Trevinyo-Rodriguez, and Velamuri, 2010; McGrath, 2010; Doz and Kosonen, 2010; Chesbrough, 2007; Wirtz, Schilke, and Ullrich, 2010), organizational change processes (Dunford, Palmer, and Beneviste, 2010), critical capabilities (Achtenhagen, Melin, and Naldi, 2013), strategic flexibility (Bock et al., 2012), and the need for strategic sensitivity, leadership unity, and resource fluidity (Doz and Kosonen, 2010). These are both antecedents to, and facilitators of, business model innovation.

"Strategic sensitivity," "sensing," and the like may in turn be determined by organizational design. Thus, the size of and division of labor within the top management team may influence how well the company reads the signals in the environment that may suggest that a change of business model is warranted. A large top management team that is closely connected to the operational levels and features functional specialists is likely to be better at picking up such signals. The degree of delegation in the company also matters. If employees (e.g., in marketing and R&D) have extensive decision rights that enable them to cooperate with external parties, they are more likely to be able to sense the need for changes in the business model or indeed a change to a new business model. Such companies may be able to start experimenting with new business models at an earlier stage than the competition, and may therefore enjoy a first-mover advantage with respect to implementing the new model. Also, multibusiness (diversified) companies may enjoy an advantage in this respect because they may find that new business models may be transferred from one business to another.

The example of the multibusiness company points to the corporate context in which the business model operates. Business models exist on the division level of the firm; that is, in multibusiness corporations, a corporate center oversees the actions of a number of discrete operating business units, each with their own competitive strategy and business model. As Santos, Spector, and Van der Heyden (chapter 3) and Casadesus-Masanell, Ricart, and Tarjizán (chapter 4) demonstrate, the corporate center may act as both a constraint on and a provider of opportunity for division-level business model change. The corporate center can play a crucial role in promoting dynamic reinforcements among the different business models at the divisional level that can be conducive to business model innovation (Casadesus-Masanell, Ricart, and Tarjizán, chapter 4). For example, corporate centers that actively promote cross-divisional knowledge exchange and learning positively influence the divisional units' ability to adapt and innovate their business models.

However, the extent to which the corporate center can act as an opportunity provider for division-level business model innovation largely depends on the type of corporate model chosen by the firm. In fact, the "corporate-model configuration" (i.e., the business model at the corporate level) can considerably increase or decrease the interactions and reinforcements between divisions in the corporation; that is, different corporate-level business models are found to have different effects on the divisional units' ability to change their business model. While in the "modular model" (corporate portfolio consisting of diverse businesses), the divisional units operate with maximum opportunity to innovate business models but low opportunity to interact, in the "linked model," the corporate center imposes operational linkages to capture synergies, which in turn places constraints on divisional units to initiate business model change because of forced linkages to other units. In contrast, promoting cross-divisional learning, divisional units in a "mutual corporate model" have flexibility to initiate business model change as well as opportunities to learn from other units (Santos, Spector, and Van der Heyden, chapter 3).

ORGANIZATION AS A MODERATOR OF BUSINESS MODEL INNOVATION

Not all firms are equally good at implementing business model innovation. The organization's ability to change its business model is influenced by its existing design and capabilities, as well as more intangible phenomena, such as the extent to which employees perceive existing roles, structures, etc. as entitlements (and therefore worth fighting for). Further, business model innovation involves a process of searching, learning, and experimentation, usually with uncertain performance prospects. A new business model is not fully and rationally planned *ex ante*, but emerges in an extended design process (Sosna, Trevinyo-Rodriguez, and Velamuri, 2010; McGrath, 2010; Dunford, Palmer, and Benveniste, 2010). However, as Stieglitz and Foss (chapter 6) argue, successful business model innovation requires the concerted and collaborative efforts of the top management team, whose leadership involvement needs to match the type of business model innovation envisioned. In fact, different business model innovations are associated with different management challenges and thus require different leadership interventions to become successful (Stieglitz and Foss, chapter 6).

Another moderating factor is power. Thus, business model innovations typically make some groups of employees more powerful and other groups less powerful inside the organization. Similarly, some business model innovations may be "competence-destroying" in that the skills/human capital of some employees may be less valuable in the context of the firm. We know very little about the implications of such shifting power constellations for decisions to adopt and implement a business model innovation. Rasmussen and Foss (chapter 12) hint that such power issues may matter in the pharmaceutical industry as the industry is innovating its business models toward models with a higher service content.

ORGANIZATION AS A PART OF BUSINESS MODEL INNOVATION: A CONFIGURATIONAL VIEW

Changing the organizational design of the firm is a key aspect of many business model innovations, particularly the more radical ones. Such a change is often complementary to changing the value proposition, the revenue model, or other modes of often highlighted components of business models.

For example, firms changing their business models toward open innovation models must also change underlying rewards, KPIs, ways of communication, and the way authority is allocated (cf. Foss, Laursen, and Pedersen, 2011). Because open business models are often based on the commercialization of ideas or on the leveraging of communities of users and developers, an important organizational requirement of these open business models is the ability to integrate external knowledge. As Colombo, Mohammadi, and Rossi-Lamastra (chapter 9) illustrate, the adoption of innovative business models in high-tech industries requires an internal organization that smoothly facilitates these interactions. To support such a shift in business model, the firm's structure, decision rights, and human resource management practices must be adapted to the need of absorbing knowledge from the external environments (Colombo, Mohammadi, and Rossi-Lamastra, chapter 9). In similar fashion, firms that aspire to shift toward "service-driven business models" (Kindström and Kowalkowski, chapter 10) need to align their existing organizational design and structure to support the new business model strategy.

Often, the managerial challenges of business model innovation are to a large extent organizational challenges that involve the redesign of organizational structure and control, as well as choices that involve the boundaries of the firm vis-à-vis other firms (Rasmussen and Foss, chapter 12). Different types of business model innovation and their accompanying organizational structures are typically followed by adjustments and/or renewal in other areas. For example, in pharmaceutical firms adopting new business models, a recurring theme is the need for new human capital to either augment the incumbent model or to drive more radical business model experimentation. To address new non-routine tasks a number of organizational practices need to be installed (such as reallocation of decision rights, lateral communication, workshops) to ease the new coordination requirements. Similarly, new performance measurement systems and KPIs are required to support the firm's new strategic reorientations (Rasmussen and Foss, chapter 12). These findings highlight that if firms are to succeed in innovating their incumbent model (especially in cases of radical change), the organizational context should be changed respectively in accordance with the new business model in order to realize complementarities and limit coordination costs (Rasmussen and Foss, chapter 12).

What this Volume Tells Us About Organization and Business Model Innovation: Emerging Themes

To launch the organizational dimension of business models and the innovation thereof as a distinct research theme, this volume contains a set of essays that deals with various organizational aspects of business model innovation. Combining organizational and strategic theory and empirical observation, the contributors specifically highlight organizational design aspects of business model innovation, focusing on how reward systems, power distributions, routines and standard operating procedures, the allocation of authority, and other aspects of organizational structure and control should be designed to support the business model the firm chooses. Also discussed are how existing organizational structures, top management team composition, capabilities, beliefs, cultures, and so on influence the firm's ability to flexibly change to new business models. These important organizational aspects of business models and the innovation thereof have so far been missing from the literature. The chapters of this book are organized around four main themes: (1) theoretical foundations, (2) organizational determinants of business model design, (3) organizational design challenges of innovative business models, and (4) firm and industry studies of business model innovation.

THEME 1: THEORETICAL FOUNDATIONS

The first Part of this edited volume lays down the theoretical foundations for business models and business model innovation. Drawing on organizational strategy, transaction-cost theory, and the organizational capability view, the following chapters highlight different aspects of business model innovation.

In chapter 2, Sunyoung Leih, Greg Linden, and David J. Teece examine the interrelationship between business model innovation, dynamic capabilities, and organizational design. By adopting a dynamic capabilities perspective, the authors argue that dynamic capabilities are key antecedents of business model innovation and implementation. Dynamic capabilities reside in the collective learning and culture of the organization and in the entrepreneurial skill of the top management team. Hence, entrepreneurial managers bear the primary responsibility for recognizing the need for business model change, for adjusting or inventing business models, for orchestrating the necessary assets, and for (re)structuring the organization as needed. The authors further argue that the organization's structure, incentives, and culture can, in turn, be more or less well suited to the recognition of new opportunities and the implementation of new structures that are integral to the dynamic capabilities of the firm. In short, the generation of new business models requires entrepreneurial managers to balance attention to customer needs and technological possibilities with the logic of organization.

Examining the implications of the organizational context for business model innovation, José Santos, Bert Spector, and Ludo Van der Heyden provide a theory of business model innovation within incumbent firms in chapter 3. The authors examine the process of business model change and innovation. In focusing on business units within large multibusiness corporations, the authors suggest that business units can be more likely to produce business model innovation if the corporation is able to create a favorable context. The dimensions of that context—what is called the "BMI-Conducive Corporation"—are explored, as are the transformational organizational changes required to produce such conduciveness. Finally, the authors present implications for both managers and researchers of the proposed theory of business model innovation within incumbent firms.

Elevating the unit of analysis from business level to the corporate level, Ramon Casadesus-Masanell, Joan Ricart, and Jorge Tarjizán analyze the fundamental economics underlying corporate business model innovations in chapter 4. The authors describe how by choosing internally consistent configurations of policies, assets, and governance structures, innovative business models integrate business units in ways that create compelling new value propositions able to fill important spaces in already crowded environments, and to capture value. Their chapter analyzes the fundamental economics underlying such corporate model innovations and highlights their organizational implications. The analysis reveals that the recommendations of transaction cost economics (TCE) as to which transactions to conduct inside the firm through authority and which ones to outsource through contracts are qualified when a business model lens is applied to corporate-level choices.

THEME 2: ORGANIZATIONAL DETERMINANTS OF BUSINESS MODEL DESIGN AND CHANGE

The second Part of this volume addresses the internal and external determinants of business model design and dynamics. The four contributions under this theme illustrate the importance of aligning business models with external contingencies as well as aligning the internal systems of management and leadership to support business model change.

In chapter 5, Julian Birkinshaw and Shaz Ansari clarify what exactly a management model is, and how it is complementary to a business model. As these authors suggest, while every company has an implicit management model, many have failed to articulate the choices they have made on these dimensions, and many have failed to align their management model with their chosen business model. Hence, reviewing the relevant bodies of academic literature on which the concept of a management model draws (e.g., structural contingency theory or organizational culture), the authors discuss how management model innovation sometimes leads and sometimes lags behind business model innovation. A future research agenda is proposed.

Chapter 6 by Nils Stieglitz and Nicolai J. Foss draws on the complementarity literature in economics and management research to dimensionalize business model innovations. Specifically, such innovation can be dimensionalized in terms of the depth and the breadth of the changes to the company's business model that they imply. Based on this, the authors identify four different types of business model innovations. These different types are associated with different management challenges and require different leadership interventions to become successful. In sum, top management is found to play a crucial role in contributing to the success of business model innovation, given that its involvement matches the type of business model innovation chosen.

Chapter 7 by Costas Markides investigates the strategic and organizational challenges of exploiting disruptive business model innovation in established firms. To address this important issue, the author examines the strategies with which incumbent firms can respond to newly created markets either by using their existing business model or by developing a new one. The findings suggest that established players cannot succeed by simply adopting their disruptors' (winning) business model in the new markets. Instead, they need to develop a business model which is different from the one they currently employ in the established market and also substantially different from the ones that disruptors use. Further, simply separating the new business model in a new unit is not enough; rather, while keeping it in a separate unit, the parent must also put in place organizational mechanisms that allow the unit to exploit synergies with the parent.

The importance of attaining alignment between the external environment and the firm's business model is further elaborated on in chapter 8. Putting forward a contingency framework, Tina Saebi examines how firms need to modify their business model in response to different threats in the business environment. Examining three different forms of business model dynamics, namely business model evolution, adaptation, and innovation, the author addresses the questions: which environmental conditions prompt which type of business model change, and by means of which capabilities firms can support change in their business models. The author argues and demonstrates how and why a fit between business model dynamics, environmental change, and dynamic capabilities is likely to be an important antecedent to firm performance.

THEME 3: THE ORGANIZATIONAL DESIGN CHALLENGES OF INNOVATIVE BUSINESS MODELS

The third Part of this edited volume investigates, both theoretically and empirically, organizational design challenges of shifting toward new forms of business models. Under investigation are organizational design challenges of innovative business models in high-tech entrepreneurial ventures (chapter 9) and transition processes toward service-based business model innovation (chapter 10).

In chapter 9, Massimo Colombo, Ali Mohammadi, and Cristina Rossi-Lamastra examine how high-tech entrepreneurial ventures should organize internally to successfully implement innovative business models. A common characteristic of innovative business models by high-tech entrepreneurial ventures is their dependence on interactions with external third parties, which provides external knowledge to be integrated with internal knowledge to deliver value to the customers. Accordingly, innovative business models by high-tech entrepreneurial ventures ask for an internal organization that smoothly favors these interactions. Specifically, the authors analyze how firms' structure, decision rights, and human resource management practices should be adapted to the need of absorbing knowledge from the external environments. Heeding a recent call in management literature, their analysis considers organizational design variables both at the individual and firm level.

Chapter 10 by Daniel Kindström and Christian Kowalkowski examines business model innovation driven by increased service focus. In their chapter, the authors discuss the external drivers and organizational implications of shifting toward service-based business models. Driven both by competition and by new customer demands, many firms find themselves moving from their traditional business models based on, primarily, product sales toward business models based on services. As business success in this setting depends as much on such organizational rearrangements (including business model redesign) as it does on new service development, examining the organizational implications of this shift becomes crucial. Hence, the authors discuss how firms can approach and understand this change to their business models, and also how their organization can become more service-oriented in order to take advantage of the emergent opportunities inherent in this shift.

THEME 4: FIRM AND INDUSTRY STUDIES OF BUSINESS MODEL INNOVATION

In the final Part of this edited volume, contributors examine business model innovation at the firm and industry level.

In chapter 11, Torben Pedersen and Henrik Sornn-Friese study the example of a business model innovation conducted by Maersk Line. The case unfolds Maersk Line's development from being a minor player in global liner shipping in 1953, through the decision to invest heavily in container-based transport systems, which changed the whole industry. Since then Maersk Line has been the main player and innovator in global shipping, and has reached its current position as the world's largest container operator with a fleet of about 650 container ships providing global "point-to-point" services.

Chapter 12 by Klement Rasmussen and Nicolai J. Foss investigates business model innovation in the pharmaceutical industry. The authors document how deep-seated changes in the pharmaceutical industry—related to increasing demands from payers, the strengthening of the role of patients, changing legal demands, and declining technological opportunity—are driving a process of experimenting with business model. Based on interviews in LEO Pharma, UCB Pharma, and Novo Nordisk, the authors distinguish between three ideal types, namely a traditionalist model (exemplified by Novo Nordisk), the full-blown service-oriented model (UCB Pharma), and the in-between model (LEO Pharma). The authors illustrate the changes to the organizational design and management processes that accompany the ongoing process of changing business models in these firms.

In chapter 13, Marcel Bogers, Kristian Sund, and Juan Andrei Villarroel explore the organizational aspect of business model innovation in the postal industry. Studying the examples of postal business model innovations from three European countries, the authors seek to understand both the organizational antecedents and impacts of these innovations. Over the past decade, postal operators across Europe and much of the developed world have seen acceleration in digital substitution, as well as a liberalization of the market, such that postal businesses today face lower volumes but higher competition. Postal operators have had to engage in a massive transformation of their organizations to meet these challenges and have simultaneously sought to diversify their businesses to seek new growth opportunities. Key challenges with postal business model innovations have included how to shield new business ventures from the rest of the organization as well as how to identify and capture value linked to synergies with existing business models.

Conclusions

Business model innovation is increasingly advocated as a necessary reaction to strategic discontinuities and disruptions, shifting base of competition, the increasing importance placed on innovation and knowledge as value-creating attributes, and emerging competition from new business models entering the market (cf. Johnson, Christensen, and Kagermann, 2008; Doz and Kosonen, 2010; Teece, 2010; Voelpel, Leibold, and Tekie, 2004). However, little is known about the organizational antecedents and barriers of business model innovation, and how business model innovation is intertwined with organizational changes. Although the notions of business models and business model innovation are shot through with broadly organizational considerations, such considerations usually appear at best as afterthoughts in the current business model literature.

This is surprising because business models need to be designed, even if the design process is incremental and experimental, and business model innovations are often major organizational change processes. This volume is based on the notions that (1) organizational considerations, notably those relating to organization design, need to be explicitly integrated in business model innovation research, and (2) the existing body of organizational research, broadly conceived, is very helpful in this regard.

The endeavor that this volume represents is a novel one, taking place within an emerging field (i.e., business models and business model innovation). This has a number of implications. First, the reader should not expect an entirely uniform terminology across chapters, although the editors have tried to impose some consistency. Second, the empirical work that is reported in this volume is all of the small-N variety. Although large-N empirical work is clearly warranted, it should also be recognized that exactly because of the emergent nature of the business model innovation/organization space; small-N research is needed and indeed justified. Third, although this volume comprises more than a dozen chapters, many issues are not discussed or only mentioned in passing. Among these are the many important potential insights into business model innovation of the organizational change and learning literatures. We are confident that future research on the organizational dimensions of business models and business model innovation will address these challenges.

■ **REFERENCES**

Achtenhagen, L., Melin, L., and Naldi, L. 2013. "Dynamics of Business Models— Strategizing, Critical Capabilities and Activities for Sustained Value Creation." *Long Range Planning*, 46 (6): pp. 427–442.

Afuah, A. 2004. *Business Models: A Strategic Management Approach*. New York: Irwin/McGraw-Hill.

Afuah, A. and Tucci, C. L. 2001. *Internet Business Models and Strategies: Text and Cases*. New York: McGraw-Hill.

Amit, R. and Zott, C. 2001. "Value Creation in e-Business." *Strategic Management Journal*, 22 (7): pp. 493–520.

Amit, R. and Zott, C. 2012. "Creating Value Through Business Model Innovation." *MIT Sloan Management Review*, 53: pp. 41–49.

Applegate, L. M. 2000. "E-Business Models: Making Sense of the Internet Business Landscape." In G. Dickson and G. DeSanctis (eds), *Information Technology and the Future Enterprise: New Models for Managers*: pp. 49–101. Englewood Cliffs, NJ: Prentice-Hall.

Baden-Fuller, C. and Morgan, M. S. 2010. "Business Models as Models." *Long Range Planning*, 43: pp. 156–171.

Birkinshaw, J. and Ansari, S. 2015. Chapter 5, this volume. "Understanding Management Models: Going Beyond "What" and "Why" to "How" Work Gets Done in Organizations."

Bock, A. J., Opsahl, T., George, G., and Gann, D. M. 2012. "The Effects of Culture and Structure on Strategic Flexibility during Business Model Innovation." *Journal of Management Studies*, 49: pp. 279–305.

Bogers, M., Sund, K. J., and Villarroel, J. A. Chapter 13, this volume. "The Organizational Dimension of Business Model Exploration: Evidence from the European Postal Industry."

Bucherer, E., Eisert, U., and Gassmann, O. 2012. "Towards Systematic Business Model Innovation: Lessons from Product Innovation Management." *Creativity and Innovation Management*, 21: pp. 183–198.

Brousseau, E. and Penard, T. 2006. "The Economics of Digital Business Models: A Framework for Analyzing the Economics of Platforms." *Review of Network Economics*, 6 (2): pp. 81–110.

Burns, T. and Stalker, G. M. 1961. *The Management of Innovation*. London: Tavistock.

Burton, R. M. and Obel, B. 2004. *Strategic Organizational Diagnosis and Design: The Dynamics of Fit*. Netherlands: Springer.

Casadesus-Masanell, R. and Ricart, J. E. 2011. "How to Design a Winning Business Model." *Harvard Business Review*, 89 (1–2): pp. 100–107.

Casadesus-Masanell, R. and Zhu, F. 2013. "Business Model Innovation and Competitive Imitation: The Case of Sponsor-Based Business Models." *Strategic Management Journal*, 34 (4): pp. 464–482.

Casadesus-Masanell, R., Ricart J., and Tarziján, J. 2015. Chapter 4, this volume. "A Corporate View of Business Model Innovation."

Chesbrough, H. W. 2007. "Business Model Innovation: It's Not Just About Technology Anymore." *Strategy & Leadership*, 35 (6): pp. 12–17.

Chesbrough, H. W. 2010. "Business Model Innovation: Opportunities and Barriers." *Long Range Planning*, 43 (2): pp. 354–363.

Chesbrough, H. W. and Rosenbloom, R. S. 2002. "The Role of the Business Model in Capturing Value from Innovation: Evidence from Xerox Corporation's Technology Spinoff Companies." *Industrial and Corporate Change*, 11 (3): pp. 529–555.

Colombo, M. G., Mohammadi, A., and Rossi Lamastra, C. 2015 Chapter 9, this volume. "Innovative Business Models for High-tech Entrepreneurial Ventures: The Organizational Design Challenges."

Daft, R. 1986. *Organization Theory and Design*. 2nd edn. St Paul, MN: West Publishing Company.

Doz, Y. L. Kosonen, M. 1986.. "Organization Theory and Design. 2nd edn. St Paul, MN: West Publishing Company..", 43 (2): pp. 370–382.

Dunford, R., Palmer, I., and Benveniste, J. 2010. "Business Model Replication for Early and Rapid Internationalisation: The ING Direct Experience." *Long Range Planning*, 43 (5): pp. 655–674.

Dubosson-Torbay, M., Osterwalder, A., and Pigneur, Y. 2002. "E-Business Model Design, Classification, and Measurements." *Thunderbird International Business Review*, 44 (1): pp. 5–23.

Economist Intelligence Unit. 2005. "Business 2010: Embracing the Challenge of Change." White paper, Economist Intelligence Unit, New York, February 2005, p. 9.

Foss, N. J., Laursen, K., and Pedersen, T. 2011. "Linking Customer Interaction and Innovation: The Mediating Role of New Organizational Practices." *Organization Science*, 22: pp. 980–999.

Galbraith, J. R. 1974. "Organization Design An Information Processing View." *Interfaces*, 4 (3): pp. 28–36.

Giesen, E., Berman, S. J., Bell, R., and Blitz, A. 2007. "Three Ways to Successfully Innovate Your Business Model." *Strategy & Leadership*, 35 (6): pp. 27–33.

Giesen, E., Riddleberger, E., Christner, R., and Bell, R. 2010. "When and How to Innovate Your Business Model." *Strategy & Leadership*, 38 (4): pp. 17–26.

George, G. and Bock, A. 2009. "The Business Model in Practice and its Implications for Entrepreneurship Research." Working paper, Imperial College, London.

George, G. and Bock, A. J. 2011. "The Business Model in Practice and its Implications for Entrepreneurship Research." *Entrepreneurship Theory and Practice*, 35: pp. 83–111.

Ho, Y., Fang, H., and Hsieh, M. 2011. "The Relationship Between Business-model Innovation and Firm Value: A Dynmaic Perspective." *World Academy of Science, Engineering and Technology*, 77 (5): pp. 656–664.

IBM Global Business Services. 2006. "Expanding the Innovation Horizon: The Global CEO Study 2006." Retrieved November 2014 from <http://www-07.ibm.com/sg/pdf/global_ceo_study.pdf>.

Jackson, J. and Morgan, C. 1982. *Organization Theory*. Englewood Cliffs, NJ: Prentice-Hall.

Johnson, M. W., Christensen, C. M., and Kagermann, H. 2008. "Reinventing Your Business Model." *Harvard Business Review*, 86 (12): pp. 57–68.

Kindström, D. and Kowalkowski, C. 2015. Chapter 10, this volume. "Service-driven Business Model Innovation: Organizing the Shift from a Product-based to a Service-centric Business Model."

Koen, P. A, Bertels H. M. J., and Elsum, I. R. 2011. "Three Faces of Business Model Innovation: Challenges for Established Firms." *Research Technology Management*, 54 (3): pp. 52–59.

Kuhn, T. S. 1970. *The Structure of Scientific Revolutions*. Chicago, IL: University of Chicago Press.

Lecocq, X., Demil, B., and Ventura, J. 2010. "Business Models as a Research Program in Strategic Management: An Appraisal Based on Lakatos." *Management*, 13 (4): pp. 214–225.

Leih, S., Linden, G., and Teece, D. J. 2015. Chapter 2, this volume. "Business Model Innovation and Organizational Design: A Dynamic Capabilities Perspective."

Levi, M. 2009. "President Obama: U.S. Automakers 'Not Quite There Yet'," CBS News, 29 March 2009. Retrieved November 2014 from <http://www.cbsnews.com/news/president-obama-us-automakers-not-quite-there-yet/>.

Lindgart, Z., Reeves, M., Stalk, G., and Deimler, M. S. 2009. *Business Model Innovation.* Boston, MA: Boston Consulting Group Report.

Margretta, J. 2002. "Why Business Models Matter." *Harvard Business Review,* 80 (5): pp. 86–92.

Markides, C. 2006. "Disruptive Innovation: In Need of Better Theory." *Journal of Product Innovation Management,* 23 (1): pp. 19–25.

Markides, C. 2015. Chapter 7, this volume. "How Established Firms Exploit Disruptive Business Model Innovation: Strategic and Organizational Challenges."

McGrath, R. G. 2010. "Business Models: A Discovery Driven Approach." *Long Range Planning,* 43 (2): pp. 247–261.

Miller, D. and Dröge, C. 1986. "Psychological and Traditional Determinants of Structure." *Administrative Science Quarterly,* 3: pp. 539–560.

Morris, M., Schindehutte, M., and Allen, J. 2005. "The Entrepreneur's Business Model: Toward a Unified Perspective." *Journal of Business Research,* 58 (6): pp. 726–735.

Osterwalder, A. 2004. "*The Business Model Ontology—A Proposition in a Design Science Approach.*" Dissertation 173, University of Lausanne, Switzerland.

Osterwalder, A. and Pigneur, Y. 2010. *Business Model Generation: A Handbook for Visionaries, Game Changers, and Challengers.* Hoboken NJ: John Wiley & Sons.

Osterwalder, A., Pigneur, Y., and Tucci, C. L. 2005. "Clarifying Business Models: Origins, Present, and Future of the Concept." *Communications of the Association for Information Systems,* 16 (1): pp. 1–25.

Ouchi, W. G. 1977. "The Relationship Between Organizational Structure and Organizational Control." *Administrative Ssience Quarterly,* 22 (1): pp. 95–113.

Pedersen, T. and Sornn-Friese, H. 2015. Chapter 11, this volume. "A Business Model Innovation by an Incumbent Late Mover: Containerization in Maersk Line."

Rappa, M. 2001. "*Business Models on the Web: Managing the Digital Enterprise.*" Retrieved November 2014 from <http://www.digitalenterprise.org/models/models.html>.

Rasmussen, K. A., and Foss, N. J. 2015. Chapter 12, this volume. "Business Model Innovation in the Pharmaceutical Industry: The Supporting Role of Organizational Design."

Saebi, T. 2015. Chapter 8, this volume. "Evolution, Adaptation, or Innovation? A Contingency Framework on Business Model Dynamics."

Santos, J. F. P., Spector, B., and Van der Heyden, L. 2015. Chapter 3, this volume. "Toward a Theory of Business Model Change."

Seelos, C. and Mair, J. 2007. "Profitable Business Models and Market Creation in the Context of Deep Poverty: A Strategic View." *Academy of Management Perspectives,* 21: pp. 49–63.

Shafer, S. M., Smith, H. J., and Linder, J. C. 2005. "The Power of Business Models." *Business Horizons,* 48: pp. 199–207.

Slywotzky, A. and Wise, R. 2003. *How to Grow When Markets Don't.* New York: Time Warner.

Stewart, D. W. and Zhao, Q. 2000. "Internet Marketing, Business Models and Public Policy." *Journal Of Public Policy and Marketing,* 19: pp. 287–296.

Stieglitz, N. and Foss, N. J. 2015. Chapter 6, this volume. "Business Model Innovation: The Role of Leadership."

Sosna, M., Trevinyo-Rodriguez, R. N., and Velamuri, S. R. 2010. "Business Model Innovation Through Trial-And-Error Learning: The Naturhouse Case." *Long Range Planning*, 43 (2): pp. 383–407.

Suddaby, R. 2010. "Editor's Comments: Construct Clarity in Theories of Management and Organization." *Academy of Management Journal* 35 (3): pp. 346–357.

Teece, D. J. 2010. "Business Models, Business Strategy and Innovation." *Long Range Planning*, 43 (2): pp. 172–194.

Timmers, P. 1998." Business Models for Electronic Markets." *Electronic Markets*, 8 (2): pp. 3–8.

Voelpel, S. C., Leibold, M., and Tekie, E. B. 2004. "The Wheel of Business Model Reinvention: How to Reshape Your Business Model to Leapfrog Competitors." *Journal of Change Management*, 4 (3): pp. 259–276.

Weill, P. and Vitale, M. R. 2001. *Place to Space: Migrating to e-Business Models*. Boston, MA: Harvard Business School Press.

Weill, P., Malone, T. W., D'Urso, V. T., Herman, G., and Woerner, S. 2005. "Do Some Business Models Perform Better Than Others?" MIT Centre for Coordination, Science Working Paper No. 226.

Winter, S. G. and Szulanski. G. 2001. "Replication as Strategy." *Organization Science*, 12 (6): pp. 730–743.

Williamson, O. E. 1996. *The Mechanisms of Governance*. Oxford: Oxford University Press.

Wirtz, B. W., Schilke, O., and Ullrich, S. 2010. "Strategic Development of Business Models: Implications of the Web 2.0 for Creating Value on the Internet." *Long Range Planning*, 43 (2): pp. 272–290.

Zott, C. and Amit, R. 2007. "Business Model Design and the Performance of Entrepreneurial Firms." *Organization Science*, 18 (2): pp. 181–199.

Zott, C. and Amit, R. 2010. "Business Model Design: An Activity System Perspective." *Long Range Planning*, 43 (2): pp. 216–226.

Zott, C., Amit, R., and Massa, L. 2011. "The Business Model: Recent Developments and Future Research." *Journal of Management*, 37 (4): pp. 1019–1042.

2 Business Model Innovation and Organizational Design

A Dynamic Capabilities Perspective

SUNYOUNG LEIH, GREG LINDEN,
AND DAVID J. TEECE[*]

Introduction

A business model is the articulation of the logic by which a business creates and delivers value to customers. Importantly, it also outlines the architecture of prices, revenues, and costs that will, when all goes well, allow the business to earn a profit (Teece, 2010a).

Some contributions to the early business model literature put the main emphasis on the content and structure of the transactions that result in value being delivered in the marketplace (e.g., Amit and Zott, 2001). While the transaction is for many purposes a highly useful unit of analysis, a focus on the content and structure of transactions risks shifting the emphasis away from what we consider to be the essence of a good business model: providing a compelling value proposition for the customer and then capturing a portion of that value (Teece, 2010a). The de-emphasis of value capture in the early literature perhaps reflected poorly thought through business practices in the real world, which might explain why many companies in the late 1990s dot-com era went bust. In short, a viable business model must support the generation of profits, not just the delivery of value to the consumer.

The "organizational dimension" of business models and business model innovation that is highlighted by all contributors to this volume emphasizes that business models are the "architecture" that provides a bridge between value for customers and profits for the business. A viable business model requires smart business logic (reflecting a good understanding of customer needs and willingness to pay) and an organizational structure that results in value being created, delivered, and captured.

Organizational design implicates firm boundaries, that is, the extent to which the firm owns and controls productive assets (Hart, 1995). Critical

* The authors are listed alphabetically.

design elements include which activities are to be managed in-house and which accessed and managed through contractual governance structures (Williamson, 1996), as well as the specific contractual modes to be used. These arrangements influence, to a large extent, the delivery of value and its division between the firm and its various stakeholders. As indicated elsewhere (Teece, 1986, 2006), the extent to which an innovating firm's business model (or asset position) enables or allows the firm to control assets that are complementary to an innovation strongly influences the extent to which the firm can garner rents from the innovation, particularly if the appropriability regime is weak.

Business model innovation may thus require changes in the boundaries of the firm, and will usually require changes in internal organizational structure and control, and even changes in company culture. How radical and encompassing these changes will be varies with the nature of the business model innovation (see, e.g., Stieglitz and Foss, chapter 6, this volume).

All business model changes are almost by definition strategic issues, for which the top management team is accountable. In particular, the design of business models typically requires the concerted and collaborative efforts of the top management team, all the more so if the changes are far-reaching.

Unfortunately, much extant thinking on business logic and organizational design, such as transaction cost economics (Williamson, 1996), while very useful to the understanding of vertical structure and lateral scope (Teece, 1980), provides little insight into business model innovation. In particular, with its focus on opportunism and recontracting hazards, transaction cost economics tends to emphasize the need for safeguards against opportunism and to de-emphasize the positive value of collaboration within and across the boundaries of an organization.[1] Opportunity is largely ignored while opportunism is given center stage.

The purpose of this chapter is to address some of the shortcomings in the existing literature by applying the dynamic capabilities framework (Teece, Pisano, and Shuen, 1997; Teece, 2007) to understanding the organizational dimensions of business model design. Fundamentally, dynamic capabilities are high-order capabilities that allow an organization to shape and deploy ("orchestrate") its resource base to meet the current and anticipated needs of consumers while also embracing technological opportunities and managing competitive responses. To a large extent, such capabilities reside at the level of the top management team, but they also involve the entire organization. Indeed, as Burgelman's (1994) study of a critical transformation at Intel makes clear, dynamic capabilities that succeed in modifying a business model may reside, in part, at lower levels in the organization.

In most cases, however, changing a firm's business model(s) in response to relevant contingencies is the key task and responsibility of the top management team. The efforts of top management can of course be compromised by the extent to which the rest of the organization is not able, or not willing, to implement and execute a new business model, or even to sense the

---

[1] A notable exception is Williamson's (1985, 1996) extensive treatment of relational contracting, which is too often ignored.

need for change (Teece, 2007). Strong dynamic capabilities require both transformational leadership and a flexible organization.

The capacity to sense the need for business model changes is vital. The ability to modify or completely redesign the business model is critical. But the capability that counts most in this context is that of actually re-engineering or displacing the existing business model.

While the ability to effectuate business model innovation is integral to dynamic capabilities, an organization's design influences the strength of its dynamic capabilities. For example, the ability to sense new threats or opportunities and to calibrate them appropriately are important to business success. Firms with a high degree of delegation and vertical communication are often better than more centralized firms at sensing and evaluating opportunities and threats. Delegation enables employees to interact more with customers, suppliers, and complementors, and open channels of communication permit information to flow to the appropriate decision-making level. In short, a high degree of coupling of the external environment to the organization ensures that "signals" from outside have a better chance of being captured, transmitted to the top management team, and acted on decisively.

The chapter begins with a brief review of the literature on the relationship of business models and organizational design, ending with a discussion of how a capabilities perspective can fill some of the gaps. This is followed by an introduction to the dynamic capabilities framework, including a discussion of two of its main components: managerial actions and organizational routines. With these foundations in place, we turn to a discussion of dynamic capabilities in the context of the organizational challenges associated with business model innovation and implementation. A key insight is that organizational design issues are central to, and intertwined with, dynamic capabilities.

Business Models and Organizational Design

A business model does not rigidly determine organizational design. Nevertheless, the way in which a company plans to deliver value to its customers must be reflected in its internal division of responsibilities and its strategic priorities. Relatedly, its tactics for capturing value will be reflected in the way it structures its boundaries and in the contracts it strikes with external parties. In an established company, the introduction of a new business model may require transforming its present structure and managing tensions between constituencies in different parts of the company.

EARLY VIEWS

Organization theorists missed the business model aspect of organizational design. For Burns and Stalker (1961), organizational design was determined merely by the nature of a company's production process. Contingency theorists claimed that systematic relations existed between external contingencies, strategic choices, and organizational design. An example would be the multidivisional organizational form that was developed to effectively manage varied activities on a large scale. In the Burns and Stalker framework, technology basically determines organizational design (see also Woodward, 1965). There was no suggestion that the business model selected by a company might somehow mediate the impact of technology on organizational design. This is a major shortcoming, and it is remarkable that it has not, to our knowledge, been pointed out before now.

Notwithstanding this, later contributions to the contingency stream of research went beyond technological determinism, highlighting the role of internal communication and access to knowledge and information as key determinants of organizational design (e.g., Galbraith, 1974). By highlighting communication and information costs, such contributions anticipated elements of the early formulation of transaction cost economics (Teece, 1982; Williamson, 1975, 1985).

Other scholars implied a link between business models and organizational design, but none were very explicit about it. For example, economic historian Alfred Chandler (1962) noted a systematic tendency of "structure" (i.e., organizational design) to be driven by "strategy." It is now understood that, while business models and strategy are different concepts, they must be compatible (Teece, 2014b).

CONTEMPORARY VIEWS

A more contemporary view is that a combination of technology, strategy, and the applicable "appropriability regime" (Teece, 1986, 2006), as well as transaction costs, jointly drive business model design and the concomitant organizational structure. The aspect of the technology–organizational design nexus that has been most developed in the economics literature is arguably the setting of the firm's boundaries, namely, which functions the firm will perform in-house and which ones it will outsource, and what these decisions imply in terms of asset ownership and the contracts struck with stakeholders (Hart, 1995; Williamson, 1996).

In the case of a business model (Teece, 2010a) built around an innovation, the necessary co-specialized complements for exploiting technological innovation—possibly including certain marketing, manufacturing, after-sale service, or distribution assets—might need to be internalized. The key factors to consider are competition in the supply of these complements and the strength of the relevant appropriability regime, which varies positively with the availability of legal protections, such as patents, and negatively with the factors influencing the imitability of the innovation, such as its complexity or tacitness (Teece, 1986, 2006). The supply-side dimensions of interest are the bargaining power of suppliers in factor markets; the cost, difficulty, and time to build assets internally; the costs of contracting upstream and downstream;

and the timing requirements for the introduction of the innovation relative to the product/process lifecycle. Where the services being procured are somewhat specialized and not readily available in a market, they should be internalized, time permitting. Although the enterprise loses some contractual flexibility, it gains the opportunity to build a valuable resource that will be costly for rivals to imitate and difficult to acquire in a market. This model is much more robust than Burns and Stalker's, which does not take into account any of these additional decision variables.

TOWARD A CAPABILITIES PERSPECTIVE ON BUSINESS MODEL DESIGN

Transaction cost approaches such as those of Williamson (1975, 1985) and Teece (1986), while insightful, are themselves incomplete. They ignore or minimize the role of learning, resource accumulation, marketing, asset orchestration, and pricing strategy. It is by exercising these capabilities that the organization can structure itself to deliver customer value while also capturing sufficient value to be viable.

Organizational structure should be responsive to shifts in the firm's strategy and business model. For example, a strategy to prioritize excellent customer service as part of the customer value proposition may entail a number of changes (see Kindström and Kowalkowski, chapter 10, this volume, for an empirical example). An outsourced service may, as a consequence, need to be supplanted with a new in-house team. The reporting level of the head of customer service may be elevated. Incentive systems need to be updated. And (cultural) norms of excellent customer service will need to be promulgated.

The influence also runs the other way. Implementation failures with respect to the structural changes noted in the previous example may necessitate a rethinking of the chosen business model (or a redoubling of implementation effort). In short, business models, organizational design, and strategy are interdependent. Transaction cost economics does not capture these considerations very well, if at all.

The organizational requirements of a new business model must be enacted coherently in order to deliver value to customers, shareholders, and other stakeholders of the enterprise. This is not to say that a business model provides a simple "recipe for change" (George and Bock, 2011). Perceiving the need for change and then accomplishing it is hardly a straightforward process. Rather, it is one that requires strong dynamic capabilities (Teece, Pisano, and Shuen, 1997; Teece, 2007).

Dynamic Capabilities and Entrepreneurial Management

Because dynamic capabilities undergird how firms create and capture value (see Table 2.1), it is vital to understand their nature.

THE NATURE AND IMPORTANCE OF DYNAMIC CAPABILITIES

Capabilities emerge through the assembling and employment of physical and human assets, which leads to collective learning. The longer an organization has been around, and the larger it is, the less its capabilities are likely to depend on particular individuals.

Ordinary and dynamic capabilities are the two main types. Ordinary capabilities, which encompass operations, administration, and governance of the firm's activities, make a firm capable of producing and selling a defined (and static) set of products and services. They support technical efficiency in performing a fixed group of activities, regardless of how well- or ill-suited the outputs are to the firm's competitive needs (Teece, 2007: 1321). Routines for new product development, quality control, knowledge transfer, and performance measurement are examples of collective activities that can be part of a firm's ordinary capabilities (Eisenhardt and Martin, 2000).[2]

Ordinary capabilities are anchored in resources that will be orchestrated by the dynamic capabilities of the firm as it aligns with its environment in the pursuit of evolutionary fitness (Helfat et al., 2007: 7). In some cases, the resources (assets, practices, and know-how) involved in ordinary capabilities will meet the criteria defined by Barney (1991) for resources that can support durable competitive advantage: valuable, rare, imperfectly imitable, and non-substitutable (VRIN). But, more often, the practices can be benchmarked and made vulnerable to imitation by competitors (Teece, 2014a).

Technical excellence in exercising ordinary capabilities is not enough to support durable competitive advantage. Something more is needed. That "something more" is dynamic capabilities.

Dynamic capabilities govern how the organization's ordinary capabilities are developed, augmented, winnowed, and combined. They can be weak or strong.

Strong dynamic capabilities enable firms to orchestrate their resources effectively. They enable a firm to identify and exploit opportunities, synchronize business processes and models with the business environment, and/or shape the business environment in its favor (Teece, Pisano, and Shuen, 1997). The real competitive strengths of a firm lie in dynamic capabilities and strategy formulation, underpinned by value-enhancing "signature" processes and other VRIN resources that the firm and its management can command. High-performance signature processes embody positive elements of a company's unique history, experience, culture, and creativity. This makes them relatively hard for rivals to imitate (Gratton and Ghoshal, 2005).

Dynamic capabilities encompass the entrepreneurial activities, processes, and leadership skills by which (1) the need for changing/innovating existing business models is recognized, and (2) the necessary assets are (a) accessed and (b) orchestrated in the pursuit of new value creation. On the

---

[2] Although earlier treatments of dynamic capabilities have included these routines, they are more likely to support ordinary capabilities unless they involve unique characteristics that make them signature processes.

organizational side this involves identifying complementarities between the various elements of the new business model, that is, how the value proposition is supported by the value-chain structure selected, and how the revenue and value capture mechanisms influence value creation (see Stieglitz and Foss, chapter 6, this volume). Dynamic capabilities also guide choices on how to secure the necessary services of assets currently missing. They determine the firm's agility and flexibility in implementing the new organizational design, including the alignment of new and existing activities and responses to the unforeseen internal and external contingencies that unavoidably accompany deploying a new business model. In short, dynamic capabilities enable a firm to identify and orchestrate the necessary resources for designing and implementing a business model that will, if employed in conjunction with a good strategy, be associated with high levels of sustainable profits (Teece, 2007).

DYNAMIC CAPABILITIES AND THE FIRM'S TOP MANAGEMENT TEAM

Dynamic capabilities are grounded in a combination of organizational learning and top management skills. They are shaped by the firm's unique history, values, and routines (Teece, 2012) and enable the firm to alter its activities as the business environment shifts. Accordingly, they contribute to the firm's evolutionary fitness, that is, its ability to survive longer term, rather than merely achieving a temporary fit. The ongoing strategizing and asset orchestration (the essence of dynamic capabilities) associated with evolutionary fitness can only be routinized in a limited sense. Indeed, the astute asset orchestration demonstrated by firms with strong dynamic capabilities is often extremely difficult, if not impossible, to routinize beyond the recognition of shared principles.

The exercise of dynamic capabilities often requires top management to make critical, high-quality "one-off" decisions. Creative managerial and entrepreneurial acts (e.g., pioneering new markets) are, by their nature, strategic and non-routine, even though there may be underlying principles that guide those choices.

Entrepreneurial managers in established firms, like entrepreneurs in startups, must excel at the scanning, learning, creative, and interpretive activities needed to sense new technological and market opportunities. They must also calibrate reasonably well how technologies will evolve and how—and how quickly—competitors, suppliers, and customers will respond. As Jack Welch (2005: 89) put it, dynamically capable managers must have "the ability to see around corners." Competitors may or may not see the same opportunity, and even if they do they may calibrate it differently.

Entrepreneurial managers in firms with strong dynamic capabilities have the time (and the necessary information) to look ahead for opportunities and openings. They avoid getting bogged down managing legacy assets and the firm's ordinary capabilities and must be able, in a distinctive and advantageous manner, to align people, processes, and assets in order to deliver value continuously as the business environment evolves. Much of the ordinary activities can be outsourced (with appropriate oversight), enabling greater focus by management on what is most important strategically.

THE KEY CLUSTERS OF DYNAMIC CAPABILITIES: SENSING, SEIZING, TRANSFORMING

As discussed in Teece (2007), dynamic capabilities can usefully be disaggregated into three clusters of processes and managerial activities: (1) sensing (the identification and assessment of opportunities), (2) seizing (the mobilization of resources internally and externally to address opportunities and to capture value from doing so), and (3) transforming (continued renewal of the organization). The first two of these clusters relate, but are not identical to, the processes of opportunity recognition and exploitation highlighted in the entrepreneurship literature (e.g., Shane, 2000; Shane and Venkataraman, 2000).

Each of the three clusters is tied to business model innovation, development, and implementation. Thus, sensing involves exploring technological possibilities, probing markets, listening to customers, and scanning the business environment. It requires management to be entrepreneurial and to build hypotheses about market and technological evolution, with an emphasis on identifying unmet needs. Although sensing activities must be embedded throughout the company, with knowledge flowing from the farthest reaches of the organization to the top management team, the development of business models that harness the most valuable knowledge is the responsibility of top management.

Seizing occurs after opportunities are properly sensed and calibrated. To seize opportunities, the firm deploys resources to create and capture value from discoveries, inventions, or innovations in which top management has identified the greatest promise. The capabilities behind seizing involve identifying, establishing control or influence over, then coordinating complementary assets, for example, by building a global supply chain, establishing alliances and joint ventures, and much more.

Transformation requires capabilities for selectively phasing out old products, adjusting lines of communication, and changing, as needed, business models, methods, and organizational culture. In some cases, it may require adopting a radically different structure, even one which may not be stable but which shakes up the organization in a way that helps it achieve an improved, durable design (Foss, 2003). Santos, Spector, and Van der Heyden (chapter 3, this volume) provide an example in which a change in Nissan's business model with its suppliers necessitated company-wide modifications.

Transformational capabilities are needed most obviously when radical new threats and opportunities need to be addressed. But they are also needed periodically to soften the rigidities that develop over time from asset accumulation and the development of standard operating procedures.

An example of these principles at work can be seen at Starbucks. The world wasn't clamoring for a coffee house on every corner, but Howard Schultz recognized and then successfully developed and exploited the potential after he bought the six-store Starbucks chain in 1987. As the company globalized starting in the late 1990s, management identified the need to adapt the Starbucks business model, particularly the products and overall experience, for a variety of tastes and cultural habits in Europe (Alderman, 2012) and, even more so, in China (Burkitt, 2012). In 2011, the location-aware business model necessitated an organizational change to ensure a better balance between local voices and corporate initiatives, leading the company to change from a functional to a regional management structure.

Start-ups generally find transformation easier than do mature firms because they have a less definite trajectory, fewer fixed assets to redeploy, and fewer established positions to re-engineer. The "lean start-up" model now popular in Silicon Valley requires the capacity to quickly test, discard, and replace ideas and business models that do not work (Ries, 2011). This is especially true for Internet companies and in circumstances where social media can provide fast feedback.

Once designed and implemented, business models must be re-assessed for relevance and potency, particularly in young industries, such as cloud-based services, and in high-velocity environments more generally. In fact, over time, all firms implementing a particular business model eventually face the need to modify it (Greiner, 1998). When dynamic capabilities are weak, the pressures build to dangerous levels with no organized management response, which sometimes leads to "ad hoc problem solving" (Winter, 2003: 993). With strong dynamic capabilities, management quickly recognizes incipient problems, and perhaps even anticipates them. A recent example is the transition of Netflix from its original physical disc-by-post business model to a streaming video-on-demand business model, which was introduced ahead of offerings by rivals such as Amazon and Blockbuster, who were in a position to exploit the same opportunities. Reed Hastings, Netflix CEO, received heavy criticism from the investor community for his prescient efforts to push subscribers toward streaming films over the Internet. By contrast, in the dynamic capabilities framework, what he did can be recognized as necessary.[3]

---

[3] Employing the framework, Teece (2010b) wrote favorably about Reed Hastings' actions at the time. Subsequent events have confirmed the correctness of Hastings' forward-thinking focus on streaming, and investors (and subscribers) have responded accordingly.

Table 2.1 Activities conducted to create and capture value (organized by clusters of dynamic capabilities)

	Sensing	Seizing	Transforming
Creating value	Spotting opportunities and threats; identifying avenues for research and development; "open" innovation; conceptualizing new customer needs and new business models	Investment discipline; commitment to research and development; building competencies; achieving new combinations	Achieving recombinations; "pivoting" as required; reinventing the business in response to new opportunities
Capturing value	Positioning for first mover and other advantages; determining desirable entry timing; lining up required complementary assets	Intellectual property qualification and enforcement; implementing business models; leveraging complementary assets; investment or co-investment in "production" facilities	Managing threats; honing the business model; developing new complements; managing the business ecosystem

Source: based on Katkalo, Pitelis, and Teece (2010).

CREATING AND CAPTURING VALUE

The understanding of dynamic capabilities can perhaps be deepened by grouping them in two essential classes of (interrelated) activities—those that (are mainly intended to) create value and those that (are mainly intended to) capture value. The former relate to the ability of firms to impact positively on the determinants of value creation, such as their human resources, technology, innovativeness, unit cost economics, and physical infrastructure. The latter relate to their ability to build value capture architectures that combine strategies, such as entry deterrence, integration, cooperation, and diversification (Pitelis, 2009), with the organizational designs that facilitate realizing such strategies.

Table 2.1 lists representative activities conducted to create and capture value, organized by the three clusters of dynamic capabilities mapped in Teece (2007). As the requisite resources for the design and building of value creation and value capture architectures are likely to differ, perhaps significantly, it is arguable that the successful intertemporal management of (the tradeoffs between) value capture and value creation-related capabilities is a critical dynamic capability in itself.

Dynamic Capabilities and the Organizational Design Dimensions of Business Model Innovation

The dynamic capabilities framework adds to the understanding of the organizational implications of business model innovation. Organizational change is a vital element of dynamic capabilities. This section covers several focus topics that further clarify how the three concepts are related.

DYNAMIC CAPABILITIES AND ORGANIZATIONAL DESIGN INTERTWINED

The notion that the successful intertemporal management of value creation and capture is a key dynamic capability puts organizational design in a central position. Ireland, Covin, and Kuratko (2009: 25), for example, identify what they call a "pro-entrepreneurship organizational architecture," encompassing a firm's structure, norms, reward systems, and resource set, that can foster entrepreneurship at all levels of the organization. Entrepreneurship is an important aspect of dynamic capabilities (Al-Aali and Teece, 2014).

Business model implementation requires that entrepreneurs and top managers go beyond merely choosing the boundaries of the firm; they must also articulate a vision, establish a culture, and build flexible organizational structures and incentives that support the creation of organizational identification and loyalty (Augier and Teece, 2009; Ireland, Covin, and Kuratko, 2009). As observed earlier, strong dynamic capabilities depend not only on the insight and orchestration capacities of entrepreneurial managers, but also on the supporting routines and resilience of the organization. Entrepreneurship can be thought of as a social process or a "state of mind" that can characterize the whole enterprise (Foss et al., 2008).

It is also the case that changes in an organization's design can improve the recognition of new opportunities. Consider, for example, the well-known case of leading hearing-aid producer, Oticon's radical organizational change in 1991. Oticon (now William Demant Holding A/S) is a Danish world leader in the hearing aids industry (Lovas and Ghoshal, 2000). The radical decentralization initiatives undertaken by CEO Lars Kolind were a key factor in the revitalization of Oticon's innovative and entrepreneurial capabilities, leading to the discovery and seizing of a series of opportunities in the hearing-aid business. The radical change of Oticon's organizational design, from a typical hierarchical structure to a largely self-organizing project-based structure backed up by powerful performance incentives, illustrates how firms, by virtue of organizational design, can fuel innovation and entrepreneurship (Foss, 2003).

In this example, the organizational redesign of Oticon was enabled by the firm's dynamic capabilities for sensing and transformation. The firm's new structure in turn helped enable its dynamic capabilities for sensing and seizing. Thus, organizational design and dynamic capabilities are intertwined. If dynamic capabilities are thought of as a latent construct, organization design is one of several indicator variables.

Similar linkages between organizational design and capabilities can be found in several research streams. In international business research, Bartlett and Ghoshal (1993) posit that the specific organizational form adopted by a multinational enterprise influences the extent to which it can recombine and leverage knowledge from across the enterprise. An emerging literature on the problem-solving theory of the firm (Nickerson and Zenger, 2004) reaches similar conclusions. Work on organizational ambidexterity increasingly points to a critical role of organizational design in the ability of a firm to successfully pursue new opportunities while maintaining existing businesses (O'Reilly and Tushman, 2004, 2008; Simsek, 2009). Ambidexterity can be enabled, for example, by segregating the new activities, encouraging experimentation, ensuring they have access to adequate resources, and shielding them from internal competition with the existing lines of business (O'Reilly and Tushman, 2004).

THE CENTRALITY OF COOPERATION IN THE DYNAMIC CAPABILITIES FRAMEWORK

The dynamic capabilities framework is also useful for understanding the internal arrangements that enable innovation, including business model innovation. This is in part because the dynamic capabilities framework, unlike some other approaches, such as transaction cost economics and agency theory, embraces cooperation and partnership.

Using the transaction cost approach, Williamson (1981: 549) explicitly addressed the "manner in which human assets are organized," and his work holds numerous implications for organizational design, personnel economics, and human resource management issues. Transaction costs, however, sometimes provide a jaundiced lens for viewing internal issues. The central notion is that "skills acquired in a learning-by-doing fashion and imperfectly transferable across employers need to be embedded in a protective governance structure" (Williamson, 1981: 563) so that they are retained within the firm to the extent possible. As with other transaction cost analyses, the emphasis here is on controlling opportunistic behavior by employee and employer alike. This is indeed an important element of organizational design, but it should not blot out equally critical issues around creating and capturing value, as opposed to merely protecting against recontracting hazards. Understanding how to address opportunity is just as important as understanding how to manage opportunism.

Williamson also addresses the metering problem raised by Alchian and Demsetz (1972). When skills are highly (asset-) specific and difficult to monitor, then Williamson recommends "relational teams" whose members are socially conditioned and assured of their job security, but adds that "it is uncertain how widespread or sustainable [such teams] are" (Williamson, 1981: 565). Since that was written, creative teams of highly skilled and relatively autonomous experts, such as engineers and social scientists, have become widespread. They are now a mainstay of innovation and strategizing.

The cooperative potential of organizations has, of course, been understood to some extent since at least since the work of Barnard (1938). The dynamic capabilities framework, however, sees internal cooperation as foundational for the firm's dynamic efficiency. In particular, the asset orchestration function, which is central to dynamic capabilities, requires strong cooperation inside the organization (and with partners). The framework also recognizes the importance of strategy along with the challenges associated with appropriability and other environmental factors ignored by Barnard and most organization theorists.

Collaboration is not an end in itself and there are numerous ways that teams and partnership arrangements go astray, including poor decision making, unproductive conflict that leads to indecision, and peer pressure that leads the group to flawed decisions. Avoiding conflict often results in low-quality decisions (Tjosvold, 1985), although the desirable type of conflict is task-related rather than merely emotional (Pelled, Eisenhardt, and Xin, 1999). More generally, encouraging the expression of "minority" or unpopular opinions can lead to higher-quality decisions (Nemeth, 2012).

As the distinction between positive and negative conflict suggests, good management of creative teams is vital and must avoid defining the goals of the team and its linkage to strategy so narrowly that real innovation is impossible. Takeuchi and Nonaka (1986: 137) call this "subtle control," which involves a monitoring function that leads to intervention (e.g., eliminating a team member) only when absolutely necessary. The generation of new knowledge is an iterative, exploratory process (Nonaka, 1994). Bogers, Sund, and Villarroel (chapter 13, this volume) provide an empirical example of this process specific to business models. Furthermore, collaborative forms of innovation, to be effective, must be embedded in a knowledge-friendly enterprise. Experts are unlikely to be productive and satisfied in a traditional hierarchical organization (Teece, 2011).

DYNAMIC CAPABILITIES, BUSINESS MODELS, AND STRATEGY

So far, we have discussed business models and capabilities without much reference to strategy.[4] Strategy, capabilities, organizational structure, and the business environment co-evolve.

A strategy is integral to a business model. It typically requires a more segmented approach to the business (Teece, 2010a). While the business model conveys the general logic of the proposed value proposition, strategic analysis differentiates it for various market segments and ensures that the planned positions are defensible. A strategy that is consistent, coherent, and

---

[4] This section is adapted from Teece (2014b).

Table 2.2 The inter-relation of dynamic capabilities and strategy

Strategy kernel	Diagnosis	Guiding Policy	Coherent Action
Related dynamic capabilities schema	Sensing	Seizing/Transformation	Seizing/transformation
Nature of managerial orchestration	Entrepreneurial	Administrative	Leadership

Source: Teece (2014a).

accommodating of innovation is needed to help achieve competitive advantage. Dynamic capabilities must be used in aid of a good strategy in order to be effective. A firm with strong dynamic capabilities is able to flesh out the details around strategic intent and to implement strategic actions quickly and effectively. Implementation is enabled (or hampered) by organizational structures at the same time that the structures must make necessary adjustments to the new strategy (Santos, Spector, and Van der Heyden, chapter 3, this volume).

To be clear, we see, following Rumelt (2011: 6), a strategy as "a coherent set of analyses, concepts, policies, arguments, and actions that respond to a high-stakes challenge." For Rumelt, a good strategy has (1) a diagnosis, (2) a guiding policy, and (3) coherent action. Rumelt's trichotomy interacts with the three clusters of dynamic capabilities: sensing, seizing, and transforming. Sensing contains a strong element of diagnosis, which is important to strategy. Seizing needs to be connected to both a guiding policy and coherent action. Transforming that protects and enhances value requires a guiding policy and coherent action. The nature of the managerial tasks for various elements of strategy and dynamic capabilities is outlined in Table 2.2.

Strategy and dynamic capabilities both occur at the line-of-business as well as the company-wide level. This is consistent with other views of modular organizations (e.g., Helfat and Eisenhardt, 2004), where company-wide strategy is different and separable from the day-to-day positioning strategy at the division level (Casadesus-Masanell, Ricart, and Tarziján, chapter 4, this volume).

Strategy, when developed properly, provides the specifics of how the firm will deploy its scarce assets to implement the business model. Strong dynamic capabilities provide the flexibility to make the necessary adjustments. As Lou Gerstner said at the start of his tenure as CEO of IBM, "you have to be fast on your feet and adaptive or else a strategy is useless" (Sellers, 1993). He might as well have said that strategy is useless without strong dynamic capabilities.

Put differently, VRIN resource accumulation and the managerial orchestration discussed earlier must be guided and informed by strategy. Frank Hoffman's (2004) analysis of the British Navy's inability in 1916 to win the Battle of Jutland seems relevant here. Despite the British Navy's numerical advantage, the battle was a stalemate. British Vice-Admiral Sir David Beatty ruefully proclaimed at the time that "there seems to be something wrong with our bloody ships today" (which can be interpreted as surprise that superior British naval resources did not prevail). Hoffman, reviewing the situation nearly a century later, concluded that "[t]he real deficiency, however, was the loss of [Vice Admiral Horatio Lord] Nelson's touch. It was not the bloody ships that were principally at fault. It was the inadequate doctrine of command and control" (2004: 70). Put differently, the British failure to leverage their superior resources into a victory reflected a failure of both (military) strategy and dynamic capabilities. It was not a lack of resources that was at fault. The British (aided by the Australians and Canadians) had 151 combat ships, including twenty-eight battleships. The Germans had ninety-nine combat ships, including sixteen battleships. Some commentators are convinced that Jellicoe missed a tremendous opportunity to annihilate the German fleet and win what would have been another Trafalgar.

Conclusion

The purpose of this chapter has been to develop a case for considering business model innovation and its organizational design ramifications in the context of the broader framework of dynamic capabilities. The dynamic capabilities approach integrates strategy and organizational design issues to show how firms can stay in alignment with, and sometimes shape, the business environment.

For practical purposes, dynamic capabilities can be decomposed into three sets of activities, namely, sensing opportunities, seizing them, and transforming the organization to do so. Business model innovation, implementation, and renewal are all key outputs from, and inputs into, these activities, suggesting that the dynamic capabilities framework can further the understanding of the role of business models in the long-run performance of the business enterprise.

The role of organizational design in dynamic capabilities is an important topic that so far has received little attention. Another purpose of this chapter has been to show that there are important overlaps and links. We are not yet able to offer a full-blown theory of the relations between dynamic capabilities, business models, strategy, and organizational design. That is a matter for future research.

At least two overall themes emerge from the discussion. Each theme suggests different causal and constitutive relations between dynamic capabilities, the dynamics of business models, and organization design.

First, the successful intertemporal management of value creation, delivery, and capture is a key dynamic capability. Yet much research indicates that such management—whether by means of organizational oscillation or structural ambidexterity—involves deploying different organizational design mechanisms to optimize value creation and capture, respectively. A fuller understanding of dynamic capabilities will require a more granular analysis of the respective organizational design aspects of value creation and capture.

Second, certain aspects of organizational design, such as shallow hierarchies and pro-entrepreneurial incentive design, are important supports for dynamic capabilities. Indeed, the dynamic capabilities framework points to the importance of a high level of internal cooperation supported by a culture of openness and knowledge-sharing. Activities such as sensing may be supported by decentralization combined with extensive internal communication.

■ REFERENCES

Al-Aali, A. and Teece, D. J. 2014. "International Entrepreneurship and the Theory of the (Long-lived) International Firm: A Capabilities Perspective." *Entrepreneurship Theory and Practice*, 38 (1): pp. 95–116.

Alchian, A. A. and Demsetz, H. 1972. "Production, Information Costs and Economic Organization." *American Economic Review*, 62 (2): pp. 777–795.

Alderman, L. 2012. "In Europe, Starbucks Adjusts to a Café Culture." *New York Times*, March 30. Retrieved November 2014 from <http://www.nytimes.com/2012/03/31/business/starbucks-tailors-its-experience-to-fit-to-european-tastes.html?pagewanted=all>.

Amit, R. and Zott, C. 2001. "Value Creation in e-business." *Strategic Management Journal*, 22 (6-7): pp. 493–520.

Augier, M. and Teece, D. J. 2009. "Dynamic Capabilities and the Role of Managers in Business Strategy and Economic Performance." *Organization Science*, 20(2): pp. 410–421.

Barnard, C. I. 1938. *The Functions of the Executive*. Cambridge, MA: Harvard University Press.

Barney, J. 1991. "Firm Resources and Sustained Competitive Advantage." *Journal of Management*, 17 (1): pp. 99–120.

Bartlett, C. A. and Ghoshal, S. 1993. "Beyond the M-form: Toward a Managerial Theory of the Firm." *Strategic Management Journal*, 14: pp. 23–46.

Bogers, M., Sund, K. J., and Villarroel, J. A. 2015. Chapter 13, this volume. "The Organizational Dimension of Business Model Exploration: Evidence from the European Postal Industry."

Burgelman, R. 1994. "Fading Memories: A Process Theory of Strategic Business Exit in Dynamic Environments." *Administrative Science Quarterly*, 39: pp. 24–56.

Burkitt, L. 2012. "Starbucks Plays to Local Chinese Tastes." *Wall Street Journal*, November 26. Retrieve November 2014 from <http://professional.wsj.com/article/SB10001424127887324784404578142931427720970.html>.

Burns, T. and Stalker, G. M. 1961. *The Management of Innovation*. London: Tavistock.

Casadesus-Masanell, R., Ricart, J. E., and Tarziján, J. 2015. Chapter 4, this volume. "A Corporate View of Business Model Innovation."

Chandler, A. D. 1962. *Strategy and Structure. Chapters in the History of the American Industrial Enterprise*. Cambridge, MA: MIT Press.

Eisenhardt, K. M. and Martin, J. A. 2000. "Dynamic Capabilities: What Are They?" *Strategic Management Journal*, 21 (10–11): pp. 1105–1121.

Foss, N. J. 2003. "Selective Intervention and Internal Hybrids: Interpreting and Learning from the Rise and Decline of the Oticon Spaghetti Organization." *Organization Science*, 14 (3): pp. 331–334.

Foss, N. J., Klein, P. G., Kor, Y. Y., and Mahoney, J. T. 2008. "Entrepreneurship, Subjectivism, and the Resource-based View: Toward a New Synthesis." *Strategic Entrepreneurship Journal*, 2 (1): pp. 73–94.

Galbraith, J. H. 1974. "Organization Design: An Information Processing View." *Interfaces*, 4: pp. 28–36.

George, G. and Bock, A. J. 2011. "The Business Model in Practice and its Implications for Entrepreneurship Research." *Entrepreneurship Theory and Practice*, 35 (1): pp. 83–111.

Gratton, L. and Ghoshal, S. 2005. "Beyond Best Practice." *MIT Sloan Management Review*, 46 (3): pp. 49–57.

Greiner, L. E. 1998. "Evolution and Revolution as Organizations Grow." *Harvard Business Review*, 76 (3): pp. 55–68.

Hart, O. 1995. *Firms, Contracts, and Financial Structure*. Oxford: Oxford University Press.

Helfat, C. E. and Eisenhardt, K. M. 2004. "Inter-temporal Economies of Scope, Organizational Modularity, and the Dynamics of Diversification." *Strategic Management Journal*, 25 (13): pp. 1217–1232.

Helfat, C. E., Finkelstein, S., Mitchell, W., Peteraf, M. A., Singh, H., Teece, D. J., and Winter, S. G. 2007. *Dynamic Capabilities: Understanding Strategic Change in Organizations*. Oxford: Blackwell.

Hoffman, F. 2004. "What We Can Learn from Jackie Fisher." *Naval Institute Proceedings*, 130 (4): pp. 68–71.

Ireland, R. D., Covin, J. G., and Kuratko, D. F. 2009. "Conceptualizing Corporate Entrepreneurship Strategy." *Entrepreneurship Theory and Practice*, 33 (1): pp. 19–46.

Katkalo, V. S., Pitelis, C. N., and Teece, D. J. 2010. "Introduction: On the Nature and Scope of Dynamic Capabilities." *Industrial and Corporate Change*, 19 (4): pp. 1175–1186.

Kindström, D. and Kowalkowski, C. 2015. Chapter 10, this volume. "Service-driven Business Model Innovation: Organizing the Shift from a Product-based to a Service-centric Business Model."

Lovas, B. and Ghoshal, S. 2000. "Strategy as Guided Evolution." *Strategic Management Journal*, 21 (9): pp. 875–896.

Nemeth, C. J. 2012. "Minority Influence Theory." In *Handbook of Theories of Social Psychology, Volume Two*, edited by P. Van Lange, A. Kruglanski, and T. Higgins: pp. 362–378. New York: Sage.

Nickerson, J. A. and Zenger, T. R. 2004. "A Knowledge-based Theory of the Firm: The Problem-solving Perspective." *Organization Science*, 15: pp. 617–632.

Nonaka, I. 1994. "A Dynamic Theory of Organizational Knowledge Creation." *Organization Science*, 5 (1): pp. 14–37.

O'Reilly, C. A. and Tushman, M. L. 2004. "The Ambidextrous Organization." *Harvard Business Review*, 82 (4): pp. 74–81.

O'Reilly, C. A. and Tushman, M. L. 2008. "Ambidexterity as a Dynamic Capability: Resolving the Innovator's Dilemma." In *Research in Organizational Behavior*, vol. 28, edited by A. P. Brief and B. M. Staw: pp. 185–206. Oxford: Elsevier.

Pelled, L. H., Eisenhardt, K. M., and Xin, K. R. 1999. "Exploring the Black Box: An Analysis of Work Group Diversity, Conflict and Performance." *Administrative Science Quarterly*, 44 (1): pp. 1–28.

Pitelis, C. N. 2009. "The Co-evolution of Organizational Value Capture, Value Creation and Sustainable Advantage." *Organization Studies*, 30 (10): pp. 1115–1139.

Ries, E. 2011. *The Lean Startup: How Today's Entrepreneurs Use Continuous Innovation to Create Radically Successful Businesses*. New York: Crown Business.

Rumelt, R. 2011. *Good Strategy/Bad Strategy: The Difference and Why It Matters*. New York: Crown Business.

Santos, J. F. P., Spector, B., and Van der Heyden, L. 2015. Chapter 3, this volume. "Toward a Theory of Business Model Change."

Sellers, P. 1993. "Can this Man save IBM?" *Fortune*, April 19: pp. 63–67.

Shane, S. 2000. "Prior Knowledge and the Discovery of Entrepreneurial Opportunities." *Organization Science*, 11: pp. 448–469.

Shane, S. and Venkataraman, S. 2000. "The Promise of Entrepreneurship as a Field of Research." *Academy of Management Review*, 25: pp. 217–226.

Simsek, Z. 2009. "Organizational Ambidexterity: Towards a Multilevel Understanding." *Journal of Management Studies*, 46: pp. 597–624.

Stieglitz, N. and Foss, N. J. 2015. Chapter 6, this volume. "Business Model Innovation: The Role of Leadership."

Takeuchi, H. and Nonaka, I. 1986. "The New Product Development Game." *Harvard Business Review*, 64 (1): pp. 137–146.

Teece, D. J. 1980. "Economies of Scope and the Scope of the Enterprise." *Journal of Economic Behavior and Organization*, 1 (3): 223–247.

Teece, D. J. 1982. "Towards an Economic Theory of the Multiproduct Firm." *Journal of Economic Behavior and Organization*, 3 (1): pp. 39–63.

Teece, D. J. 1986. "Profiting from Technological Innovation." *Research Policy*, 15 (6): pp. 285–305.

Teece, D. J. 2006. "Reflections on Profiting from Innovation." *Research Policy*, 35 (8): pp. 1131–1146.

Teece, D. J. 2007. "Explicating Dynamic Capabilities: The Nature and Microfoundations of (Sustainable) Enterprise Performance." *Strategic Management Journal*, 28 (13): pp. 1319–1350.

Teece, D. J. 2010a. "Business Models, Business Strategy and Innovation." *Long Range Planning*, 43 (2–3): pp. 172–194.

Teece, D. J. 2010b. "Technological Innovation and the Theory of the Firm: The Role of Enterprise-level Knowledge, Complementarities, and (Dynamic) Capabilities." In *The Handbook of the Economics of Innovation 1*, edited by N. Rosenberg and B. Hall, pp. 679–730. Amsterdam: Elsevier.

Teece, D. J. 2011. "Human Capital, Capabilities and the Firm: Literati, Numerati, And Entrepreneurs In The 21st-century Enterprise." In *The Oxford Handbook of Human Capital*, edited by A. Burton-Jones and J.-C. Spender: pp. 527–562. Oxford: Oxford University Press.

Teece, D. J. 2012. "Dynamic Capabilities: Routines Versus Entrepreneurial Action." *Journal of Management Studies*, 49 (8): pp. 1395–1401.

Teece, D. J. 2014a. "A Dynamic Capabilities-based Entrepreneurial Theory of the Multinational Enterprise." *Journal of International Business Studies*, 45 (1): pp. 8–37.

Teece, D. J. 2014b. "The Foundations of Enterprise Performance: Dynamic and Ordinary (Managerial and Organizational) Capabilities in an (Economic) Theory of Firms." *Academy of Management Perspectives*, published ahead of print March 25, 2014, doi:10.5465/amp.2013.0116.

Teece, D. J., Pisano, G., and Shuen, A. 1997. "Dynamic Capabilities and Strategic Management." *Strategic Management Journal* 18 (7): pp. 509–533.

Tjosvold, D. 1985. "Implications of Controversy Research for Management." *Journal of Management*, 11 (3): pp. 21–37.

Welch, J. 2005 *Winning.* New York: HarperBusiness.

Williamson, O. E. 1975. *Markets and Hierarchies.* New York: The Free Press.

Williamson, O. E. 1981. "The Economics of Organization: The Transaction Cost Approach." *American Journal of Sociology*, 87 (3): pp. 548–577.

Williamson, O. E. 1985. *The Economic Institutions of Capitalism.* New York: The Free Press.

Williamson, O. E. 1996. *The Mechanisms of Governance.* Oxford: Oxford University Press.

Winter, S. G. 2003. "Understanding Dynamic Capabilities." *Strategic Management Journal*, 24 (10): pp. 991–995.

Woodward, J. 1965. *Industrial Organization: Theory and Practice.* Oxford: Oxford University Press.

3 Toward a Theory of Business Model Change

JOSÉ F. P. DOS SANTOS, BERT SPECTOR, AND LUDO VAN DER HEYDEN

Despite the ongoing flood of attention being paid to business models and the promise of *business model innovation*, a significant gap in the literature remains: what is the relationship between a company's *business model* and the organizational context in which that business model is embedded? That gap has challenged existing companies in their attempts to implement a new business model, when, unlike start-ups, these companies operate with an incumbent business model. The task, then, is to engage in a process we label *business model change* (BMC).

In this chapter, we analyze the dynamics of the change process required to implement a new business model in a company with an incumbent model. We set as our task the generation of a series of typologies and propositions regarding the BMC process. Our approach has both academic and applied implications. Much of the extant academic literature on business models focuses on models developed by start-ups (see, e.g., Amit and Zott, 2001; Zott and Amit, 2007). Managers of start-ups face numerous challenges, of course. Addressing the requirement to change an incumbent business model is not among them. The existing literature adds little to an understanding of BMC and the organizational context in which that process unfolds.

In terms of business practice, our point for executives in existing companies is to advise them to consider not only what new business model to adopt, but also how to move from an incumbent model to a new one. Miscalculating the costs, complexity, and dynamics associated with BMC will likely undermine effective implementation. US-based retailer J. C. Penney recently experienced the difference between a fascination with an attractive business model—in this case, Apple's retailing model—and the challenge of engaging in an effective process of replacing a decades-old business model with a new one (Tuttle, 2013). After moving from Apple retailing to J. C. Penney in 2011, Ron Johnson proved to be spectacularly incapable of orchestrating the transformation needed to support his vision for a new retailing model, and his tenure came to an abrupt end after only seventeen months.

The title of our chapter includes "*toward* a theory" because our goal is to offer a preliminary set of typologies and propositions concerning the BMC process. Following the theory-building framework described by Dubin (1978), we start with a definition of business models. We then generate a set of typologies and propositions concerning BMC that explicitly recognizes the people who perform activities within the model, while acknowledging the organizational implications of the BMC process. Propositions are not testable in and of themselves. The generation of propositions, however, is an indispensable step in the process of theory building. The next step, which we are hoping to encourage with this chapter, would be the construction of empirical indicators within our propositional statements that could be used to develop testable hypotheses. Real-world examples will be used throughout the chapter not as evidence—typologies and propositions are statements of logic rather than empiricism—but rather to provide concrete illustrations of our points and the issues we seek to address.

Defining Business Models

Despite years of attention to business models, clarity of definition remains elusive. Much of that lack of clarity stems from a conflation of two related but separable concepts: "business strategy" and "business model." A *business strategy* is specified by the answer to three questions: *what* is the offer, *who* constitutes the targeted market segment, and *how* is the offer delivered to the customer? There is a growing consensus, although hardly definitive, across the literature that the business model resides within the *how* question (see, e.g., Amit and Zott, 2001; Chesbrough, 2006; Santos, Spector, and Van der Heyden, 2009; Spector, 2013b; Teece, 2010; Zott and Amit, 2007, 2008, 2010). Businesses often compete with the same product offered to the same targeted market segments but with different business models. For instance, GAP, ZARA, and H&M all compete in the same product market, each with quite distinct business models.

That conceptualization of a business model as the component of competitive strategy that focuses on how product is delivered to the chosen market segment builds on existing strains of strategy theory. Porter introduced the notion of activities and their linkages in his analysis of a business's value chain: the activities involved in producing and delivering a good or a service to a market (Porter, 1985). Value-chain analysis points to *activities*—say, inbound logistics, operations, outbound logistics, marketing, sales, and so on—as well as *linkages* across activities. Porter understood a linkage largely in economic terms: the value flow (gains and losses) across activities, with emphasis on how one activity impacts the cost of another.

Stabell and Fjeldstad (1998) expanded the notion of value "chain" to value "network." In a value network, the business organizes and facilitates a complex set of exchanges among "actors, people, and organizations" (427). Rather than flowing sequentially from marketing to design to manufacturing, as in a traditional linear chain, these domains may interact simultaneously and continually. Because people are involved in the linking activities—employees who exchange information—value networks depend on people and how they relate to each other (see also Allee, 2003; Normann and Ramírez, 1998; Mintzberg and Van der Heyden, 1999).

Zott and Amit focused their definition of a business model on that value chain, starting at transactions between the focal company and "all of its *external* constituencies in factor and product markets [emphasis added]" (Zott and Amit, 2008: 183). Their business model concept reached outside of the focal company to include "external constituencies" but, at the time, did not include activities performed and linkages enacted entirely *within* the company. By relying on transaction cost economics to define the governance of linkages between activities, Zott and Amit posited a business model choice between market governance for inter-company transactions (outsourcing) and hierarchical governance for intra-company transactions (insourcing). The make/buy decision that resided at the heart of this conceptualization of business model design rested on rational—that is, self-interested—decisions concerning transaction costs.

A subtle but significant alteration in the conceptualization of business models occurred when *intra*-company activities were embraced as part of a business model design itself rather than just as the outcome of in/outsourcing decision (Santos, Spector, and Van der Heyden, 2009; Zott and Amit, 2010). That change brought the organization and its specific context into play, demanding consideration.

At the base of all business model definitions is an activity, which can be understood as a technologically separable node of an exchange (Williamson, 1975, 1991). A transaction, which involves the movement of a good or service between activities, is governed either by market forces with their appeal to incentives, by hierarchical forces with their appeal to authority, or by a hybrid of the two. Williamson (1981) recognized that activities were performed by "parties," which we will label *organizational units*. By organizational units, we mean the individual or individuals who perform a single, separable activity. Some activities may be performed by an individual, but companies typically have multiple individuals performing the same activity. These individuals, in turn, create a social context in which the activities are performed and linked.

Organizational units engage in inter-unit transactions, of course. But they do more. They also enact interdependent relationships. To parallel the transactional linkage between activities, we call on Thompson's (1967) concept of interdependence to classify non-economic linkages between organizational units. Thompson noted that organizational "parts"—his term for organizational units—are bound together by one of three types of interdependence: pooled interdependence in which "each part renders a discrete contribution to the whole and is supported by the whole" (54); sequential interdependence in which "direct interdependence can be pinpointed" and "the order of that interdependence can be specified" (54); and reciprocal interdependence in which "the outputs of each become the inputs for the others" (55). Altering interdependence among organizational units may involve either reordering the specified sequence—say, from A → B to B → A—or moving from one type of interdependence to another—say, from sequential to reciprocal.

A TWO-TIERED CONSTRUCT

By including the people who perform an activity either individually or collectively, we offer a definition of a business model that departs from earlier definitions by juxtaposing two systems: a system of *activities* and a system of *organizational units*. Our definition accounts for the different types of linkages among them: *transactions* between activities and *interdependencies* between organizational units:

> A business model is a configuration of activities, the organizational units that perform those activities, the company boundaries in which the organizational units reside, and the linkages among them.

That definition is presented schematically in Figure 3.1.

Our definition recognizes that organizational units are embedded within the borders of a larger organization: a function or a geographic/product division. Because business models link organizational units across these organizational boundaries, the interdependence among them takes on additional complexity which must be addressed in the BMC process.

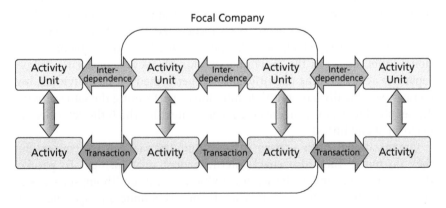

Figure 3.1 The business model

A BMC TYPOLOGY

To help analyze BMC in existing businesses, we offer a typology. Typologies are theoretical constructs that separate a given set of items' multi-dimensionality (Smith, 2002). We follow Bailey (1994) in distinguishing between a typology and a taxonomy, the latter being a classification system based on empirically observable and measureable characteristics. Our typology, which is presented in Table 3.1, proposes four BMC categories, with two subdivisions in each:

- *Reactivating*: an alteration that either adds to or removes an activity from the incumbent business model. In 2001, Apple added retail stores to its business model and removed the activity of selling through third-party retailers. More recently, that activity was added again to Apple's business model. There are examples in which the business may remove an activity and "outsource" that third-party activity to the customer. IKEA did that in the early days of their evolving business model when it removed assembly and delivery from its business model, asking the customer to enact these activities.

Table 3.1 Typology of business model change

Classification	Type	What Changes
Reactivating—altering the set of activities performed by the company	Adding	The activity set of a company's business model by adding
	Removing	The activity set of a company's business model by removing
Relinking—altering the linkages between activities	Regoverning	The governance of transactions between market, hierarchy, and hybrid
	Resequencing	The order in which organizational units perform activities Or The interdependence among organizational units between pooled, sequential, and reciprocal
Repartitioning—altering the boundaries of the focal company by moving an organizational unit across business boundaries	Insourcing/outsourcing	The location of an organizational unit moves from outside to inside the company or from inside to outside the company
	Reassigning	The location of an organizational unit moves from one unit to another within the company
Relocating—alerting the (physical, cultural, and institutional) location between organizational units performing activities	Off-shoring	The geographic location of an organizational unit from inside to outside the company's home country to a foreign country
	On-shoring	The geographic location of an organizational unit from a foreign-country activity unit into the home country

- *Relinking*: an alteration that involves either changing the transaction governance among activities or the interdependence among organizational units in the incumbent model. Relinking may involve moving a transaction between market, hierarchy, and hybrid. When Netflix changed its transaction with content suppliers from a licensing contract to a revenue-sharing one, it moved from market to hybrid governance of the transaction. Relinking may also involve altering the interdependence among organizational units either by changing the order of input–output sequence or changing the nature of the interdependence between units among pooled, sequential, and reciprocal. Under its "Made for You" program, McDonald's reversed its long-standing practice of assembling the burger *before* a customer placed an order, now sequencing the activities so as the hamburger was cooked first and assembled only after the order was taken. In its pursuit of a fast fashion strategy, ZARA moved from sequential to reciprocal interdependence among design, supply, and store management units. For each product category, such as baby garments or women's classics, the managers of those three units were co-located, actually working at the same table, to facilitate reciprocity to support speed.
- *Repartitioning*: an alteration that moves the organizational unit performing an activity. Repartitioning may involve insourcing or outsourcing: Apple insourced the chip design activity and Levi's outsourced jean assembly. It may also involve moving an activity from one organizational unit to another within the same company, as Taco Bell did when it moved food preparation from its stores to a central kitchen. In each of these cases, the activities remained the same but the organizational boundaries in which the organizational units were embedded changed.
- *Relocating*: an alteration that maintains the existing activity set of the incumbent model while moving the organizational unit to another country. Ford first off-shored and then on-shored assembly work. By placing organizational units in different countries, the nature of the transaction link is altered by virtue of the new national context in which the organizational unit operates; the nature of the interdependence link is altered by physical, cultural, and psychic distance.

Business models are situated within the business units of a company—the *how* to complement the *what* and *who* of a business strategy—and, therefore, BMC occurs within that business unit. Our primary level of analysis is therefore the company. We recognize that many business units operate within a multibusiness corporation, a configuration that includes multinationals. Multibusiness corporations are enterprises characterized by a corporate center and relatively autonomous, discrete operating business units (often called divisions or subsidiaries), each with its own competitive strategy (Chandler, 1962; Williamson, 1975; Porter, 1987). The executives who comprise the corporate center engage in a set of (corporate) activities clearly distinguished from those at the divisional level.

We will discuss the organizational implications of corporate context later in the chapter. For now, we would like to make the point that from the perspective of the business unit, other divisions in the corporation should be classified as *non-focal*. Thus, a division may outsource to or insource from another division—say, Verizon Wireless purchasing access to network infrastructure from Verizon Landline—in the same corporation. Transactions between divisions in the same company may be governed by market-like forces (usually through transfer pricing mechanisms), hierarchy, or hybrid techniques (Williamson, 1975).

THE TRANSFORMATIVE POWER OF BMC

BMC may be used by a business to improve internal efficiencies, thus lowering costs, and/or enhancing value appropriation. BMC helped transform the once-ailing Nissan Motors, which received an equity investment from Renault and joined the Renault-Nissan Alliance in 1999 (Magee, 2003). A number of management missteps at Nissan had kicked off a debilitating and long-lasting decline starting in the 1980s. Less obvious than the missteps but more troubling was Nissan's inability to find flexibility and efficiency in its relationship with suppliers. Nissan's cost of parts was significantly higher (in the 15–20 percent range), than its Japanese competitors. Aggressive competition from Honda in the United States forced Nissan to take a $1,000 discount on its cars. Sales declined, but costs did not. Despite several restructuring plans, Nissan executives achieved little real improvement. The company had to borrow money from the government-owned Japan Development Bank to stay afloat. Forced by its creditors to seek potential partners, Nissan entered into an alliance with France-based Renault. As a precondition for the alliance, Nissan executives agreed that Renault's second-in-command, Carlos Ghosn, would come to Japan as COO.

With the recommendations from nine cross-functional teams that Ghosn oversaw, he and the Nisan executive committee pulled together what became known as the Nissan Revival Plan. That plan maintained the company's product/market matrix. What Ghosn changed dramatically was the business model as he reconfigured activities and organizational units. Among those sweeping business model changes were:

- *Relinking by regoverning*: The nature of the relation with suppliers changed from a "keiretsu" close partnership (hybrid) to a more arms-length, competitive kind of relation with a reduced number of suppliers (market). In parallel, by selling Nissan's ownership stake in suppliers—that ownership stake is what made the transaction governance in the incumbent model a hybrid—the company was able to free up much-needed cash.

- *Relinking by regoverning and resequencing and repartitioning by out-sourcing and reassigning*: Manufacturing of certain models for specific markets was outsourced to Renault (and vice versa). Certain procurement and IT activities were outsourced to joint-venture units with Renault. New car platforms were developed jointly with Renault using multicultural, dispersed teams. New model introductions and market development activities were coordinated between Nissan and Renault via the Renault–Nissan Alliance. In addition, market research activities were resequenced to be included at the front end of the new car development process.
- *Relocating by off-shoring*: Production capacity was cut in Japan and increased in the United States.

Nissan's BMC required vast changes in both values and organization structure. Nissan's core values of technical excellence and loyalty were supplemented by customer satisfaction and performance metrics. Decision-making processes and incentives also changed. And people changed, mostly at the highest management levels. Ghosn brought with him twenty executives from Renault. Ghosn's dramatic BMC returned Nissan to profitability in three years.

The Organizational Implications of BMC

When companies look to the possibilities of introducing a new business model, they face two options. The first is what we call *additive* BMC. In this case, companies introduce a new business model while simultaneously maintaining their incumbent model. The second option is *replacive* BMC, by which we mean that the incumbent model is abolished and replaced by the new model. It is possible, of course, that a company might adopt a new business model to serve the same product/market matrix while continuing to maintain its incumbent business model. This would be additive BMC. Typically, however, these parallel business models are assigned to separate divisions within the same multibusiness corporation. That is what Wal-Mart did when it created its online model to target its traditional customers with the same products. More recently, Netflix separated its streaming-delivery model and its mail-delivery model into different divisions.

Because our definition of business model includes organizational units and because of the social nature of people and their interactions, we propose that the impact of additive and replacive BMC will have a different effect on the people who perform the acridities in the business model:

> **Proposition 1**: *The organizational impact of replacive BMC will likely be greater than the organizational impact of additive BMC.*

To explore why this is, we call on two categories: social capital and competency.

SOCIAL CAPITAL

By recognizing the centrality of interactions among people in the enactment of business models, we offer the following proposition:

> **Proposition 1a**: *Replacive BMC will alter existing social interactions between the organizational units in the incumbent business model.*

Interdependencies are enacted across relational linkages (Coleman 1988; Nahapiet and Ghoshal 1998). Social capital has been found to facilitate interdependencies by encouraging the flow of information among actors located within a social structure, enhancing the capacity for actors to influence the behaviors of others, and reinforcing reciprocal behaviors by assigning positive support to and reinforcement of those behaviors (Lin, 2001). Social capital reduces uncertainty by increasing the possibility of predictable decision making among actors.

BMC, especially when it is replacive, has the potential for disrupting social ties and reducing social capital. That disruption will act as a constraint on the ability to implement BMC effectively. To understand that disruption, we can look at the BMC process at the Joplin Clinic (a disguised name), a full-service medical clinic. After fifty years in operation, the Clinic purchased two small, highly successful family practices in the hopes of capturing greater value through a flow of referrals. The BMC in this case involved relinking by regoverning and repartitioning by insourcing. Despite those business model innovations, the behaviors remained unchanged. The Joplin Clinic had, over its fifty-plus years of existence, developed considerable social capital among its physician partners. It quickly became apparent, however, that the BMC had failed to strengthen relationships. Doctors in the purchased clinics continued their previous referral pattern. Even though the BMC had changed the nature of the transaction—as part of the Joplin Clinic, the new doctors shared in its profitability—the relationship ties remained untouched. It had not forged new relational ties. When it became clear that no such alteration had occurred, the Clinic made a commitment to investing in social capital by focusing on community building. That investment impacted referrals in a positive way, allowing the Clinic to leverage its BMC into financial gain. Effective enactment of BMC, therefore, may require an investment in training and other methodologies to build skills and knowledge as well as social relationships.

COMPETENCY DOMAIN

Replacive BMC will impact the collective competencies of a company, leading to our next proposition:

> **Proposition 1b**: *Replacive BMC will be competency destructive.*

Competencies refer to skills and/or knowledge in the possession of the individuals who comprise the organizational units performing a given activity.

The notion of competency-destructive innovation comes from Tushman and Anderson (1986), who identified the destruction caused by new technologies that "are so fundamentally different from previous dominant technologies that the skills and knowledge base required to operate the core technology shift" (442). Hence, BMC may require both new skills and new knowledge on the part of the individuals who comprise the affected activity units and the elimination of the need for previous core skills and knowledge.

Take the case of BMC within the Hardware Engineering division of Auratek (a disguised name). That BMC outsourced the organizational unit performing the verification activity that identified flaws in chip design prior to fabrication. Cost savings were achieved by reducing the division's internal verification group from thirty-three to six engineers. To manage the interface between internal and external organizational units, the verification engineers at headquarters were expected to act as liaisons between internal design engineers and the external verification activity unit. Few of those engineers had competencies to effectively enact this added activity as coordinators and liaisons, and were in any case not interested in developing these competencies. They were engineers, they insisted, not administrators. A number of them threatened to resign. Outsourcing was accompanied by off-shoring (repartitioning and relocating) that made the requirements for new competencies all the more urgent. Additionally, literal competency destruction—the elimination of twenty-seven engineering jobs within the incumbent organizational unit—undermined commitment on the part of the remaining engineers to change.

Auratek countered with stock options and retention bonuses to induce them to stay. Even so, four left. The remaining verification engineers found themselves under increasing pressure to pick up the workload, not just that of the division-based engineers who had left, but also of the outsourced verification engineers. BMC led to delayed product releases and lengthened cycle time to fix defects. "Maybe we saved $2 million in salaries," concluded a manager, "but I am afraid to even consider what we've lost in present and future sales."

Competency-destructive processes require transformational behavior change (Spector, 2013a). Individuals who make up the organizational units will be required to gain new competencies. Businesses will need to invest in training, assuming of course that the targeted individuals are motivated to learn new competences. A misfit between extant and newly required competencies may well require removal and replacement. The cost of BMC will be high if the business does not deal adequately with the competency domain.

THE TRANSFORMATIONAL CHALLENGE

It may be the reluctance to engage in replacive BMC that leaves businesses in the awkward position of holding onto an old model long past the replacement time for that model. Sears, a business unit within Sears Holding, used the additive rather than replacive strategy for BMC. Sears started to sell some of its private brands (Kenmore appliances and Craftsmen tools) through competing retail stores, while continuing to sell those same brands in its own unprofitable retail outlets (having the impact of lowering the revenues of those stores even further). The "logic" of replacive BMC can butt up against organizational dynamics that support the status quo. Unlike start-ups, existing companies have incumbent business models, and the power of incumbency is considerable, particularly in terms of resilience in the face of challenge. Our proposition regarding the power of incumbency is:

> **Proposition 2**: *The power of incumbency may work to slow the response of management in existing companies to the need for replacive BMC.*

The concept of dominant logic (Bettis and Prahalad, 1995; Prahalad and Bettis, 1986) helps to explain that response.

Managers are often unable to perceive the significance of either the challenge or the opportunity presented by a new business model. Shih, Kaufman, and Spinola (2009), for instance, demonstrated how unresponsive executives at Blockbuster were to the potent threat being offered by a new business model in the home entertainment business: Netflix's direct delivery of DVDs by mail. Blockbuster's 2002 annual 10-K did not list the threat posed by online rental services under its mandatory "Risk" section, and the company did not respond with its own online service until 2004, seven years after Netflix's founding. In 2011, a bankrupted Blockbuster was acquired at auction by Dish Network. Currently, there are no bricks-and-mortar DVD rental chains left in the United States.

Relying heavily on cognitive psychology literature, Prahalad and Bettis proposed dominant logic as a concept to help understand how organizational leaders may ignore or undervalue relevant data concerning threats and opportunities. The dominant logic of an existing business—a mindset created through experience and reinforced by shared schemas and cognitive maps—acts to narrow the stem through which data are funneled into the process of organizational learning. Thus, Blockbuster executives "saw"—that is, they were aware of—the rise of an alternative business model but discounted the competitive threat and held on to their incumbent model. All existing companies have a dominant logic that resides, of course, in people, not in activities. Dominant logic creates a cognitive bias, although some businesses have a wider stem than others, allowing for greater adaptation.

Replacive BMC has the property of unseating not just incumbent models but also the social capital, competencies, and behaviors of organization unit members, demanding a replacement of the status quo. For that reason, our next proposition addresses the requirement for a more fundamental change:

> **Proposition 3**: *Replacive BMC will require systemic organizational transformation.*

Optimally, transformational change occurs in a systemic and strategic way: aligning multiple design elements with the new business model. Often, however, organizational leaders prefer to avoid such fundamental change, opting instead for incremental, piecemeal approaches when systemic change is needed. Miller (1990) has documented the tendency of once-successful organizations to hold on to, with only occasional tinkering, the designs and arrangements that provided success in the past. Replacive BMC will require more than tinkering.

We can return to the Nissan example to witness an executive facing just this challenge. "For a company that had been losing money for seven years out of eight," Carlos Ghosn observed, "there is not enough of a sense of urgency. People should be banging their heads on the walls everywhere" (quoted in Thorton, 1999: 54). Ghosn proved to be masterful at building support for BMC. Before determining what the new business model would be, Ghosn toured Nissan plants, subsidiaries, and dealerships in Japan, the United States, Europe, and Taiwan. Rather than imposing a solution, he allowed key employees in the business to propose solutions. Changes imposed from "above"—top executives telling employees what the new business model will be and what they must change in order to enact it—is likely to engender resistance from the organizational units—activities, after all, do not resist—that must enact the new business model. When people participate in designing the new model, as was the case at Nissan, they are more likely to feel that they are making an informed choice and to develop a commitment to the choice as well as a sense of responsibility for implementing the new design.

To harvest the embedded knowledge and gain the commitment of employees, Ghosn pulled together nine cross-functional teams to examine all aspects of the business operation: from business development to manufacturing and logistics to supplier relationships to organizational structure. Each had ten members, all from middle management. Teams could also create subteams to help them collect data. In total, the effort involved about 500 people. Ghosn gave the teams three months to review the company's operations and make recommendations. By managing the organizational transformation process effectively and engaging middle management in its design, Nissan succeeded in replacing the incumbent business model.

The Corporation as Context

For companies that operate as part of a multibusiness corporation, that corporation is an element of the organizational context for BMC. Business models exist at the divisional level, not at the corporate level. In their proximity to operations, customers, and competitors, division managers are best positioned to make judgments about the optimum configuration of activities and units that will deliver the product and/or services to the intended market.

The corporate center exists both outside and above the division, and corporate executives have the duty of looking after the interests of the entire corporate entity, not just a single division. In order to fulfill that mandate, corporations create corporate models that specify the framework for governing corporate center/division linkages. Academic literature on business models tends to blur that distinction. Amit and Zott (2012), for instance, refer to business models at Apple, HTC, and IBM (all multibusiness corporations) alongside references to Taco Bell, Bancolumbia Retail, and Nespresso (all divisions within multibusiness corporations). Corporate models are not the same as business models; rather, they are context to business models. Multibusiness corporations such as Inditex (with divisions including ZARA, Massimo Duttim, and Bershka) and ACCOR (with divisions including Mercure, Novotel, and Ibis) leave business model choices to their divisions. The role of the corporation in that regard is key.

In that regard, we propose that the corporate center plays a dual role vis-à-vis BMC:

Proposition 4: *The corporate center may act as both a constraint on and a provider of opportunity for division-level BMC.*

Let's examine these two possibilities in turn.

THE CORPORATION AS A POTENTIAL CONSTRAINT

At first glance, it would seem that corporate interest would be entirely aligned with division-level BMC. After all, the purpose of BMC is to generate value. However, the corporate center has interests that could mitigate BMC support in three regards:

1. *BMC potentially alters the scope of the corporation.* BMC can alter the scope of the individual business, either by outsourcing (broadening) or insourcing (narrowing), as well as by relocating. Changes in business scope on the part of divisions impacts the scope of the entire corporation, and thus requires corporate approval. As a number of global corporations with apparel businesses recently learned, the risk of outsourcing and off-shoring production of a business—in this case, to Bangladesh—can impact the entire corporation.

2. *BMC potentially impacts the strategic operations of other units.* Relinking and repartitioning on the part of one division may have an impact on other divisions within the corporation, particularly in corporations that pursue operational synergies. Any of these decisions may have a positive impact on a division's performance while placing another division at a disadvantage. Outsourcing information technology (IT) activities by one division may impact the performance of the corporate IT function and work to the detriment of another division. Conversely, centralizing IT, which typically accompanies enterprise resource planning

implementation, can generate opposition from divisions that may be less well served by the new system and/or lack the competencies to deal with the complex interface that a new system is likely to impose.

3. *BMC potentially changes the risk exposure of the organization.* Corporate risk is a function of the risk assumed by each individual division. An alteration in a division's business model may alter the division's risk or perception of risk as expressed by its beta coefficient, that is, its measure of systematic risk. This may simply be the effect of analysts' views of the division if the innovation results in placing that division in a different "industry" (expressed by a different standard industrial classification code) or by a change in the geographic risk of the unit by outsourcing organizational units in its business model. That perception of changed risk exposure will impact the share price of the whole corporation and its cost of capital.

Some BMC alterations will attract little attention from the corporate center. But others demand substantial involvement in and likely the approval of the corporate center. The constraints of corporate membership are typically felt by the divisions on business model choices more due to central costs and synergy imperatives than on product/market choices, which are more naturally within the score of divisional strategic choices.

Table 3.2 offers a set of propositions concerning the degree to which the different classifications and sub-classifications of BMC will demand corporate attention.

THE CORPORATION AS A POTENTIAL SOURCE OF OPPORTUNITY

Multibusiness corporations such as General Electric (GE), Nestlé, and Samsung house a variety of business models across their divisions. That variety creates a potential for cross-divisional learning, adaptation, and innovation. That opportunity grows out of the corporation's capacity to encourage

Table 3.2 A typology of corporate attention to division-level BMC

Classification	Type	Level of Corporate Attention
Reactivating	Adding	Low
	Removing	Low
Relinking	Regoverning	Moderate
	Resequencing	Low
Repartitioning	Insourcing/outsourcing	High
	Reassigning	Low
Relocating	Off-shoring	High
	On-shoring	High

knowledge exchange and learning among division managers and corporate executives. Corporate membership offers an opportunity for both deep and timely learning concerning the possibility of other divisions' business models.

Although knowledge transfer within a multibusiness corporation can and often is hampered by stickiness (Szulanski, 2000), institutional distance among divisions of the same corporation can be overcome. Corporations can and do undertake actions designed explicitly to lower barriers to cross-divisional learning: Disney relies on socialization to build bonds among newly hired executives in all divisions, GE develops division-level executives into corporate assets through a shared culture and regular cross-divisional transfers, and Accor and Dannon convene regular "innovation fairs" that encourage cross-business sharing. All of these activities have the potential to increase trust and lower the distance and institutional barriers to sharing knowledge. The goal of these corporate-sponsored activities is to offer the opportunity for divisional managers to embed and acquire knowledge that "transcends one's own limited perspective and boundary" in order to create opportunities for "interdependent innovation" among divisions (Burgelman and Doz, 2001; Dunford, Palmer, and Benveniste, 2010; Kleinbaum and Tushman, 2007; Teece and Pisano, 1994).

The development of learning opportunities for division managers who initiate BMC and corporate executives who judge the final merit of innovation proposals will depend on an organizational context that allows for, even encourages, both initiative and risk-taking behaviors. Risk taking will be subdued if the organizational context is seen by divisional managers as punishing to risk takers. Because it is mainly the division managers who possess the knowledge for BMC, these managers will require a context of psychological safety in which they can offer innovative ideas both to each other and to the corporate center without fear of punishment or personal rejection (as opposed to rejection of an idea) (Edmundson, 1999). Therefore, we propose two factors, relating to both structure and process, will impact the likelihood of BMC emergence within corporate divisions.

MUTUALITY IN CORPORATE STRUCTURE

The literature on corporate strategy offers different design options for what might be thought of as a corporate model (see, e.g., Goold, Campbell, and Alexander, 1994):

- *The modular model.* Corporations pursuing a portfolio strategy adopt a modular corporate model. A portfolio corporation seeks to create wealth by investing in different and diverse businesses, often referred to as assets. The modular model removes the corporate center from any direct role in managing the business units, which are largely autonomous. Under the modular model, corporate executives appoint the division heads and monitor the financial requirements (capital and investments budgets) and outcomes. Warren Buffet, chairman of Berkshire Hathaway, describes the modular model as "a collection of private businesses" in which the division heads "need to make decisions as if they own 100% of the company" (quoted in Larcker and Tayan, 2009: 2).

- *The linked model.* Many corporations seek to create value not simply by investing in a portfolio of business à la Berkshire Hathaway, but rather by exploiting opportunities for synergies. Shared services, common supply-chain elements, single-face-to-the-customer teams are all attempts to locate value in cross-business linkages. Under a linked model, corporate executives focus on those opportunities in order to reduce overall costs and improve corporate profitability. TJX, a multibusiness retail-based corporation, for instance, requires its divisions—Marmaxx, Home Goods, and TK Maxx among them—to share credit operations along with buying activities. Alcoa's Global Business Services centralizes global credit, procurement, information services, and other activities as a way to seek economies of scale. The key element of the linked model is that the corporate center *requires* that divisions participate in synergistic activities.

- *The mutual model.* A mutual corporate model welcomes synergistic activities among divisions. Unlike the linked model, however, the mutual model does not impose linkages; rather, it allows the divisional managers to identify linkage opportunities based on enlightened self-interest. The mutual model identifies as a key role for the corporate center the creation of opportunities to learn from and share across divisions, an opportunity that transcends the necessarily limited perspective and boundaries of each business. As a result, synergies may be identified and exploited by divisional managers and supported by corporate executives.

Each model—modular, linked, and mutual—has advantages and require a different value-adding role of the corporate center and different behaviors on the part of corporate and divisional executives. We are not proposing that one model is superior to the others in all respects, only in the specific case of BMC (see Table 3.3). The linked model is intended to create efficiencies, but will do

Table 3.3 How the corporate model impacts business-unit-level BMC

Model Choice	Role of Corporate Center	Impact on BMC
Modular model	Selects which businesses to invest in and allocates capital among units	Units operate with maximum opportunity to innovate business models but low opportunity to learn from other corporate members
Linked model	Imposes operational linkages to capture synergies	Units constrained to initiate BMC because of linkages to other units
Mutual model	Creates opportunities for exploiting mutual self-interest among business units	Units have flexibility to initiate BMC as well as opportunities to learn from other units

so typically at the expense of divisional autonomy. In the modular model, each autonomous division can pursue BMC on its own without concern about its impact on other units. However, what each unit gains in autonomy it loses in the opportunity to share business model knowledge across units. Our proposition, then, is:

> **Proposition 5**: *The mutual corporate model will maximize opportunities and minimize constraints on division-level BMC.*

The mutual model with its embrace of enlightened self-interest becomes the corporate model most conducive to BMC.

ORGANIZATIONAL JUSTICE IN CORPORATE PROCESSES

Structure must be supplemented by processes, particularly concerning the relationship between the corporate center and the division heads. In any corporation, a dual asymmetry of knowledge and authority is likely to exist. Division managers will have greater knowledge of their current business, including customers, suppliers, and competitors than do corporate executives: knowledge asymmetry. At the time, corporate executives have greater authority in imposing new business models on the divisions and vetoing division-generated proposals for BMC: power asymmetry.

Such situations call for organizational justice, the perception among organizational members that decisions are fair, both in terms of the process by which they are derived (procedural justice) and the content of the decisions (distributive justice). Organizational justice will be especially salient in circumstances that involve change, the presence of status and power differences, resource scarcity, and the potential for negative outcomes for some (Greenberg and Cropanzano, 2001). A major result of organizational justice is that decisions will generate resistance when those impacted perceive that the decision-making and implementation process were unfair, whereas those impacted negatively will be more likely to accept the outcome if they view the process by which decisions were made to have been transparent and fair.

A key characteristic of organizational justice is *voice*: the ability for those affected to provide input and be heard (without fear of retaliation). Given the disparity of power between the corporate center and the divisions, there is always a danger that BMC imposed by the corporate center violates the requirement for voice. An example can be found in the history of General Motors (GM). When Frederic Donner, an accountant who worked his way up the ranks of GM corporate by virtue of being a "true financial genius," took over the CEO role from the retiring Alfred Sloan in 1958, he set out to dismantle Sloan's carefully constructed and balanced system of "participative decentralization" (Freeland, 2001).

Sloan's participative decentralization was built by co-participation by corporate executives and division managers on planning committees and other cross-functional committees. Co-membership had assured that corporate executives and divisional managers would fully share information about operations in the divisions, as well as about the overall policies of the corporation. Donner, with his lack of operating experience, saw the separation of policy formulation from execution as a useful step toward greater discipline and lower costs. As a result, he removed divisional managers from all top corporate committees. Now, instead of being fully engaged in policy decisions, divisional managers would be told what to do and how to do it. The managers of GM's many divisions lost their voice in corporate policy making.

Another potential barrier to the process of BMC lies in the motivation of the division manager. For the most part, BMC will emerge from within the divisions. The closeness of the business units to customers, suppliers, and competitors provides the source of innovation. Unless division managers feel confident that the corporate center wants to engage them in BMC, they will not strongly pursue such opportunities. It is the belief that organizational justice pervades the corporation—and embodied at its top levels by corporate executives—that will support the pursuit of BMC within divisions.

A telling contrast can be seen in the example of ABC, a disguised name for a European-based multinational (Van der Heyden, 2014). ABC needed a major strategic change involving a renewed focus on organic growth and improved operational efficiencies. The CEO called in all his division heads during summer vacation, and gave them voice in a collective exercise where he challenged them in groups to operationalize the new strategy. One of the frictions among divisions—that played out in each country—had been the lack of collaboration between the company's multiple brands, leading each country manager to make allocation decisions concerning brand budgets and deployment which often would be regarded as sub-optimal from a global viewpoint. The summer vacation retreat of the division managers resulted very quickly in overcoming year-long problems, including, for example, the creation of a new (corporate) activity called "brand management," as well as global "key account" management, which had proven elusive until then.

Comparing the GM and ABC experiences leads to a proposition concerning the role of organizational justice:

> **Proposition 6**: *The presence of organizational justice within a corporation will encourage the development, sharing, and implementation of BMC across divisions.*

The BMC-conducive corporation will, therefore, adopt the mutual model and embed processes to ensure organizational justice.

Conclusion

A useful way to start our conclusion might be to take a moment to consider what this chapter was *not* about. We did not address innovative business models in start-up companies. We did not evaluate the advantages and disadvantages of different business models, nor did we attempt to address optimal models for particular strategies and/or industries. Our concerns were specifically focused on one particular facet of business model innovation: the organizational implications that come into play when a company attempts to change or replace its incumbent business model.

The organizational units that perform the activities in a business model are, in our view, an integral part of that model, and not incidental to it. Because the bulk of existing business model literature focuses on start-ups, the role of actors—except perhaps for the leading entrepreneurs themselves—has not been explicitly addressed. In this chapter, we focused not on the end-state of business model innovation but rather on the process of business model change.

Existing companies possess incumbent models. A body of competencies, a web of relationships, and a set of emotions attach themselves not to the activities but to the individuals in and across the units that perform them. Furthermore, when a business operates within the context of a multibusiness corporation, another set of competencies, relationships, and emotions come into play when a company attempts to change its business model.

By bringing organizational units into the business model construct rather than consigning them to the outskirts or ignoring them altogether, we have complemented existing definitions, and also opened the construct to strikingly different propositions pertaining for example to corporate structure and processes. We believe that without the organizational unit, the business model construct runs the danger of either over- or under-specification. An overly specified definition of business models tends to erase the boundary between a business model and organizational design. Conversely, under-specification allows for the conflation of business model and business strategy.

▪ REFERENCES

Allee, V. 2003. *The Future of Knowledge: Increasing Prosperity Through Value Networks*. London: Butterworth-Heinemann.

Amit, R. and Zott, C. 2001. "Value Creation in e-business." *Strategic Management Journal*, 22 (June–July): pp. 493–520.

Amit, R. and Zott, C. 2012. "Creating Value Through Business Model Innovation." *MIT Sloan Management Review*, 53 (3): pp. 41–49.

Bailey, K. D. 1994. *Topologies and Taxonomies: An Introduction to Classification Techniques*. Thousand Oaks, CA: Sage.

Bettis, R. A. and Prahalad, C. K. 1995. "The Dominant Logic: Retrospective and Extension." *Strategic Management Journal*, 16 (1): pp. 5–14.

Burgelman, R. A. and Doz, Y. L. 2001. "The Power of Strategic Integration." *Sloan Management Review*, 42 (3): pp. 28–38.

Chandler, A. D. 1962. *Strategy and Structure: Chapters in the History of the Industrial Enterprise*. Cambridge: MIT Press.

Chesbrough, H. W. 2006. *Open Business Models: How to Thrive in the New Innovation Landscape.* Boston, MA: Harvard Business School Press.

Coleman, J. S. 1988. "Social Capital in the Creation of Human Capital." *American Journal of Sociology,* 94 (1): pp. 95–121.

Dunford, R., Palmer, I., and Benveniste, J. 2010. "Business Model Replication for Early and Rapid Internationalization: The ING Direct Experience." *Long Range Planning,* 43 (2-3): pp. 655–674.

Dubin, R. 1978. *Theory Building: Revised Edition.* New York: Free Press.

Edmundson, A. 1999. "Psychological Safety and Learning Behavior in Work Teams." *Administrative Science Quarterly,* 44 (2): pp. 350–383.

Freeland, R. F. 2001. *The Struggle for Control of the Modern Corporation: Organizational Change at General Motors, 1924–1970.* Cambridge: Cambridge University Press.

Goold, M., Campbell, A., and Alexander, M. 1994. *Corporate-level Strategy: Creating Value in the Multibusiness Company.* New York: John Wiley.

Greenberg, J. and Cropanzano, R. 2001. *Advances in Organizational Justice.* Stanford: Stanford University Press.

Kleinbaum, A. M. and Tushman, M. L. 2007. "Building Bridges: The Social Structure of Interdependent Innovation." *Strategic Entrepreneurship Journal,* 1 (1–2): pp. 103–122.

Larcker, D. F. and Tayan, B. 2009. *The Management of Berkshire Hathaway.* Boston, MA: Harvard Business School Publishing.

Lin, N. 2001. *Social Capital: A Theory of Social Structure in Action.* Cambridge: Cambridge University Press.

Magee, D. 2003. *Turnaround: How Carlos Ghosn Rescued Nissan.* New York: HarperCollins.

Miller, D. 1990. *The Icarus Paradox: How Exceptional Companies Bring About their Own Downfall.* New York: Harper Business.

Mintzberg, H. and Van der Heyden, L. 1999. "Organigraphs: Drawing How Companies Really Work". *Harvard Business Review,* 77 (5): pp. 88–94.

Nahapiet, J. and Ghoshal, S. 1998. "Social Capital, Intellectual Capital, and the Organizational Advantage." *Academy of Management Review,* 23 (2): pp. 242–266.

Normann, R. and Ramírez, R. 1998. *Designing Interactive Strategy: From Value Chain to Value Constellation.* San Francisco: Wiley.

Porter, M. E. 1985. *Competitive Advantage: Creating and Sustaining Superior Performance.* New York: Free Press.

Porter, M. E. 1987. "From Competitive Advantage to Corporate Strategy." *Harvard Business Review,* 65 (May–June): pp. 43–60.

Prahalad, C. K. and Bettis, R. A. 1986. "The Dominent Logic: A New Linkage Between Diversity and Performance." *Strategic Management Journal,* 7 (6): pp. 485–501.

Santos, J. F. P., Spector, B. A., and Van der Heyden, L. 2009. "Toward a Theory of Business Model Innovation in Incumbent Firms." Fontainebleau: INSEAD Working Papers, Collection 16.

Shih, W., Kaufman, S., and Spinola, D. 2009. *Netflix.* Boston, MA: Harvard Business School Publishing.

Smith, K. B. 2002. "Topologies, Taxonomies, and the Benefits of Policy Classification." *Policy Studies Journal,* 30 (3): pp. 379–395.

Spector, B. A. 2013a. *Implementing Organizational Change: Theory Into Action*, 3rd edition. New Jersey: Pearson.

Spector, B. A. 2013b. "The Social Embeddedness of Business Model Enactment: Implications for Theory and Practice." *Journal of Strategy and Management*, 6 (1): pp. 27–39.

Stabell, C. B. and Fjeldstad, Ø. 1998. "Configuring Value for Competitive Advantage: On Chains, Shops, and Networks." *Strategic Management Journal*, 19 (5): pp. 413–437.

Szulanski, G. 2000. "The Process of Knowledge Transfer: A Diachronic Analysis of Stickiness." *Organizational Behavior and Human Decision Processes*, 82 (1): pp. 9–27.

Teece, D. J. 2010. "Business Model, Business Strategy, and Innovation." *Long Range Planning*, 43 (2–3): pp. 172–194.

Teece, D. and Pisano, G. 1994. "The Dynamic Capabilities of Firms: An Introduction." *Industrial and Corporate Change*, 3 (3): pp. 537–556.

Thompson, J. D. 1967. *Organizations in Action: Social Science Bases of Administrative Theory*. New York: McGraw-Hill.

Thorton, E. 1999. "Remaking Nissan." *Business Week* (November 15): 70.

Tushman, M. L. and Anderson, P. 1986. "Technological Discontinuities and Organizational Environments." *Administrative Science Quarterly*, 31 (3): pp. 439–465.

Tuttle, B. 2013. "The 5 Big Mistakes that Led to Ron Johnson's Ouster at J. C. Penny." *Time*, 9 April. Retrieved November 2014 from <http://business.time.com/2013/04/09/the-5-big-mistakes-that-led-to-ron-johnsons-ouster-at-jc-penny/>.

Van der Heyden, L. 2014. "Planning and Realizing Corporate Strategy ay ABC SpA." Fontainebleau: INSEAD Working Papers.

Williamson, O. E. 1975. *Markets and Hierarchies: Analysis and Antitrust Implications*. New York: Free Press.

Williamson, O. E. 1981. "The Economics of Organization: The Transaction Cost Approach." *American Journal of Sociology*, 87 (3): pp. 548–577.

Williamson, O. E. 1991. "Comparative Economic Organizations: The Analysis of Discrete Structural Alternatives." *Administrative Science Quarterly*, 36 (2): pp. 269–296.

Zott, C. and Amit, R. 2007. "Business Model Design and the Performance of Entrepreneurial Firms." *Organization Science*, 18 (2): pp. 181–199.

Zott, C. and Amit, R. 2008. "The Fit Between Product Market Strategy and Business Model: Implications for Business Performance." *Strategic Management Journal*, 29 (1): pp. 1–26.

Zott, C. and Amit, R. 2010. "Business Model Design: An Activity System Perspective." *Long Range Planning*, 43(2–3): pp. 216–226.

4 A Corporate View of Business Model Innovation

RAMON CASADESUS-MASANELL,
JOAN E. RICART, AND JORGE TARZIJÁN

Introduction

Corporations have experienced immense changes in the last few decades. Drivers such as technological change, deregulation, and competition (to name but a few) have forced companies to continuously re-examine and re-configure their boundaries externally, as well as internally. As a result, new forms of organizations have arisen challenging conventional wisdom and the academicians' and practitioners' toolkit, forcing them to further analyze corporate issues such as the determination of firms' boundaries and the organizational structure of multibusiness companies.

Many changes in corporations have been fueled by changes in their business models. Business models in a corporation not only interact externally but also internally. Corporations can change, develop, or even invent business models and novel combinations of business models in what we call corporate models. In this chapter we develop the corporate-level view of business models and business model innovation. Whereas the analysis of the business model of a multibusiness corporation will be equivalent to the analysis of a set of individual business models (each at the business level) when the corporation's businesses do not interact with one another, the analysis of the business model at the corporate level is needed when there are interactions between the businesses of an organization, or between those and the corporate center.

The advantages arising from a well-designed corporate model do not entail only a static sharing of resources but also the creation of value, thanks to dynamic reinforcements or complementarities. Dynamic reinforcement is associated with how well the combination of businesses allows the organization to attain its goal as time passes, and as such, it represents a dynamic version of static complementarities. Dynamic reinforcement might also enable the generation of resources and/or capabilities that without the corporate model would not be available. The generation of these new resources and capabilities might represent an important business model innovation at the corporate level that may differentiate one corporation from another. Our corporate view helps to detect, analyze, and manage such dynamic forces.

The chapter is organized as follows. After this introduction, the following section develops the theoretical background by reviewing the concept of the business model and its extension to corporate strategy by focusing on business model innovation and design. This perspective and the underlying value drivers are illustrated with three case studies in the third section. From the examples, in the fourth section, we extend the concept of complementarity from a static perspective to a dynamic and systemic one. The final section concludes and develops some managerial implications.

Theory Review

A business model shows "the logic of the firm, the way it operates and how it creates value for its stakeholders" (Baden-Fuller et al., 2008: 1). Grounding on this, and to provide a more concrete definition, we posit that a business model is defined by two sets of elements that explain value creation and value capture by the focal organization: (a) the concrete choices made by management about how the organization must operate, and (b) the consequences of those choices (Casadesus-Masanell and Ricart, 2011). Choices can be policies (e.g., everyday low prices), investment in assets (e.g., distribution centers), or governance choices (e.g., the leasing or purchasing of a truck). Whatever the type, every choice has consequences: for example, the addition of a new product line might allow the sharing of resources to achieve economies of scope, but it might also add bureaucratic and coordination costs, whereas the outsourcing of a previously integrated activity may reduce costs but increase hold-up risks and affect the neat performance of the firm's activities. Consequences can be flexible or rigid. A consequence is flexible if it is sensitive to the choice that generates it. An example of a flexible consequence is sales volume falling (rapidly, perhaps) as a consequence of price increases. A consequence is rigid when it does not change rapidly with the choices that generate it (Casadesus-Masanell and Ricart, 2010). Especially relevant are rigid consequences such as brand equity, reputation, or an installed base, because they might become important strategic resources or capabilities (Dierickx and Cool, 1989) that enable choices otherwise not feasible. Because consequences are essential to describe the way the firm operates, we include them in our definition of a business model. Based on this definition, we consider business model innovations (BMI) as logics of value creation and value capture that are new to the industry/product market.

The literature on strategic management typically distinguishes between business-level (BL) strategy and corporate-level (CL) strategy (Bowman and Helfat, 2001), in which the former deals with the ways in which an individual business competes within a particular industry, and the latter with the ways in which a corporation manages a set of businesses together (Grant, 1995). Consistent with this, business models must also be associated with business-level (BL) and corporate-level (CL) constructs, in which a BL business model shows the logic of the business and the way it operates and creates value, and a CL business model shows the logic of the corporation and the way it operates and creates value for its stakeholders. Because businesses are part of corporations, these two logics, although related, are at different levels of analysis.

Our definition of business model enables us to analyze them from the aforementioned levels of aggregation. By zooming out from a business model and looking at it from a distance, we will be able to bundle together detailed choices and consequences into larger constructs. These larger constructs generally correspond to businesses (usually organizational units but not always). When such businesses do not closely interact with one another they can be analyzed in isolation (BL business models) and the study of the business model of a multibusiness organization will be equivalent to the analysis of a set of individual BL business models. On the other hand, the interactions among the sets of choices and consequences that originate the BL business model are observed by zooming in on these sets, which enables us to look at the business model of the whole corporation from a shorter distance. Thus, the model that shows the full array of businesses and the interactions among them, and between them and the corporate center, corresponds to the CL business model. The analysis of the CL business model has become consistent with the renewed interest in corporate-level effects on performance (Martin and Eisenhardt, 2010; Joseph and Ocasio, 2012; Gulati, Puranam, and Tushman, 2012) and thus, a closer re-examination of the corporate-business unit relationship in diversified firms is warranted (Joseph and Ocasio, 2012).

Whereas a BL business model creates willingness to pay for customers, willingness to sell for suppliers, sets prices for customers and suppliers, and produces and sells a particular volume of goods or services (Brandenburger and Stuart, 1996), a CL business model mainly refers to the choices of businesses, which we call the business scope choice, and the choices of the organizational structure of the firm, which will show, among other things, the degree of interdependence among businesses and between them and the corporate center.[1] Thus, the CL business model may include a number of different BL business models, where the number, diversity, and interdependence of these business models are related to the scope and organizational structure

---

[1] Certainly, organizational-structure decisions also involve decisions that are different from the degree of interdependency among businesses, such as those related to the determination of the roles, power, and responsibilities inside the organization and how they are controlled and coordinated. Other organizational-structure decisions are related to how communication and information flows are managed and how decision rights are granted.

of the CL business model. To simplify, we will also refer to the CL business model as the "Corporate Model."

A company can choose from many different corporate models, each involving a different overall logic of value creation and value capture at the corporate level. Studying the corporate model is important, as it enables us to investigate topics such as the management of a portfolio of business models, synergies, conflicts, and cannibalization among businesses. This discussion leads us to conclude that business models (and the innovations thereof) are located both at the individual business level (BL) and at the corporate-model level (CL). However, as there are more interdependencies among the businesses and between them and the corporate center, the CL view of the business model, or corporate model, becomes relatively more important.

When analyzed at the CL, a business model innovation involves reconfigurations of the corporate choices (e.g., business scope and/or organizational structure choices), which results in logics of value creation and value capture at the CL that are new to the market. Thus, innovations in business models at the CL may be fostered by changes in the business scope and in the organizational structure that create compelling new value propositions.

In fact, one can claim that the CL is needed for innovation of the business model even at the BL, as the leadership of the business may not have either the full perspective or the right incentives to innovate the BL business model when such innovation interacts at the CL or it represents an important change in the dominant logic of the business (Prahalad and Bettis, 1986). Because a BMI is defined as new to the industry, it generally represents a mindset different from that which the industry, and therefore the business, are used to. To make this change possible, this new logic of the business may need to be introduced by someone outside the business itself, showing the relevance of the corporate level for such BMI to take place.

Consider the case of LAN (Casadesus-Masanell and Tarziján, 2012), one of the most thriving airlines in the world, which successfully operates three businesses simultaneously: full service for long-haul international passengers, air-cargo, and no-frills passenger service for domestic flights. Whereas LAN's business-scope decision has been to participate in those three businesses, the firm's organizational-structure decision has been to jointly operate the long-haul passenger and cargo businesses, and to separately operate the short-haul passenger business. The sharing of resources promoted by the joint business model for cargo and international passengers has allowed the company to decrease the break-even load factors and thus to fly to more places more times of the day, which has promoted a higher willingness to pay for passenger and cargo customers, and lower costs. LAN manages the operation of the no-frills domestic passenger business separately because there are no strong complementarities with its other businesses. The way LAN has selected and combined its different businesses represents an innovative corporate model, without parallel in the industry, which has allowed the company to offer new value propositions based on more flights, routes, and service in competitive markets.

LAN would not have the same route structure without the cargo and passenger combination, or if both businesses were managed as completely separate entities. There is not, a priori, a dominant corporate arrangement, and different organizations can choose different configurations of corporate choices out of many possible sets of alternatives. The task of crafting innovative corporate models to maximize a firm's value is one of the cornerstones of a successful corporate strategy.

The analysis of the CL view of the business model is also interesting because it has not yet been explicitly studied. We add to this literature by analyzing some important corporate-level issues with a business model lens. Our development agrees with authors such as Teece (1982), Collis and Montgomery (1998), Porter (1987), Bowman and Helfat (2001), Martin and Eisenhardt (2001), and Joseph and Ocasio (2012), in that we emphasize the importance of interactions, complementarities, and resource-sharing for a successful corporate performance.

Interactions are relevant when considering the crafting of business models at the CL, given that the effects of the business scope and the organizational-structure choices are heavily dependent upon them. There are internal and external interactions. Internal interactions are those that arise among the businesses of the same corporation. Two BL business models interact when they affect one another. Companies should seek positive interactions, which are associated with the well-known concept of complementarity (Teece 1980, 1982; Milgrom and Roberts, 1995). Two BL business models are complements if doing more of any one increases the returns of doing more of the other (Milgrom and Roberts, 1995). When there are complementarities, the proper management of interdependencies enables obtaining certain consequences that are useful and different from those that will arise if the businesses were managed separately. Those consequences may be based, for example, on the performance of certain common activities between businesses, the generation of new resources and capabilities that without the interaction will not be achieved, or the cannibalization of the products or services sold by the business units. External interactions, on the other hand, are those that arise when the effectiveness of a business model depends, to a large extent, on the design of the business models of other players with whom it interacts (Casadesus-Masanell and Ricart, 2010).[2] Therefore, the success of a given business model depends, at least partially, on internal and external interactions.

Advantages arising from a well-designed corporate model are richer than the static sharing of resources, as they might also entail a dynamic reinforcement. Dynamic reinforcement is associated with how well the combination

---

[2] For space constraint reasons, in this chapter we focus on internal interactions, thus we do not expand further on external interactions.

of businesses allows the organization to attain its goal as time passes, and it represents a dynamic version of the concept of static reinforcement. Dynamic reinforcement might also enable the generation of resources and/or capabilities that represent an important business model innovation at the CL.

Our concept of a business model is intrinsically dynamic because the relationship between choices and consequences occurs over time. This happens because, in addition to choices yielding consequences, consequences enable choices, thus generating feedback loops that can strengthen some component of the CL business model. For example, in the case of LAN, the combination of cargo and international passengers (choice) decreases the break-even load factor (BELF), which enables more flights to more places (a consequence) and to profitably set higher prices (a choice). We define systemic reinforcement as the greater value that can be obtained by implementing an innovative corporate model, reconfiguring the basic corporate choices and as such, it includes the concepts of static and dynamic reinforcements. Thus, the combination of static, dynamic, and the overall systemic reinforcements is endogenous to the choices of the corporate model.

Business-level and Corporate-level Business Models: Examples of Corporate-level Reconfigurations

In this section we present three examples of corporate-model reconfigurations. These companies have reconfigured both their BL and their CL business models and the examples are useful to understand the static, dynamic, and systemic reinforcements behind the CL business model innovations that are discussed later.

THE CASE OF LAN

LAN (Casadesus-Masanell, Tarziján, and Mitchell, 2010) successfully operates three businesses: full-service passenger business for international long-haul, cargo business, and a no-frills passenger service for domestic operations. The full-service international passenger-carrier business is operated in much the same way as other global carriers. It offers frequent flights to major destinations through its own hubs, and via alliances with other airlines (LAN is part of the *oneworld* alliance), and it has two classes of service (coach and business), offering amenity-filled services featuring complimentary hot meals and beverages, multilingual personal-entertainment units in coach, and fully flat beds in business class. On numerous occasions, the company had received awards for its high level of service, including "Best Business Class in Latin America" by *Business Traveler* magazine, "Best Airline in South America" by the official *Airline Guide*, the "Best Latin American Airline" by the *Global Finance Magazine*, and the best A-340 operator in the world by Airbus.

LAN also operates a no-frills operation for domestic and short-haul routes. That operation is a lower-cost, lower-overhead model characterized by fewer amenities, Internet ticketing, shorter turnaround times, and a uniform fleet of single-aisle planes from which the kitchens have been removed to increase seating capacity. LAN adopted a no-frills business model for domestic flights to stimulate demand in price-sensitive segments and to increase capacity utilization. With more passengers, the airline could use newer, more efficient planes, which could be in flight more hours per day, thus exploiting economies of scale and reducing costs. The low fares have also kept competitors out.

The cargo business also has an extensive international-route network and offers a high level of service. It transports salmon from Chile, asparagus from Peru, fresh flowers from Ecuador, and other such perishables to the United States and Europe, while flying high-value-to-weight merchandise such as computers, mobile phones, and small car parts from the United States and Europe to Latin America. LAN carries about two-thirds of its cargo shipments in specialized freighters and one-third in the belly of passenger aircrafts. The company's international cargo operations are based on facilities located at different international airports. Its storage capacity, equipment, and extensive refrigeration units have made LAN the largest Latin American airline with dedicated cargo assets on US soil.

Each of these three businesses has a different logic for value creation and value capture to given sets of customers and suppliers. Each business creates willingness to pay for its potential customers, sets prices for them, and sells a particular volume of services. The premium long-haul passenger and cargo businesses drive an important willingness to pay from less price-elastic passenger and corporate clients, whereas the low-cost, short-haul operations charge low prices that are aimed at more price-sensitive customers.

The high level of integration between the international passenger and cargo businesses has allowed LAN to be unusual among passenger carriers in its reliance on cargo revenue—accounting for almost 35 percent of its total revenues (compared with less than 5 percent for American, Delta, and United-Continental). That is, without the international-passenger business, LAN could not be as strong in cargo as it currently is. Although Korean Air and Cathay Pacific also derive about a third of their revenue from cargo, LAN is distinctive in that it transports a larger percentage of its shipments in the belly of wide-body passenger aircraft (Casadesus-Masanell and Tarziján, 2012). The bulk of LAN's cargo business operates on the same route network as its passenger business.

However, LAN cannot benefit from combining passenger and cargo businesses on domestic routes given the competition in cargo from trucks, trains, and boats. Moreover, the local markets generated little demand for the perishables that LAN was transporting farther abroad, and the narrow-body aircraft used on the short-haul routes were not big enough to carry sufficient cargo. The high price elasticity of domestic air travel implied that a direct way to increase capacity utilization for domestic flights was with low fares, made possible solely by offering a basic level of service to drive down costs. As a result, whereas the no-frills model seeks to fill planes to the maximum possible extent so as to take advantage of economies of scale, the "cargo" and the long-haul passenger businesses also attempt to do this, albeit doing so by taking advantage of economies of scope.

By choosing original configurations of choices, LAN operates an innovative CL business model that integrates business in ways that have helped the company to create compelling new value propositions. Until 2006, LAN's corporate model included the operation of two interdependent businesses: full-service passengers and cargo. However, that year LAN reconfigured its passenger model to include a separate, low-cost business for short-haul passengers that does not have a high interdependency with the cargo business. The reconfiguration of LAN BL business models resulted in a reconfiguration of choices that originated an innovative CL business model or corporate model.

THE CASE OF AMAZON

Amazon has also innovated in terms of its corporate-model configuration (Casadesus-Masanell and Thaker, 2012). Launched online in 1995 as the "Earth's Biggest Bookstore," in 1998, the company entered the music and video business, extending the retail capabilities it had developed for books. Soon thereafter the company launched toys, electronics, and tools (among other categories). In order to grow and compete, Amazon invested aggressively in its supply-chain and distribution network. In addition, Amazon spent heavily on "Technology and Content," which included its technology infrastructure and the expansion of product categories. Other main choices involved in the retail business were Amazon's heavy investments in its inventory, fulfillment, and distribution capabilities, including buying, warehousing, and merchandising, a feedback and a payment system, a recommendation engine, a single-product detail page, and fraud protection policies. Most of these choices were aimed at leveraging economies of scale to offer low prices.

In 1999, Amazon took its first steps toward expanding beyond its retail model into a marketplace platform for e-commerce. In January 2000, the company decided to adopt a "single-store" strategy in which third-party merchants would be allowed to sell their products to consumers alongside Amazon's own goods in the primary "product-detail" pages. For example, a product page for a particular book or DVD would include options to buy the product from Amazon, shipped from its distribution centers, or from third-party sellers. Jeff Bezos reorganized the company to support this strategy by making general managers for category stores responsible for income statements reflecting the operations of both Amazon and third-party sellers.

The reconfiguration of Amazon's corporate model to enable its participation in a marketplace platform to increase selection on its site was done by adding some choices that aimed to offer a full suite of services to attract merchants to its platform. Its WebStore service helped merchants build and operate a direct-to-customer business across multiple channels, its Checkout service offered merchants a complete payments solution, and companies could advertise on Amazon product pages. In addition, the service known as "Fulfillment by Amazon" allowed third-party sellers to use Amazon's vast distribution and warehousing network to ship and store their products. The idea was to leverage the vast capacity of the network to attract third-party sellers, which might also benefit consumers.

Amazon has innovated its corporate model by choosing a business scope (online retail and marketplace platform) and an organizational structure based on the close interdependency (complementarity) between its businesses. By adding the marketplace-platform business to the retail business, a significant benefit was added because high traffic and volume, in addition to leading to economies of scale, now also attracted third-party sellers to the site. This, in turn, broadened Amazon's selection, which again attracted greater traffic and volume. This innovation at the corporate level has created compelling new value propositions for final consumers and merchants, and has increased the attractiveness of Amazon's individual businesses.

THE CASE OF ARAUCO

Arauco, as described by Casadesus-Masanell, Tarziján, and Mitchell (2009), is another interesting example of a corporate-level model reconfiguration. Owning over 1.2 million hectares of forests in Chile, Argentina, Brazil, and Uruguay, Arauco is one of the world's two largest producers of pulp sold in the open market (the other is the Brazilian company Aracruz) and an important producer of other wood products such as panels, sawn timber, and remanufactured products.

Arauco was established in 1967, aiming to build a pulp mill to produce and sell wood pulp. Soon thereafter, Arauco started the development of its own forest resources. Later, in the early 1990s, Arauco began its diversification by creating new business units, which were associated with sawn timber, energy, and plywood. A key reason for the creation of these new businesses was the need to optimize the value of the forest, given that different parts of the tree have different economic values according to their use. The top part of the tree is ideal for pulplogs and the lower half is best for sawn timber. The opportunity cost of using the lower part of the tree for pulp is much greater than that of the top part, implying that the economic cost of pulp is lower by jointly operating the different businesses. By producing a wide range of products, Arauco can use corporate resources such as logistics, transport, distribution, ports, and R&D in all of them.

The reconfiguration of Arauco's corporate model to enable its participation in new businesses was done by adding choices that seek to optimize the use of the tree. In addition to the necessary investments in mills and logistics to produce different products, one important choice was the acquisition and operation of a "log-merchandizing" process, which involves the use of a computer-driven scanner to identify the log's diameter, the shape of the knots, and the optimal points for the cuts. After a log is cut, it is automatically grouped and then sent to one of three destinations: sawmills for timber, plywood production, or the chip plant for pulp production. Another key choice associated with the reconfiguration of Arauco's corporate model was the R&D function, which seeks a genetic manipulation of the tree coherent with the company's scope choice, that is, a tree that can be optimized by using it according to Arauco's choice of businesses.

Each of Arauco's businesses has logic for value creation and value capture for given sets of customers and suppliers. Each business creates willingness to pay for its potential customers, sets prices for them, and sells a particular volume of services. As an example, whereas the plywood businesses drive an important willingness to pay from less price-elastic customers, the pulp operations are sold in a more commoditized market. Besides its participation in different businesses, Arauco's corporate model is based on the close interdependency among its businesses. This interdependency can be seen best in the log-merchandizing process and the R&D activity, which were important for the efficiency of the whole set of Arauco's business units. Without a close interdependency among the different businesses, it would be extremely difficult to efficiently operate the log-merchandizing and the R&D activities.

LAN, Amazon, and Arauco show that different configurations of scope and organizational-structure choices can foster innovations in CL business models. As implied by the three previous examples, a fundamental task of the strategist is to choose a corporate model that maximizes the value created and captured by the firm. All the previously mentioned cases show that BL and CL business models are closely related and intertwined. BL decisions affect the functioning, operation, and performance of the CL business model, and the design and performance of the latter affect the BL business models.

Value Creation and Value Capture at the Corporate Level

We have argued that it is important to evaluate the combination of businesses to be performed and their interactions because they imply different logics for value creation and value capture at the CL. Two businesses managed by the same company are complements if the performance of each of them increases the returns of operating the other (Milgrom and Roberts, 1995). Corporate models must seek advantages from complementarity (i.e., positive interactions). The success of the marketplace business model in Amazon's case is not only dependent on the design and organization of that business model, but also on how the marketplace business model interacts with the more traditional Amazon's retail business model, whereas the effectiveness of LAN's international passenger business model depends not only on its organization, but also on how it interacts with the cargo business model. Amazon and LAN corporate models make possible some actions that affect the ability of their BL business models to grow through the exploitation of synergies.

The interactions between the business models of different businesses of the same corporation can potentially be very complex because the choices of a BL business model affect the consequences of other BL business models. In addition to the full richness of choices and consequences of individual BL business models, there is a full richness of potential interdependencies among them. The type and intensity of interdependencies are partly endogenous because they depend on how players have decided to configure their corporate models. The seeking of positive interdependencies (i.e., complementarities) must be a priority in the design of a CL business model. Next, we discuss how two important drivers of interdependencies at the corporate level are static and dynamic reinforcements. Finally, we discuss the potential presence of systemic reinforcement.

STATIC REINFORCEMENT

Complementarities between businesses are explained by positive static and/or dynamic reinforcement between them. A positive reinforcement means that two choices complement each other well (Casadesus-Masanell and Ricart, 2008). For example, assuming that business A is associated with online sales, business B with in-store sales, and that the company's objective is to maximize revenues, A and B will reinforce each other if the effect of online sales in net revenues is larger when the company also offers its products in physical stores.

Static reinforcements emerge, for example, from asset sharing or from advantages derived from product bundling. Resource sharing generally arises because the joint performance of businesses may require fewer resources than the sum of the resources required to operating them separately. Synergies resulting from sharing of resources have been an important determinant of a successful corporate strategy (e.g., Collis and Montgomery, 1998; Porter, 1987). In LAN's case, there are a number of resources that are shared by the different businesses, such as the brand, maintenance personnel, pilots, and yield-management systems. In the case of Amazon, there is also sharing of resources, such as those related to the development and improvement of the web page, clearing, payment systems, and the client's strategic information. Arauco shares a central corporate management function, R&D, a brand name, certain information technology activities, and more importantly, the tree, among others.

While our examples may not be the best illustrations of the static reinforcement emerging from product bundling, it is well known that product bundling facilitates price discrimination, and thus allows the firm to capture more value when the demands for the bundled products are negatively correlated.

Static reinforcement is closely related to the well-known idea in strategy of internal consistency or fit (Rivkin and Siggelkow, 2003; Siggelkow and Rivkin, 2005). The strategy wheel, the value chain, and activity systems (developed by Andrews, 1971; Porter, 1985; and Porter, 1996, respectively) provide interesting applications of the fit concept. As we discuss below, a novel element of our approach is that by separating choices and consequences, we consider the dynamics of internal consistency.

DYNAMIC REINFORCEMENT

The degree of dynamic reinforcement between businesses is associated with how well the combination of businesses allows the organization to attain its goal as time passes, and as such, it is a dynamic version of the concept of static reinforcement. There is a positive dynamic reinforcement between businesses A and B when performing one of them facilitates and speeds up value creation and capture of the other, while there would be a negative dynamic reinforcement when the performing of one of them hurts and slows down value creation and capture of the other.

An important driver of dynamic reinforcement is the set of rigid consequences, such as brand name or reputation. Most of the rigid consequences are built over time. Once rigid consequences are well developed they become a very powerful resource or capability that might enable the corporate model to function better. The choice of the organizational structure of the CL affects the development of rigid consequences. A joint CL business model might promote the achievement of rigid consequences that facilitate the emergence of resources and/or capabilities that, without that organizational structure, would not be available. These additional resources and/or capabilities are helpful to increase revenues or decrease costs over time and thus represent an important driver of dynamic reinforcement. The additional resources sometimes even go beyond the increase in revenues or decrease in costs, as we see in the next section, and are instrumental to the design of a difficult-to-imitate business model innovation.

In LAN's case, an important rigid consequence arising from the joint cargo–passenger business operation is the denser route network. The expanded route network is a valuable resource that emerges from the corporate model because the ability to fly more routes profitably creates a "virtuous circle": more routes and frequencies imply more value to customers, enabling LAN to charge premium prices, which generates extra revenues to support more routes and to eventually become the one-stop shop for cargo distribution in Latin America (Casadesus-Masanell, Tarziján, and Mitchell, 2010).

In Amazon's case, the combination of the retail and marketplace platform businesses enables the company to have a larger network of sellers (a rigid consequence) increasing traffic and product variety, and attracting more buyers. All of this reinforces the positive network effects between buyers and sellers, and facilitates the speeding up and working of some of the main company's virtuous circles, which positively impacts volume, revenues, and economies of scale, enabling a more efficient cost structure.

In Arauco's case, the addition of the plywood and sawn timber businesses promotes the investment in the log-merchandizing process, which increases the value obtained from the tree and promotes additional investments in forests (a rigid consequence). Moreover, the idiosyncratic R&D in forest genetics facilitates the growing of a certain type of tree that is coherent with its diversified corporate model.

In the three cases, rigid consequences fueled a value-enhancing cycle that creates increasing value and promotes growth, making each of these companies a tremendous success story. All of these examples also show that the rigid consequences generated by a corporate model facilitate an endogenous change in the firm's corporate model, for example promoting the emergence of new business units. This generation of new resources can represent an important consequence of innovative choices (e.g., choices related to business units and organizational structure) in corporate models and a way to foster business model innovations. An implication of this discussion is that dynamic reinforcement cannot be analyzed considering only what happens under the restrictions imposed by the current corporate model.

Lack of static and dynamic reinforcement presents the opportunity for a firm to improve by discontinuing some businesses or adding new ones. Among the main drivers of the lack of reinforcement are the risks of cannibalizing an existing brand or product affecting the existing distribution channel, image, reputation, and quality of the company's offerings. Larger monitoring costs, bureaucracy, and a suboptimal sharing of resources because of an excessive demand for them may also provoke negative interdependencies.

Reinforcement between businesses requires the existence of points of contact. One of the points of contact in LAN's case is the aircraft. Figure 4.1 shows that LAN's participation in the passenger business promotes a better functioning of its cargo business, whereas a higher profitability of the cargo business helps to have more resources to invest in certain assets and activities necessary for the development of the passenger business. Interestingly, a company can choose the degree of intensity of the interdependency between

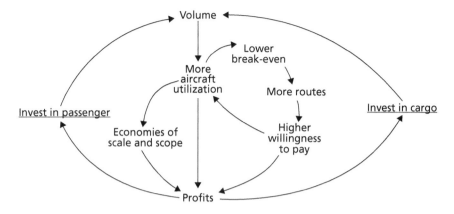

Figure 4.1 LAN cargo and passenger value loops

Source: Casadesus-Masanell and Tarziján (2012).

its businesses through an organizational-structure decision. LAN may make the decision of participating in the cargo and passenger businesses simultaneously with the decision of operating them jointly. However, the company also has the possibility of operating both businesses separately, or even to not operate either one of those businesses at all. The choice of the degree of interdependency will affect the generation of rigid consequences and the achievement of static and dynamic reinforcement.

Reinforcement comes together with some level of commitment. Managing interdependent businesses in a corporate model is always complex and, at some point, good decisions at the corporate level may involve suboptimal decisions for at least one of the businesses. For example, LAN's operating decisions should consider the opportunity of adding a new passenger or an additional ton of cargo as a function of the already-compromised overall weight in a given flight and the expected demands in each business. This also means that the incentive to innovate BL business models that take advantage of the corporate model will essentially be at the corporate level and not at the business level, an important organizational consideration associated with BMI. Therefore the role of the corporate-level view in business strategy can be very relevant when opportunities for business model innovation are available.

Although most of the literature has analyzed situations associated with static reinforcement, there has also been some (more implicit) discussion of dynamic effects. Porter (1987) focuses on three types of inter-relationships among business units: tangible, intangible, and competitive. He sees the role of corporate officers as exploiting such inter-relationships among business units. Exploiting tangible relationships is essentially related to static reinforcement, while both intangible and competitive interrelationships, although presented as static reinforcement, have some inner implicit dynamic. For instance, knowledge (intangible) is not only shared but has to be created and maintained at the same time. Prahalad and Hamel (1990) focus directly on these dynamics by introducing the concept of core competence. They acknowledge that some core businesses may have the function of generating core competences exploited in other business units. Collis and Montgomery (1995, 1998) generalize this idea by focusing both on businesses and resources, understanding the existence of a virtuous cycle from businesses to resources and back to businesses, generating a coherent corporate model that improves the performance of the underlying businesses.

Martin and Eisenhardt (2001) also consider a time dimension by defining a cross-business synergy as the value that is created, over time, by the sum of the businesses together relative to what their value would be separately. They suggest that the specific sources of cross-business synergy are constantly changing as markets evolve, and that we should look at the strategic processes (a dynamic concept) to understand the creation of new synergies. Two strategic processes that are especially relevant in the multibusiness firm are knowledge transfer (i.e., deployment of experience, skills, information, routines) and co-evolving (i.e., the business unit processes of routinely changing the collaborative links and relationships among the business units to exploit changing market opportunities).

In sum, although static and dynamic reinforcements are important, we focus more on the dynamic version, both because it has not been analyzed in detail elsewhere and because it is important to determine the success of the CL business model reconfigurations. One of our contributions over existing literature is to make a more explicit treatment of dynamic reinforcement by stressing the relationship between choices and consequences, and the possible emergence of new resources and capabilities through time, which are specially relevant when analyzing corporate models because the choices in one BL business model can have consequences that affect other BL business models and the whole corporate model. This endogenous emergence of resources and capabilities can be the result of an innovative corporate model that seeks to generate these resources through its business scope and organizational-structure choices. Moreover, the emergence of these resources and capabilities can support the sustainable growth of innovations at the CL business model level. Going back to LAN's case, the growing revenues provided by cargo operations enables a better service to passengers and vice versa, increasing the customers' willingness to pay for both offerings, and fostering a competitive advantage that is difficult for competitors to overcome.

SYSTEMIC REINFORCEMENT

In order to better understand the concepts behind interactions and corporate-model configurations, let us consider that a firm that undertakes one business (e.g., business A) selects a set of assets, policies, and governance choices needed to perform it. This set of choices generates a set of consequences. The BL business model of business A is jointly defined by the set of choices and consequences associated with this business. Similarly, the independent business model B has a BL business model defined by its particular set of choices and consequences. Therefore, we can consider, as an initial point, a company operating in these two businesses, A and B, with independent BL business models.

The company may reconfigure its set of choices to operate the same or different sets of businesses. For instance, it can choose a different configuration of choices to jointly operate businesses A and B. This reconfiguration may be composed of different proper subsets or supersets of the union of choices associated with businesses A and B independently (e.g., because by adding a few new choices, the firm can perhaps incorporate other additional businesses), or by any other possible combination of choices. CL reconfigurations involve the assessment and selection of different combinations of choices.

Because business models are made up of choices and consequences, a complete analysis must explicitly consider the consequences. By jointly performing businesses A and B, a firm may obtain certain consequences that are different from those obtained by undertaking both businesses separately.

Any firm should consider different combinations of the business it chooses to operate (say A and B), or it may consider operating. Each possible combination of the businesses the firm chooses to operate corresponds to a different CL business model. The search for the best possible CL business model is a process of business model innovation undertaken by the firm. Out of this process, the firm defines its corporate model as the combination of choices and consequences of those businesses that allows the corporation to create and capture more value than alternative combinations.

As explained, the firm can start by exploiting the complementarities associated with the static and dynamic reinforcements between the businesses. If the company succeeds in finding a superior business model innovation, it will develop a CL business model that captures more value than the alternative corporate models it may consider. We call this extra value a systemic reinforcement.[3] We named this reinforcement as systemic because this concept

[3] According to this definition, the systemic reinforcement of corporate model A is computed relative to a second corporate model B. Thus, the degree of systemic reinforcement exhibited by a given corporate model varies depending on the particular corporate model used for the comparison. An alternative approach to deal with this issue is to always use the corporate model with independent BL business models for the comparison. Systemic reinforcement would then be defined as the excess value obtained by the firm by crafting its corporate model differently from operating each of its businesses as independent BL business models. Note that both definitions are closely related. In particular, given the systemic reinforcements of two corporate models compared to a corporate model with independent BL business models, we can easily compute (through subtraction) the systemic reinforcement of one corporate model relative to the other. For example, consider a firm operating corporate model A, which has systemic reinforcement $250 when compared to the corporate model with independent BL business models. Suppose that a different corporate model, corporate model B, has systemic reinforcement $150 when compared to that same reference. Then, the systemic reinforcement of corporate model A relative to B is $250–$150 = $100. In this chapter, we use the relative-form definition because it is simpler and easier to understand and to act on.

is related to the idea that systems and their properties should be viewed as wholes, not as collections of individual parts. Any gain in systemic reinforcement above the one obtained by purely exploiting static and dynamic reinforcements has to be associated with the overall configuration of choices and consequences of the innovative CL business model. For instance, some consequences of the joint cargo–passenger business model in LAN's case are the decreasing probability of entry into LAN's markets because of its more ample route network, and the increasing attractiveness for LAN of entering into new businesses, such as express mail delivery. While these additional gains can partly be explained by static and dynamic reinforcements among particular subsets of LAN's choices, it is the whole set of choices and consequences that really sustain the emergence of those new consequences.

The higher value of a corporate model that innovates the crafting of business scope and organizational structure can originate in a number of (intricate) inter-relationships. These inter-relationships grow from the functioning of whole sets of choices (e.g., from the interaction of business units or from the emergence of endogenous resources and capabilities). As such, the concept of systemic reinforcement recognizes that the interactions between choices or businesses are not only related to the static sharing of some resources, but they can become much more complicated, for example, the acquisition of knowledge can dynamically affect several activities/businesses simultaneously.[4] As such, static, and mainly dynamic, reinforcement are key drivers of what we call systemic reinforcement.

In real life there are many possible configurations of business-scope and organizational-structure choices, and therefore there are many possible sets of consequences. The company should reconfigure its choices as long as a systemic reinforcement exists, and should stop when it is exhausted, that is, when there is no reconfiguration of choices that delivers more value. Corporate-model innovations may be an important driver of systemic reinforcement, for instance because they can promote the emergence of endogenous capabilities that can generate dynamic feedback loops or sharing of resources that are not available to competitors that implement different corporate models.

In the case of Amazon, the advantages of adding the platform business to the retail activity are not restricted to just static cost advantages, but involve the whole functioning of the joint business units, for example, through the achievement of stronger network effects. The greater network of buyers and sellers, and the addition of services such as WebStore and Checkout, facilitate an expansion of the Amazon corporate model toward the offering of more services to merchants (e.g., IT services), which may result in more loyalty and increased switching costs. The generation of rigid consequences by a joint CL business model

---

[4] This is the case of the R&D activity in Arauco's case. This activity spans several Arauco's businesses because it aims to genetically modify the quality of the tree in order to more efficiently produce the different products manufactured by the company.

complements the concept of envelopment introduced by Eisenmann, Parker, and Van Alstyne (2011), which involves entry by one platform provider into another's market by bundling its own platform's functionality with that of the target's so as to leverage shared-user relationships and common components.

Conclusions

The business model has been considered as a new unit of analysis (e.g., Zott, Amit, and Massa, 2011; Demil and Lecocq, 2010), which spans or bridges traditional units of analysis, such as the firm or the network. In this chapter we posited that this unit of analysis must also consider important corporate strategy issues such as the choices of businesses and organizational structure. This is important because different business scope and organizational arrangements can affect the logics of value creation and value capture at the overall corporate level, as well as at the individual BL business model level.

Innovations at the corporate-level model may foster new logics of value creation and value capture. As such, a new dimension of business model innovation is the creation of new corporate models, that is, new configurations of business scopes and organizational structures. Novel corporate models can be a source of corporate advantage and a new way to distinguish a firm from its competitors.

An important determinant of a CL business model is the intensity of the interdependency among the firm's businesses. This intensity is endogenous because it depends on how a company has decided to configure its corporate model. Positive interactions between businesses are generally explained by static and dynamic reinforcements. Dynamic reinforcement is driven by the presence of rigid consequences, which might originate endogenous resources and capabilities that can foster difficult-to-imitate corporate model innovations. Corporate-model reconfigurations can be especially important to increase or decrease the interactions between businesses and individual choices. The achievement of static and dynamic reinforcement among the different choices and businesses requires a high level of cross-unit coordination. Managers must analyze what parts of their businesses should be integrated, what parts should be kept separated, and the appropriate levels of coordination between the businesses and their parts. Our analysis, based on the dynamic interactions between choices and consequences, goes one step beyond the more traditional synergy analysis, which is at the heart of the rationales for the existence of a multibusiness firm (Martin and Eisenhardt, 2001).

An important goal of corporate-model reconfigurations is the achievement of systemic reinforcement. Systemic reinforcement can originate in a number of intricate inter-relationships that are the result of the functioning of a whole set of choices and not necessarily a result of the breaking down of the company's activities into smaller bits. Static and dynamic reinforcements are important drivers of systemic reinforcement. The concept of systemic reinforcement illustrates the importance of considering the dynamic aspects of business model reconfiguration and innovation. By choosing the right configuration, a company can take advantage of positive internal interactions among businesses.

The development of corporate models that create systemic reinforcement is complex. It is an intricate exercise of design where organizational and management innovation can be necessary. It usually involves difficult balances, compromises, and tradeoffs that require complex allocations of decision rights and sophisticated management systems. In addition, timing is very important. Until some rigid consequences reach a particular level, perhaps some solutions are not yet possible or feasible. Therefore, one needs dynamic organizing more than static organizational design. All of this implies constant change and self-renewal.

Finally, fluid boundaries are usually involved, generating novel and interesting tradeoffs where issues of contracting should be combined with the relevance of the activities for the good working of the value loops in the different businesses inside the corporation (Kogut and Zander, 1992). Therefore, standard transaction cost reasoning (Williamson, 1975, 1991) will have to be complemented with our business model view of corporate models to search for the right boundaries of the firm and/or relationships with possible partners (Jacobides and Billinger, 2006).

It is important to realize that the corporate level is the adequate level for business model innovation. Of course, this seems quite obvious when the change on the different business models is due to a change in the corporate model. However, even when the innovation is in one individual business model, the business level can have problems with implementing such change and it needs to be initiated at the corporate level. Thus, factors associated with organizational structures (Chandler, 1977; Williamson, 1975), control of business unit performance and of coordination and cohesiveness of business units (Bowman and Helfat, 2001), and the role of top management teams in corporate transformations (Hambrick, Nadler, and Tushman, 1998) are important to determine corporate performance in relation to business model innovation.

Value creation through CL business models involves a very complex, interconnected set of exchange relationships and activities among eventually multiple business units. To excel in this difficult arena some companies, as the ones mentioned in this chapter, develop a dynamic capability: the renewal of the corporate model to take advantage of the opportunities feasible at each point in time and made feasible by the accumulated rigid consequence of their past and current CL business models. We hope the discussion presented in this chapter helps to identify some important issues to be taken into account when analysing a business model innovation with a corporate view.

▓ REFERENCES

Andrews, K. 1971. *The Concept of Corporate Strategy*. Homewood, IL: Dow Jones-Irwin.

Baden-Fuller, C., MacMillan, I., Demil, B., and Lecocq, X. 2008. *Long Range Planning*, Call for papers for the Special Issue on "Business Models."

Brandenburger, A. and Stuart, H. 1996. "Value-based Business Strategy." *Journal of Economics & Management Strategy*, 5: pp. 5–24.

Bowman E. and Helfat, C. 2001. "Does Corporate Strategy Matter?." *Strategic Management Journal*, 22 (1): pp. 1–23.

Casadesus-Masanell, R. and Ricart, J. E. 2008. "Competing Through Business Models (A)." *Harvard Business School*, Conceptual Note: 708–452.

Casadesus-Masanell, R. and Ricart. J. E. 2010. "From Strategy to Business Models and onto Tactics." *Long Range Planning* (special issue), 43 (2): pp. 195–215.

Casadesus-Masanell, R. and Ricart, J. E. 2011. "How to Design a Winning Business Model." *Harvard Business Review*, 89 (1–2): pp. 100–107.

Casadesus-Masanell, R. and Tarziján, J. 2012. "When One Business Model Isn't Enough." *Harvard Business Review*, 90, January–February: pp. 80–87.

Casadesus-Masanell, R. and Thaker, A. 2012. "eBay, Inc. and Amazon.com (A)." *Harvard Business School*, Case: 712–405.

Casadesus-Masanell, R., Tarziján, J., and Mitchell, J. 2009. "Arauco (A): Forward Integration or Horizontal Expansion?." *Harvard Business School*, Case: 705–474.

Casadesus-Masanell, R., Tarziján, J., and Mitchell, J. 2010. "LAN Airlines in 2008: Connecting the World to Latin America." *Harvard Business School*, Case: 711–461.

Chandler, A. 1977. *The Visible Hand: The Managerial Revolution in American Business*. Cambridge, MA: Harvard University Press, Belknap Press.

Collis, D. and Montgomery, C. 1995. "Competing on Resources: Strategy in the 1990s." *Harvard Business Review*, July–August 73 (4): pp. 118–128.

Collis, D. and Montgomery, C. 1998. "Creating Corporate Advantage." *Harvard Business Review*, May–June 76 (3) : pp. 70–83.

Demil, B. and Lecocq, X. 2010. "Business Model Evolution: In Search of Dynamic Consistency." *Long Range Planning*, 43 (2): pp. 227–246.

Dierickx, I. and Cool, K. 1989. "Asset Stock Accumulation and Sustainability of Competitive Advantage." *Management Science*, 35 (12), pp. 1504–1511.

Eisenmann, T., Parker, G., and Van Alstyne, M. 2011. "Platform Envelopment." *Strategic Management Journal*, 32 (12): pp. 1270–1285.

Grant, R. 1995. *Contemporary Strategy Analysis*. Oxford: Blackwell.

Gulati R., Puranam, P., and Tushman, M. 2012. "Meta-Organization Design: Rethinking Design in Interorganizational and Community Contexts." *Strategic Management Journal* (special issue), 33: pp. 571–586.

Hambrick, D., Nadler, D., and Tushman, M. 1998. *Navigating Change: How CEOs, Top Teams, and Boards Steer Transformation*. Boston, MA: Harvard Business School Press.

Jacobides, M. and Billinger, S. 2006. "Designing the Boundaries of the Firm: From 'Make, Buy, or Ally' to the Dynamic Benefits of Vertical Architecture." *Organization Science*, 17 (2): pp. 249–261.

Joseph, J. and Ocasio, W. 2012. "Architecture, Attention, and Adaptation in the Multibusiness Firm: General Electric from 1951 to 2001." *Strategic Management Journal* (special issue), 33: pp. 633–660.

Kogut, B. and Zander, U. 1992. "Knowledge of the Firm, Combinative Capabilities, and the Replication of Technology." *Organization Science*, 3: pp. 383–397.

Martin J. and Eisenhardt, K. 2001. "Exploring Cross-business Synergies." *Academy of Management Proceedings*: H1–H6.

Martin J. and Eisenhardt, K. 2010. "Rewiring: Cross-business-unit Collaborations in Multibusiness Organizations." *Academy of Management Journal*, 53 (2): pp. 265–301.

Milgrom, P. and Roberts, J. 1995. "Complementarities and Fit Strategy, Structure, and Organizational Change in Manufacturing." *Journal of Accounting and Economics*, 19 (2–3): pp. 179–208.

Porter, M. E. 1985. *Competitive Advantage*. New York: Free Press.

Porter, M. E. 1987. "From Competitive Advantage to Corporate Strategy." *Harvard Business Review*, May–June 65 (3): pp 43–59.

Porter, M. E. 1996. "What is Strategy?." *Harvard Business Review*, November–December 74 (60): pp. 61–78.

Prahalad, C. and Bettis, R. 1986. "The Dominant Logic: A New Linkage Between Diversity and Performance." *Strategic Management Journal*, 7 (6): pp. 485–501.

Prahalad, C. and Hamel, G. 1990. "The Core Competence of the Corporation." *Harvard Business Review*, 68 (3): pp. 79–91.

Rivkin, J. and Siggelkow, N. 2003. "Balancing Search and Stability: Interdependencies Among Elements of Organizational Design." *Management Science*, 49 (3): pp. 290–311.

Siggelkow, N. and Rivkin, J. 2005. "Speed and Search: Designing Organizations for Turbulence and Complexity." *Organization Science*, 16 (2): pp. 101–122.

Teece, D. 1980. "Economies of Scope and the Scope of the Enterprise." *Journal of Economic Behavior and Organization*, 1: pp. 223–247.

Teece, D. 1982. "Towards an Economic Theory of the Multiproduct Firm." *Journal of Economic Behavior and Organization*, 3: pp. 39–63.

Williamson, O. 1975. *Markets and Hierarchies: Analysis and Antitrust Implications*. New York: The Free Press.

Williamson, O. 1991. "Strategizing, Economizing and Economic Organization." *Strategic Management Journal*, 12: pp. 75–94.

Zott, C., Amit, R., and Massa, L. 2011. "The Business Model: Recent Developments and Future Research." *Journal of Management*, 37 (4): pp. 1019–1042.

5 Understanding Management Models

Going Beyond "What" and "Why" to "How" Work Gets Done in Organizations

JULIAN BIRKINSHAW AND SHAZ ANSARI

Over the last decade, the term 'business model' has been increasingly used by executives, consultants, and academics. The term came into popular usage during the dot-com revolution, as new online companies started to compete with very different revenue and costs structures to traditional bricks-and-mortar companies. The term was subsequently applied much more widely, and nowadays it is used to refer, in essence, to the basic choices a firm makes regarding its revenues and costs, and thereby its formula for making money. Within a given industry, say airlines, there will often be two or three distinct business models co-existing. A critical element of strategic thinking for executives is to be clear on their business model, as many other decisions flow from that basic choice.

The academic literature on business models is now quite extensive. A concept distinct from strategy (Casadesus-Masanell and Ricart, 2010) which is a description, plan, or process for how to move from the current situation to a desired future state, a business model is "a system of interdependent activities" which together comprise the way in which a firm does business and creates value (Zott and Amit, 2010: 216; Arend, 2013). In other words, it is "the translation of a company's strategy into a blueprint of the company's logic of earning money" (Osterwalder, 2004: 14).

A key challenge for firms, and an important theme in this literature, is the concept of *business model innovation,* that is, how a firm changes its business models. While many innovative business models are created by start-up firms, there are also cases of established firms experimenting with new business models as a way of responding to or forestalling the competitive threats from start-ups (Markides, 2000). This process of business model innovation is risky, as firms are restricted by path dependencies, and institutional and cultural constraints, but it is an important phenomenon that deserves greater scrutiny (Arend, 2013; Hamel, 2000).

A much less well-established concept is the *management model* of a firm. We will describe this concept in more detail later, but in essence a firm's management model is the basic choices it makes about how work gets done, for example, how activities are coordinated, how decisions are made, how objectives are set, and how employees are motivated. Every firm has an implicit management model. Just as with business models, there are often several different management models co-existing within the same industry sector. Microsoft, Google, and Linux, for example, have very different management models, especially in terms of the ways they coordinate the activities of their programmers to create software products, and yet they are direct competitors in several markets. And just as with business models, a key issue facing firms is how to change from one model to another, that is, the process of management model innovation (Birkinshaw, Hamel, and Mol, 2008).

A firm's management model is likely to be linked to its business model but at the same time it is conceptually distinct. "Management model" refers to choices at the level of "how" work gets done, rather than choices in terms of "who" the customer is and "what" the products and services offered are. Indeed, as we discuss in this chapter, those firms that understand their management model and use it to complement and support their business model will potentially generate competitive advantage from their efforts.

The purpose of this chapter is to provide a detailed explanation of management models, and how they relate to business models, in both static and dynamic terms. We first review the relevant bodies of academic literature to which the concept of a management model is linked (e.g., contingency theory and organizational culture). Second, we put forward a framework for defining and operationalizing a firm's management model. Third, we examine the notion of management model innovation, that is, how a management model changes over time, and how this form of innovation might lead or lag business model innovation. We conclude by proposing a research agenda in this area.

Theoretical Background

BUSINESS MODELS AND MANAGEMENT MODELS

Peter Drucker argued that a firm's business model—the "theory of the business" in his words—has three parts: assumptions about the environment of the organization, the specific mission of the organization, and the core competencies needed to accomplish the organization's mission (Drucker, 1994). Together these assumptions define what an organization gets paid for, what results it considers meaningful, and what it must excel at to maintain its competitive position.

Subsequent studies emphasized three business model elements that have received substantial support in the literature: the delivery of a value proposition to customers, the activities required for such delivery, and a logic of how these activities create profits for the firm (Amit and Zott, 2001; Chesbrough and Rosenbloom, 2002; Johnson, Christensen, and Kagermann, 2008; Magretta, 2002; Teece, 2010; Zott and Amit, 2010; Zott, Amit, and Massa, 2011). Although the revenue model has received most attention, the business system—the collection of all activities by which the value proposition is delivered—has been argued to be the true substance of the business model (Itami and Nishino, 2010). Thus, the business model is understood as a detailed specification of the activities a firm undertakes to exploit an identified opportunity (Morris, Schindehutte, and Allen, 2005). It is based on the information and knowledge through which a firm brings together partners, suppliers, customers, and other parties in its network (Voelpel, Leibold, and Tekie, 2004). Besides this objective definition of the business model, the business model also consists of *subjective* components (Doz and Kosonen, 2010). These are the cognitive aspects with regards to the boundaries of the firm, competition, and the economic, competitive, and institutional contexts that affect the industry in which a firm is active, and the benefits that should be included in a product offering (Doz and Kosonen, 2010). Table 5.1 lists the major business model elements (see Osterwalder, 2004).

Business model *innovation* is about creating a new value proposition and reconfiguring the business system in a way that supports this value proposition (Markides, 2000; Osterwalder, 2004). Through strategic sensing, businesses can identify opportunities created by environmental changes, and then capitalize on such developments through changes in various elements of the business model.

Scholars have suggested that firms generally pursue two main activities to create or adapt business models: experimentation and effectuation. Morris, Schindehutte, and Allen (2005) argue that the innovation process is emergent rather than planned in nature and relies heavily on rules of thumb and a process of trial-and-error. Due to the uncertainty that firms face when building or renewing business models, effectuation is another process to aid business model development (Sarasvathy, 2008). Because the benefits of analysis are limited in such contexts, knowledge is instead expanded through enacting the situation (McGrath, 2010).

The crux of business model innovation is not solely the reconfiguration of the objective elements of the business model (Chesbrough, 2010). Instead, firms are generally well aware of the changes required to their business model but encounter significant organizational barriers when carrying them out. The literature on organizational change and strategic renewal provides insights into how organizations move through change processes. For example,

Table 5.1 Business model elements

Study	Value Proposition	Revenues and Costs	Activity System	Relationship with the Customer	Partners
Afuah and Tucci (2003)	Customer value	Pricing; revenue source; cost structure	Connected activities; value configuration		Partners
Alt and Zimmerman (2001)		Source of revenues; business logic	Structure; processes	Processes	Structure
Amit and Zott (2001)	Transaction component		Architectural configuration		Transaction component
Applegate (2001)	Product and service offered	Benefits returned to the firm; financial performance	Operating model	Marketing sales model; brand and reputation	Partners
Bonaccorsi, Giannangeli, and Rossi (2006)		Income; cost structure			
Brousseau and Penard (2006)		Revenue steam; cost structure; income generation	Assembly costs	Knowledge management	Transaction costs
Chesbrough and Rosenbloom (2002)	Value proposition	Cost structure	Structure of the value chain		Position in the value chain
Gordijn (2002)	Value offering	Value exchange	e3-value configuration		Actors
Hamel (2000)	Product/market scope	Pricing structure	Core processes	Relationship dynamics	Suppliers; partners; coalitions
Linder and Cantrell (2001)	Value proposition	Pricing model; revenue model	Commerce process model	Commerce relationship	
Magretta (2002)	What does the customer value?	How do we make money in this business?			

Bock et al. (2012) document the effects of culture and structure on a firm's strategic flexibility during business model innovation, while on a more applied basis both Hamel (1999) and Markides (2000) offer insights into the challenges executives face in implementing new business models.

While this growing body of literature on business models provides important insights into the way a firm configures itself vis-à-vis external actors, it has less to say about the internal workings of the firm. Of course, this literature doesn't entirely focus on external factors: Zott and Amit (2010), for example, highlight internal governance as a key component of a firm's business model. But nonetheless, there are important features of the internal organization of a firm, in terms of the systems, processes, and style of working through which business activities are managed, that do not get addressed in the business model literature.

This is where the notion of a management model comes in: it is a way of characterizing the internal workings of the firm.

A firm's management model is the choices it makes about *how* work gets done—how activities are coordinated, how decisions are made, how objectives are set, and how employees are motivated (Birkinshaw, 2012). It is linked to the firm's business model, often as a way of operationalizing some of the business model choices that have been made, but it is also something that can be identified and understood in its own right.

Of course, there are many existing bodies of literature that characterize, in various ways, the internal workings of the firm, so it is important for us to show how the notion of a management model is distinct from them, and therefore why it is a useful concept to develop further. We focus on two such bodies of literature—contingency theory in the field of organization studies, and the culture literature in organizational behavior.

CONTINGENCY THEORY

One of the longest-established lines of inquiry in the field of organization studies has been the desire to understand why organizations are often structured and managed in different ways. Groundbreaking work by Burns and Stalker (1961), Woodward (1965), Lawrence and Lorsch (1967), among others, gave rise to what became known as contingency theory—the notion that an organization's internal form depended, to a large degree, on the environmental contingencies it was facing. For example, Burns and Stalker (1961) made a distinction, still used today, between "mechanistic" structures that were more appropriate in a relatively stable and predictable environment and "organic" structures that were better suited to uncertain or fast-changing environments.

Contingency theory has remained an important line of thinking in organization research for fifty years, and it spawned a related body of research often called "configuration theory." This moves away from a focus on "fit" occurring between one element of the organization and the environment to a view that fit is about multiple elements of the organization working together in mutually supportive ways, so that they collectively support a chosen position in the task environment (e.g., Doty, Glick, and Huber, 1993; Meyer, Tsui, and Hinings, 1993).

While this approach to understanding a firm's internal workings has been valuable, our view is that most of these studies characterize the organization in structural terms (indeed, this field is often referred to as *structural* contingency theory), and with little regard for the underlying processes and sometimes informal systems through which work actually gets done. So while this literature is not flawed, neither is it complete. Our concept of management—and therefore our concept of a firm's management model—helps to bring out aspects of the internal workings of the firm that are not considered in this body of literature.

ORGANIZATIONAL CULTURE

A very different way of characterizing the internal workings of the firm is through the study of organization culture. Again, there is a very long tradition here dating back to the 1950s, though often the related term organizational climate was used in this era (see Denison, 1990, for a discussion of culture vs climate).

Organization culture is a pattern of shared assumptions, beliefs, and expectations that guide members' interpretations and actions by defining appropriate behavior within the organization (e.g., Fiol, 1991; O'Reilly and Chatman, 1996). A key unifying element of this definition is the shared nature of culture (e.g., Martin, 2002; Ravasi and Schultz, 2006). Researchers have agreed less about the explicitness of organizational culture, with some viewing culture as mostly tacit and implicit (e.g., Schein, 1985) and others focusing more on its behavioral manifestations (e.g., Harrison and Carroll, 2006; O'Reilly, Chatman, and Caldwell, 1991). Culture content refers to the actual attitudes and behaviors that characterize an organization's norms. For example, cultures can shape and support risk taking and cooperation (Smith, Collins, and Clark, 2005), meritocracy (Castilla and Benard, 2010), stability and predictability, flexibility or standardization, collectivism or individualism, and transparency or openness. An example is the culture of secrecy at Apple. Apple's founder and former CEO, the late Steve Jobs even risked violating SEC disclosure rules by withholding information about his serious health issues as CEO (Stone and Vance, 2009).

One of the major themes in the organization culture literature is that cultures vary in systematic and predictable ways from company to company (e.g., Denison and Mishra, 1995; Goffee and Jones, 2003), partly as a reflection of the industry environment in which the company is operating, partly as a function of its chosen position in the market, its history, and its current leadership. It would be expected, for example, that a Silicon Valley company would have an informal, free-wheeling culture, while a government bureaucracy might have a more formalized and conservative culture.

So there is, in other words, some overlap between the concept of a firm's culture and its management model. However, there are also important points of difference. First, by definition culture has a strong informal or tacit component: it cannot be written down in a way that fully captures its essence. A management model, in contrast, is much more conducive to codification and objective verification. Second, and linked to the first point, a culture is not something that can be easily manipulated. While it is possible to change a firm's culture, the process typically takes many years. A management model, in contrast, includes elements that can be more readily altered by those in positions of seniority.

Essentially, then, a firm's management model is more tangible and readily manipulated than its culture; and it is more comprehensive, in terms of how things actually get done in the firm, than the formal structures or systems studied in contingency theory. There are, of course, overlaps between the concepts in terms of the things they focus on, but we believe there are sufficient differences between them for the management model to become a concept worth studying in its own right.

A Framework for Operationalizing a Firm's Management Model

In this section we develop our concept of a management model in detail. This section draws to a large degree from Birkinshaw (2012).

To shed light on what "management model" means, we need to start with a point of view on management. For us, management is simply about "getting work done through others." Drawing from the writings of Drucker (2008), Fayol (1967), Gulick and Urwick (1937), and Mintzberg (2009), we view management as comprising four activities: coordinating activities, making decisions, defining objectives, and motivating effort. It therefore follows that a firm's management model can be viewed as the choices made by the executives of a firm regarding how these four things get done, that is, how activities are coordinated, decisions made, objectives defined, and effort motivated.

This definition has a few important features. First it is about making choices. In the airline industry there are several co-existing business models, and every firm knows it has to make an explicit choice about which business model it will adopt. Similarly, some industries already feature competing management models. As noted earlier, Linux, Google, and Microsoft all operate with very different management models (Linux is run through an open-source software community; Google has a highly informal, university-like model; Microsoft has a more traditional, hierarchical structure), yet they compete head-to-head in the desktop operating system market. Toyota operated for decades with a different management model from those of GM and Ford, despite having a very similar business model. Thus, while management models are related to business models, different organizations can have similar business models but different management models, or different business models but similar management models.

The second feature of the definition is that we do not assume that the work of management is limited to a small number of senior executives at the top of the firm. Thus for example we talk about "how activities are coordinated" rather than "how executives coordinate activities." As will become clear, the whole argument here rests on the possibility that many of the activities of management can transpire in a bottom-up way as well as top-down.

DEFINING THE PRINCIPLES OF MANAGEMENT

For each of the four dimensions of management, in fact, we can identify two underlying principles, or belief systems, about how they should work. The first might be considered the *traditional principle* that firms have implicitly used for generations. The second is the *alternative principle* that is either just beginning to be adopted, or has been talked about for a long time but has not been widely used.

(A note on terminology: We view a management principle as something like "extrinsic motivation" which is an underlying belief about a causal relationship between two things. Principles are manifested in organizations through processes, such as the resource allocation process or the budgeting process, and also through specific practices, such as 360-degree feedback, quality circles, or scenario planning.)

Putting these two dimensions together, we end up with the framework shown in Figure 5.1 with four traditional principles and four alternative principles, as follows.

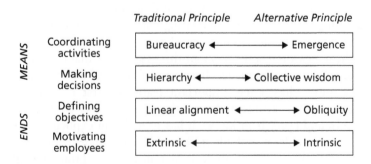

Figure 5.1 Management model framework

The traditional view of managerial coordination can be traced back to Weber (1978) and is called bureaucracy—a means of coordinating economic activity that relies on formal rules and procedures to ensure conformity of behavior and to generate consistent outputs. The alternative view of coordination has come from the application of complexity theory to social science (e.g., Anderson, 1999) and can be called emergence—the spontaneous coordination of activities achieved through the self-interested behaviors of independent actors.

Decision making or resource allocation more generally is traditionally managed through the principle of hierarchy—the notion that managers have legitimate authority over their subordinates. Hierarchy, as a concept, can be traced back to ancient Greek times (Hedlund, 1994). In recent years, it has been increasingly challenged by the alternative principle of collective wisdom, which suggests that under certain conditions the aggregated expertise of a large number of people can produce more accurate forecasts and better decisions than those of a small number of experts (Surowiecki, 2004). Hierarchy can, of course, be viewed as one element of bureaucracy (Weber, 1978) but we believe it is useful to view it as a separate dimension, with bureaucracy being about managing *across* and hierarchy being about managing *down*.

Objective setting has traditionally been managed through a linear approach to alignment—the notion that we can work back logically from an end-point and define the objectives through which every team and individual will contribute to the overall objective. This principle has been around for at least a hundred years; but recently some studies have suggested that it may not be quite right. Specifically, John Kay (2010) described the notion of obliquity, which states that goals are often best achieved when pursued indirectly.

Finally, the two competing principles for motivating employees have long been recognized, for example by McGregor (1957). The traditional principle here is extrinsic motivation, which comes from outside the person, for example money, coercion, and the threat of punishment. The alternative principle is intrinsic motivation, which comes from the rewards inherent to a task or activity itself, for example playing the piano or solving a puzzle.

In sum, the purpose of this framework is to provide a means of describing a firm's management model. Each dimension represents a choice: for example, do we want to rely more on hierarchy or collective wisdom to make decisions? Put the four choices together, and one ends up with a profile for a particular firm, that is, its overall management model. This model can then be evaluated in terms of whether it is supporting the firm's business model and/or whether it is appropriate for the business environment in which the firm is operating. It can also be evaluated in terms of its novelty vis-à-vis its competitors: does the firm have any unique aspects to its management model? Are there certain principles that might help it to differentiate itself?

FOUR ARCHETYPAL MODELS OF MANAGEMENT

The management model framework also allows us to identify four archetypes (Greenwood and Hinings, 1993), by separating out the "means" (coordinating activities and making decisions) from the "ends" (defining objectives and motivating employees).

Figure 5.2 provides a graphical depiction of the four archetypes. The horizontal axis refers to the *means* of management (coordinating activities, making decisions); the vertical axis refers to the *ends* of management (setting objectives, motivating people). For each axis, the scale runs from *tight* to *loose*, with the traditional principles of management at the tight end and the alternative principles of management at the loose end.

The Planning Model

Many large firms operate with narrow, short-term objectives, clearly defined management processes, and with strict hierarchical decision making. And importantly these are often among the highest-performing firms on the stock market—most people would place ExxonMobil and Wal-Mart in this quadrant of the matrix. While less "progressive" than the other models, it is evidently a viable model in certain business settings, typically those that are slower moving or where the benefits of scale and scope are significant.

The Quest Model

One alternative to the planning model is to loosen up the "means" of management while retaining tight control over the "ends"—telling employees what to do, but not how to do it. This is one of the hallmarks of high-growth companies, where the founder has a clear view of what she is trying to achieve and encourages her employees to pursue those objectives through a variety of means. It is also increasingly popular in large firms that are seeking to recapture their vitality. In such cases, the intention is typically to simplify or get rid of the bureaucratic and hierarchical elements that are getting in the way.

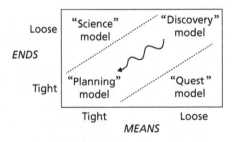

Figure 5.2 Four management model archetypes

The Scientific Model

The other alternative path away from the planning model is to free up the ends, while keeping control of the means. This is how science makes progress: there is a canon of knowledge, taught through texts and through university lectures; and there are clear rules of engagement, in the form of peer review, citation of others, open disclosure of results, and so on. But the objectives of science are deliberately framed in the broadest possible sense: the pursuit of knowledge.

Many organizations use a version of the scientific model. For example, Arup, a world-leading consulting engineer, provides enormous scope to its employees to bid for projects that they believe are interesting and consistent with the values of the firm, while also expecting them to apply their shared understanding of how high-quality engineering work should be conducted.

The Discovery Model

If both the means and ends of management are deliberately loose, there is a risk of chaos and confusion, but for certain activities, and for certain periods of time, it can be effective. The discovery model is suitable for many start-up ventures operating in highly ambiguous environments, where there are multiple potential ways forward, of varying levels of potential, and success is achieved through trial and error. Google, for example, used the discovery model for perhaps the first ten years of its existence, though as it has grown it has moved closer to the quest model.

As with any such framework, the interesting part of the story is how a given firm shifts its management model from one archetype to another over time. This process of change has a proactive component, as we will discuss later, but there is also an implicit life-cycle at work. When a firm is founded, its competitive environment usually feels highly ambiguous, and progress depends a great deal on trial and error. As a result, goals are typically vague and flexible, people work long hours for little pay, and work gets coordinated and defined through informal mechanisms. As it grows and becomes more successful, its positioning in the marketplace becomes established, and its positioning vis-à-vis competitors becomes clear. Internally, operations tend to become more structured, decision making more formalized, and objectives more clearly defined. There is, in other words, a natural drift over time from the discovery model toward the planning model, typically via the quest or science model.

Management Model Innovation

The challenge of innovation at various levels of analysis has long attracted academic and managerial attention. For example, Ahuja, Lampert, and Tandon

(2008) provide an overview of innovation across four broad headings—industry structure, firm characteristics, intra-organizational attributes, and institutional influences. Under the rubric of firm characteristics, they consider the many externally observable attributes of a firm such as its size, scope, access to external sources of knowledge (such as through alliances), and performance. Under the heading of intra-organizational attributes, they look at the inside of the firm, the firm's organizational structure and processes, corporate governance arrangements including compensation and incentive structures, the backgrounds of managers, and organizational search processes.

Management model innovation is therefore one useful way of characterizing innovation at the intra-organizational level, and it is a topic that has attracted a reasonable amount of research attention over the years (Birkinshaw, Hamel, and Mol, 2008).

How does management model innovation manifest itself in practice? Using our terminology, it should involve significant changes on one or more of the four dimensions of management. For example, Gary Hamel (1999) argued that most large firms have management structures inspired more by Soviet-style central planning than by free-market principles, and that we should develop Silicon Valley-style *internal markets* for allocating people and capital to ideas—in essence by moving from "bureaucracy" to "emergence" on the coordinating activities dimension, and from "hierarchy" to "collective wisdom" on the making decisions dimension. Many companies have picked up on this idea—for example, Hamel (1999) described GameChanger, Royal Dutch Shell's successful process for seed-funding innovative technology projects. But Enron also followed a variant of this model, by giving its employees enormous freedom to pursue opportunities and jobs within the company's internal market, with disastrous consequences. Management model innovation, just like other forms of innovation, doesn't always have successful outcomes.

Similarly, management models may influence why some Western companies underperform in non-traditional markets. Even high-performing companies such as Google and eBay have failed to make significant inroads in mainland China. Non-relational Western models may face difficulties in markets characterized by guanxi (networks of trust, mutual obligation, and shared experience); non-linear temporal orientations, and holistic worldviews (Chen and Miller, 2011). For example, the founder of Alibaba.com (the company eBay faltered against) terms his company a customer-to-business operation (existing to solve social problems) rather than the more conventional business-to-customer designation (existing to seize business opportunities). His emphasis is on facilitating good relationships between buyers and sellers of goods, fostering enriching and enduring relationships among employees, and maintaining a more peripheral relationship with "opportunistic" investors (Chen and Miller, 2011). This is in stark contrast to traditional Western models.

Changes in a management model need to be considered alongside other changes such as those in the firm's business model. Consider, for example, the case of Linux, the open-source software movement. Linux's management approach has been described as "centrally facilitated yet organizationally distributed" based on interactions among contributors across space and time (Garud, Jain, and Tuertscher, 2008; Lanzara and Morner, 2005). A combination of technological and social rules worked in concert to keep its innovative business platform from falling apart. These mechanisms were buttressed by an "overarching meritocracy" within the community in which developers focus on providing new code and modules that added features and functionality to the platform. Others, based on their reputation and prior contributions, assumed the task of maintenance which involved evaluating code submitted by developers for inclusion into new versions (Garud and Kumaraswamy, 2005). The management model developed by Linux has enabled access to knowledge, encouraged constant adaptation, and curbed private appropriation and free riding—aspects that are necessary for its business model to work. A more tightly controlled bureaucratic model would have been less appropriate, given the challenges of accommodating the contradictory requirements of Linux's heterogeneous community.

Another example is innovative business models for new ventures in the Bottom of the Pyramid (BoP)—the part of the world's population that lives on less than two dollars a day (Ansari, Munir, and Gregg, 2012; Prahalad, and Hammond, 2002). Current literature has extensively addressed the issue of business model innovations required for such ventures; the products or services offered should be affordable and relevant to the local population (Anderson and Markides, 2007), products should address a fundamental need of the poor (Garrette and Karnani, 2010), and businesses should include the poor not as passive customers but as partners (London, 2007). Most current debates in this area center around external barriers that could prevent a more widespread adoption of such ideas, for example, lack of infrastructure, corruption of local governments, problems with distribution networks, low educational levels, and lack of buying power. Yet there are likely to be significant organizational ramifications to these initiatives, and the successful players will surely be looking for innovative ways of setting objectives, motivating their employees, and coordinating their activities, given the very distinctive business challenges they are facing.

When companies seek to enhance their competitive advantage through efforts to implement new sustainability initiatives, they may inadvertently overlook the need to develop or adapt their management model, and this in turn may hamper the implementation of some of the most novel and promising business initiatives. Moreover, aspects of their existing management models may prevent cognitive shifts and skill acquisition, which are required for organizational learning to take place, for new routines to emerge, and for capabilities to develop. In short, innovative business models need to be accompanied by appropriate management models if they are to gain traction. Figuring out the "how" is just as important as figuring out the "what" and the "why."

Conclusion: A Research Agenda

By formalizing and operationalizing the management model concept, we are opening up some potentially interesting avenues for future research, and in this final section we explore what some of these might be.

First, it would be useful to study management models as a phenomenon in their own right. Building on the methodologies used in configuration theory and in studies of organization culture, it would be possible to operationalize the various dimensions of a firm's management model and to examine how they fit together to enable a firm to generate superior performance. It would also be interesting to examine how a firm's management model changes over time, by collecting data over multiple time periods. It is often the case, for example, that executives express a desire to shift their management model to the right side of the framework (i.e., toward the alternative principles), but our hunch is that few actually make the intended transition. A careful academic study of this phenomenon would be very promising.

Second, there is scope for linking analysis of a firm's management model to its business model, and indeed for studying management model innovation and business model innovation as linked processes. A promising exercise to adapt business models in response to external or internal drivers for change is to map the elements of the business model and the processes that underlie them (Chesbrough, 2010). Here, innovation is about creating a superior value proposition, a business system to deliver that value proposition, and a revenue model to specify the ways in which these activities accrue profits for the firm (Itami and Nishino, 2010).

As noted earlier, the crux of business model innovation is not necessarily the reconfiguration of the objective elements of the business model (Chesbrough, 2010). Rather, firms are generally well aware of the changes required to their business model but encounter significant organizational barriers when carrying them out. The literature on organizational change and strategic renewal, including changes in organizational structure and culture, provides insights into how organizations move through change processes (Lewin, 1951; Schalk, Campbell, and Freese, 1998; Todnemby, 2010). However, the concept of a management model may help to explain the linkages between organizational change and business models, and how the cognitive elements need to undergo change in order to accommodate new business models. For example, working in the BoP or other novel contexts may involve collaboration with external partners, relationships with local producers, and public–private partnerships. However, the firm's management model may simply be ill-equipped or ill-configured to manage these new and evolving relationships that a new business model may require.

When pursuing innovative business models, firms frequently encounter organizational conflicts that pose barriers to business model innovation. Some of these are structural in nature, such as poorly suited evaluation targets and counterproductive incentive structures and discrepant mandates (Olsen and Boxenbaum, 2009). Few studies have, however, addressed the *entire* process by which firms innovate their management model and/or provided a holistic picture of the innovation journey. More theorization is therefore, needed on management model innovation in novel environments. In commercializing new products and services, the management model may require thorough reconfiguration such that the model, the objectives of the innovation, and the business model elements to deliver this innovation are well aligned.

Finally, it is interesting to consider the phasing of change in organizations in terms of our notions of business and management models. One logic might be for a firm to change its business model first, and then to adjust its management model accordingly, so that it supports the business model. But the opposite sequencing is equally plausible. For example, one could argue that Google's distinctive management model, with a high degree of individual freedom to experiment with new business ideas, has made it possible for new businesses to emerge, some of which have very different business models to traditional Google businesses. In this case, an innovative management model caused the emergence of an innovative business model, rather than vice versa. While there have been some studies on the relative timing of management vs technological innovations (e.g., Damanpour, 1987), there have not been any studies, to our knowledge, on this related question.

What methodologies are appropriate for studying management models? For the most part, a case study design is most appropriate (Marshall and Rossman, 1995), because the intention is to understand an organizational phenomenon where events are linked across time toward the attainment of a goal. Studying processes can result in an articulation of routines and practices that remain relatively constant over time or of diachronic changes that emerge chronologically across time. Case-based research is particularly appropriate for capturing processes which are fluid across both space and time and hard to isolate (Pettigrew, 1992). Management model development is such a process, where individual phases are hard to separate from each other and likely to manifest themselves on multiple levels of analysis (Langley, 1999, 2007). Furthermore, organizational context is a crucial element of management model development and innovation and process research accommodates the inclusion of such a context (Pettigrew, 1992).

■ **REFERENCES**

Afuah, A. and Tucci, C. L. 2003. *Internet Business Models and Strategies*. Boston, MA: McGraw Hill.

Anderson, P. 1999. "Complexity Theory and Organization Science." *Organization Science*, Vol. 10, No. 3: pp. 216–232.

Ahuja, G., Lampert, C., and Tandon, V. 2008. "Chapter 1: Moving Beyond Schumpeter: Management Research on the Determinants of Technological Innovation." *The Academy of Management Annals*, 2 (1): pp. 1–98.

Alt, R. and Zimmermann, H. D. 2001. "Introduction to Special Section on Business Models." *Electronic Markets*, 11 (1): pp. 3–9.

Amit, R. and Zott, C. 2001. "Value Creation in e-business." *Strategic Management Journal*, 22: pp. 493–520.

Anderson, J. and Markides, C. 2007. "Strategic Innovation at the Base of the Pyramid." *MIT Sloan Management Review*, 49 (1): pp. 83–88.

Ansari, S., Munir, K., and Gregg, T. 2012. "Impact at the 'Bottom of the Pyramid': The Role of Social Capital in Capability Development and Community Empowerment." *Journal of Management Studies*, 49 (4): pp. 813–842.

Applegate, L. M. 2001. *Emerging e-business Models: Lessons from the Field*. HBS No. 9-801-172, Harvard Business School, Boston, MA.

Arend, R. 2013. "The Business Model: Present and Future—Beyond a Skeumorph." *Strategic Organization*, 11 (4): pp. 390–402.

Birkinshaw, J. 2012. *Reinventing Management. Smarter Choices for Getting Work Done*. San Fransisco: John Wiley & Sons Ltd.

Birkinshaw, J., Hamel, G., and Mol, M. 2008. "Management Innovation." *Academy of Management Review*, 33: pp. 825–845.

Bonaccorsi, A., Giannangeli, S., and Rossi, C. 2006. "Entry Strategies Under Competing Standards: Hybrid Business Models in the Open Source Software Industry." *Management Science*, 52: pp. 1085–1098.

Bock, A. J., Opsahl, T., George, G., and Gann, D. M. 2012 "The Effects of Culture and Structure on Strategic Flexibility During Business Model Innovation." *Journal of Management Studies*, 49 (2): pp. 279–305.

Brousseau, E. and Penard, T. 2006. "The Economics of Digital Business Models: A Framework for Analyzing the Economics of Platforms." *Review of Network Economics*, 6 (2): pp. 81–110.

Burns, T. and Stalker, G. M. 1961. *The Management of Innovation*. London: Tavistock.

Casadesus-Masanell, R. and Ricart, J. E. 2010. "From Strategy to Business Models and to Tactics." *Long Range Planning*, 43: pp. 195–215.

Castilla, E. J. and S. Benard. 2010. "The Paradox of Meritocracy in Organizations." *Administrative Science Quarterly*, 55: pp. 543–576.

Chen, M.-J. and Miller, D. 2011. "The Relational Perspective as a Business Mindset: Managerial Implications for East and West." *The Academy of Management Perspectives*, 25(3): 6–18.

Chesbrough, H. W. 2010. "Business Model Innovation: Opportunities and Barriers." *Long Range Planning*, 43: pp. 354–363.

Chesbrough, H. W. and Rosenbloom, R. S. 2002. "The Role of the Business Model in Capturing Value from Innovation: Evidence from Xerox Corporation's Technology Spinoff Companies." *Industrial and Corporate Change*, 11: pp. 533–534.

Damanpour, F., 1987. "The Adoption of Technological, Administrative, and Ancillary Innovations: Impact of Organizational Factors." *Journal of Management*, 13: pp. 675–688.

Denison, D. R. 1990. *Corporate Culture and Organizational Effectiveness*. New York: Wiley.

Denison, D. R. and A. K. Mishra. 1995. "Toward a Theory of Culture and Effectiveness." *Organization Science*, 6: pp. 204–223.

Doty, H., Glick, W., and Huber, G. 1993. "Fit, Equifinality, and Organizational Effectiveness: A Test of Two Configurational Theories." *Academy of Management Journal*, 36 (6): pp. 1196–1250.

Doz, Y. L. and Kosonen, M. 2010. "Embedding Strategic Agility." *Long Range Planning*, 43: pp. 370–382.

Drucker, P. 1994. "The Theory of the Business," *Harvard Business Review*, September–October: pp. 95–104.

Drucker, P. 2008. *Management*. Fourth edition. New York: Collins Business.

Fayol, H. 1947. *General and Industrial Management* (Administration, industrielle ET generale). London: Pitman.

Fayol, H. 1967. *General and Industrial Management*. London: Pitman.

Fiol, C. 1991. "Managing Culture as a Competitive Resource: An Identity-based View of Sustainable Competitive Advantage." *Journal of Management*, 17 (1): pp. 191–211.

Garud, R. and Kumaraswamy, A. 2005. "Vicious and Virtuous Circles in the Management of Knowledge: The Case of Infosys Technologies." *MIS Quarterly* 29 (1): pp. 9–33.

Garud, R., Jain, S., and Tuertscher, P. 2008. "Incomplete by Design and Designing for Incompleteness." *Organization Studies*, 29: pp. 351–371.

Garrette, B. and Karnani, A. 2010. "Challenges in Marketing Socially Useful Goods to the Poor." *California Management Review*, 52 (4): pp. 29–47.

Goffee, R. and G. Jones, 2003. *The Character of a Corporation*. Second edition. London: Profile Books.

Gordijn, J. 2002. *Value-based Requirements Engineering—Exploring Innovative e-Commerce Ideas*. Amsterdam: Vrije Universiteit.

Greenwood, R. and Hinings, C. R. 1993. "Understanding Strategic Change: The Contribution of Archetypes." *Academy of Management Journal*, 36 (5): pp. 1052–1081.

Gulick, L. and Urwick, L. 1937. *Papers on the Science of Administrating*. New York: Institute of Public Administration.

Hamel, G. 1999. "Bringing Silicon Valley Inside." *Harvard Business Review*, September–October 5 (77): pp. 70–84.

Hamel, G. 2000. *Leading the Revolution*. Boston, MA: Harvard Business School Press.

Harrison, J. R. and G. R. Carroll. 2006. *Culture and Demography in Organizations*. Princeton, NJ: Princeton University Press.

Hedlund G. 1994. "A Model of Knowledge Management and the N-form Corporation." *Strategic Management Journal*, 15: pp. 73–90.

Itami, H. and Nishino, K. 2010. "Killing Two Birds with One Stone: Profit for Now and Learning for the Future." *Long Range Planning*, 43: pp. 364–369.

Johnson, M. W., Christensen, C. M., and Kagermann, H. 2008. "Reinventing your Business Model." *Harvard Business Review*, 86 (12): pp. 50–59.

Kay, J. 2010. *Obliquity: Why Our Goals are Best Achieved Indirectly*. London: Profile Books.

Langley, A. 1999. "Strategies for Theorizing from Process Data." *Academy of Management Review*, 24 (4): pp. 691–710.

Langley, A. 2007. "Process Thinking in Strategic Organization." *Strategic Organization*, 5 (3): pp. 271–282.

Lanzara, G. F. and Morner, M. 2005. "Artefacts Rule! How Organizing Happens in Open Source Software Projects." In B. Czarniawska and T. Hernes, eds, *Actor-Network-Theory and Organizing*. Copenhagen: Copenhagen Business School Press, pp. 67–90.

Lawrence, P. R. and Lorsch, J. W. 1967. *Organization and Environment.* Boston, MA: Harvard University, Graduate School of Business Administration.

Lewin, K. 1951. *Field Theory in Social Science.* New York: Harper and Row.

Linder, J., and Cantrell, S. 2001. "Changing Business Models: Surveying the Landscape." Working paper, Accenture Institute for Strategic Change.

London, T. 2007. "A Base-of-the-Pyramid Perspective on Poverty Alleviation." Working paper, The William Davidson Institute, Ann Arbor.

Magretta, J. 2002. "Why Business Models Matter." *Harvard Business Review*, May 80 (5): pp. 86-92.

Markides, C.C. 2000. *All the Right Moves.* Cambridge, MA: Harvard Business Press.

Marshall, C. and Rossman, G. B. 1995. *Designing Qualitative Research.* Thousand Oaks, CA: Sage Publications.

Martin, J. 2002. "Organizational Culture: Mapping the Terrain." Thousand Oaks, CA: Sage Publications.

McGrath, R. G. 2010. "Business Models: A Discovery Driven Approach." *Long Range Planning*, 43: pp. 247–261.

McGregor, D. 1957. "The Human Side of Enterprise." *Management Review*: pp. 22–28, 88–92.

Meyer, A. D., Tsui, A. S., and Hinings, C. R. 1993. "Configurational Approaches to Organizational Analysis." *Academy of Management Journal*, 36: pp. 1175–1195.

Mintzberg, H. 2009. *Managing.* San Francisco: Berrett Koehler.

Morris, M., Schindehutte, M., and Allen, J. 2005. "The Entrepreneur's Business Model: Toward a Unified Perspective." *Journal of Business Research*, 58: pp. 726–735.

O'Reilly, C. A. and Chatman, J. A. 1996. "Culture as Social Control: Corporations, Cults, and Commitment." *Research in Organizational Behavior*, 18: pp. 157–200.

O'Reilly, C. A., Chatman, J. A., and Caldwell, D.F. 1991. "People and Organizational Culture: A Profile Comparison Approach to Assessing Personorganization Fit." *Academy of Management Journal*, 34: pp. 487–516.

Olsen, M. and Boxenbaum, E. 2009. "Bottom-of-the-Pyramid: Organizational Barriers to Implementation." *California Management Review*, 51 (4): pp. 100–125.

Osterwalder, A. 2004. "The Business Model Ontology—A Proposition in a Design Science Approach." Dissertation 173, University of Lausanne, Switzerland.

Pettigrew, A. 1992. "The Character and Significance of Strategy Process Research." *Strategic Management Journal*, 13 (S2): pp. 5–16.

Prahalad, C. K. and Hammond, A. 2002. "Serving the World's Poor, Profitably." *Harvard Business Review*, 80 (9): pp. 48–57.

Ravasi, D., and Schultz, M. 2006. "Responding to Organizational Identity Threats: Exploring the Role of Organizational Culture." *Academy of Management Journal*, 49 (3): pp 433–458.

Sarasvathy, S. D. 2008. *Effectuation: Elements of Entrepreneurial Expertise.* London: Edward Elgar, New Horizons in Entrepreneurship Series.

Schalk, R., Campbell, J. W., and Freese, C. 1998. "Change and Employee Behaviour." *Leadership and Organization Development Journal*, 19 (3): pp. 157–163.

Schein, E. H. 1985. *Organizational Culture and Leadership.* San Francisco, CA: Jossey-Bass.

Smith, K. G., Collins, C. J., and K. D. Clark. 2005. "Existing Knowledge, Knowledge Creation Capability, and the Rate of New Product Introduction in High-Technology Firms." *Academy of Management Journal*, 48 (2): pp. 346–357.

Stone, B. and Vance, A. 2009. "Apple's Obsession With Secrecy Grows Stronger." *New York Times*, June, 22.

Surowiecki, J. 2004. *The Wisdom of Crowds*. New York: Doubleday, Anchor.

Teece, D. J. 2010. "Business Models, Business Strategy and Innovation." *Long Range Planning*, 43: pp. 172–194.

Todnemby, R. 2010. "Organizational Change Management, A Critical Review." *Journal of Change Management*, 5 (4): pp. 369–380.

Voelpel S. C., Leibold M., and Tekie E. B. 2004. "The Wheel of Business Model Reinvention: How to Reshape your Business Model to Leapfrog Competitors." *Journal of Change Management*, 4 (3): pp. 259–276.

Weber, M. 1978. *Economy and Society: An Outline of Interpretive Sociology*. Berkeley, CA: University of California Press.

Woodward, J. 1965. *Industrial Organization: Theory and Practice*. Oxford: Oxford University Press.

Zott, C. and Amit, R. 2010. "Business Model Design: An Activity System Perspective." *Long Range Planning*, 43 (2-3): pp. 216–226.

Zott, C., Amit, R., and Massa, L. 2011. "The Business Model: Recent Developments and Future Research." *Journal of Management*, 37 (4): pp. 1019–1042.

6 Business Model Innovation

The Role of Leadership

NILS STIEGLITZ AND NICOLAI J. FOSS

Introduction

In spite of the massive attention in the practitioner and research literature over the last decade to business models and the innovation thereof (cf. Massa and Tucci, 2013; Zott, Amit, and Massi, 2011), little or no research so far has dealt with the leadership aspects of business model innovation (BMI) in a systematic manner. And yet, BMI can be a massive organizational change process that places very heavy demands on top management and potentially strains the organization. Moreover, BMIs are far from homogenous. Some may involve relatively minor connected changes in, for example, the customer segments that are addressed and the revenue model in a business unit. Other BMIs may be massive corporate-wide processes that involve basically all employees and all processes and activities. It seems reasonable to argue that different BMIs therefore pose different leadership requirements.

However, we know of no analysis that systematically links BMI, appropriately dimensionalized, to an understanding of the different competences of leadership and organizational design that are required to cope with the challenges represented by different kinds of BMIs. This is not to say that organizational and leadership challenges associated with business models and BMI have been neglected; in fact, this is far from being the case (e.g., Chesbrough and Rosenbloom, 2002; Margretta, 2002; Casadesus-Masanell and Ricart, 2010; Chesbrough, 2007, 2010; Demil and Lecoq, 2010; Doz and Kosenen, 2010; Teece, 2010; Zott and Amit, 2010; Amit and Zott, 2012). However, existing research does not offer a contingency perspective. A key reason is that the unit of analysis is not clearly characterized. Specifically, existing research does not adequately represent the heterogeneity of BMI, and therefore does not dimensionalize BMI. In turn, the different leadership challenges that different kinds of BMI give rise to are not identified.

Accordingly, in this chapter we take some preliminary steps toward developing a theory of the leadership requirements of BMI, given a theoretically grounded dimensionalization of BMI. The theory is fundamentally a contingency theory and leaves out many important process aspects. Our reasoning starts from noting the inherently *systemic* character of business models. Indeed, as argued elsewhere in this volume (e.g., Foss and Saebi, chapter 1, this volume), the main contribution that the business model literature has brought to macro-management theory may well in retrospect turn out to be an emphasis on the need for integration of and coherence among strategic choices related to value proposition, segments, value-appropriation models, and value-chain organization. It is well known from the literature on coordination in complex systems that system elements may stand in different relations of specificity and complementarity to each other (Lachmann, 1956; Milgrom and Roberts, 1990; Williamson, 1996; Levinthal, 1997). The need for leadership and a planned approach to the allocation of responsibilities, roles, and tasks—that is, organizational design—derive from such interdependencies. We argue that a key dimension along which business models (and hence the innovation thereof) may differ is exactly in terms of the strength of the interdependencies, or, as we shall say, "complementarities," between their constituent components.

The purpose of this chapter is to unfold this overall theme. By placing "complementarity" centrally in our thinking about BMI, we add to the literature by (1) developing a taxonomy of BMI that is based on a dimensionalization of BMIs in terms of complementarity; (2) identifying limits/constraints to successful BMI; and (3) highlighting the role of the top management interventions in terms of making BMIs successful.

Business Models and Complementarities

BUSINESS MODELS IN THE SPACE OF STRATEGIC MANAGEMENT THEORY

Although science can make progress even in the presence of considerable conceptual ambiguity, there is little doubt that scientific advances are assisted by the presence of construct clarity (Suddaby, 2010), particularly clarity of the key constructs that organize and differentiate research efforts, streams, and programs. Distinct research streams thrive by organizing research around core constructs that are clearly delineated from core constructs in other, neighboring research streams. The concept of a business model was coined several decades ago (Bellman and Clark, 1957; Jones, 1960), and sustained, cumulative academic work that is explicitly organized around the business model construct has been going on for at least a decade-and-a-half (e.g., Chesbrough and Rosenbloom, 2002).[1] And yet, no single, clear, unifying

---

[1] We do not here pursue the theme of whether earlier research (e.g., Teece, 1986) in actuality dealt with business models, even though it did not use the term.

definition of the construct that is also clearly delineated from related constructs has been advanced. What we have instead is a plethora of definitions (see also Foss and Saebi, chapter 1, this volume), many of which bear a distinct resemblance to existing constructs in strategic management. For this reason, many of the proponents of the business model construct have often been at pains to differentiate it from more established strategic management constructs (e.g., Casadesus-Masanell and Ricart, 2011). Sometimes business models are seen as subordinate and sometimes as superordinate to business strategy. Our position is that the business model concept has drawn attention to a fundamental perspective in strategy that arguably was present at the inception of strategy thinking but was forgotten as academic specialization came to characterize strategic management. The perspective is outlined in the following quotation (Rumelt, Schendel, and Teece, 1991: 5):

> ... firms have choices to make if they are to survive. Those that are *strategic* include: the selection of goals; the choice of products and services to offer; the design and configuration of ... competitive strategy; the choice of an appropriate level of scope and diversity; and the design of organization structure, administrative systems and policies used to define and coordinate work ... It is the *integration* (or reinforcing pattern) among these choices that makes a set a strategy.

This definition of strategy accords well with, for example, Zott, Amit, and Massa's (2011: 1037) argument that a business model is a "system level concept" that contains a "systemic and holistic understanding of how an organization orchestrates its system of activities for value creation" (Massa and Tucci, 2014: 9). What makes it "systemic" is exactly the notion that the choices can be reinforcing, as suggested by Rumelt, Schendel, and Teece (1991).

DEFINING BUSINESS MODELS

Teece (2010: 172) provides a neat definition of a business model as the "... architecture that the company has chosen for its value creation and appropriation mechanisms." The key word in this definition is "architecture." We define an architecture as the set of relations among elements in a system (Simon, 1969), where these relations can be characterized in such terms as directionality (i.e., are relations sequentially or reciprocally dependent?), strength, and content (notably, information content). The architecture can in turn be characterized in terms of complexity.

In the context of a business model, extant literature suggests that the relevant elements are clusters of activities that can be grouped under the headings of the company's overall value proposition ("What?"), the market segments it addresses with this value proposition ("Who?"), its mechanisms of value appropriation ("How much?"), the structure of the value chain required to create and distribute the offering, the complementary resources needed to support the firm's position in this chain, and the processes and internal organization of the firm that support the other elements in the business model ("How?"). Thus, a business model is a system made up of the interdependent activities that allows the company to address the "What?," "Who?," "How?," and "How much?" questions.

While much discussion of business models mentions interdependencies (notably Amit and Zott, 2012), there has been a strong tendency in the more applied literature to emphasize one or two elements of a business model; for example, "freemium" business models, which call attention to only the value proposition and the revenue model or "cutting-out-the-middleman" models that only highlight value-chain aspects. Why this is so is an interesting issue from the point of view of managerial cognition. However, the point here is that such discussions typically neglect the interdependencies between activities underlying a business model—and accordingly neglect the distinct organizational and leadership challenges present in systems with interdependencies. Although interdependencies are fundamentally choice variables (Milgrom and Roberts, 1990) and there may be business models with weak interdependencies between activities, they certainly cannot always be neglected. The case of the BMI of Danish toy producer, Lego, may illustrate this (Foss et al., 2012).

BUSINESS MODEL INNOVATION IN LEGO

Lego, headquartered in Billund, Denmark, is currently the world's second largest toy producer with 10,000+ employees worldwide, and 2012 sales of approximately 4.5 billion USD and profits of about a billion USD. Though not a big company internationally it has undoubtedly exhibited a high performance over the last decade, growing from a position as the seventh largest toy producer to the second place in a stagnant industry. However, in 2004 the company was on the verge of bankruptcy, arguably as a result of an ambitious diversification strategy. Partly prompted by the expiration of the basic Lego brick patent in 1983, the company had diversified into theme parks, merchandise, and products that essentially had little to do with the emphasis on construction and creative play that had been core values since the inception of the company. This had been accompanied by a strategy of pursuing a high degree of vertical integration.

Massive losses and a decline in sales toward the end of 2004 led to the dismissal of the CEO and the appointment of a new CEO, Jørgen Vig Knudstorp who, with a PhD in business administration, a previous career as a McKinsey consultant and a Lego career as the manager of Lego's internal strategic planning unit, combined the right mix of inside and outside perspectives with strong analytical capabilities. Over the coming years he essentially innovated the Lego business model in four key dimensions. Specifically, Knudstorp trimmed the product offering and the number of inputs into Lego products;

restructured the supply chain in terms of engaging in substantial outsourcing and off-shoring; made the company's boundaries vis-à-vis customers and users substantially more permeable by creating user communities and engaging in joint new product development efforts with major customers; and stepping up the digitalization content of both operations and products.

With respect to the trimming of the product portfolio and the use of component inputs, Lego phased out production of most non-construction Lego toys (many licensing agreements have been kept, however), sold off major assets, notably the Lego theme parks, and reduced the number of sourced product components from 12,700 to currently approximately 6,000. Knudstorp's moves here were explicitly influenced by organizational economics, as he reasoned that reducing products and inputs would strongly reduce managerial complexity and bring down internal transaction costs. Similarly, the many changes in Lego's supply chain away from the highly vertically integrated model was explicitly inspired by the belief that hierarchy is the option of last resort (Williamson, 1996) and that firms in general do well by relying on the high-powered incentives of the market. Thus, much actual production activity was outsourced to Flextronics, a Fortune 500 company and one of the world's leading supply chain service firms. Many of the outsourced activities (in Hungary and the Czech Republic) had already been off-shored from Denmark to save costs. Lego kept the production of more advanced products (such as Lego Technic and Bionicle) in Billund, close to headquarters. Difficulties of maintaining plastic quality later led Lego to insource some of those activities that had been outsourced to Flextronics.

In terms of reaching out to users and customers, Lego engaged in a series of activities, such as Lego Factory, which encouraged children to build their own designs using Lego Digital Designer Software (the activity was closed in 2012, though the software remains in the public domain); close cooperation on the new product development with Wal-Mart and Toys "R" Us; and the establishment of Lego Certified Professionals, thirteen adult "super users" worldwide who are allowed to use the Lego concept in, for example, the production of lamps or customized solutions for select customers (e.g., building company headquarters in Lego bricks).

The above initiatives were supported by a consistent digitalization process, not only internally and with respect to sourcing partners, but also with respect to customers and users.

These changes, which played out between 2004 and 2008, involved a set of interrelated changes in business model components. In terms of the earlier simple distinction between the "What?," "Who?," "How?," and "How much?" components of a business model, Lego's BMI involved changes in all four components. Thus, in the "What?" dimension, the change amounted to a change back to construction as the core, in harmony with the key company value "creative play." This change was consistent with the increased emphasis on digitalization to the extent that this may be seen as being about leveraging the creativity dimension in virtual space. These changes included changes in the

Table 6.1 Mapping complementarities in the Lego business model innovation

	What?	Who?	How?	How Much?
What?		"Back to basic" → Δ segments	Construction aspect strengthened by digitalization	Selling off theme parks, etc. boosted revenue and cut cost
Who?			New segments can be reached through digitalization	New profitable segments were reached
How?				Outsourcing is a tool for cost-cutting
How Much?				

"Who?" dimension. Of course, those segments that demand traditional non-construction toys were eliminated from the Lego customer portfolio, while Lego strengthened its outreach to sophisticated, adult users. In terms of the "How?" dimension, Lego engaged in substantial outsourcing and off-shoring, as explained earlier, and also made numerous changes in terms of strengthening incentives and changing the allocation of decision rights inside the company. In particular, the company's purchasing functions were decentralized to support the strong reduction in the number of sourced components that had exploded because engineers held decision rights to initiate component purchase on their own. The increased emphasis on permeable downstream company boundaries, that is, working closely with sophisticated buyers and users, was also a change in the "How?" dimension as this organization allowed the company to execute an open innovation strategy. Finally, in the "How much?" dimension Lego's performance was strongly improved by the trimming of the product and component portfolios, off-shoring and outsourcing, and a continuous emphasis on cost-cutting and striving to become lean.

As indicated, the various changes in the Lego business model fed on each other. A simple way to represent this is captured in Table 6.1, which juxtaposes the four business model elements in Lego and how its process of BMI over the 2004–2008 period involved interconnected changes in these elements.[2]

And yet, the fact that the changes were implemented sequentially rather than simultaneously suggests that the changes did not possess maximum interconnectedness (in which case they would have had to be implemented exactly simultaneously). However, once implemented the changes in the Lego business model constituted an interlocking system because each element of the model feeds on the other ones. The technical term for this systemic property is "complementarity" and the individual business model elements are "complements." As we argue next, the complementarity framework provides a convenient, choice–theoretic approach to thinking about BMI in terms of definition, performance consequences, and the difficulties of implementing it.

---

[2] The figure can be refined in a number of ways, e.g., by detailing the activities underlying the various business model elements.

COMPLEMENTARITIES AND BUSINESS MODEL INNOVATION

A basic assumption in the complementarity framework is that if changes in activities can be made separately, changes can also be made simultaneously (Brynjolfsson and Milgrom, 2013: 15). A broad definition then states that complementarity obtains if the profits from doing the activities jointly is higher than the sum of the profits from doing the activities in isolation. If the changes involve design decisions relating to fixing the levels of a set of variables (say, x and y), complementarity obtains when choosing a higher level of x raises the returns of choosing a higher level of y and vice versa (more precise definitions, based on lattice algebra, may be found in Milgrom and Roberts, 1990; Brynjolfsson and Milgrom, 2013). The connection to Table 6.1 is easily seen (cf. also Brynjolfsson, Renshaw, and Van Alstyne, 1997).

From the point of view of a strategist and organizational designer, complementarities represent both opportunities and constraints. Because of the fundamental synergistic property of complementarities they represent opportunities for additional value creation. In fact, if all activities are not completely flexible in the short run (which they virtually never are) opportunities tend to be larger in the long run than in the short run in systems with complementarities. The reason is that some decisions will have to be fixed in the short run but can be made flexible in the long run (as in the textbook economics analysis of the firm's production decision). For this reason systems of complementarities will typically exhibit momentum in the sense that doing x at time t_0 will make it more attractive to do y at t_1 and perhaps z at t_2. Lego's process of BMI from 2004 to 2008 seems to exhibit such a dynamic: The initial reduction of the product offering allowed for a concentration of fewer suppliers and realizing scale economies in purchasing. Concentrating purchasing in turn eased the more widespread use of outsourcing. Outsourcing and off-shoring drove massive cost savings that helped support the company's increased emphasis on digitalization, which in turn facilitated a stronger engagement with users and customers. Given this momentum it is not surprising that Lego announced its highest profits after its BMI was completed.

Although realizing complementarities would seem to be a key goal of the strategic organization designer, systems with complementarities may be complex and have multiple local equilibria that can usually be ranked on some performance criterion (notably productivity, or profitability). Usually the global optimum is by no means given to the decision maker, but can only be approximated through a process of more or less deliberate search (Levinthal, 1997; Gavetti and Levinthal, 2000; Stieglitz and Heine, 2007). Such search processes may reveal the existence of hidden complementarities that represent further opportunities for increasing profits. Conversely, search may reveal the existence of "anti-complementarities" or organizational substitutes (Siggelkow, 2002). Thus, Brynjolfsson, Renshaw, and Alstyne (1997) document an instance of business process re-engineering where new, flexible manufacturing equipment was installed but used for the purpose of long, uninterrupted product runs by a supervisor and a team that relied on decades-old heuristics developed for traditional manufacturing practices (Brynjolfsson and Milgrom, 2013: 27).

SEARCH, LEARNING, AND BUSINESS MODEL INNOVATION

In management research, the NK model, originally developed in evolutionary biology, has developed into a workhorse model to capture complex tasks such as the design of business models (Kauffman, 1993; Levinthal, 1997). In the model, parameter K captures interactions between design elements and shapes the ruggedness of search space. The more pervasive the interactions (the higher the K), the more local optima exist, and the more difficult and uncertain is the identification and development of a high-performing business model. How an organization structures and manages its search process becomes critical for ultimate performance. At the same time, the NK model also reveals that complementarities, while challenging BMI, also serve as an effective barrier to imitation (Rivkin, 2000; Lenox, Rockart, and Lewin, 2010) that isolates the innovator from imitative competition (Rumelt, 1984) (if not from other kinds of competition). The tighter the fit among business model elements, the harder it becomes for competitors to imitate the basis for competitive advantages, and the more likely it is that imitation of only parts of the business model deteriorates performance (Rivkin, 2000; Ryall, 2009). Thus, complementarities are a bane to successful BMI, but a blessing for protecting its rewards.

Viewed from the complementarity perspective, BMI is very much a process of search, learning, and experimentation, usually with uncertain performance prospects. Recall that it took Lego four years to develop and execute its new business model, and many of its new elements were not in place when the top management began the re-design. Given that a new business model is not planned *ex ante*, but usually emerges in an extended design process (Mintzberg and Waters, 1985; Gavetti and Rivkin, 2007), the emphasis shifts toward how to structure and manage the process of innovating the business model. Leadership and organizational design may facilitate, channel, or even impede the search for a new business model. However, while prior research has focused on the benefits and the outcomes of BMI, the leadership and organizational design challenges of BMI are strongly under-researched. However, there are certainly indications in the literature. For instance, Chesbrough (2010) suggests that (1) barriers to BMI may be caused by underlying asset configurations, and that (2) such barriers may be overcome by constructing maps of present potential business models and by conferring authority within the hierarchy for experimentation to rejuvenate traditional business models.

In the following, we further develop such ideas by (a) suggesting that BMIs can be dimensionalized in terms of the complementarities they involve; (b) that different kinds of BMIs create distinct managerial and organizational challenges; and (c) that they require distinct leadership intervention and organizational design configurations to tackle these challenges successfully.

DIMENSIONALIZING AND MAPPING BUSINESS MODEL INNOVATIONS

As alluded to earlier, not all BMIs are created equal. Innovations may have a differential impact on existing complementarities (Henderson and Clark, 1990; Stieglitz and Heine, 2007) and the scope for BMI is constrained by the complementarities that are in place. For example, contrast Amazon's Kindle business model with the restructuring of Lego. In the case of Lego, many elements changed and Knudstorp changed decisively the overall Lego architecture by re-wiring many elements of the business model. In retrospect, many of the individual changes to business model elements may not have been that radical, such as making more use of outsourcing, selling off theme parks, and so on. The Lego BMI may in retrospect have been more of an architectural change of numerous elements, feeding on each other. In particular, Lego did not enter new business areas (rather, they exited some).

In contrast, the Kindle eReader was a radical departure for Amazon, since it took the company into entirely new business domains. At the same time, Amazon's traditional e-commerce business was (so far) hardly affected by the new Kindle business model. The Kindle devices have been developed by lab126, a subsidiary of Amazon and a dedicated business unit that focuses on the underlying business model.

Obviously, the system-wide, architectural changes of Lego confront business model designers with different challenges to the more modular, autonomous BMI of the Kindle. Thus, Lego and Amazon differ in terms of the breadth of changes in the business model. Modular changes to a business model are confined to particular business units or departments, while not changing elements in other parts of the firm. Architectural changes rewire complementarities across business units and departments.

Furthermore, BMIs may differ in the depth of changes (Katila and Ahuja, 2002). The Amazon Kindle offers a new value proposition—the "What?" in the context of the business model—that represents a radical departure from the company's e-commerce activities. In contrast, Lego did not radically alter its answers to the "What?" and "Who?" questions: Products were not changed dramatically and the company did not go forcefully after a new customer segment.

By combining the two dimensions of BMI—the depth and the breadth of (intended) changes to an existing BMI—we propose a 2 × 2 matrix to classify four forms of BMI; see Table 6.2.

Note that BMI is distinct from product innovations and we only invoke product names to fix ideas.

The upper-right-hand corner represents the continuous refinement of an existing business model, akin to incremental process innovations. To illustrate, consider continuous BMI at Google. Google's core business model remains the Internet search engine, with a clear value proposition and an appropriation regime that offers free content and revenues from advertisement. At the same time, the business model has been honed for the last decade

Table 6.2 Dimensionalizing business model innovation

Depth of BM Changes Breadth of BM Changes	Incremental	Radical
Modular	(I) Continuous BMI Example: Google's search engine	(II) Ambidextrous BMI Example: Amazon's Kindle
Architectural	(III) Evolutionary BMI Example: Mobile Facebook	(IV) Revolutionary BMI Example: Apple's iModel

by evolving the underlying organizational and information architecture. In the upper left-hand, we locate the Kindle case, where changes are radical relative to Amazon's existing business model, but they are primarily contained in a loosely coupled business unit. Because of the organizational separation of old and new business models, we call this type ambidextrous BMI (e.g., O'Reilly and Tushman, 2004).

Facebook's attempt to integrate and monetize mobile access to their social network is an illustration of BMI that is incremental—the "What?" and the "Who?" do not change substantially—while being architectural in nature, affecting the entire system of value-creating and value-capturing activities, thereby changing fundamentally the logic of the underlying business model. Because the focus is on the gradual transformation of the business model we refer to it as evolutionary BMI. Finally, Steve Jobs' restructuring of Apple is a primary example for a revolutionary BMI that is both radical and architectural. The new business model—creating a device-independent ecosystem—required new hardware devices, integrated software development of operating systems, a different approach to application software, and new retail structures.

Amazon has launched multiple versions of the Kindle device—and these product innovations follow the logic of the business model. In fact, BMI often precedes product innovation by spelling out the logic of value creation and value appropriation and thereby providing the organizational architecture for product development.

Leading and Designing Companies for Business Model Innovation

CHALLENGES OF BUSINESS MODEL INNOVATIONS

Because of the complementarities among elements of a business model, innovating existing business models presents unique challenges whose severity depends on the form of the BMI that the company seeks to implement (cf. Table 6.2). In particular, the complementarity framework directs attention to three challenges: First, inertial forces caused by the existing set of complementary elements in the traditional business model; second, the limits to *ex ante* planning; and, third, the problem of maintaining coherence among business model elements.

The first challenge relates to the inertia caused by the system of existing elements of a business model. Given that the existing logic may have gradually emerged over long stretches of time, the present model typically offers a tight fit of elements and a compelling logic, especially if it made the firm successful in the past. Incremental interventions, that is, changing just a few elements, might improve upon the *status quo*, but they will not radically alter the existing business model (Milgrom and Roberts, 1990). Moreover, isolated and uncoordinated changes often fail to improve performance; the new initiative does not fit to the existing business model and will therefore be discarded (Rivkin and Siggelkow, 2003). That is, the system is set up for the incremental and modular improvement of the existing business model (continuous BMI in Table 6.2), but other forms of BMI are much harder to initiate and sustain successfully due to the conservative pull of the existing complementarities.

The second challenge is caused by the complexity of complementary elements. Due to the inherent complexity when there are many interacting elements, it is not easy to forecast the true performance implications of internal changes (Rivkin, 2000). For example, in the Lego case it was obvious that the turn "back to the brick" would lead to cost savings, for example, because of reduced coordination costs and diseconomies of scope, but the impact of trimming the product portfolio firm boundaries, product development, and user involvement were much harder to discern *ex ante*. The problem of estimating performance implications becomes more difficult when changes are architectural and more radical. Architectural changes affect many complementary elements at the same time. More radical changes imply a sharper departure from the current knowledge about the business model and take the designer into new, as yet unexplored territory (Levinthal and March, 1993). The problem is magnified by uncertainty about market conditions; that is, the internal uncertainty about the "How?" is magnified by uncertainties about the value creation ("What?"), the relevant customer segment "Who?," and the competitive dynamics (the "How much?"). When Amazon launched the Kindle, the market for eReaders and tablet PCs was just in its formative stages. The overall implication is that Knightian uncertainty (Foss and Klein, 2012)—pervasive uncertainty about probabilities and outcomes—often challenges BMI, especially the revolutionary BMI in Table 6.2.

Finally, the third challenge relates to the requirement of establishing and maintaining coherence among business model elements. The major insight emerging from a complementarity perspective is that individual elements have to fit to each other to realize their full potential (Milgrom and Roberts, 1990). Establishing coherence requires search and learning about how elements complement (or substitute for) each other, while maintaining coherence calls for stabilizing and integrating the relationship between elements. This presents a clear tension to the business model designer because she needs to balance the conflicting demands of search and coordination. Otherwise, the company runs the risk of performance-damaging over-exploration (Siggelkow and Rivkin, 2006) that might entrap the company (March, 1991) and explorative search-reducing performance, in turn triggering more exploration and failure in a destructive cycle. For example, the failing social network site MySpace has undertaken several unsuccessful business model redesigns during the last few years to stay viable and prevent bankruptcy.

In sum, the challenges stemming from complementary elements in a business model become more severe with increasing depth and breadth. Increasing depth of changes invalidates prior knowledge about the underlying system of complementary elements and thereby puts a premium on search and learning. Increasing the breadth of changes disrupts coherence to a larger extent and coordinated action becomes critical for BMI. In the next steps, we address how leadership and organization design may be aligned with the BMI to address these outlined challenges.

LEADING BUSINESS MODEL INNOVATIONS

Because the types of BMI differ in associated challenges, the role of top management in leading the BMI process correspondingly differs (Table 6.3).

Top Management as Monitor

When BMI is modular and incremental, that is, it is basically a refinement of an existing business model, most development activities can be decentralized to subordinates. The organization supports the execution of the current business model while providing for its continuous improvement. Interfaces are largely standardized, with the set of complementary relationships firmly in place and offering routine integration across departments. Mutual adjustment therefore is kept to a minimum, while the primary role of incentives is to motivate optimal effort in executing the tasks inherent in the current business model.

Table 6.3 The role of top management different business model innovations

Depth of BM changes Breadth of BM changes	Incremental	Radical
Modular	TM as monitor Decentralization—very limited role for top management intervention	TM as sponsor Decentralization—but sponsor in top management team Top management pays attention to organizational externalities
Architectural	TM as moderator Strategic intent—top management provides roadmap and active participation in mutual adjustment	TM as architect Active involvement—in everyday decision making, attention to detail, centralized decisions, highly aligned top management team

Partial inertia here is value enhancing, because it preserves the core of the business model, and that is also the strategic intent of the BMI. The idea is to continuously improve value creation and value appropriation, although without questioning the existing answers to the "What?," "Who?," "How?," and "How much?" questions. Top management's primary function is to act as the central monitor, without active involvement in the daily development of the business model. The monitoring role is to ensure that employees do not overstep their mandates and that changes to the business model do not go against its core logic. Put differently, employees tasked with business model development exercise derived judgment (Foss and Klein, 2012). On the level of incentives, top management must ensure that improvements to the current business are properly incentivized and rewarded through the design of key performance indicators (KPIs) and performance measurement systems.

Of course, this type of BMI runs the risk of being replaced by disruptive changes in the market environment. For example, Nokia engaged in largely modular and incremental improvement of their business model in the late 2000s, assuming wrongly that the smartphone era were just an evolution of feature phones (where Nokia ruled supreme). This points to the second dimension of top management as a monitor: It is top management's responsibility to track external environments and make judgment calls as to whether the existing business model remains viable. Another implication is that this BMI form is ill-suited to address disruptive changes that threaten the viability of the traditional business model or to get the company out of a crisis. For example, Lego's turnaround was only made possible by a major architectural BMI.

Top Management as Sponsor

In the case of a modular, radical BMI, the top management team needs to act as the sponsor for the business unit (Smith and Tushman, 2005). Separation of new and old business models will often be key, and this can be achieved by what earlier literature has termed structural ambidexterity (O'Reilly and Tushman, 2004): Old and new business units are separated organizationally as far as necessary, with linkages either regulated through standardized or by infrequent mutual adjustments sponsored by top management. The idea here is to provide for a loose coupling, so that the new unit can effectively experiment and concentrate on a radical new organizational design. This is especially relevant in terms of reward structures that need to engrain milestones and growth targets rather than productivity and profits. For example, the Kindle initiative at Amazon requires different KPIs than managers charged with Amazon's e-commerce services.

Strategic and tactical decision making is largely delegated to the new unit that may concentrate fully on the new business model, without having to integrate it with the existing business model logic in other parts of the organization. For instance, most business model decisions for the Amazon Kindle were taken by Gregg Zahr, the president of Amazon's subsidiary lab126. lab126 has a different vision statement from Amazon. While Amazon projects its vision to become the "Earth's most customer-centric company for four primary customer sets: consumers, sellers, enterprises, and content creators,"[3] lab126 focuses more narrowly on the seamless provision of digital content: "to make available in less than 60 seconds every book, ever written, in any language, in print or out of print; and bring the same ease-of-use, deep integration and superior selection of content to movies, TV shows, music, magazines, apps, games, and more."[4] The conservative pull of the existing business model therefore is not much of a challenge, precisely because old and new initiatives are largely separated. The key task is search and experimentation—and a decentralized leadership style supports this.

Yet, the hands-off approach to this BMI form still places unique responsibilities on the top management team. First, radical BM innovations are more exploratory, implying more uncertain and distant rewards (March, 1991). The radical nature implies a higher degree of uncertainty, thereby calling for different performance metrics and KPIs that are currently in place for the established business unit. In terms of leadership challenges this primarily has an impact on the performance dimensions along which resources are allocated (Noda and Bower, 1996). Senior management has to act as an active sponsor of the new initiative, especially against internal pressures for capital re-allocations. Second, while largely modular in nature, relevant complementarities with the rest of the organization often still exist. For example, a critical element of the Kindle business model is to develop the Amazon marketplace into a platform for digital products. That obviously requires coordination choices about how to integrate digital products into the marketplace, how to communicate with Kindle users, etc. To provide for coherence, the top management team must act as residual boundary spanner between the old and the new business model. A critical task in that regard is to overcome inertia in the traditional business model as the conservative pull there is especially strong. If top management refuses to get involved as a sponsor, this form of BMI often ultimately fails, because it is unable to leverage firm-wide capabilities and competitive advantages (Smith and Tushman, 2005; Carmeli and Halevi, 2009).

Top Management as Moderator

Compared to the two BMI forms discussed so far, the architectural and incremental changes in an evolutionary BMI put more demands on top management leadership. The innovation affects the entire business model and changes are not neatly confined to a separate business unit. Top management here has to act as the moderator that (a) provides a coarse roadmap of system-wide interventions to innate and guide search; and (b) moderates the many conflicts and changes to re-establish coherence. The two roles of the moderator address the outlined challenges for BMIs.

---

[3]   <http://phx.corporate-ir.net/phoenix.zhtml?c=97664&p=irol-faq_pf#14296> (February 10, 2014).

[4]   <http://www.lab126.com/our-vision.htm> (February 10, 2014).

A roadmap of system-wide interventions is required to shake up the existing set of complementarities, to trigger a broad search for a new business model, and to guide its evolution (Lovas and Ghosal, 2000). The roadmap also signals the commitment of senior management to BMI, an important behavioral component given that a tolerance for failure is an important part for enabling search and experimentation (Levinthal and March, 1993). At the same time, the roadmap also gives purpose and direction to the search process, preventing mission creep and too much experimentation. Prior theoretical work on organizational search demonstrated that decentralization of search may result in performance-decreasing over-exploration (Siggelkow and Rivkin, 2006). For example, Facebook's successful evolution toward mobile advertisement was engineered by top management because it required many changes to core parts of its business model.

The other role of the top management moderator is to establish and maintain coherence among business elements. That requires the resolution of conflicts among business units, a task that often needs centralized intervention (Williamson, 1991). For example, at Lego, conflicts between the design studio and manufacturing emerged: While the reduction of standard Lego bricks offered economies of scale and reduced production costs, it constrained designers in the development of new construction sets. Only after that conflict was resolved in favor of manufacturing did Lego realize that the reduction of the designers' toolbox also facilitated user involvement in the product development process.

The broad picture here is what operations researchers have called a simulated annealing process (Carley and Svoboda, 1996): The initial heating up of the search to unfreeze a system and, in turn, the gradual cooling down of search intensity. Critically, simulated annealing does not happen naturally in organizations, but demands to be carefully managed. Top management must provide the initial heat-up and the subsequent cooling-down by establishing what works and what does not work and then readjusting search away from elements that proved to be value enhancing.

Because the organization can rely less on standardized interfaces in the BMI process, the organization design must support mutual adjustment by providing for formal and informal arenas for communication and coordination. It is important that the reward structures are realigned with the new business model roadmap. The reward system is a primary instrument to communicate the roadmap and to motivate the development of the new business model (Siggelkow and Rivkin, 2003; Kaplan and Henderson, 2005). The incentive system therefore becomes an important complement to the leadership approach of the design team: Senior management may only fruitfully act as a moderator if the criteria for moderation are clear, and one way is to communicate clearly what it expected from subordinates and employees.

Top Management as Architect

The revolutionary BMI—that is, architectural and radical changes—is the most challenging and risky one. It takes the firm into new territory and is associated with a high level of Knightian uncertainty. It requires entrepreneurial judgment by the top management team—and its communication to the entire organization. Top management becomes the architect who not just provides a broad roadmap, but who is actively involved in everyday experimentation and decision making to realize the perceived potential of her original entrepreneurial judgment. Steve Jobs' leadership at Apple exemplifies this leadership style (Isaacson, 2011). He was obsessed with technical and business details. This also implies that many decisions are taken centrally and are not delegated to subordinates, because their derived judgment may not be aligned with the original conception of the new business model (Foss and Klein, 2012).

Architectural, radical BMI by its very nature limits the value of standardized interfaces, but also of decentralized mutual adjustment. At the same time, incentives may only offer limited guidance, because the Knightian uncertainty inherited in the type of BMI defeats the goal of specifying and incentivizing relevant performance metrics. Indeed, the risk here is that incentives privilege easy-to-measure tasks over hard-to-measure tasks and thereby drive out search, experimentation, cooperation, and communication (e.g., Roberts, 2010). These tasks are of critical importance to address the outlined challenges of experimentation and coherence in revolutionary BMI.

Conclusions

In this chapter, we have outlined a contingency theory of BMI. Our starting point is that to make progress regarding the understanding of the leadership and other organizational challenges of BMI, it is necessary to dimensionalize the unit of analysis. Drawing on innovation theory (Henderson and Clark, 1990) and work on complementarities (Milgrom and Roberts, 1990; Brynjolfsson and Milgrom, 2013), we suggest that BMIs differ in terms of the strength of the complementarities between the elements of the business model that are being innovated. Some BMIs are more modular, while others are more architectural. Also, BMIs can be dimensionalized in terms how radical they are. We argued that the leadership challenges systematically depend on the nature of the relevant BMI, and suggested, but did not systematically unfold, that organizational design requirements similarly systematically vary with the nature of the BMI.

While the framework we have sketched is in principle a self-contained, testable contingency theory, it is also clear that it can be extended and refined in many ways. For example, although we have directed attention to internal organization as an important aspect of how top management can support BMI, we have not touched on the broader organizational design issues that involve the boundaries of the firm. It is clear, however, that firm boundaries must inherently be part of business model design and therefore also BMI; after all, business models involve backstream and upstream vertical linkages that transcend the boundaries of the firm. Ultimately, activities, assets, and transactions are internalized within the boundaries of the firm because this affords control and authority (Hart, 1995). When activities, etc. are placed outside of the boundaries of the firm, the level of control is smaller. For example, Lego outsourced many of its plastic operations to Flextronics, a major international supply chain solutions company, but had to realize that this diminished Lego's control over plastic quality to an extent that Lego was not willing to accept. As a result, a number of initial outsourcing decisions were later reversed (Foss et al., 2012). In terms of the theory we have presented in this chapter, the import of the point about the boundaries of the firm is that these somehow need to be controlled for in empirical work on BMI.

Another omission is that we have neglected key process aspects of BMI. Thus, we have not addressed issues of managerial cognition related to sensing the need for BMI. It is also intuitive that dynamics in the top management team can influence the success of the business model, depending on the nature of the BMI. Thus, architectural BMIs, particularly when these are also radical (cf. Table 6.2) require an effective, aligned top management team. It may also require a relatively large top management team with many functional specialists in order to ensure that the team is close to those operations and processes that not only need to be changed but where those changes also need to be tightly coordinated. Future work will address these issues.

■ REFERENCES

Amit, R. and Zott, C. 2012. "Creating Value Through Business Model Innovation." *MIT Sloan Management Review*, 53: pp. 41–49.

Bellman, R. and Clark, C. 1957. "On the Construction of a Multi-stage, Multi-person Business Game." *Operations Research*, 5 (4): pp. 469–503.

Brynjolfsson, E. and Milgrom, M. 2013. "Complementarity in Organizations." In R. Gibbons, and J. Roberts, eds, *Handbook of Organizational Economics*. Princeton, NJ: Princeton University Press.

Brynjolfsson, E., Renshaw, A., and Van Alstyne, M. 1997. "The Matrix of Change." *MIT Sloan Management Review*, 38: pp. 37–54.

Carley, K. M. and Svoboda, D. M. 1996. "Modeling Organizational Adaptation as a Simulated Annealing Process." *Sociological Methods & Research*, 25 (1): pp. 138–168.

Carmeli, A. and Halevi, M. Y. 2009. "How Top Management Team Behavioral Integration and Behavioral Complexity Enable Organizational Ambidexterity: The Moderating Role of Contextual Ambidexterity." *The Leadership Quarterly*, 20 (2): pp. 207–218.

Casadesus-Masanell, R. and Ricart, J. E. 2010. "From Strategy to Business Models and onto Tactics." *Long Range Planning*, 43: pp. 195–215.

Casadesus-Masanell, R. and Ricart, J. E. 2011. "How to Design a Winning Business Model." *Harvard Business Review*, 89 (1–2): pp. 100–107.

Chesbrough, H. W. 2007. "Business Model Innovation: It's Not Just About Technology Anymore." *Strategy and Leadership*, 35: pp. 12–17.

Chesbrough, H. W. 2010. "Business Model Innovation: Opportunities and Barriers." *Long Range Planning*, 43 (2): pp. 354–363.

Chesbrough, H. W. and Rosenbloom, R. S. 2002. "The Role of the Business Model in Capturing Value from Innovation: Evidence from Xerox Corporation's Technology Spin-Off Companies." *Industrial and Corporate Change*, 11 (3): pp. 529–555.

Demil B. and Lecocq, S. 2010. "Business Model Evolution: In Search of Dynamic Consistency." *Long Range Planning*, 43: pp. 227–246.

Doz, Y. and Kosenen, M. 2010. "Embedding Strategic Agility: A Leadership Agenda for Accelerating Business Model Renewal." *Long Range Planning*, 43: pp. 370–382.

Foss, N. J., and Klein, P. G. 2012. *Organizing Entrepreneurial Judgment: A New Approach to the Firm*. Cambridge: Cambridge University Press.

Foss, N. J., Schultz, M., Pedersen, T., and Pyndt, J. 2012. *Management Innovation*. Cambridge: Cambridge University Press.

Gavetti, G. and Levinthal, D. 2000. "Looking Forward and Looking Backward: Cognitive and Experiential Search." *Administrative Science Quarterly*, 45 (1): pp. 113–137.

Gavetti, G. and Rivkin, J. W. 2007. "On the Origin of Strategy: Action and Cognition Over Time." *Organization Science*, 18 (3): pp. 420–439.

Hart, O. 1995. *Firms, Contracts, and Financial Structure*. Oxford: Clarendon Press.

Henderson, R. M. and Clark, K. B. 1990. "Architectural Innovation: The Reconfiguration of Existing Product Technologies and the Failure of Established Firms." *Administrative Science Quarterly*, 35, pp. 9–30.

Isaacson, W. 2011. *Steve Jobs*. New York: Simon & Schuster.

Jones, G. M. 1960. "Educators, Electrons, and Business Models." *Accounting Review* 35 (4): pp. 619–626.

Kaplan, S. and Henderson, R. 2005. "Inertia and Incentives: Bridging Organizational Economics and Organizational Theory." *Organization Science*, 16 (5), pp. 509–521.

Katila, R. and Ahuja, G. 2002. "Something Old, Something New: A Longitudinal Study of Search Behavior and New Product Introduction." *Academy of Management Journal*, 45 (6): pp. 1183–1194.

Kauffman, S. 1993. *The Origins of Order: Self Organization and Selection in Evolution*. Oxford: Oxford University Press.

Lachmann, L.M. 1956. *Capital and Its Structure*. 1978 reissue. Menlo Park: Institute for Humane Studies.

Lenox, M. J., Rockart, S. F., and Lewin, A. Y. 2010. "Does Interdependency Affect Firm and Industry Profitability? An Empirical Test." *Strategic Management Journal*, 31 (2): pp. 121–139.

Levinthal, D. A. 1997. "Adaptation on Rugged Landscapes." *Management Science*, 43 (7): pp. 934–950.

Levinthal, D. A. and March, J. G. 1993. "The Myopia of Learning." *Strategic Management Journal*, 14 (S2): pp. 95–112.

Lovas, B. and Ghoshal, S. 2000. "Strategy as Guided Evolution." *Strategic Management Journal*, 21 (9): pp. 875–896.

March, J. G. 1991. "Exploration and Exploitation in Organizational Learning." *Organization Science*, 2 (1): pp. 71–87.

Margretta, J. 2002. "Why Business Models Matter." *Harvard Business Review*, 80 (5), pp. 86–92.

Massa, L. and Tucci, C. L. 2014. "Business Model Innovation." In M. Dodgson, D. M. Gann, and N. Phillips (eds), *The Oxford Handbook of Innovation Management*, pp. 420–441. Oxford: Oxford University Press.

Milgrom, P. and Roberts, J. 1990. "The Economics of Modern Manufacturing: Technology, Strategy, and Organization." *The American Economic Review*, 100: pp. 511–528.

Mintzberg, H. and Waters, J. A. 1985. "Of Strategies, Deliberate and Emergent." *Strategic Management Journal*, 6 (3): pp. 257–272.

Noda, T. and Bower, J. L. 1996. "Strategy Making as Iterated Processes of Resource Allocation." *Strategic Management Journal*, 17 (S1): pp. 159–192.

O'Reilly, C. A. and Tushman, M. L. 2004. "The Ambidextrous Organization." *Harvard Business Review*, 82 (4): pp. 74–83.

Rivkin, J. W. 2000. "Imitation of Complex Strategies." *Management Science*, 46 (6): pp. 824–844.

Rivkin, J. W. and Siggelkow, N. 2003. "Balancing Search and Stability: Interdependencies Among Elements of Organizational Design." *Management Science*, 49 (3): pp. 290–311.

Roberts, J. 2010. "Designing Incentives in Organizations." *Journal of Institutional Economics*, 6 (1): pp. 125–132.

Rumelt, R. P. 1984. "Toward a Strategic Theory of the Firm." In R. Lamb, ed., *Competitive Strategic Management*. Englewood Cliffs, NJ: Prentice Hall, pp. 550–570.

Rumelt, R. P., Schendel, D., and Teece, D. J. 1991. "Strategic Management and Economics." *Strategic Management Journal*, 12: 5–29.

Ryall, M. D. 2009. "Causal Ambiguity as a Source of Sustained Capability-based Advantages." *Management Science*, 55 (3): pp. 389–403.

Siggelkow, N. 2002. "Misperceiving Interactions Among Complements and Substitutes: Organizational Consequences." *Management Science*, 48 (7): pp. 900–916.

Siggelkow, N. and Rivkin, J. W. 2006. "When Exploration Backfires: Unintended Consequences of Multilevel Organizational Search." *Academy of Management Journal*, 49 (4): pp. 779–795.

Simon, H. A. 1969. *The Sciences of the Artificial*. Harvard, MA: MIT Press.

Smith, W. K. and Tushman, M. L. 2005. "Managing Strategic Contradictions: A Top Management Model for Managing Innovation Streams." *Organization Science*, 16 (5): pp. 522–536.

Stieglitz, N. and Heine, K. 2007. "Innovations and the Role of Complementarities in a Strategic Theory of the Firm." *Strategic Management Journal*, 28 (1): pp. 1–15.

Suddaby, R. 2010. "Editor's Comments: Construct Clarity in Theories of Management and Organization." *Academy of Management Journal*, 35 (3): pp. 346–357.

Teece, D. J. 1986. "Profiting from Innovation: Implications for Integration, Collaboration, Licensing and Public Policy." *Research Policy*, 15: pp. 285–305.

Teece, D. J. 2010. "Business Models, Business Strategy and Innovation." *Long Range Planning*, 43: pp. 172–194.

Williamson, O. E. 1991. "Comparative Economic Organization: The Analysis of Discrete Structural Alternatives." *Administrative Science Quarterly*: pp. 269–296.

Williamson, O. E. 1996. *The Institutions of Governance*. Oxford: Oxford University Press.

Zott, C. and R. Amit. 2010. "Business Model Design: An Activity System Perspective." *Long Range Planning*, 43: pp. 216–226.

Zott, C., Amit, R., and Massa, L. 2011. "The Business Model: Recent Developments and Future Research." *Journal of Management*, 37: pp. 1019–1042.

7 How Established Firms Exploit Disruptive Business Model Innovation

Strategic and Organizational Challenges

COSTAS MARKIDES

The growing literature on disruptive innovation has already alerted us to the fact that disruptive business models grow not only by cannibalizing customers from the established firms but also—and more importantly—by attracting new customers into the market (Gilbert, 2003). In fact, as originally demonstrated by Christensen and later by other researchers, it is *new* customers that are initially attracted to the invading business model and give it the initial support that it needs to grow (Christensen, 1997; Gilbert and Bower, 2002). It is only later that established customers switch to the new offering. Thus, disruptive business models end up creating entirely new markets on the periphery of the established markets, which are composed of two types of customers: the existing customers who desert the established business model and new customers that are attracted into the market for the first time. This implies that *for an established player,* disruptive business models are not only threats to defend against but also opportunities to exploit (Gilbert, 2003).

How then can established firms exploit the markets that get created by disruptive innovation on the periphery of the main market? Recent work has argued that the decision to enter and exploit the market space that the new business model has created is not (and should not be) an automatic one (Markides and Oyon, 2010). There are instances when the established firm is better off by *not* going after the new market. For example, if the new market created is small or non-growing or the established firm's competences are not suitable for the new market, it may be better to focus one's attention and resources on the established market.

If (and only if) an established firm makes the strategic decision to enter the new market, it then has two basic strategic options in how it goes about exploiting it: it could utilize its *existing* business model or it could develop a *different* business model from the one it currently employs in its established market. Both options are viable alternatives and what the firm chooses depends on a number of variables, including how different the new market is relative to the established market and how aggressively the established firm wants to go after the new markets (e.g., Johnson, Christensen, and Kagermann, 2008). The fact that there is no "right" strategy explains why established firms in the *same* industry that faced the *same* disruption ended up adopting *different* strategies to exploit the disruption—for example, most established banks have treated online banking as just another distribution channel and adopted it as part of their existing business model. By contrast, ING has looked at it as a totally different way of competing in the banking market and created a separate unit (ING Direct) with its own dedicated business model to exploit it.

This chapter focuses on the *subset* of established firms that decide to enter the new markets by using different business models from the ones they employ in their established market. It examines these firms in order to answer the question: "What separates success from failure in those (established) firms that create separate units (and adopt different business models) to exploit a new market created by business model innovation?" For example, why did BA (with its separate unit *GO*), KLM (with *Buzz*), United (with *Ted*) and Continental (with Continental *Lite*) fail to make inroads in the low-cost, no frills, point-to-point airline market while companies such as Qantas (with *Jetstar*) and Singapore Airlines (with *Tiger Air*) appear to be doing just fine? Similarly, why are major banks such as HSBC (with *First Direct*), ING (with *ING Direct*), the Cooperative Bank (with *Smile*) and BNP Paribas (with *Hello Bank*) doing well in the online banking market whereas banks such as Lloyds TSB (with *Evolve*), Santanter (with *Cahoot*) and Banque d'Escompte (with *First-e*) failed to crack this market?

Past research has identified some of the factors that could lead to success (e.g., Gilbert and Bower, 2002; Ghoshal and Gratton, 2003; Govindarajan and Trimble, 2005; Tushman and O'Reilly, 1996). These included: approaching the task of responding to the invading business model as *both* an opportunity and a threat (Gilbert and Bower, 2002); creating a separate unit to exploit the new market (Christensen and Raynor, 2003); funding the new unit in stages (Gilbert, 2003); cultivating outside perspectives in the new unit (Govindarajan and Trimble, 2005); appointing an active integrator between the new unit and the parent (O'Reilly and Tushman, 2004); putting in place active integrating mechanisms between the unit and the parent (O'Reilly and Tushman, 2004; Gulati and, Garino 2000; Govindarajan and Trimble, 2005); modularizing integration between the unit and the parent company (Gilbert, 2003); committing resources to the new unit in stages and over time (Cooper and Smith, 1992); being patient with the new unit when it comes to revenues but not profits (Christensen and Raynor, 2003); and remaining committed to the unit over a long period (Cooper and Smith, 1992). While all these insights are useful, they have all been developed through case research without any subsequent large sample empirical testing. In addition, no academic study to date has explored whether the specific *strategy* that established firms utilize to enter and exploit the new market can explain success or failure. Our study aims to use large-sample survey data along with case research to explore the organizational and strategic factors that differentiate success from failure in adopting a second business model in the same industry.

Research Design

To answer our research question, we first sent out a detailed questionnaire survey to 740 firms whose industries had been invaded by a disruptive business model. We received ninety-eight usable questionnaires from companies in a number of industries (see Table 7.1). Of these, sixty-eight firms responded to the disruption while thirty firms chose not to. Of the sixty-eight firms that responded to the disruption, twenty-six did so by using their existing business model while forty-two did so by developing a different business model. It is these forty-two firms that formed the main sample for our analysis. Using the methodology described in the Appendix, we determined that ten of them had succeeded with their new business model while thirty-two failed. We used simple statistical and regression analyses to compare the successful firms to the unsuccessful ones and so uncover, *on average*, what worked and what did not work.

Since we are fundamentally interested not only in what works *on average* but also on the outlier firms that do better than the average, we supplemented our large-sample quantitative research with case research on eighteen other firms. This was *not* a random sample of firms. Instead, for a number of

Table 7.1 Distribution of industries represented in the questionnaire sample

Industry	No. of companies in the sample	% of sample
UK banking	13	13.3%
UK general insurance	9	9.2%
UK life insurance and pensions	7	7.1%
UK retail supermarkets	10	10.2%
UK retail brokerage	4	4.1%
European airlines	10	10.2%
European stock exchanges	12	12.2%
US general insurance	8	8.2%
US life and health insurance	9	9.2%
US retail brokerage	9	9.2%
US and Canadian stock exchanges	7	7.1%
Total sample	98	100%

Table 7.2 Field research sample firms

Industry	Disruption	Respond by Developing a New Business Model Success/Failure	
Airline	Point-to-point low-cost flying	Qantas Jetstar Singapore Silk Air	Qantas Australia Air Buzz
Pharmaceuticals	Generic	Novartis SANDOZ	Sanofi Aventis
FMCGs	Private label & natural products	Estee Lauder	L'Oreal
Banking	Online distribution	ING Direct	First-e
Newspaper	Online distribution	*Guardian*	*London Times*
Newspaper	Free newspapers	*Evening Standard*	Edipresse
Supermarkets	Online groceries	Waitrose	Sainsbury
Coffee	Nespresso	Sara Lee DE Senseo	Kraft Tassimo

industries, we identified one firm in that industry that succeeded in exploiting the new market and one firm that did not do as well (see Table 7.2). In this way, we were able to compare their actions and strategies while keeping the industry context and the nature of the disruption constant. Our goal was to understand why firms in the same industry (that faced the same disruption), fared so differently in their success rate.

What follows are some of the lessons derived from our research. As already pointed out, we only examined firms that entered the new markets *by using a different business model* (rather than using their existing business model). Therefore, the generalizations that we propose here are only relevant to this subset of firms.

Separate and Integrate Simultaneouly

According to Porter (1980, 1996), the challenge in attempting to manage two different business models in the same market is that the two models (and their underlying value chains) could *conflict* with one another. For example, if a Fast-Moving Consumer Goods (FMCG) company that competes primarily through differentiation decides to adopt the low-cost, private-label strategy, it risks damaging its existing brands and diluting its culture for innovation. Similarly, if an established airline company decides to adopt the Southwest (or easyJet) business model, it risks cannibalizing its existing customer base. The existence of such tradeoffs and conflicts means that a company that tries to compete in both positions simultaneously risks paying a huge straddling cost and degrading the value of its existing activities (Porter, 1996).

The primary solution that academics have offered to solve this problem is to keep the two business models (and their underlying value chains) physically separate in two distinct organizations. Doing so will protect the new business model from the managers of the established business who—because of all the conflicts—are likely to view the new business model as a threat to them. However, the separation strategy is not without its own problems. One of the biggest is the fact that by keeping the two businesses separate, the parent fails to exploit any synergies between the two. For example, a study by a group of McKinsey consultants found that: "... the simple injunction to cordon off new businesses is too narrow. Although ventures do need space to develop, strict separation can prevent them from obtaining invaluable resources and rob their parents of the vitality they can generate" (Day, Mang, Richter, and Roberts, 2001: 21). Similarly, a team of MIT researchers reported that: "... spinoffs often enable faster action early on but they later have difficulty achieving true staying power in the market. Even worse, by launching a spinoff, a company often creates conditions that make future integration very difficult" (Iansiti, McFarlan, and Westerman, 2003: 58).

This suggests that simply separating the new business model from the parent should not be enough to ensure success. To be successful, a firm must not only place the new business model in a separate unit but must also put in place integrating mechanisms that allow for the exploitation of synergies between the unit and the parent. This is a recommendation that several academics have made (e.g., Govindarajan and Trimble, 2005; Gulati and Garito, 2000; O'Reilly and Tushman, 2004). Our first task, therefore, was to test whether this idea was supported by our data.

Consider the forty-two sample firms that separated the new business model into an independent unit. As noted earlier, ten of these firms were classified as successful and thirty-two as not successful. Table 7.3 compares the two groups along the following dimensions: (1) how much strategic, financial, and operational autonomy was given to the unit (measured on a scale of 1 to 5, with

Table 7.3 Administrative mechanisms in the firms that created a separate unit

Administrative Mechanism	Successful Firms (10)	Unsuccessful Firms (32)
Strategic autonomy (1–5)	3.0	3.2
Financial autonomy (1–5)	4.1	2.9
Operational autonomy (1–5)	4.4	3.1
Different culture (1–6)	4.6	4.0
Different budgetary policies (1–6)	4.5	3.9
Different incentive systems (1–6)	3.2	3.6
Different rewards (1–6)	3.2	3.2
Appointed CEO (0–1)	0.8	0.6
CEO from inside (0–1)	0.8	0.6

(Autonomy is measured on a scale of 1–5, with 1 being "no autonomy to the separate unit" and 5 being "the unit makes all decisions." Other variables are measured on a 1–6 scale, with 1 meaning that the policies between the main business and the unit are very similar and 6 being very different.)

Table reproduced from Markides (2008), 103.

high scores implying that decision-making autonomy was granted to the unit); (2) how different the culture, budgetary and investment policies, evaluation systems, and rewards of the unit were relative to the parent (measured on a scale of 1 to 6 with high scores implying that these policies were very different); (3) whether the new unit was assigned a new CEO to manage it; and (4) whether the new CEO was hired from outside the firm or transferred internally.

It is obvious from this table that successful firms gave much more operational and financial autonomy to the units than unsuccessful firms. They also allowed the units to develop their own cultures and budgetary systems and to have their own CEO. All these policies allowed the new units to operate with the necessary freedom and autonomy to serve their markets as they saw fit. However, this autonomy did not come at the expense of synergies: the parent still kept close watch over the strategy of the unit (as shown by the low score on strategic autonomy); cooperation between the unit and the parent was encouraged through common incentive and reward systems; and the CEO of the units was transferred from inside the organization so as to facilitate closer cooperation and active exploitation of synergies. These findings suggest that successful firms are able to find the right balance between, on the one hand, protecting the new business unit by placing it in a separate unit and, on the other hand, exploiting synergies between the unit and the parent by putting in place appropriate integrating mechanisms.

Table 7.3 identifies a few of the integrating mechanisms that companies used to exploit synergies between the parent and the unit—things such as common incentives and using "insiders" as CEOs of the unit. Our field research suggested several others, including:

- strong shared values between the parent and the unit;
- transfer of people between the two and use of common conferences to make them feel part of one company;
- subjective incentives that encourage cooperation between the two;
- hiring outsiders to staff the unit but using an insider to lead it;
- having the general manager of the unit sit on the Board of the parent;
- using common projects to get people working together; and
- using common goals that both could aim for.

Perhaps the most important integrating mechanism that emerged from our field research was the decision by the firm to separate some activities of the unit's value chain while keeping other activities integrated with the parent. In many cases, the unit was given autonomy to develop its own dedicated *customer-facing* activities (such as marketing, pricing, advertising, and customer relations) but had to share the parent's existing *back-office* activities (such as accounting, HR, and IT systems). This finding is consistent with the work of Gulati and Garino (2000), who suggested that the question that established firms need to ask is not: "Should we create a separate unit or not?" but instead: "What activities in our value chain do we separate and what activities do we keep integrated?" (Gulati and Garino, 2000: 107).

Agility is Key

The decision on what to separate and what to keep integrated is always taken at a point in time. At that point, given the existing conditions, the organization chooses what it considers to be the appropriate balance between integration and separation. But over time conditions change—for example, the conflicts between the two business models may become more or less acute; the synergies between the two businesses may grow or decrease; learning on how to manage the two accumulates. This suggests that the appropriate balance between separation and integration changes over time (Nickerson and Zenger, 2002). This is how one senior executive articulated the challenge to us:

> Early on, the new unit is like a new baby. It needs constant care and attention. But then it becomes a teenager; and then an adult. Obviously, the way you treat an adult is and should be different from the way you treat a baby.

This suggests that the organizational policies that the parent puts in place to manage the unit need to continuously evolve. For example, incentive systems that were appropriate early on in the life of the new unit may become counter productive later on and have to be changed. The same goes for the structures and processes that have been put in place to integrate the parent and the unit. Even the appropriate degree of structural separation needs to be continuously evaluated. A business model that was originated placed in a separate unit may need to be re-integrated into the parent organization or may need to be totally divorced from the parent (through a spinoff) as it grows. For example, the Danish bank Lan & Spar Bank started out in internet banking by creating a separate unit. After three years, the online unit was re-integrated into the existing bank. Charles Schwab did the exact same thing with its online brokerage unit e.Schwab. By contrast, the British supermarket giant Tesco Plc grew its home delivery service within the existing organizational infrastructure before spinning it off as a totally separate company.

The point is that what is appropriate at one point in time may not be so at another time. The organization must, therefore, develop the agility to change its choices over time. Doing so in a timely and efficient manner requires the ability to sense when it is time for change and then act quickly to implement the change needed. Sensing when to make a change may be a function of appropriate control systems but implementing change is purely a cultural competence. This is how the Managing Director of a major newspaper company in the UK put it to us:

> The only thing that can give us competitive advantage is speed. We need to react to challenges or exploit new opportunities faster than our competitors. This is not something you can impose from above—it has be part of our cultural fabric.

Of course, everybody talks about the importance of an agile culture. But very often, such cultures perish in the face of the organization's formal controls and incentives that encourage short-term behaviors and an emphasis on exploiting the current business. The trick, therefore, is to design control and incentive systems that encourage behaviors that promote exploitation of the core business and short-term orientation while at the same time fostering a culture that encourages long-term orientation, questioning, experimentation, and collaboration. It is the correct management of this *tension* that determines success from failure. Managing this tension between the firm's formal and informal systems is obviously extremely difficult but it is an idea consistent with the findings of other academic studies (Gulati and Puranam, 2009).

What Business Model to Adopt in the New Market

Putting in place the appropriate *organizational arrangements* between the parent and the unit and managing their evolution over time was the first major source of difference between successful and unsuccessful firms in our sample. A second source of difference was the extent to which the new unit was allowed to develop *a differentiated business model of its own.*

Whether established firms will be successful in exploiting the new market depends to a large extent on the nature and characteristics of the new market. For example, past research has explored whether the new market is related to the established market and whether the new business model is "disruptive" to the established business model (as measured by the number of conflicts between the two). It has been proposed that the higher the conflicts and the more dissimilar the new market, the more difficult it is for established firms to succeed in the new market (Charitou, 2001).

Our research has found support for this proposition. Specifically, simple regression analysis showed that *on average*, the higher the degree of conflict, the less effective was the established firm in using the new business model to exploit the new market. Similarly, the more strategically related the two markets, the more effective was the established firm in the new market. These results were as expected and in accordance with existing theory on disruptive innovation (Christensen, 1997; Porter, 1996). However, they do raise one interesting question: as shown in Table 7.2, firms in the same industry, facing the same conflicts (low or high) fared differently in their success rate. What could explain this?

Our field research on the sample firms listed in Table 7.2 pointed to a possible reason for this. The one consistent result to emerge when we compared the business models that the successful firms in Table 7.2 adopted relative to the unsuccessful ones was the following: established firms that entered the new markets using the *same* business model as the disruptors ended up doing worse than companies that entered on the back of a business model that was differentiated from *that of the disruptor*. Note that in both cases the established firms adopted a business model which was different from the one they employed *in their main market*. But this was not enough. To succeed, established companies had to develop a business model that was not only different from the one they employed in their established market but was also different from the one the disruptors were using. Thus, a key insight to emerge from our field research is that *established firms cannot rely on the disruptors' (winning) business model to exploit the new market*.

Consider, for example, the coffee industry. This industry was revolutionized[1] in the early 1990s with the introduction of the Nespresso system by Nestle. The system consisted of stylish coffee machines designed to make espresso using thimble-sized capsules filled with highest quality coffees. It allowed for the quick preparation of single-serve, high-quality espressos and cappuccinos at home. The new system gave rise to the premium, single-portion coffee market, which quickly grew to dominate the overall coffee market, at the expense of more traditional R&G coffee. The rapid growth of this market attracted entry from all the established coffee players. For example, Kraft introduced Tassimo in 2004; Lavazza introduced Espresso Point in 1994; Procter and Gamble introduced Home Café in 2004; Sara Lee's Dutch subsidiary, Douwe Egberts, introduced the Senseo system in 2001; and Melitta, introduced the Melitta One:One system in 2003. Of all these market entries by established firms, the only one that proved to be a success in the first ten years since its introduction was Sara Lee DE's entry with Senseo.

The big difference between Sara Lee DE and all the others was the *business model* that they used to enter the single-serve coffee market. Whereas all other players adopted a business model that was similar to the one that Nespresso pioneered, Sara Lee DE adopted a totally different one. For example, rather than target wealthy households (as Nespresso did), Senseo went after the mass market. Rather than focus on espresso-drinking countries like Switzerland, Italy, and France (as Nespresso did), Senseo focused on roast and ground (R&G) coffee-drinking countries like Germany and the Netherlands. Rather than offer machines that prepared espresso and cappuccino coffee (as Nespresso did), Senseo offered single-serve American coffee. Rather than position its product as a luxury item and distribute it through exclusive department stores (as Nespresso did), Senseo was positioned as a mass-market product, sold through mass-market department stores. In short, Senseo entered the market on the back of a business model that was radically different from the business model that Nespresso introduced (and all other players imitated) in this market. The end result was that Senseo was the only one to make any inroads in the new market that Nespresso created.

You see this generalization playing out in other industries. For example, in 1993 Continental Airlines created a separate subsidiary called Continental Lite

---

[1] For example, in Switzerland in 1990, Roast and Ground (R&G) coffee accounted for 65% of consumption of coffee at home. By 2004, this share had dropped to 25% while single-serve consumption increased from nothing to take 60% of the market. The growth rates in the different segments revealed clearly where the future lay—the capsules and pods segment was growing at 25% per year, the R&G segment at 1%, and the instant coffee segment at 0%.

and set about capturing market share in the low-cost, no-frills, point-to-point airline market that Southwest had pioneered. Unfortunately for Continental, the strategy adopted by its Lite subsidiary was almost an exact replica of the Southwest strategy. As a result, it failed to make any inroads and Continental shut the unit down in 1994. European airline companies like BA (with its *GO* subsidiary) and KLM (with its *Buzz* subsidiary) had the exact same experience as Continental: they entered the new market using the same business model as the (European) disruptors—in this case easyJet and Ryanair—and ended up selling or shutting down their operations within a few years of entry.

The same pattern emerged in the newspaper industry. For example, in 2005 the Swiss newspaper company Edipresse entered the huge new market created by advertiser-funded *free* daily newspapers that were distributed through major cities' public transportation systems during the peak morning commute. It did so by developing its own free newspaper (called *Le Matin Bleu*) and started distributing it in Geneva and Lausanne using the same business model as the original disruptor, Sweden-based Metro International. Inevitably, the venture failed and was shut down in 2009.

Compare these failed entry attempts with the success of, for example, Nintendo, who fought against its disruptors Sony and Microsoft in the games console market by adopting a totally different business model from the one that they used to attack Nintendo. The end result was the tremendous success of the Nintendo Wii. Similarly, in the watch industry in the mid-1980s, SMH entered the low-end segment created by disruptors such as Seiko and Timex, not by adopting their strategy but by developing a new and innovative strategy around the Swatch watch. This catapulted the Swiss back to industry leadership.

Therefore, a key insight to emerge from our field research is: the disruptors' business model has served them well and has helped them to create and dominate the new market. But this does not mean that it is the appropriate business model for the established firms to adopt in the new market. Instead, they should counter-attack the disruptors by developing a differentiated business model.

WHY BEING BETTER IS NOT ENOUGH

One might wonder why the established players cannot rely on adopting the disruptors' winning business model or cannot win by simply being *better* than them in the new markets. After all, they are not just adopting any business model—they are embracing the business model that made the disruptors a success in the first place. On top of this, they bring into the battle distinct advantages over the disruptors: resources, knowledge, and assets from the established market. Why isn't this enough?

The answer to this becomes obvious when we consider the academic evidence on new market entry (e.g., Geroski, 1995). One of the most robust findings from academic studies on new market entry is that most new entrants fail. For example, several studies of market entry in the United States, Canada, and the United Kingdom have reported that about 5–10 percent of new entrants disappear within a year of entry, 20–30 percent disappear within two years and some 50 percent disappear within five years of entry (Geroski, 1991). These results are consistent with a study by Dunne, Roberts, and Samuelson (1989), which found that 64 percent of their sample of new US firms had exited within five years of entry while a full 79 percent had ceased trading ten years after commencing operations. The failure rate of new entrants is so high that economists have come up with the "revolving door" analogy to describe the entry process: new entrants are like people going through a revolving door, exiting the room as soon as they enter it (Audretsch, 1995).

Another robust finding on new market entry is that most entrants imitate the incumbents when they enter. Imitative entry has been estimated to be 90 percent of all entry, with the remaining 10 percent being taken over by entrants that utilize innovative strategies (Geroski, 1991). Yet another finding is that it takes between ten and twelve years for the profitability (ROI) of the entrant to be equal to that of the mature business, a fact that has serious implications on how patient new entrants ought to be before giving up (Biggadike, 1979).

The high failure rate of new entrants should not be a surprise. When they enter a new market, entrants are in effect attacking the established players there. By virtue of being in the market before the entrants, these established firms enjoy first-mover advantages, such as economies of scale, knowledge of the market, control of scarce assets, and consumer inertia. In addition, the market under attack is their home, which implies that incumbents will fight to the death before giving it up. This suggests that unless the entrants have some serious advantages over the established firms (such as superior and patented technology) or unless they utilize an innovative strategy to attack, the established firms will most likely win out. Since we know that 90 percent of all entrants use imitative entry to attack, it should not come as a surprise to know that most of them fail, and they do so fairly regularly and fairly quickly (Geroski, 1991).

Looking at market entry from the entrants' perspective, these same facts carry a serious implication: the probability of success in attacking established competitors through market entry is increased if the entrant adopts an innovative strategy, one that avoids imitation and instead disrupts the established players. As proposed by Porter (1985): "The cardinal rule in offensive strategy is not to attack head-on with an imitative strategy, regardless of the challenger's resources or staying power." Adopting such strategy does not guarantee success but it improves the odds of success for the entrants.

Consider, now, the new markets created by disruptive innovation. Who are the incumbents in these markets who enjoy the first-mover advantages? They are none other than the disruptors themselves. And who are the new entrants in these markets? They are the firms that are currently incumbents in the established market. By entering the new markets on the back of the disruptors' business model, the established players are trying to beat the disruptors at their own game by trying to be better than them. As the academic research on market entry suggests, this is not enough. To succeed, they need to enter the new markets using a different business model—just like the disruptors did when they entered the established market in the first place.

An Entrepreneurship Mindset is Important

The need to *not* imitate the disruptor's business model should be obvious enough. But our research has also uncovered another less obvious key to success: the need to avoid wholesale "exporting" of the *established* business model and the established firm's existing competences into the new market. While the desire to transfer the firm's strengths and competences into the new market is understandable, our results suggest that this should be undertaken with great care and in moderation.

Table 7.4 compares the successful firms to the unsuccessful ones on a specific issue—how different is the product offering in the new market compared to the product offering in the established market? The one consistent result that emerges from this comparison is that compared to their established business, successful firms develop a fundamentally different product with a different value proposition that targets a different customer base in the new market. By contrast, unsuccessful firms try to "export" their existing products and services into the new market.

The difference in approach toward the new market was obviously important but what was the source of this difference? Our field research unearthed a possible explanation, one that highlights the importance of developing *an entrepreneurial mindset* within the established firm. Many of the unsuccessful

Table 7.4 How different is the new product/service to the established one?

Product Characteristic	Successful Firms (10)	Unsuccessful Firms (32)
Targeted customer segment	5.2	3.5
Level of personal service provided	4.8	2.9
Price	5.4	3.1
Overall product/service characteristics	4.6	3.0
Quality	4.8	3.9
Expressed value proposition	5.2	3.6
Advertising message	5.1	4.2

(The question asked was: "Compare the products or services you offer in the new business with those you offer in your established business." Answers were provided on the following scale: 1 = Same; 2 = Similar; 3 = Somewhat similar; 4 = Somewhat different; 5 = Different; and 6 = Very different.)

firms approached the market being created by disruption *as simply an extension* of the established market. After all, what is the difference between the low end of the airline market and the established market? Aren't they simply two segments of the same market? We found that firms that started their thinking in this way approached market entry as a lateral move from their established market. Thus, rather than attempt entry like an entrepreneur with a clean slate, they became pre-occupied with how to leverage their existing assets in the new market. Rather than start out with the realities of the new market and work backwards to design a strategy appropriate for it, they started out with what they had in the established market and attempted to transfer it in the new market. As a result, they often imitated their disruptors' successful business model and tried to out-compete them using their existing strengths.

By contrast, the successful firms were alert enough to appreciate that even though the new market *appeared* similar to the established market, this was nothing but an illusion. They therefore *approached the new market like entrepreneurs* by asking themselves: "If I were to enter this new market, what strategy should I adopt?" Rather than focus on defending their existing market, their goal was to attack the new market. And since we know from past research that new market entry almost always ends up in failure unless the attacker adopts an innovative business model, the successful established firms entered the new markets by adopting a radical new strategy.

THE NINTENDO EXAMPLE

As an example of this point, consider the home games console market. Throughout the early years, games consoles were viewed as toys, *primarily targeted at young teenage boys* with non-violent titles such as Super Mario, Donkey Kong, Zelda (all Nintendo), and Sega's Sonic the Hedgehog. Nintendo dominated this market with its 16- and 32-bit cartridges and with its popular Super NES console, introduced in 1991. This dominance came to an abrupt end in 1994 with the entry of Sony into the market. Sony's Playstation was an immediate success because it emphasized a *different value proposition* from Nintendo and, as a result, attracted a *different* customer. With superior graphics, CD-quality sound playing techno tracks, and a full range of games titles, the Playstation was unlike anything seen before. It targeted *18–24 year olds (mainly males)* who had grown up on early game consoles but were no longer catered for. As a result, Playstation broke out of the toy niche. Games were targeted at young adults who had larger disposable incomes to purchase new titles. The games themselves were darker, more sophisticated, and more violent. Sony's audience was on average aged 22, with a third over the age of 30.

Nintendo was caught out with nothing to offer but its SNES cartridge-based console. Its traditional market of easy-to-play, non-violent games that appealed to all age groups across different cultures was no longer what the primary gaming audience wanted. Things got worse for Nintendo with the arrival of Microsoft's Xbox in May 2001, which effectively pushed Nintendo into third position.

The three-way battle focused the manufacturers on a continual and seemingly unending battle for technological advancement and superiority of hardware. Consoles had to have faster processing speeds and higher definition graphics. The games became more and more complex, requiring gamers to invest time learning how to play. An entire allied industry sprang up with websites and magazines that offered gamers tips on strategies to win as well as how to actually use the games controllers with their combinations of buttons and joysticks. Gamers themselves were seduced into immersing themselves ever deeper into these increasingly sophisticated fantasy worlds.

Tipped by industry analysts to withdraw altogether from the console marketplace, Nintendo had other ideas. In 2002, it appointed Satoru Iwata as fourth President and CEO of Nintendo. He came to believe that the relentless pursuit of technology by Sony and Microsoft was counterproductive—customers were driven away and the market was shrinking because of the complexity of the games and the time required to learn and also to play them. This "barrier to entry" was a big disincentive for novice gamers and an effective deterrent for non-gamers to start playing. Even occasional gamers had stopped playing due to other priorities in their busy lives.

Rather than follow Sony and Microsoft, Iwata took a different tack with Nintendo.[2] He recognized that there was a huge potential market of people who wanted to play simple, fun games for a few minutes at a time and *potentially with family members and friends*. These same people might currently be playing games on their PCs in their odd moments of free time but wouldn't dream of buying a games console. Nintendo's strategy was essentially to expand the market by developing consoles that would support simple, real-life games that could be learnt quickly and played by all members of the family including the very youngest and the very oldest.

Nintendo's engineers decided they would neither re-create a console based on the popular DS nor follow the joystick/button consoles of Sony and Microsoft. The developers looked beyond technical specifications, creating instead a console that was quiet, used less electricity, and that enabled households to play every Nintendo game ever made, rather than having to keep old consoles. Pricing was key, capped at approximately $200. What resulted from the 'back-to-scratch' approach was the Nintendo Wii. Launched in November 2006, the Wii targeted working *women with families*.[3] Nintendo emphasized the Wii's family-friendly advantages: encouraging family members of all ages to play together, helping children (and adults) get physical through the body movements allowed by the motion sensors. The women who got to try out the Wii at a marketing event often left saying they wanted one for themselves, as much to play with their girlfriends as with their families (Nuttal, 2006)!

---

[2] "Playing a Different Game." *The Economist* (print edition), October 26, 2006.
[3] N.a. 2008. "Survival Through Innovation." *Strategic Direction*, 24 (1): pp. 21–24.

The strategy seems to have paid off. By 2007, the launch of the Wii led to household penetration of consoles rising for the first time in twenty-five years. The console outsold the PS3 three to one in the Japanese market and five to one in the United States. It has also been crowned the fastest selling console in history in the United Kingdom after one million units were sold in just eight months (Fildes, 2007). Nintendo, the dominant giant brought to its knees, has now re-emerged as a dominant player in the videogames industry.

This example highlights the importance of attacking a competitor by emphasizing a *different* value proposition. Doing so attracts a *different* customer, something that delays retaliation. Sony did this against Nintendo in the mid-1990s with the launch of the Playstation that targeted young adults rather than teenagers. Nintendo is now doing it against Sony (and Microsoft) with the launch of the Wii, targeting mothers and families rather than young adults. But to be able to do this requires that the established firm does not look at the new market as just an extension of the established market and treat it, like an entrepreneur, as a brand new market.

Attitudes Matter

One of the questions on our questionnaire survey asked the firms to specify the reasons why they decided to enter the new market. The majority of those firms classified as "successful" replied that they did it so as to defend their existing market, but also to attract new customers. By contrast, more than 60 percent of those firms classified as "unsuccessful" replied that they decided to enter the new market primarily as a defensive move so as to prevent the loss of existing customers. Thus, an important determinant of success appears to be the attitude with which the new market was approached.

These survey results found strong support in our field research. Consider, for example, the following two quotes from senior managers at two US firms. The first is VP at a major office supplies firm, whose company was rated as very *successful* in adopting internet distribution (Markides and Charitou, 2004: 28):

> We got onto the Internet long before anybody else knew what the Internet was. In fact, our biggest problem for the first two years was persuading our customers to use it! But we persisted because I knew in my bones that the Internet was it. This new technology was going to be the future. It would be the medium that would allow us to do great new things.

The second quote is from the CEO of a major bookseller whose company was rated as *unsuccessful* in adopting online distribution of books (Markides and Charitou, 2004: 28):

> We were late in implementing [it] but not in evaluating it. And our evaluation was that this thing did not make sense. Yet, every time I tried to explain our reasons why we wouldn't do it to Wall Street, my share price went down! Even

in 1997 when online distribution of books went from zero to 6%, superstores increased their share from 10% to 22%—yet our stock price dropped by 40%. So in the end, we decided we had to do something.

Thus, it appears that unsuccessful firms look at the invading disruptive business model more as a *threat* to their established business than as an opportunity to exploit (Gilbert, 2003). As a result, they approach it with a defensive attitude and they set about *defending* against it. More often than not, they do so by adopting the same disruptive business model (usually in a separate unit) and then use it to compete with the disruptors head-on. They believe that this will be enough to make them successful because they assume that they will be *better* than the disruptors. What gives them confidence that they can beat the disruptors is the fact that they are much bigger than them (i.e., have more resources) plus the fact that they already have certain skills and competences (from their main market) that they can leverage in the new market and so start out with an advantage over the disruptors. As already pointed out, the strategy of being "better" rarely succeeds when it comes to new market entry.

Not only do established firms make the mistake of utilizing the wrong business model, but they also bring the wrong *attitudes* into the battle. Their goal and emphasis is to defend and protect their main market rather than exploit the new market that the disruptors have created. Inevitably, this defensive attitude leads them to short-term-oriented actions and behaviors that compromise the viability of their chosen strategy. More often than not, their response ends in failure.

In short, the companies that fail in their response make four fundamental mistakes:

- They assume that the new market created by the disruption is *similar* to their core market.
- They adopt the *same* business model as the disruptors (usually in a separate unit) and compete head-on with them, hoping to win by being better than them.
- They view the disruptive business model as a *threat* to their market, an attitude that leads them into a defensive mindset.
- They display short-term behaviors and limited commitment to the new market, probably as a direct result of their *defensive mindset*.

By contrast, the firms that tend to succeed in their forays into the new markets accept that the disruption is damaging to their main market but they also recognize that the new business model has created a new market adjacent to their main market. They therefore attack the new market in an effort to attract new customers.

In short, the companies that succeed in their entry do four things right:

- They approach the new market created by the disruption as fundamentally *different* market from their core market.
- They enter the new market by adopting a business model that is fundamentally *different* from the one that the disruptors are using.

- They view the disruption not only as a threat to their existing business but also as an *opportunity* to develop a brand new market.
- They approach the new market with commitment and *long-term* orientation.

Summary and Discussion

A basic insight that emerged from our study is that established players cannot rely on adopting the winning business model of their disruptors to exploit the new markets created by disruptive innovation. Instead, they need to develop a business model which is different from the one they currently employ in the established market but also different from the one that disruptors use. Doing so does not guarantee success but it does *increase the probability* that they will successfully attack the disruptors in the markets that they created.

The following quote about Microsoft's attempts to exploit the huge market that Google's disruption has created captures the essence of this finding well:[4]

> For several years now, Microsoft has spent hundreds of millions (and likely close to billions) trying to out-do Google at search. Now, the folks in Redmond have something new up their pale blue Oxfords. Microsoft is debuting a search engine, code-named "Kumo." Chief executive Steve Ballmer is likely to show it off at a conference next week. If it's anything like Google, no one will care. There are lots of good-enough search alternatives out there. Yahoo! ranks second with 20% market share. Little Ask.com is still eeking out a meagre 3.8% share. Would-be Google killers have come and gone ... These rivals' strategies seem to be: Search is a big market so all we need is just a sliver to make a nice business. So they aim to be just a little different ... To unseat Google, Microsoft has to be sly. Building a "more robust search experience" won't do. Microsoft will have to shock and awe. This might be about rethinking where we do our searching or how we come up with search queries ...

The idea sounds simple but in reality, established firms face formidable obstacles in carrying it out. First, there is the issue of actually coming up with an innovative business model capable of disrupting the disruptors—Microsoft's inability to do so in the search business should be an indication of how difficult such a task is. But even when an established company succeeds in designing an innovative strategy, serious problems with implementation inevitably surface. Prominent among them is the fact that success in the new market often requires sacrifices in the main market of the established firm. For example, if Sony decides to go after the new market that the Nintento Wii

---

has created, what happens to Sony's Playstation market and the value proposition that Sony is promoting in that market (i.e., more complex and graphic games)? Similarly, if BA decides to go into the low-cost market aggressively, what would be the effect on its brand image and the margins in its established high-margin market? It is *conflicts* like these that undermine a firm's ability to compete in the new markets aggressively and forces the managers of the established business to abandon any attempts to exploit the new markets after just a few years.

Obviously these organizational challenges are not insurmountable and this chapter has suggested that the firm can make the task more manageable by housing the new business model in a separate unit and then putting in place integrating mechanisms to exploit any synergies between the unit and the parent. But even then, managing two conflicting business models at the same time requires strong leadership, ambidextrous mindsets, and the ability to continuously juggle ever-changing balances between conflicting demands and priorities. Recent work by O'Reilly and Tushman (2011) suggests that the task is quite formidable and the probability of failure high.

This chapter has examined only *one* possible strategy that established firms can use to exploit the market created by business model innovation—and that is the strategy of entering the new market using a different business model. We don't want to give the impression that this is the only way to exploit the new market. Under certain circumstances, the established firm is better off using its existing business model to exploit the new market. In fact, there were twenty-six firms in our questionnaire sample that chose this strategy. Of those, seventeen were successful and nine failed. What explained the different fortunes of these firms?

We found that a key variable determining the outcome was the relative success that firms had in achieving two things *simultaneously*: (a) matching the disruptors in whatever value proposition they were offering; *and* (b) improving their own value proposition to such an extent that consumers stopped considering the disruptor's offering as "good enough." Companies that succeeded in doing these two things were able to make the following claim to customers: "I am good enough in whatever the disruptors are offering and I am far superior to them in my own value proposition."

Consider for example the well-known case of Swatch. In the early 1980s, the Swiss watch manufacturers responded to Seiko's low-cost disruption by introducing the Swatch. This proved to be a tremendous success and allowed the Swiss to recapture lost market share. What were the ingredients of the successful Swatch strategy? The new watch did not pretend to be better than Seiko (or Timex) in price or features. Instead, it emphasized *different* product attributes—style and variety—where it could claim that it was superior to its competitors. But it did not ignore the requirement to achieve proximity in what the disruptors were emphasizing (i.e., price). By eliminating many product attributes that they thought were unnecessary, by automating manufacturing, and by reducing the number of components that went into the watch (thus reducing complexity and materials used), they were able to reduce the cost of making the Swatch and thus its price. This allowed the Swiss to make the claim that: "We are good enough in price and superior in style and design." By being good enough in price, they achieved proximity in what the disruptors were offering; and by being superior in style and design, they achieved competitive advantage over their disruptors. In addition, by utilizing a business model that delivered low cost *and* differentiation at the same time, they were able to delay any response from the disruptors. Since its launch in 1983, Swatch has become the world's most popular time piece, with more than 100 million sold in over thirty countries.

For this strategy to work, the established firms must not only match the disruptors in their value proposition (such as price) but must also find ways to improve their own value proposition in a *radical* way. In our interviews with sample firms we explored in depth how they could do this. We identified two possible strategies.

The first was to shift the basis of competition altogether *away from* their original value proposition (which was targeted by the disruptors) onto another product benefit. This is what Swatch did to perfection. The second was by focusing on the product's *existing* value proposition and improving that in a *radical* way. By doing this, they kept raising the bar on what was good enough and thus made life difficult for disruptors.

Consider, for example, how Gillette responded to Bic's low-cost disruption. After seeing a quarter of the market being won over by Bic (in less than ten years), Gillette set about changing people's perceptions on what to expect from their razor. Through a series of innovative product introductions (such as the Sensor, the Mach 3, and the Fusion), Gillette redefined what "performance" meant in this market. They also innovated in the disposable space—for example, in 1994 they introduced the Custom Plus line that was a disposable with a lubricating strip. In late 2002, they announced the introduction of a new line of disposable razors with proprietary technology (rumored to be a disposable version of a triple-blade razor, its premier product in refillables.) By successfully raising the bar in this market, Gillette managed to convince consumers that they should expect more from their razors and that Bic was not really "good enough" for them. In the process, they succeeded in maintaining their leadership position in refillables while capturing a 45-percent market share in disposables. The Swatch and Gillette examples highlight a simple point: the more successful the incumbents are in changing consumers' expectations of what is "good enough" in their markets, the less successful would the disruptors be in disrupting them.

Whether companies choose to exploit the markets created by disruption through their existing business model or through a different business model depends on their specific circumstances. But the ingredients of success for whatever strategy they choose are the same: innovation (in developing innovative business models to face up to the disruptors' own innovative business models) and leadership (in managing the conflicting demands that the two business models create). Only firms that succeed in overcoming these strategic and organizational challenges in ever-changing markets will be successful in exploiting the markets created by disruptive business model innovation.

■ APPENDIX: RESEARCH DESIGN

A thirteen-page questionnaire was sent to 740 established companies in eleven industries. We received 115 completed questionnaires from ninety-eight different companies. Of these, sixty-eight responded to the disruptive business model while thirty opted not to respond. Of the sixty-eight that responded, twenty-six did so by using their existing business model and were, therefore, excluded from further analysis. Our analysis focuses on the forty-two firms that responded to the disruptive business model by creating a separate unit.

Our questionnaire allowed us to measure a number of variables for each of these firms—such as the degree of conflicts between the two business models and the strategic similarity between the two markets that the two business models were serving. For the purposes of this chapter, we were particularly interested in determining which firms responded successfully to the invasion of the disruptive business model and which failed in their response.

We used three complementary approaches to determine "success." We first asked all responding firms to assess their own effectiveness in adopting a new business model in the new market along nine performance criteria. Specifically, we asked them to assess whether by embracing the new model, they: (a) prevented the new business model from expanding into the traditional business and hurting existing operations; (b) prevented existing customers from leaving the company; (c) attracted new customers; (d) increased revenues and improved profitability; (e) developed new skills and competencies; (f) improved the quality of products and services; (g) cut costs; (h) became more competitive overall in the industry; and (i) became part of the new, growing business. A six-point scale was used, ranging from "Very ineffective" (= 1) to "Very effective" (= 6). The average score of these nine items was calculated as the measure for statistical analysis. The higher the score, the higher the firm's effectiveness in adopting the new business model and competing in the two strategic positions simultaneously. Values ranged from 2.56 to 6, with an overall mean of 4.6 (Cronbach's alpha = 0.72).

As a second measure of success, we asked the responding firms to give us an overall assessment (on a scale of 1 to 6) of how effectively they thought they had adopted the new business model. Finally, to reduce self-reporting bias, we also employed a third measure of success: industry analysts from seven fund management companies in London were asked to rate each of our responding firms on an "overall effectiveness" scale. The analysts rated only companies in the industries that they covered, and they used the same 1–6 scale.

A firm was rated as "successful" if it scored 6 and above on the "overall effectiveness" scale *or* 5 and above on the scale calculated as the mean of the nine performance criteria *and* also received a rating of 6 from the analysts. In total, ten firms were rated as successful and thirty-two as unsuccessful.

■ REFERENCES

Audretsch, D. 1995. *Innovation and Industry Evolution.* Cambridge, MA: MIT Press.

Barret, V. 2009. "Disrupting the Disruption." Forbes.com, May 20. Retrieved November 2014 at: <http://www.forbes.com/2009/05/20/google-microsoft-search-intelligent-technology-barret.html>.

Biggadike, R. 1979: "The Risky Business of Diversification." *Harvard Business Review,* May–June 60 (3): pp. 103–111.

Charitou, C. 2001. *"Responses by Established Firms to Strategic Innovation."* Unpublished doctoral dissertation, London Business School.

Christensen, C. M. 1997. *The Innovator's Dilemma: When New Technologies Cause Great Firms to Fail.* Boston, MA: Harvard Business School Press.

Christensen, C. M. and Raynor, M. 2003. *The Innovator's Solution.* Boston, MA: HBS Press.

Cooper, A. C. and Smith, C. G. 1992. "How Established Firms Respond to Threatening Technologies." *Academy of Management Executive,* 6: pp. 55–70.

Day, J. D., Mang, P. Y., Richter, A., and Roberts, J. 2001. "The Innovative Organization: Why New Ventures Need More Than a Room of Their Own." *The McKinsey Quarterly,* 37 (2): pp. 21–31.

Dunne, T., Roberts, M., and Samuelson, L. 1989. "The Growth and Failure of US Manufacturing Plants." *Quarterly Journal of Economics,* November, 104 (4): pp. 671–698.

Fildes, N. 2007. "Game on: Console Makers in Three-way Shoot-out." *The Independent,* October 26. Retrieved November 2014 at <http://www.independent.co.uk/news/business/analysis-and-features/game-on-console-makers-in-threeway-shootout-395364.html>.

Geroski, P. 1991. *Market Dynamics and Entry.* Oxford: Blackwell, p. 27.

Geroski, P. 1995. "What Do We Know About Entry?" *International Journal of Industrial Organization,* 13, pp. 421–440.

Ghoshal, S. and Gratton, L. 2003. "Integrating the Enterprise." *Sloan Management Review,* 44 (1): pp. 31–38.

Gilbert, Clark. 2003. "The Disruption Opportunity." *Sloan Management Review,* Summer, 44 (4): pp. 27–32.

Gilbert, C. and Bower, J. 2002. "Disruptive Change: When Trying Harder is Part of the Problem." *Harvard Business Review,* May 80 (5): pp. 94–101.

Govindarajan, V. and Trimble, C. 2005. *Ten Rules for Strategic Innovators: From Idea to Execution.* Boston, MA: HBS Press.

Gulati, R. and Garino, J. 2000. "Get the Right Mix of Bricks and Clicks." *Harvard Business Review,* May–June 78 (3): pp. 107–114.

Gulati, R. and Puranam, P. 2009. "Renewal Through Reorganization: The Value of Inconsistencies Between Formal and Informal Organization." *Organization Science,* March–April, 20 (2): pp. 422–440.

Iansiti, M., McFarlan, F.W., and Westerman, G. 2003. "Leveraging the Incumbent's Advantage." *Sloan Management Review,* Summer, 44 (4): p. 58.

Johnson, M., Christensen, C. M., and Kagermann, H. 2008. "Reinventing your Business Model." *Harvard Business Review,* December 86 (12): pp. 50–59.

Markides, C. 2008. *Game-changing Strategies: How to Create New Market Space in Established Industries by Breaking the Rules,* San Francisco, CA: Jossey-Bass, a Wiley Imprint.

Markides, C and Charitou, C. 2004. "Competing with Dual Business Models: A Contingency Approach." *Academy of Management Executive*, 18 (3): pp. 22–36.

Markides C. and Oyon, D. 2010. "What to Do Against Disruptive Business Models: When and How to Play Two Games at Once." *Sloan Management Review*, Summer, 51 (4): pp. 25–32.

Nickerson, J. and T. Zenger. 2002. "Being Efficiently Fickle: A Dynamic Theory of Organizational Choice." *Organization Science*, September-October, 13 (5): pp. 547–566.

Nuttal, C. 2006. "Console Makers Go For a Slam Dunk." *The Financial Times*, November 17, p. 10.

O'Reilly, C. III and Tushman, M. 2004. "The Ambidextrous Organization." *Harvard Business Review*, 82 (4): pp. 74–81.

O'Reilly, C. III, and Tushman, M. 2011. "Organizational Ambidexterity in Action." *California Management Review*, 53 (4): pp. 5–22.

"Playing a Different Game." The Econonist (print edition), October 26, 2006.

Porter, M. E. 1980. *Competitive Strategy*. New York: Free Press.

Porter, M. E. 1985. *Competitive Advantage*. New York: Free Press.

Porter, M. E. 1996. "What is Strategy?" *Harvard Business Review*, November–December 74 (6): pp. 61–78.

N.a. 2008. "Survival Through Innovation." Strategic Direction, 24 (1): pp. 21–26.

Tushman, M. L. and O'Reilly III, C. A. 1996. "Ambidextrous Organizations: Managing Evolutionary and Revolutionary Change." *California Management Review*, 38 (4): pp. 8–30.

8 Evolution, Adaptation, or Innovation?

A Contingency Framework on Business Model Dynamics

TINA SAEBI

Introduction

A business model reflects management's hypothesis about what the customer wants and how the firm can organize best to create, deliver, and capture that value (Doz and Kosonen, 2010; Teece, 2010; Tikkanen et al., 2005). Once articulated, the logic of the business model is subjected to the market test and needs to be modified and retested in the face of changing environmental conditions (Teece, 2010). Hence, far from being static, business models need to be in a continuous flux, responding to opportunities and threats in the firm's external environment.

Yet, not all firms succeed in adapting their business model to new market demands or competitive threats. From a contingency theory perspective, organizational responses need to match environmental conditions (cf. Venkatraman and Prescott, 1990; Zahra, 1996; Zahra and Bogner, 2000). That is, different environmental conditions need to be matched with appropriate adjustments in the firm's business model. However, systematic examinations of what the relevant drivers of business model change are and what kind of change they cause are missing to date from extant business model literature.

Moreover, from an organizational perspective, the firm's ability to change its business model is further influenced by its existing design and capabilities. That is, firms may cultivate a preparedness for business model change by developing dynamic capabilities that enable them to change their business models in a systematic way (Foss and Saebi, chapter 1, this volume). While the notion of business model change as a dynamic capability has been implicitly articulated in business model literature (cf. Doz and Kosonen, 2010; Demil and Leqcoq, 2010; Achtenhagen, Melin, and Naldi, 2013), research has not differentiated the capabilities needed to support different business model dynamics.

To address these shortcomings, this study puts forward a contingency framework on business model dynamics, environmental change, and dynamic capabilities. This framework sheds light on the questions: (1) which environmental conditions prompt what type of business model change, and (2) which dynamic capabilities are essential in supporting different types of business model change.

In answering these questions, this study makes two contributions to the business model literature. First, the study demonstrates how and why a fit between business model dynamics, environmental change, and dynamic capabilities is likely to be an important antecedent to firm performance. As investing in and implementing business model change can be costly and time-consuming, managers need to carefully consider the external and internal organizational conditions under which business model change can be most fruitful. Hence, this contingency framework can guide practitioners in the choice of business model change under different environmental conditions.

Second, differentiating three types of business model change (business model evolution, adaptation, and innovation), the proposed framework delineates their distinct implications for the development of dynamic capabilities, and thereby sheds light on the organizational dimension of business model dynamics. With extant literature either emphasizing the disruptive capacity of new business models (cf. Chesbrough, 2010; Teece, 2010; Voelpel, Leibold, and Tekie, 2004) or the need for them to adapt over time (cf. Doz and Kosonen, 2010; Demil and Lecocq, 2010), we know little about how firms can develop the organizational capability to manage and implement business model change in a systematic way.

On the Need for a Contingency Model

In extant business model literature, there is the widely shared view that dynamic business models are essential to firm performance (cf. Sosna, Trevinyo-Rodriguez, and Velamuri, 2010; Teece, 2010; Ho, Fang, and Hsieh, 2011; McGrath, 2010). However, not all business model change seems to lead to superior firm performance. Four possible reasons emerge from extant literature.

One line of research ascribes the inter-firm performance heterogeneity to differences in types of business model change. Here, studies assume a main-effect relationship between the type of business model change (e.g., business model innovation, adaptation, renewal, replication) and firm performance (cf. Voelpel, Leopold, and Tekie, 2004; Chesbrough, 2010). Such effects may correspond to actual practice, where creating a disruptive business model is likely to contribute more significantly to a firm's competitive advantage than aligning the business model to the environment.

As this is usually somehow moderated by, for example, the environmental context, a second line of research investigates the effect of environmental drivers on the propensity for business model change (cf. de Reuver, Bouwman, and MacInnes, 2009). However, while these studies highlight the strategic relevance of business model change in the face of changing environmental conditions, they do not differentiate between the kinds of business model change these drivers cause.

A third line of research ascribes the inter-firm performance heterogeneity to differences in the firm's *ability* to change its business model effectively. Studies that fall within this group refer to dynamic capability theory either implicitly (cf. Doz and Kosonen, 2010; Demil and Leqcoq, 2010) or explicitly (cf. Achtenhagen, Melin, and Naldi, 2013), suggesting that the firm is in need for organizational and managerial processes to support the process of business model change. However, while these studies mention a number of managerial actions to support business model change, they do not differentiate the dynamic capabilities underlying different types of business model change.

Integrating these three perspectives, a fourth reason for performance differentials may stem from the fact that different environmental conditions prompt different types of business model change, which in turn require different types of dynamic capabilities. Thus, as firms may not be equally good at matching the type of business model change with environmental conditions and dynamic capability development, this can result in performance differentials. Hence, the contingency between environmental dynamics, business model change, and dynamic capabilities is likely to be an important antecedent to firm performance.

As relatively little has been written on this issue from a business model perspective, I complement the literature review on types, drivers, and facilitators of business models change with findings from strategy and organizational literatures to develop a contingency model.

Business Model Dynamics

AN ORGANIZATIONAL VIEW ON BUSINESS MODEL CHANGE

In line with recent literature (Zott and Amit, 2010; Santos, Spector, and Van der Heyden, 2009), I define business models as the firm's configuration of intra-organizational and extra-organizational activities and relations geared toward creating, delivering, and capturing value. *Activities* refer to "what" the firm offers and to "whom," that is, value proposition and target customers of the firm. *Relations* specify the organizational units performing those activities and the ways in which these units are linked and governed, thus determining "how" the firm creates, delivers, and captures value.

At the organizational level, these activities and relationships are articulated in procedures and contracts, and embedded in routines and capabilities (Doz and Kosonen, 2010). Thus, while these structures and processes contribute to stability and increased operational efficiency in existing business models, they can result in a growing rigidity that constricts the firm's ability to change its business model in the face of environmental dynamics.

Further, business model literature has unequivocally ascribed the occurrence of business model change to disruptions in the firm's environment (cf. Doz and Kosonen, 2010; Teece, 2010; Voelpel, Leibold, and Tekie, 2004). Business model change can thus be defined as the process by which management *actively alters* the intra-organizational and/or extra-organizational systems of activities and relations of the business model *in response to changing environmental conditions.* This suggests that changes made to an existing business model are of intentional and deliberate nature and occur in response to environmental contingencies.

The following sections further elaborate on the notion of business model change by delineating different types of business model dynamics, which will be subsequently linked to environmental contingencies and dynamic capabilities.

TYPES OF BUSINESS MODEL DYNAMICS

Dynamic business models have entered the research arena rather recently. The notion of business models has received wide popularity since the late 1990s as it has been an effective response to difficulties in using existing frameworks to describe the emergence and business logic of online businesses (Zott, Amit, and Massa, 2011). This, however, resulted in a predominantly static view on business models, focused on conceptualizing its various components (cf. Amit and Zott, 2001; Osterwalder, Pigneur, and Tucci, 2005) or highlighting the innovative capacity of new forms of business models (cf. Chesbrough and Rosenbloom, 2002; Chesbrough, 2007). It is only recently that this predominantly static view has been replaced by a more dynamic and transformational take on business models.

Perhaps due to the nascent stage of this research stream, there is a lack of a unified typology of business model change. Table 8.1 provides a brief overview of the most commonly found types of business model dynamics reported in extant business model literature.

Despite varying definitions reported in Table 8.1, three types of business model change are discernible. The first type of business model change refers to the effective standardization, replication, implementation, and maintenance of the existing business model, manifested in the "fine tuning process involving voluntary and emergent changes in and between permanently linked core components" (Demil and Lecocq, 2010: 239). This type of evolutionary change process can be referred to as *business model evolution.* The second type of business model change process refers to the need for continuous adaptation of business models to fit changing market conditions (cf. Doz and Kosonen, 2010;

Table 8.1 Types of business model change

Concept	Definition	Author(s)
Business model evolution	"A fine tuning process involving voluntary and emergent changes in and between permanently linked core components"	Demil and Lecocq (2010: 239)
Business model renewal	*(No definition provided)*	Doz and Kosonen (2010)
Business model replication	*(No definition provided)*	Dunford, Palmer, and Beneviste (2010)
Business model learning	An established firm modifies its business model in the face of competition from a new business model	Teece (2010)
Business model erosion	The declining competitiveness of established business models	McGrath (2010)
Business model lifecycle	"A business model lifecycle involving periods of specification, refinement, adaptation, revision and reformulation. An initial period during which the model is fairly informal or implicit is followed by a process of trial-and-error, and a number of core decisions are made that delimit the directions in which the firm can evolve."	Morris, Schindehutte, and Allen (2005: 732–3)
Business model reconfiguration	"We use the term to capture the phenomenon by which managers reconfigure organizational resources (and acquire new ones) to change an existing business model. Thus the process of reconfiguration requires shifting, with different degrees of radicalism, from an existing model to a new one."	Massa and Tucci (2014: 11)
Business model innovation	"Business model innovation is the discovery of a fundamentally different business model in an existing business"	Markides (2006: 20)
	"Business model innovation is a reconfiguration of activities in the existing business model of a firm that is new to the product service market in which the firm competes"	Santos, Spector, and Van den Heyden (2009: 14)

Teece, 2010; Sosna, Trevinyo-Rodriguez, and Velamuri, 2010). *Business model adaptation* can thus be defined as the process by which management actively aligns the internal and/or external system of activities and relations of the business model to a changing environment. In contrast, the third type of business model change process refers to the need to create disruptive innovation in response to environmental dynamics (cf. Voelpel, Leibold, and Tekie, 2004; Chesbrough, 2010; McGrath, 2010). Hence, *business model innovation* can be defined as the process by which management actively innovates the internal and/or external dimensions of the business model to disrupt market conditions. As business model evolution, adaptation, and innovation have been studied separately in extant literature and lack clear conceptualization, the next section characterizes each type of business model change and discusses their differences.

BUSINESS MODEL EVOLUTION, ADAPTATION, AND INNOVATION

In this section, the different types of business model change are contrasted with regard to planned outcome, scope of change, degree of radicalness, frequency of change, and degree of novelty (cf. Robertson, Roberts, and Porras, 1993).

Business model evolution

Business model evolution refers to the effective standardization, replication, implementation, and maintenance of the existing business model. Change processes are geared toward incremental and continuous adjustments in the firm's existing system of activities and relations, such as improvements in the activities offered to the firm's customers, strengthening ties with suppliers or making adjustments in operating routines to increase operational efficiency. The scope of change is limited to a few areas at a time and does not significantly alter core-repeated standard processes of the firm's business model.

Business model adaptation

Attaining alignment with the environment is the main motivation of business model adaptation. Numerous dimensions of the business model can be affected simultaneously with varying degrees of radicalness. This is in line with extant literature, suggesting that the use of business models is a process of continuous selection, adaptation, and improvement to fit a changing environment (cf. Dunford, Palmer, and Benveniste, 2010; Doz and Kosonen, 2010; Demil and Lecocq, 2010; Teece, 2010; Casadesus-Masanell and Ricart, 2010; Ho, Fang, and Hsieh, 2011). Business models "have to be tested and retested, adjusted and tuned as the evidence with respect to provisional assumptions becomes clarified" (Teece, 2010: 188). Finally, while novelty might be a likely outcome of business model adaptation, it does not constitute a necessary requirement.

Business model innovation

The main motivation to innovate business models is to shape markets or industries by means of creating disruptive innovations (cf. Markides, 2006, Voelpel, Leibold, and Tekie, 2004). Notably, while business model evolution and adaptation always entail changes to the existing business models, the process of business model innovation may or may not result in the creation of a distinct business model for a separate unit, or it can imply changes to an existing business model. Often, the process of business model innovation is likely to affect various components of the business model simultaneously and entails reconfiguration and/or creation of new core activities and processes within the business model. Business model innovations can yield different innovative outcomes. For instance, Giesen et al. (2007) mention "industry model innovation" (i.e., redefining existing industries), "revenue model innovation" (i.e., innovating how revenue is generated by changing or re-configurating the offering in addition to the pricing models) and "enterprise model innovation" (i.e., changing the value-chain position through the value network with employees, suppliers, and customers, in addition to capability and assets configurations).

Table 8.2 contrasts the main characteristics of business model evolution, adaptation, and innovation.

Table 8.2 Evolution, adaptation, and innovation

	Business Model Evolution	Business Model Adaptation	Business Model Innovation
Planned outcome	Natural, minor adjustments	Align with the environment	Disrupt market conditions
Scope of change (areas affected)	Narrow	Narrow–wide	Wide
Degree of radicalness	Incremental	Incremental–radical	Radical
Frequency of change	Continuous, gradual changes	Periodically	Infrequently
Degree of novelty	Not applicable	Novelty is not a requirement	Must be novel to the industry

In sum, business model evolution and adaptation are similar to the degree that they entail organizational processes that bring about adjustments (as opposed to disruptions) to the business models. They differ, however, in the way that evolutionary change processes occur more naturally and incrementally over the lifespan of the firm's business model, while business model adaptation reflects purposeful changes made in response to changing environmental conditions. Further, this typology indicates that firms operating in dynamic environments can either (1) aim to attain alignment with the environment by adapting the business model to changing external conditions (i.e., business model adaptation), or (2) innovate the business model to shape market conditions by means of creating disruptive innovation (i.e., business model innovation).[1] It thus becomes important to discern the environmental contingencies prompting these different types of business model change.

Environmental Dynamics and Business Model Change

DRIVERS OF BUSINESS MODEL CHANGE

Scanning and interpreting the environment, firms have to make appropriate decisions with regard to both internal arrangement and external alignment (Tan and Litschert, 1994). In fact, the link between environmental conditions and organizational response has been established in a number of streams in the strategic and organizational literatures for several decades (e.g., Burns and Stalker, 1961; Perrow, 1967; Harvey, 1968; Galbraith, 1973; Hannan and Freeman, 1977; Chakravarthy, 1982; Nelson and Winter, 1982; Hrebiniak and

---

[1] The distinction between business model innovation vis-à-vis adaptation is in line with research based on organizational change theory, where episodic, discontinuous, and intermittent change is contrasted against change that is continuous, evolving, and incremental (e.g., see Weick and Quinn, 1999; Porras and Silvers, 1991).

Joyce, 1985; Teece, Pisano, and Shuen, 1997). Building upon this logic, one can expect different types of environmental change to prompt or require different changes to a firm's business model.

However, to date, business model literature has paid relatively little attention to the drivers of business model change. To illustrate, the majority of studies on business model dynamics describe the environment in highly abstract terms, often to provide a *general* context in which a particular type of business model change (e.g., renewal, innovation, etc.) is examined in more detail. For example, Doz and Kosonen (2010: 370) mention "strategic discontinuities and disruptions, convergence and intense global competition," as drivers for business model renewal. Johnson, Christensen, and Kagermann (2008) advocate the need for business model innovation to respond to competitive pressure or to a shifting base of competition. Similarly, other studies discuss the need for "business model learning" (Teece, 2010) or "business model erosion" (McGrath, 2010) in light of competition from new business models entering the market. Along the same lines, Voelpel, Leibold, and Tekie (2004: 264) mention "major and unpredictable changes in the business environment, the increasing importance placed on innovation and knowledge as value-creating attributes, and the accelerating pace of the business environment" as driving forces for business model innovation.

In contrast, another group of studies examine the effect of a *particular* environmental driver on firms' propensity to innovate their business model. For example, in their cross-industry study, de Reuver, Bouwman, and MacInnes (2009) analyze the influence of external factors on the propensity for business model innovation, indicating that regulatory drivers are less important drivers of business model change as compared to technological and market-related forces. Other studies examine the influence of, for example, ICT technologies on the emergence of new business models in the context of e-commerce (cf. Wirtz, Schilke, and Ullrich, 2010; Pateli and Giaglis 2005).

With these generic descriptions of the environment, there is little differentiation with regard to what drives different types of business model change. A more fine-grained typology of environmental dynamics is proposed in the next section.

TYPES OF ENVIRONMENTAL DYNAMISMS

Based on Jansen, Van Den Bosch, and Volberda (2006), Suarez and Oliva (2005), *and others*, three main types of environmental dynamics can be discerned. Table 8.3 contrasts these types of environmental dynamics along the dimensions of *frequency* (i.e., the amount of environmental disturbances per unit of time), *amplitude* (i.e., the magnitude of the deviation from initial conditions caused by a disturbance), *predictability* (i.e., the degree of irregularity in the overall pattern of change), and *velocity* (i.e., the rate/pace of change of disturbances) (cf. Bourgeois and Eisenhardt, 1988; Wholey and Brittain, 1989; Davis, Eisenhardt, and Bingham, 2009; McCarthy et al., 2010).

Table 8.3 Patterns of environmental dynamics

	Regular Change	Environmental Competitiveness	Environmental Shift
Frequency	Low	High	Low
Amplitude	Low	Low–moderate	High
Predictability	High	Moderate	Low
Velocity	Low	High/continuous	Punctuated (two stages)

Matching Environmental Dynamics With Business Model Change

Regular environmental change

Regular change describes fairly stable environments that experience low-intensity gradual changes (Suarez and Oliva, 2005). The degree of irregularity in the overall pattern of change is highly predictable and deviations from initial conditions caused by changes in the environment are minimal. Although the pace of change is slow and the amplitude of change is limited, firms are likely to experience the need for incremental adjustments and improvements in their business model. One can thus expect that in such settings, firms are likely to allow for the natural evolution of their business model to take place and merely engage in adjustment and fine-tuning activities that are simple and iterative.

Environmental shifts

Environmental shifts or "punctuated equilibria" (Tushman and Romanelli, 1985) can be described as dramatic or discontinuous changes to a firm's environment, often brought about by disruptive technologies (Tushman and Anderson, 1986; Christensen, 1992), new competitors (Sirmon, Hitt, and Ireland, 2007), or major regulatory or political regime changes (Suarez and Oliva, 2005; Dixon, Meyer, and Day, 2014). These shifts occur infrequently and rarely repeat themselves. The amplitude of these shifts can be severe, often termed as "competence destroying change" (Tushman and Anderson, 1986). Environmental shifts are highly unpredictable and cause a high degree of instability in the environment (Dess and Beard 1984). The velocity of an environmental shift has two paces: periods of incremental change are punctuated by disruptions (e.g., technological breakthroughs), which significantly increase both environmental uncertainty and munificence (Tushman and Anderson, 1986).

Because environmental shifts can be competence destroying (Tushman and Anderson, 1986), they make current products and services obsolete (Jansen, Van Den Bosch, and Volberda, 2006, Sorensen and Stuart 2000). This might render "the core of the firm largely useless in its current product market" (Agarwal and Helfat, 2009: 283). For example, Danneels (2011) describes the case of Smith Corona, a manufacturer of mechanical typewriters, whose long-term viability was threatened during the transition from mechanical to electronic products.

Thus, environmental shifts are often found to prompt organizations to respond with "revolutionary change" (Greenwood and Hinings, 1996), "discontinuous transformations" (Agarwal and Helfat, 2009), or "reorientations" (Tushman and Romanelli, 1985). These radical types of organizational change affect all parts of the organization, including a shift in the firm's core values and beliefs as well as the firm's strategy, structures, and control systems (Agarwal and Helfat, 2009).

Hence, one can anticipate that environmental shifts not only prompt a large amount of organizational change, but also require change along multiple dimensions of the firm's business model. Because gradual and incremental adaptations of the firm's business model may not be sufficient, I argue for the important role of business model innovation in the face of environmental shifts. I suggest that business model innovation provides an effective way for firms to get ahead of the competition and to "rewrite" the rules of the game by introducing a novel way of creating, delivering, and capturing value. This idea is in line with organizational learning and innovation studies, which highlight the important role of exploratory innovations in the face of environmental shifts (cf. Jansen, Van Den Bosch, and Volberda, 2006), as a way to capitalize on changing circumstances (Zahra, 1996) by innovating their offering and targeting premium market segments (Levinthal and March 1993; Zahra and Bogner, 2000) or creating new niches (Lumpkin and Dess, 2001).

Environmental competitiveness

"Environmental competitiveness" (Jansen, Van Den Bosch, and Volberda, 2006), "hypercompetition" (D'Aveni, 1994; Brown and Eisenhardt, 1997; Eisenhardt and Tabrizi, 1995; Hanssen-Bauer and Snow, 1996), or "environmental turbulence" (Easterby-Smith, Lyles, and Peteraf, 2009) describe high-velocity environments that are in perpetual flux or churn (Eisenhardt and Tabrizi, 1995). Characterized by intense competition (Matusik and Hill 1998; Miller 1987), companies are required to continuously evolve their basis of competitive advantage (Burgelman, 1994). Hypercompetitive environments are associated with intensive pressures for higher efficiency and lower prices (Matusik and Hill 1998; Pablo et al., 2007) and to keep pace with rapid innovations in product markets (Lee et al., 2010; Galunic and Eisenhardt, 2001; Rindova and Kotha, 2001).

Given the need for continuously evolving their basis of competitive advantage, one can expect business model innovation to be ineffective and even harmful in the face of environmental competitiveness. Research has shown that operating in hypercompetitive markets, firms have fewer resources available for innovations, and that outcomes of innovations would rapidly diffuse over the population of competitors (cf. Miller and Friesen, 1983; Zahra, 1996; Zahra and Bogner, 2000; Levinthal and March 1993). Thus, with periodically changing competitive demands on the firm, the firm cannot afford to continuously uproot, deconstruct, and innovate its extant business model. Hence, I argue for the need for business model adaptation to reach temporary alignment with the environment. These adaptations can affect the core and non-core dimensions of the firm's business model and allow the firm to respond quickly to new market demands.

Dynamic Capabilities and Business Model Change

BUSINESS MODEL CHANGE AS A DYNAMIC CAPABILITY

Drawing on the dynamic capability view of the firm, one can assume that an organization's ability to systematically change its business model in the face of environmental dynamics is influenced by its existing design and capabilities. Organizations may cultivate a preparedness for business model change by developing dynamic capabilities that enable them to change their business models in a systematic way. As business model change can be considered as a key process in organizational and strategic renewal, it is suitable to adopt a dynamic capability perspective to describe the organizational and managerial processes underlying business model change.

The view of business model change as a firm's dynamic capability has been implicitly (e.g., Doz and Kosonen, 2010; Demil and Leqcoq, 2010) and explicitly (e.g., Achtenhagen, Melin, and Naldi, 2013) articulated in extant business model literature, suggesting the need for underlying organizational and managerial practices to facilitate business model change. For example, authors emphasize the need for "strengthening strategic sensitivity, leadership unity and resource fluidity" to accelerate business model renewal (Doz and Kosonen, 2010: 656) or "clarification, localization, experimentation and co-option" processes for business model replication (Dunford, Palmer, and Benveniste, 2010: 655). Along similar lines, Achtenhagen, Melin, and Naldi (2013: 7) argue for the need for "critical capabilities," including an orientation toward experimentation, a balanced way of using resources, clear leadership, and strong organizational culture and employee commitment. The role of experimentation in particular has been repeatedly emphasized with regard to generating business model innovation (e.g., Sosna, Trevinyo-Rodriguez, and Velamuri, 2010; McGrath, 2010; Doz and Kosonen, 2010; Chesbrough, 2007; Wirtz, Schilke, and Ulrich, 2010; Achtenhagen, Melin, and Naldi, 2013).

However, which dynamic capabilities are most effective given different types of business model dynamics has not been addressed so far. Thus, the following sections first briefly review types of organizational capabilities before linking them to different types of business model change.

TYPES OF ORGANIZATIONAL CAPABILITIES

Dynamic capability studies differentiate between three levels of capabilities. The first level of capabilities, *operational capabilities*,[2] facilitates efficient and effective use of existing resources, for example in "performing an activity, such as manufacturing a particular product" (Helfat and Peteraf, 2003: 999).

---

[2] Operational capabilities are also referred to as "first-order capabilities" (Danneels, 2002; Collis, 1994), "zero-level capabilities" (Winter, 2003), "substantive capabilities" (Zahra, Sapienza, and Davidsson, 2006), or "resource base" (Helfat et al., 2007; Ambrosini, Bowman, and Collier, 2009).

The second level of capabilities refers to *dynamic capabilities*,[3] defined as the "capacity of an organization to purposefully create, extend or modify its resource base" (Helfat et al., 2007: 4).[4] In contrast to operational capabilities, dynamic capabilities do not involve production of a good or provision of a marketable service (Helfat and Peteraf, 2003). Instead, dynamic capabilities refer to deliberate efforts to change a firm's resources and operational capabilities (Zahra, Sapienza, and Davidsson, 2006; Helfat et al., 2007). That is, while resources (physical, human, organizational) are available to all firms, the "capability" to deploy and alter them productively differs among firms. By altering the resource base—acquiring new resources or recombining existing ones—companies are able to generate new value-creating strategies (Grant, 1996; Pisano, 1994; Henderson and Cockburn, 1994; Teece, Pisano, and Shuen, 1997).

A third level of capabilities is referred to as "meta capabilities" (Collis, 1994), "higher order capabilities" (Winter, 2003), or "regenerative capabilities" (Ambrosini, Bowman, and Collier, 2009) and denotes the capacity to modify or create new dynamic capabilities (Winter, 2003).

Capabilities consist of "routines to execute and coordinate the variety of tasks required to perform the activity" (Helfat and Peteraf, 2003: 999). Routines are "repetitive, highly patterned activities or behavior that are learned" (Nelson and Winter, 1982: 97). While skills are embodied in individuals, routines are found at the organizational level, where they act as "rules of conduct" or "best practices" for the members of the organization. The notion of routines is crucial for the definition of capabilities (operational or dynamic) as routines imply that the organization must have reached some threshold level of practiced activity. On a micro-level, the antecedents of capabilities and routines are suggested to be embodied in individuals, organizational and managerial activities and practices, and structures (cf. Felin et al., 2012).

Matching Dynamic Capabilities for Business Model Change

Analogous to the hierarchy with which capabilities evolve in an organization (cf. Collis, 1994; Winter, 2003), one can expect the process of business model change to involve different types of organizational capabilities. In this

---

[3] Dynamic capabilities are also referred to as "first-order capability" (Winter, 2003) or "second-order capability" (Danneels, 2002) throughout extant literature.

[4] The "resource base" is defined to include "tangible, intangible, and human assets (or resources) as well as capabilities which the organization owns, controls, or has access to on a preferential basis" (Helfat et al., 2007: 4).

section, I illustrate how business model evolution and adaptation are akin to dynamic capabilities in that they involve alterations to the firm's extant set of operating capabilities and resources on a continuous basis. In contrast, the process of business model innovation is more likely to be akin to "meta capabilities" in that it challenges the firm's existing ways of doing business, thereby effecting changes in the sets of extant dynamic capabilities.

Further, similar to dynamic capabilities, the processes of evolution, adaptation, and innovation need to be institutionalized through routines, organizational structure, and incentives to facilitate the ongoing and repeated processes of evolutionary, adaptive, or innovative change. This further warrants that a certain threshold level of practiced activity is maintained to ensure effectiveness in change processes. Hence, I argue that firms need to develop *"business model change capability,"* defined as the firm's capacity to adjust, adapt, and innovate its business model in the face of environmental dynamics. Developing this capability can help the firm to overcome core rigidities of its existing business model and implement change processes in a structured and systematic way. Contingent on the environmental setting and the type of business model change required, I illustrate the need for different types of capabilities to facilitate evolutionary, adaptive, and innovative change.

Evolutionary change capability

As argued earlier in this study, firms operating in environments characterized by low-intensity and gradual changes are in need of incremental adjustments and fine-tuning activities to support the evolution process of their business model. This evolution process centres on standardization, implementation, and maintenance of the existing business model. For this purpose, change processes are geared toward incremental and continuous adjustments in the firm's existing system of activities and relations, such as improvements in the activities offered to the firm's customers, strengthening ties with external stakeholders, or increasing efficiency in the way value is delivered and captured. Although the scope of change is limited to one or few areas at a time, effective business model evolution requires managers to have a deep understanding of how business models operate and what changes are required to maintain or improve the effectiveness of the existing business model. This is why Doz and Kosonen highlight the need for "dynamic consistency," defined as the "capability to anticipate change sequences" manifested in managers' understanding "what their BM is, how it works, and what the relationships are between its core components, that seem to at first sight be only loosely coupled. A progressive process of discovering more about these relations over time will enable managers to fine-tune their BM more effectively and preserve its efficiency" (2010: 243). Thus, to guide and implement business model evolution, firms need evolutionary change capabilities. I define these as those organizational processes that facilitate effective standardization, replication, and maintenance of the existing business model and thus guide its evolution process.

Adaptive change capability

As argued previously, operating under conditions of environmental competitiveness requires firms to respond with swift adaptations of their business models with the aim of aligning their business model to the environment, rather than to incrementally adjust or radically disrupt it. For example, in highly competitive environments, innovation-based advantages resulting from disruptive business model innovations may well be rapidly eroded. Business model adaptation, as compared to evolution or innovation, takes place periodically and is likely to affect a number of business model dimensions simultaneously.

Two important barriers are likely to impede business model adaptation. First, operating under conditions of environmental competitiveness can make it difficult for the firm to detect and anticipate new market demands. As environmental competitiveness is spurred by continuously shifting customer needs (D'Aveni, 1994; Jarrat and Fayed, 2001; Nath and Newell, 1998) it becomes imperative to sense and respond quickly to changes in customer preferences (Day, 1994; Jayachandran, Hewett, and Kaufman, 2004; Hult, Ketchen, and Slater, 2005). From a dynamic capability perspective, "organizational agility" or "customer agility" has been suggested as an important determinant of firm success in hyper-competitive environments, suggesting that a firm may be less or more agile than its competitors (cf. Haeckel, 1999; Zaheer and Zaheer, 1997). As firms can be agile in more than one domain, such as responding to changes in customer needs, supply-chain activities, or system development (cf. Sambamurthy, Bharadwaj, and Grover, 2003; cited in Roberts and Grover, 2012), I argue that developing organizational agility is an important prerequisite for successful business model adaptation. Organizational agility is conceptualized to consist of two complementary dimensions: Sensing capabilities and responding capabilities, manifested in the firm's ability to scan, learn, and interpret market and competitors activities, and as the ability to mobilize the firm's existing resources and processes to respond quickly (cf. Teece, 2007; Jayanchandran, Hewett, and Kaufman, 2004).

However, the need for organizational agility is likely to impose contradictory demands on the firm, requiring it to balance the tension between "stability and agility" (cf. Doz and Kosonen, 2010; Agarwal and Helfat, 2009). As Agarwal and Helfat (2009: 284) point out (in reference to Nelson and Winter, 1982), continuous adaptation "may be hard for organizations to manage effectively, because this may conflict with routines that enable companies to perform current tasks well." To solve this tension, I argue that firms need to institutionalize continuous adaption through the use of routines, organizational structure, and incentives that facilitate ongoing adaptation activities. For instance, routines for search (Helfat, 1998) or exploitative learning processes (March, 1991) support the firm to align with changing competitive conditions, by broadening and building on existing knowledge and reinforcing skills, processes, and structures (cf. Abernathy and Clark 1985; Levinthal and March 1993; Danneels 2002; Benner and Tushman, 2003). The importance of exploitative learning for organizational adaptation has further been highlighted in extant dynamic capability literature (cf. Dixon, Meyer, and Day, 2014; Jansen, Van Den Bosch, and Volberda, 2006).

Moreover, the firm can develop dynamic capabilities and install dedicated organizational units in charge of specific types of renewal activities such as alliances or acquisitions to help institutionalize adaptation within the organization (cf. Agarwal and Helfat, 2009). Further, while authors emphasize the need for "strategic flexibility" (Wang and Ahmed, 2007) or "resource fluidity" (Doz and Kosonen, 2010) on the organizational level, flexibility has its antecedents on the individual level, manifested in terms of cognitive decision styles, reflecting the individual's belief system or cognitive content (Nutt, 1993). These are shaped by antecedents such as culture (Lorsch, 1986), past experience (Brief and Downey, 1983; Prahalad and Bettis, 1986), and learning (Lord and Maher, 1990).

In sum adaptive change capability can be defined as the firm's capacity to align its business model in response to conditions of environmental competitiveness by means of institutionalizing routines, processes, and incentives that facilitate adaptation activities on a continuous basis. I propose that firms can develop this capability by employing organizational and managerial routines and processes associated with organizational agility (sensing and responding), exploitative learning processes, strategic flexibility (on organizational and individual levels), and boundary-spanning processes for resource renewal (e.g., alliances and acquisitions).

Innovative change capability

Environmental shifts are often brought about by disruptive technologies, new competitors, or major regulatory or political regime changes. The amplitude of these shifts can be severe in the way that it renders the firm's knowledge and competence base useless (cf. "competence destroying change": Tushman and Anderson, 1986). To respond to these shifts, continuous adaptations of the firm's business model are often not sufficient. Rather, business model innovation can provide an effective way for firms to get ahead of the competition and to "rewrite" the rules of the game by introducing a novel way of creating, delivering, and capturing value. Thus, exploratory learning processes become a key process of business model innovation.

Further, two types of barriers, cognitive and organizational, are likely to obstruct the process of business model innovation. On a cognitive level, management might be unable or unwilling to perceive the need for change. This inability has been primarily associated with the constricting effect of the dominant logic (Prahalad and Bettis, 1986) or path-dependency of the firm (Coombs and Hull, 1998), and has been referred to as the "bias of the current business model" (Chesbrough, 2007). As environmental shifts occur infrequently and rarely repeat themselves, managers might be unable to detect the need for change in time or fail to recognize opportunities outside their current logic of doing business.

Further, the inherent complexity and uncertainty of the change process is likely to impede the process of business model innovation. As demonstrated earlier, business model innovation requires change along multiple dimensions of the firm's business model. Thus, assessing the many interrelated, heterogeneous elements and evaluating new ideas can pose a difficult task for business leaders (Osterwalder and Pigneur, 2002; Pateli and Giaglis, 2005).

To address these cognitive challenges, management is needed for a comprehensive understanding of the firm's business model and its underlying assumptions. Hence, augmenting and internalizing relevant business model know-how on a formal and informal basis (e.g., by means of internal or external training programs, information sessions, or handbooks) contributes to the firm's capability to innovate its business model. These learning processes need to be supplemented by the development and usage of analytical tools to determine and assess current business models.

On an organizational level, the firm is likely to experience challenges idiosyncratic to organizational change, such as a lack of clear roles and responsibility in conducing the change process, also termed "business model innovation leadership gap" (Chesbrough, 2007). Particularly in cases of business model innovation, often no single person has been given the authority and the capability to innovate the business model. Chesbrough (2007) finds that while top leadership should assume this responsibility, CEOs are likely to delegate the responsibility for the business model to the general manager of the business unit, who in turn is often unwilling or unable to change the status quo as their familiarity with the existing model inhibits them from challenging the existing model.

To address the organizational challenges of coordination and authority, I propose the development of dedicated organizational units and functions (e.g., chief officer of business model innovation) that oversee and manage decisions and activities pertaining to business model innovation. Similar uses of "innovation offices" have been proposed in open innovation literature (Chesbrough, 2006) or alliance management literature (Dyer, Kale, and Sing, 2001).

In sum, innovative change capability can be defined as the firm's capacity to innovate its business model in response to conditions of environmental shifts. This innovative change capability rests upon learning processes pertaining to explorative innovation and the accumulation and internalization of relevant business model know-how. Further, this capability resides within management operating in the organizational unit, functions, and roles dedicated to the coordination and management of the business model innovation process.

Table 8.4 presents my contingency framework on business model dynamics, environmental change, and dynamic capabilities.

A number of similarities and dissimilarities between evolutionary, adaptive, and innovative business model change become apparent. First, all three types of business model change occur in response to environmental dynamics and require deliberate managerial action for the change to be anticipated and implemented. Second, this further requires a certain threshold of understanding within the organization about the firm's business model and its underlying assumptions. Third, developing the capability for business model change is required in all of the three cases of business model dynamics.

Table 8.4 A contingency framework

	Environmental Dynamics		
	Regular change	Environmental competitiveness	Environmental shift
Type of business model change	Business model evolution	Business model adaptation	Business model innovation
Type of dynamic capability	Evolutionary change capability	Adaptive change capability	Innovative change capability
Underlying capability dimensions	• Dynamic consistency (Doz and Kosonen, 2010)	• Customer agility (Roberts and Grover, 2012), • Strategic flexibility (Wang and Ahmed, 2007), • Exploitation (March, 1991; Jansen et al., 2006; Dixon et al., 2014)	• Exploration (March, 1991; Jansen et al., 2006; Dixon et al., 2014) • Business model know-how • Dedicated org. units and functions for business model innovation

However, the constituent elements of these business model change capabilities differ among the three types of business model dynamics. The proposed organizational and managerial routines are tailored to address and overcome the specific challenges idiosyncratic to the different types of business model change. Thus, business model evolution merely requires processes to maintain dynamic consistency, that is, the fine-tuning between the linked core components of the business model. Conversely, requiring adaptive activities on a continuous basis, business model adaptation necessitates an effective level of strategic flexibility within the organization, supported by standardized routines pertaining to exploitative learning, as well as sensing and responding to the environment. In contrast, affecting change along multiple dimensions of the firm's business model simultaneously, the process of business model innovation requires the highest level of relevant business model know-how, analytical tools, exploratory learning mechanisms, and institutionalized organizational units, functions, and roles to ensure effective coordination and implementation of the new business model.

Concluding Discussion

In this brief study, I examined the contingencies between environmental dynamics, business model change, and dynamic capabilities and illustrated that these contingencies are indeed important antecedents to firm performance. In doing so, this study has contributed to a clearer conceptualization of business models and a typology of business model dynamics. While business model literature commonly studies types of business model dynamics separately (e.g., adaptation or innovation), examining three types of dynamics in one framework takes into account the heterogeneity with which firms can alter their existing business model. Further, examining the environmental contingencies of business model change contributed to a more systematic treatment of the drivers of business model change, which to date had been presented on an abstract and generic level. Moreover, differentiating dynamic capabilities for different business model dynamics sheds light on the organizational dimension of business model change and highlights that firms can cultivate a preparedness for business model change.

It is clear that the framework outlined in this chapter requires additional work, both conceptual/theory and empirical. Conceptually speaking, my study rests upon two main assumptions. The first assumption is that management assesses environmental dynamics "objectively" and subsequently recognizes the need for business model change. However, it is conceivable that realized organizational behavior reflects managerial perceptions of how stable or turbulent the environment is rather than its objective characteristics (Child, 1972; Duncan, 1972). The second assumption is that when faced with the need to change, management will choose from among three alternative courses of action (business model evolution, adaptation, and innovation). However, environmental conditions are often not clear cut and neither are types of business model dynamics. For example, in cases of environmental scenarios entailing elements of both intense competition and continuous market disruptions, firms may need to develop capabilities that support both the exploration and exploitation of knowledge, and to facilitate strategic flexibility while experimenting with new business model designs.

Further empirical research is required to generate taxonomies on business model dynamics and to test the moderating roles of environmental dynamics and dynamic capabilities on the performance implications of business model change. The main purpose of this study, however, has been to develop *a priori* behavioural theory of business model dynamics.

■ REFERENCES

Abernathy, W. J. and Clark, K. B. 1985. "Innovation: Mapping the Winds of Creative Destruction." *Research Policy*, 14 (1): pp. 3–22.

Achtenhagen, L., Melin, L., and Naldi, L. 2013. "Dynamics of Business Models-Strategizing, Critical Capabilities and Activities for Sustained Value Creation." *Long Range Planning*, 46 (6): pp. 427–442.

Agarwal, R. and Helfat, C. E. 2009. "Strategic Renewal of Organizations." *Organization Science*, 20 (2): pp. 281–293.

Ambrosini, V. R., Bowman, C., and Collier, N. 2009. "Dynamic Capabilities: An Exploration of How Firms Renew Their Resource Base." *British Journal of Management*, 20 (1): pp. S9-S24.

Amit, R. and Zott, C. 2001. "Value Creation in e-business." *Strategic Management Journal*, 22 (7): pp. 493–520.

Benner, M. J. and Tushman, M. L. (2003). "Exploitation, Exploration, and Process Management: The Productivity Dilemma Revisited." *Academy of Management Review*, 28(2), 238–256.

Bourgeois, L. J. and Eisenhardt, K. M. (1988). Strategic Decision Processes in High Velocity Environments: Four Cases in the Microcomputer Industry." *Management Science*, 34 (7): pp. 816–835.

Brief, A. P. and Downey, H. K. 1983. "Cognitive and Organizational Structures: A Conceptual Analysis of Implicit Organizing Theories." *Human Relations*, 36 (12): pp. 1065–1089.

Brown, S. L., and Eisenhardt, K. M. 1997. "The Art of Continuous Change: Linking Complexity Theory and Time-Paced Evolution in Relentlessly Shifting Organizations." *Administrative Science Quarterly.* 42(1): pp. 1–34.

Burgelman, R. A. 1994. "Fading Memories: A Process Theory of Strategic Business Exit in Dynamic Environments." *Administrative Science Quarterly*, 39 (1): pp. 24–56.

Burns, T. and Stalker, G. M. 1961. *The Management of Innovation*. London: Tavistock Publications.

Casadesus-Masanell, R. and Ricart, J. E. 2010. "From Strategy to Business Models and onto Tactics." *Long Range Planning*, 43 (2): pp. 195–215.

Chakravarthy, B. S. 1982. "Adaptation: A Promising Metaphor for Strategic Management." *Academy of Management Review*, 7 (1): pp. 35–44.

Chesbrough, H. W. 2006. *Open Business Models: How to Thrive in the New Innovation Landscape*. Boston, MA: Harvard Business School Press.

Chesbrough, H. W. 2007. "Business Model Innovation: It's Not Just About Technology Anymore." *Strategy & Leadership*, 35 (6): pp. 12–17.

Chesbrough, H. W. 2010. "Business Model Innovation: Opportunities and Barriers." *Long Range Planning*, 43 (2): pp. 354–363.

Chesbrough, H. W., and Rosenbloom, R. S. 2002. "The Role of the Business Model in Capturing Value from Innovation: Evidence from Xerox Corporation's Technology Spinoff Companies." *Industrial and Corporate Change*, 11 (3): pp. 529–555.

Child, J. 1972. "Organizational Structure, Environment and Performance: The Role of Strategic Choice." *Sociology*, 6 (1): pp. 1–22.

Christensen, C. M. 1992. "Exploring the Limits of the Technology S-curve, Part 1: Component Technologies." *Production and Operations Management*, 1 (4): pp. 334–357.

Collis, D. J. 1994. "Research Note: How Valuable Are Organizational Capabilities?" *Strategic Management Journal*, 15 (S1): pp. 143–152.

Coombs, R., and Hull, R. 1998. "Knowledge Management Practices and Path-Dependency in Innovation." *Research Policy*, 27 (3): pp. 237–253.

Danneels, E. 2002. "The Dynamics of Product Innovation and Firm Competences." *Strategic Management Journal*, 23 (12): pp. 1095–1121.

Danneels, E. 2011. "Trying to Become a Different Type of Company: Dynamic Capability at Smith Corona." *Strategic Management Journal*, 32 (1): pp. 1–31.

D'Aveni, R. A. 1994. *Hypercompetition: Managing the Dynamics of Strategic Maneuvering: Free Press.* New York: EEUU.

Davis, J. P., Eisenhardt, K. M., and Bingham, C. B. 2009. "Optimal Structure, Market Dynamism, and the Strategy of Simple Rules." *Administrative Science Quarterly*, 54 (3): pp. 413–452.

Day, G. S. 1994. "The Capabilities of Market-driven Organizations." *The Journal of Marketing*, 58 (October): pp. 37–52.

De Reuver, M., Bouwman, H., and MacInnes, I. 2009. "Business Models Dynamics for Start-ups and Innovating e-businesses." *International Journal of Electronic Business*, 7 (3): pp. 269–286.

Demil, B., and Lecocq, X. 2010. "Business Model Evolution: In Search of Dynamic Consistency." *Long Range Planning*, 43 (2): pp. 227–246.

Dess, G. G. and Beard, D. W. 1984. "Dimensions of Organizational Task Environments." *Administrative Science Quarterly*, 29 (1): pp. 52–73.

Dixon, S., Meyer, K., and Day, M. 2014. "Building Dynamic Capabilities of Adaptation and Innovation: A Study of Micro-foundations in a Transition Economy." *Long Range Planning*, 47 (4): pp. 186–205.

Doz, Y. L. and Kosonen, M. 2010. Embedding Strategic Agility: A Leadership Agenda for Accelerating Business Model Renewal." *Long Range Planning*, 43 (2): pp. 370–382.

Duncan, R. B. 1972. "Characteristics of Organizational Environments and Perceived Environmental Uncertainty." *Administrative Science Quarterly*, 17 (3): pp. 313–327.

Dyer, J., Kale, P., and Singh, H. 2001. "How to Make Strategic Alliances Work." *Sloan Management Review*, 42 (4): pp. 37–43.

Dunford, R., Palmer, I., and Benveniste, J. 2010. "Business Model Replication for Early and Rapid Internationalisation: The ING Direct Experience." *Long Range Planning*, 43 (5): pp. 655–674.

Easterby-Smith, M., Lyles, M. A., and Peteraf, M. A. 2009. "Dynamic Capabilities: Current Debates and Future Directions." *British Journal of Management*, 20 (s1): pp. S1–S8.

Eisenhardt, K. M. and Tabrizi, B. N. 1995. "Accelerating Adaptive Processes: Product Innovation in the Global Computer Industry." *Administrative Science Quarterly*, 40 (1): pp. 84–110.

Felin, T., Foss, N. J., Heimeriks, K. H., and Madsen, T. L. 2012. "Microfoundations of Routines and Capabilities: Individuals, Processes, and Structure." *Journal of Management Studies*, 49 (8): pp. 1351–1374.

Foss, N. J. and Saebi, T. 2015. Chapter 1, this volume. "Business Models and Business Model Innovation: Bringing Organization into the Discussion."

Galbraith, J. R. 1973. *Designing Complex Organizations*. Reading, MA: Addison-Wesley Longman Publishing Co., Inc.

Galunic, D. C. and Eisenhardt, K. M. 2001. "Architectural Innovation and Modular Corporate Forms." *Academy of Management Journal*, 44 (6): pp. 1229–1249.

Giesen, E., Berman, S. J., Bell, R., and Blitz, A. 2007. "Three Ways to Successfully Innovate Your Business Model." *Strategy & Leadership*, 35 (6): pp. 27–33.

Grant, R. M. 1996. "Toward a Knowledge-based Theory of the Firm." *Strategic Management Journal*, 17: pp. 109–122.

Greenwood, R. and Hinings, C. R. 1996. "Understanding Radical Organizational Change: Bringing Together the Old and the New Institutionalism." *Academy of Management Review*, 21 (4): pp. 1022–1054.

Haeckel, S. H. 1999. *Adaptive Enterprise: Creating and Leading Sense-and-Respond Organizations*. Boston, MA: Harvard Business School Press.

Hannan, M. T., and Freeman, J. 1977. "The Population Ecology of Organizations." *American Journal of Sociology*, 82 (5): pp. 929–964.

Hanssen-Bauer, J. and Snow, C. C. 1996. "Responding to Hypercompetition: The Structure and Processes of a Regional Learning Network Organization." *Organization Science*, 7 (4): pp. 413–427.

Harvey, E. 1968. "Technology and the Structure of Organizations." *American Sociological Review*, 33 (2): pp. 247–259.

Helfat, C. E. 1998. "Simple Indicators of Adaptation Versus Rigidity in History-dependent Firm Activities and Decision Rules." *Industrial and Corporate Change*, 7 (1): pp. 49–75.

Helfat, C. E. and Peteraf, M. A. 2003. "The Dynamic Resource Based View: Capability Lifecycles." *Strategic Management Journal*, 24 (10): pp. 997–1010.

Helfat, C. E., Finkelstein, S., Mitchell, W., Peteraf, M., Singh, H., Teece, D. J., and Winter, S. G. 2007. *Dynamic Capabilities: Understanding Strategic Change in Organizations*. Malden, MA: Blackwell.

Henderson, R. and Cockburn, I. 1994. "Measuring Competence? Exploring Firm Effects in Pharmaceutical Research." *Strategic Management Journal*, 15 (S1): pp. 63–84.

Ho, Y., Fang, H., and Hsieh, M. 2011. "The Relationship Between Business-model Innovation and Firm Value: A Dynamic Perspective." *World Academy of Science, Engineering and Technology*, 77: pp. 656–664.

Hrebiniak, L. G. and Joyce, W. F. 1985. "Organizational Adaptation: Strategic Choice and Environmental Determinism." *Administrative Science Quarterly*, 30 (3): pp. 336–349.

Hult, G. T. M., Ketchen, D. J., and Slater, S. F. 2005. "Market Orientation and Performance: An Integration of Disparate Approaches." *Strategic Management Journal*, 26 (12): pp. 1173–1181.

Jansen, J. J. P., Van Den Bosch, F. A. J., and Volberda, H. W. 2006. "Exploratory Innovation, Exploitative Innovation, and Performance: Effects of Organizational Antecedents and Environmental Moderators." *Management Science*, 52 (11): pp. 1661–1674.

Jarratt, D. G. and Fayed, R. 2001. "The Impact of Market and Organizational Challenges on Marketing Strategy Decision-Making." *Journal of Business Research*, 51 (1): pp. 61–72.

Jayachandran, S., Hewett, K., and Kaufman, P. 2004. "Customer Response Capability in a Sense-And-Respond Era: The Role Of Customer Knowledge Process." *Journal of the Academy of Marketing Science*, 32 (3): pp. 219–233.

Johnson, M. W., Christensen, C. M., and Kagermann, H. 2008. "Reinventing Your Business Model." *Harvard Business Review*, 86 (12): pp. 57–68.

Lee, C.-H., Venkatraman, N., Tanriverdi, H. S., and Iyer, B. 2010. "Complementarity Based Hypercompetition in the Software Industry: Theory and Empirical Test, 1990–2002." *Strategic Management Journal*, 31 (13): pp. 1431–1456.

Levinthal, D. A. and March, J. G. 1993. "The Myopia of Learning." *Strategic Management Journal*, 14 (S2): pp. 95–112.

Lord, R. G. and Maher, K. J. 1990. "Alternative Information-processing Models and Their Implications for Theory, Research, and Practice." *Academy of Management Review*, 15 (1): pp. 9–28.

Lorsch, J. W. 1986. "Managing Culture: The Invisible Barrier to Strategic Change." *California Management Review*, 28 (2): pp. 95–109.

Lumpkin, G. T. and Dess, G. G. 2001. "Linking Two Dimensions of Entrepreneurial Orientation to Firm Performance: The Moderating Role of Environment and Industry Life Cycle." *Journal of Business Venturing*, 16 (5): pp. 429–451.

March, J. G. 1991. "Exploration and Exploitation in Organizational Learning." *Organization Science*, 2 (1): pp. 71–87.

Markides, C. 2006. "Disruptive Innovation: In Need of Better Theory." *Journal of Product Innovation Management*, 23 (1): pp. 19–25.

Massa, L. and Tucci, C. L. 2013. "Business Model Innovation." In M. Dodgson, D. Gann, and N. Phillips (eds), *The Oxford Handbook of Innovation Management*, pp. 420–441. Oxford: Oxford University Press.

Matusik, S. F. and Hill, C. W. L. 1998. "The Utilization of Contingent Work, Knowledge Creation, and Competitive Advantage." *Academy of Management Review*, 23 (4): pp. 680–697.

McCarthy, I. P., Lawrence, T. B., Wixted, B., and Gordon, B. R. 2010. "A Multidimensional Conceptualization of Environmental Velocity." *Academy of Management Review*, 35 (4): pp. 604–626.

McGrath, R. G. 2010. "Business Models: A Discovery Driven Approach." *Long Range Planning*, 43 (2): pp. 247–261.

Miller, D. 1987. "The Structural and Environmental Correlates of Business Strategy." *Strategic Management Journal*, 8 (1): pp. 55–76.

Miller, D. and Friesen, P. H. 1983. "Strategy-making and Environment: The Third Link." *Strategic Management Journal*, 4 (3): pp. 221–235.

Morris, M., Schindehutte, M., and Allen, J. 2005. "The Entrepreneur's Business Model: Toward a Unified Perspective." *Journal of Business Research*, 58 (6): pp. 726–735.

Nath, D. and Newell, S. E. 1998. "Organizational Responses to a Hypercompetitive Environment: A Case Study of Pepsi Canada." *Journal of Business Research*, 41 (1): pp. 41–48.

Nelson, R. R. and Winter, S. G. 1982. *An Evolutionary Theory of Economic Change*. Cambridge MA: Belknap Press of Harvard University Press.

Nutt, P. C. 1993. "Flexible Decision Styles and the Choices of Top Executives." *Journal of Management Studies*, 30 (5): pp. 695–721.

Osterwalder, A. and Pigneur, Y. 2002. "An e-business Model Ontology for Modeling e-business." Paper presented at the 15th Bled Electronic Commerce Conference.

Osterwalder, A., Pigneur, Y., and Tucci, C. L. 2005. "Clarifying Business Models: Origins, Present, and Future of the Concept." *Communications of the Association for Information Systems*, 16 (1): pp. 1–25.

Pablo, A. L., Reay, T., Dewald, J. R., and Casebeer, A. L. 2007. "Identifying, Enabling and Managing Dynamic Capabilities in the Public Sector." *Journal of Management Studies*, 44 (5): pp. 687–708.

Pateli, A. G. and Giaglis, G. M. 2005. "Technology Innovation-induced Business Model Change: A Contingency Approach." *Journal of Organizational Change Management*, 18 (2): pp. 167–183.

Perrow, C. 1967. "A Framework for the Comparative Analysis of Organizations." *American Sociological Review*, 32: pp. 194–208.

Pisano, G. P. 1994. "Knowledge, Integration, and the Locus of Learning: An Empirical Analysis of Process Development." *Strategic Management Journal*, 15 (S1): pp. 85–100.

Porras, J., and Silvers, R. 1991. "Organizational Development and Transformation." *Annual Review of Psychology*, 42 (1): pp. 51–78.

Prahalad, C. K. and Bettis, R. A. 1986. "The Dominant Logic: A New Linkage Between Diversity and Performance." *Strategic Management Journal*, 7 (6): pp. 485–501.

Rindova, V. P. and Kotha, S. 2001. "Continuous 'Morphing': Competing Through Dynamic Capabilities, Form, and Function." *Academy of Management Journal*, 44 (6): pp. 1263–1280.

Roberts, N. and Grover, V. 2012. "Leveraging Information Technology Infrastructure to Facilitate a Firm's Customer Agility and Competitive Activity: An Empirical Investigation." *Journal of Management Information Systems*, 28 (4): pp. 231–270.

Robertson, P. J., Roberts, D. R., and Porras, J. I. 1993. "Dynamics of Planned Organizational Change: Assessing Empirical Support for a Theoretical Model." *Academy of Management Journal*, 36 (3): pp. 619–634.

Sambamurthy, V., Bharadwaj, A., and Grover, V. 2003. "Shaping Agility Through Digital Options: Reconceptualizing the Role of Information Technology in Contemporary Firms." *MIS Quarterly*, 27 (2): pp. 237–263.

Santos, J. F. P., Spector, B., and Van der Heyden, L. 2009. "Toward a Theory of Business Model Innovation Within Incumbent Firms." Fontainebleau: INSEAD Working Papers Collection 16.

Sirmon, D. G., Hitt, M. A., and Ireland, R. D. 2007. "Managing Firm Resources in Dynamic Environments to Create Value: Looking Inside the Black Box." *Academy of Management Review*, 32 (1): pp. 273–292.

Sorensen, J. B. and Stuart, T. E. 2000. "Aging, Obsolescence and Organizational Innovation." *Administrative Science Quarterly*, 45 (1): pp. 81–113.

Sosna, M., Trevinyo-Rodriguez, R. N., and Velamuri, S. R. 2010. "Business Model Innovation Through Trial-and-Error Learning: The Naturhouse Case." *Long Range Planning*, 43 (2): pp. 383–407.

Suarez, F. F. and Olivia, R. 2005. "Environmental Change and Organizational Transformation." *Industrial and Corporate Change*, 14 (6): pp. 1017–1041.

Tan, J. and Litschert, R. J. 1994. "Environmental Strategy Relationship and Its Performance Implications: An Empirical Study of the Chinese Electronics Industry." *Strategic Management Journal*, 15 (1): pp 1–20.

Teece, D. J. 2007. "Explicating Dynamic Capabilities: The Nature and Microfoundations of (Sustainable) Enterprise Performance." *Strategic Management Journal*, 28 (13): pp. 1319–1350.

Teece, D. J. 2010. "Business Models, Business Strategy and Innovation." *Long Range Planning*, 43 (2): pp. 172–194.

Teece, D. J., Pisano, G., and Shuen, A. 1997. "Dynamic Capabilities and Strategic Management." *Strategic Management Journal*, 18 (7): pp. 509–533.

Tikkanen, H., Lamberg, J.-A., Parvinen, P., and Kallunki, J.-P. 2005. "Managerial Cognition, Action and the Business Model of the Firm." *Management Decision*, 43 (6): pp. 789–809.

Tushman, M. L. and Anderson, P. 1986. "Technological Discontinuities and Organizational Environments." *Administrative Science Quarterly*, 31 (3): pp. 439–465.

Tushman, M. L. and Romanelli, E. 1985. "Organizational Evolution: A Metamorphosis Model of Convergence and Reorientation." In L. L. Cummings and B. M. Staw (eds), *Research in Organizational Behavior*, Vol. 7: pp.171–222. Greenwich, CT: JAI Press.

Venkatraman, N. and Prescott, J. E. 1990. "Environment–Strategy Coalignment: An Empirical Test of Its Performance Implications." *Strategic Management Journal*, 11 (1): pp. 1–23.

Voelpel, S. C., Leibold, M., and Tekie, E. B. 2004. "The Wheel of Business Model Reinvention: How to Reshape Your Business Model to Leapfrog Competitors." *Journal of Change Management*, 4 (3): pp. 259–276.

Wang, C. L. and Ahmed, P. K. 2007. "Dynamic Capabilities: A Review and Research Agenda." *International Journal of Management Reviews*, 9 (1): pp. 31–51.

Weick, K. E. and Quinn, R. E. 1999. "Organizational Change and Development." *Annual Review of Psychology*, 50: pp. 361–386.

Wholey, D. R. and Brittain, J. 1989. "Research Notes: Characterizing Environmental Variation." *Academy of Management Journal*, 32 (4): pp. 867–882.

Winter, S. G. 2003. "Understanding Dynamic Capabilities." *Strategic Management Journal*, 24 (10): pp. 991–995.

Wirtz, B. W., Schilke, O., and Ullrich, S. 2010. "Strategic Development of Business Models: Implications of the Web 2.0 for Creating Value on the Internet." *Long Range Planning*, 43 (2): pp. 272–290.

Zaheer, A. and Zaheer, S. 1997. "Catching the Wave: Alertness, Responsiveness, and Market Influence in Global Electronic Networks." *Management Science*, 43 (11): 1493–1509.

Zahra, S. A. 1996. "Technology Strategy and Financial Performance: Examining the Moderating Role of the Firm's Competitive Environment." *Journal of Business Venturing*, 11 (3): pp. 189–219.

Zahra, S. A. and Bogner, W. C. 2000. "Technology Strategy and Software New Ventures' Performance: Exploring the Moderating Effect of the Competitive Environment." *Journal of Business Venturing*, 15 (2): pp. 135–173.

Zahra, S. A., Sapienza, H. J., and Davidsson, P. 2006. "Entrepreneurship and Dynamic Capabilities: A Review, Model and Research Agenda." *Journal of Management Studies*, 43 (4): pp. 917–955.

Zott, C. and Amit, R. 2010. "Business Model Design: An Activity System Perspective." *Long Range Planning*, 43 (2): pp. 216–226.

Zott, C., Amit, R., and Massa, L. 2011. "The Business Model: Recent Developments and Future Research." *Journal of Management*, 37 (4): pp. 1019–1042.

9 Innovative Business Models for High-tech Entrepreneurial Ventures

The Organizational Design Challenges

MASSIMO G. COLOMBO, ALI MOHAMMADI,
AND CRISTINA ROSSI-LAMASTRA

Introduction

New customers' preferences, deregulation, and technological changes are currently facilitating the emergence of new business models, and *business model innovation* (BMI) is increasingly attracting the attention of scholars and practitioners (Casadesus-Masanell and Zhu, 2013; Zott, Amit, and Massa, 2011; Massa and Tucci, 2014). BMI refers to "the search for new logics of the firm and new ways to create and capture value for its stakeholders; it focuses primarily on finding new ways to generate revenues and define value propositions for customers, suppliers, and partners" (Casadesus-Masanell and Zhu, 2013). In this chapter, we concentrate on BMI in the context of high-tech entrepreneurial ventures and study how BMI challenges the organizational design of these firms. We adopt a broad definition of BMI as deviation from the traditional ways in which "an organization orchestrates its system of activities for value creation" (Massa and Tucci, 2014: 9). Hence, the terms *business model innovation* and *innovative business models* (which we use interchangeably in this chapter) refer to these deviations from the traditional ways.

Academic literature on BMI has devoted attention to high-tech entrepreneurial ventures (e.g., Amit and Zott, 2001; Zott and Amit, 2007) showing that BMI creates entrepreneurial opportunities (Markides, 2008) and affects venture performance (Zott and Amit 2007, 2008). However, so far the literature has been silent on how BMI shapes the organizational design of high-tech entrepreneurial ventures. We contend that such an aspect is of paramount importance for these firms. High-tech entrepreneurial ventures operate in a high-velocity and uncertain environment where rapid changes require decision makers to process a large amount of information (Galbraith, 1974). A proper organizational design is thus fundamental for the effectiveness of high-tech entrepreneurial ventures' decision processes and ultimately for their performance. This holds even more true as the organizational design of a venture in its early years has an enduring effects on the organizational design that the firm adopts in subsequent phases of its lifecycle (Baron, Hannan, and Burton, 1999).

The lack of research on the relation between BMI and high-tech entrepreneurial ventures' organizational design is part of a more general gap in the organizational design literature. Indeed, scholars in this field have not devoted much attention to the organizational design of entrepreneurial ventures (Colombo and Rossi-Lamastra, 2013). Conventional wisdom suggests that entrepreneurial ventures are different from established firms in several aspects. They have limited financial, technological, and human resources (Becker and Gordon, 1966), lack sophisticated governance structures (Ambos and Birkinshaw, 2010) and legitimacy (Stinchcombe, 1965). Hence, knowledge on organizational design of established firms cannot be generalized to apply to entrepreneurial ventures.

In this chapter, we contribute to filling this gap by discussing the challenges posed to the organizational design of high-tech entrepreneurial ventures[1] by two innovative business models that these firms are increasingly adopting. Namely, we consider the business model based on collaboration with communities of users and developers (hereafter: *community collaboration BM*) and the business model based on market for ideas (hereafter: *market-for-ideas BM*). Traditionally high-tech entrepreneurial ventures rely on internal research and development (R&D) and commercialize their innovations by moving along the value chain and internalizing downstream complementary assets such as production facilities, marketing channels, and so on. Prominent examples of entrepreneurial ventures adopting this traditional business model are Dell and Hewlett-Packard in their early years. Many firms are now innovating this traditional approach across its two main dimensions: the *organization of R&D* and the *control of downstream complementary assets*. In the former case, high-tech entrepreneurial ventures insource external knowledge generated by communities of users and developers to cope with the surge in development costs and competition. In so doing, these firms move the locus of innovation outside their boundaries by engaging in an increasingly salient type of open innovation (Chesbrough, 2003).[2] Collaboration between high-tech

---

[1] The discussion here is highly relevant for newly established ventures, which are adopting one of these models and build their organizational design accordingly. We do not claim that there are similar issues for established firms, which want to innovate their business model. Indeed, established firms already have an organizational structure and transition from one business model to another is different from newly established ventures. For arguments about challenges of BMI for established firms see, e.g., Santos, Spector, and Van der Heyden, chapter 3 of this volume.

[2] The two business models presented here also echo mainstream notions in open innovation, namely *inbound* (community collaboration BM) and *outbound* (market-for-ideas BM) open

entrepreneurial ventures operating in the software industry and the community developing open-source software (hereafter: *OSS entrepreneurial ventures*) is a case in point (Bonaccorsi, Giannangeli, and Rossi, 2006).

In the case of market-for-ideas BM, high-tech entrepreneurial ventures generate value by commercializing their ideas instead of their products. These firms focus on developing technologies, whilst other firms that possessed the required complementary assets commercialize products based on these technologies (Arora, Fosfuri, and Gambardella, 2001a). High-tech entrepreneurial ventures with a market-for-ideas BM capture value from a variety of technological exchanges like licensing, cross-licensing, R&D joint ventures, technological partnerships, and so on (Arora, Fosfuri, and Gambardella, 2001a; Gambardella and McGahan, 2010; Grindley and Teece, 1997).

Figure 9.1 summarizes the above discussion. The situation in which firms conduct R&D internally and revenues result from the commercialization of technology-based products corresponds to the *traditional BM* of high-tech entrepreneurial ventures. Conversely, the situation in which a venture focuses on developing technological knowledge instead of products and the control of downstream complementary assets is external configures the *market-for-ideas BM*. The situation in which a high-tech entrepreneurial venture opens up its R&D processes and relies more on external ideas developed by communities of users and developers configures the *community collaboration BM*. Finally, a *mixed model* is possible, which is characterized by external R&D and external control of downstream complementary assets.

We do not claim that these business models are discrete alternatives. They can indeed co-exist in the same firm, being suitable for different transactions with different customers.[3] However, for the sake of simplicity, in this chapter, we analyze the market-for-ideas BM and the community collaboration BM separately and set aside the mixed model. As regards the organizational design dimensions considered in this chapter, we root in mainstream research (Galbraith, 1974; Colombo and Delmastro, 2008) and focus on the *organizational structure* (i.e., hierarchy and task specialization) and *delegation of decision authority*.

The chapter is organized as follows. The second section illustrates the two innovative business models we are focusing on in this chapter. The third section discusses the challenges that these business models pose to the organizational

---

innovation. Inbound open innovation refers to internalizing of external knowledge, while outbound open innovation refers to the transfer of a firm's technology to other actors (Chesbrough and Crowther, 2006).

[3] It is worth noting that besides being based on the leveraging of innovative technological knowledge, the market-for-ideas BM and the community collaboration BM differ regarding their approach toward intellectual property (IP) protection. While in the former business model, IP protection is essential in order to facilitate transactions in market for ideas, in the latter loose IP protection is necessary to foster knowledge exchange and sharing with communities of users and developers. High-tech entrepreneurial ventures are more likely to adopt a market-for-ideas BM when the appropriability regime of the industry in which they operate is *tight*.

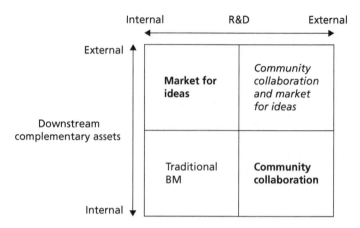

Figure 9.1 BMI in high-tech entrepreneurial ventures

design of high-tech entrepreneurial ventures and offers possible solutions to them. Finally, the fourth section concludes and summarizes possible promising avenues for future research.

BMI FOR HIGH-TECH ENTREPRENEURIAL VENTURES

The business model (BM) of a firm reflects the "management hypotheses about what customers want, how they want it, and how an enterprise can best meet those needs and get paid for doing so" (Teece, 2010: 172). Hence, the BM of a firm sketches the business logic of how to manage resources and exploit knowledge, how to create and capture value for stakeholders and define the landscape that venture operates in (Amit and Zott, 2001; Trimi and Berbegal-Mirabent, 2012; Casadesus-Masanell and Ricart, 2010). The BM depicts the design of *transaction content, structure,* and *governance* to create value through the exploitation of business opportunities. Governance refers to who is responsible for activities and controls resources and to incentives. Structure defines how transactions are linked and determines their *flexibility, adaptability,* and *scalability.* Content refers to what is exchanged and what resources are required for the exchange (Amit and Zott, 2001). Referring to this BM definition, any change in conventional business models namely changes in content, structure, or governance of transactions turns out to be a BMI.

Chesbrough (2006) argues that the rise in development cost and the shorter product lifecycle force firms to modify their BM regarding where to get the ideas and how to commercialize the ideas. The new BM, which is different from traditional BMs where firms discover, develop, and commercialize technologies internally, creates new opportunities for entrepreneurial ventures to create and capture value despite their limited financial resources, scant specialized employees, and lack of downstream complementary assets (Van de Vrande et al., 2009). In a typology of BMI developed by Santos, Spector, and Van der Heyden, chapter 3 in this volume, this change is categorized in repartition, that is, "altering the boundaries of the focal company by moving an organizational unit across business boundaries. The location of an organizational unit moves from outisde to inside the company or from inside to outside the company" (p. 47). As Figure 9.1 shows, in the community collaboration BM the research development expands outside boundaries of firm and in the market-for-ideas BM the downstream complementary assets, which are necessary for commercialization, are controlled by external actors. In this section, we discuss these two BMs, which are deviations from traditional business model adopted by high-tech entrepreneurial ventures.

THE MARKET-FOR-IDEAS BM

While Lamoreaux and Sokoloff (1996, 1999) have documented the existence of a lively market for patented technologies in the nineteenth century, in the last thirty years there has been a surge in markets for ideas with a variety of technological exchanges through R&D joint ventures, partnerships, licensing, cross-licensing, and so on (Arora, Fosfuri, and Gambardella, 2001a). Empirical studies point out the increasing role of licensing in high-tech industries around the globe since the 1990s (Grindley and Teece, 1997; Dengan, 1998; Sheehan, Martinez, and Guellec, 2004; Zuniga and Guellec, 2008; Arora, Fosfuri, and Gambardella, 2001b), driven mainly by information-and communication technology (ICT) and by the bio-pharmaceutical industry.

According to Arora, Fosfuri, and Gambardella (2001a), markets for technologies are highly beneficial for high-tech entrepreneurial ventures, which suffer from liability of newness and lack of size despite having competitive advantage in technology development. These firms indeed produce high-quality technology,[4] but usually lack the resources and complementary assets needed to manufacture and commercialize technology-based products. Also, there is the risk that the life span of these downstream activities might be longer than the lifecycle of the technology,[5] generating under-utilized assets, which lead to pressures for developing new technologies. When markets for ideas are well-developed, high-tech entrepreneurial ventures lacking resources and complementary assets have the option of focusing on developing technology and transferring it to third parties (usually larger firms), which possess resources and downstream assets (Grindley and Teece, 1997). Gambardella

---

[4] Technology can take the form of technological services, intellectual property, or software code, design, or product (Arora, Fosfuri, and Gambardella, 2001a), on so on.

[5] This frequently happens in the pharmaceutical industry, where the life of a molecule is limited to patent life and the development of a new molecule is very uncertain and often depends on serendipity.

and McGahan (2010) provide a comprehensive list of entrepreneurial ventures in different industries, which primarily focus on markets for ideas. These firms are for instance common in the biotech industry. While in the 1980s, the ideal path for a biotech was to become a drug manufacturer, in recent years biotech entrepreneurial ventures mainly focus on the development of a molecule of a drug to be licensed to large pharmaceutical firms (Arora and Gambardella, 1995; Gambardella and McGahan, 2010). Other examples are specialized engineering firms in chemical-processing industries and firms designing chips in semiconductor and software firms (Arora and Gambardella, 1998, 2010; Hall and Ziedonis, 2001; Cockburn and MacGarvie, 2011).

The main concern for high-tech entrepreneurial ventures adopting a market-for-ideas BM consists in not appropriating the full value from their technology (Caves, Crookell, and Killing, 1983). These firms are indeed largely dependent on downstream manufacturers and providers of complementary assets and thus are plagued by inefficiency of contracts and lack of bargaining power (Arora, Fosfuri, and Gambardella, 2001a).

In particular, value appropriation by high-tech entrepreneurial ventures with a market-for-ideas BM is easier in the short term than in the long term as licensing a technology causes its diffusion and increases the risk of imitation. A high-tech entrepreneurial venture usually protects itself from the risk of imitation by innovating and producing new technologies. However, this is hard to achieve due to the toughness of the innovation race and to the heterogeneous value of technologies (Arora and Gambardella, 2010). Alternatively, a high-tech entrepreneurial venture can provide complementary services associated with its technologies such as modifications and improvements of other technologies. However, this strategy is also not straightforward and requires significant investment. Having said that, the difficulty of long-term success for high-tech entrepreneurial ventures adopting a market-for-ideas BM makes them potential acquisition targets for large firms, with acquisition being the natural outcome of this model.

Moreover, high-tech entrepreneurial ventures adopting a market-for-ideas BM may have an advantage in focusing on *general-purpose technologies* (Arora and Gambardella, 2010). Indeed, developing general-purpose technologies allows technologies to be licensed within a wider range of markets and industries, thus obtaining revenues from numerous customers (Thoma, 2009). A large number of customers also create positive network externalities, which favor the attraction of more customers. Moreover, general-purpose technologies are not dependent on limited specialized downstream assets. This makes high-tech entrepreneurial ventures less vulnerable in negotiation and less dependent on the success of a single downstream manufacturer (Gambardella and McGahan, 2010). Examples of general-purpose technology suppliers are common in the software industry (Giarratana, 2004).

However, the development of general-purpose technologies poses two major challenges. The wide range of potential applications is associated with higher competition. Furthermore, capturing the full potential of general-purpose technologies requires marketing insights in addition to technological skills (Gambardella and McGahan, 2010). As it is difficult to predict the industries and markets in which these technologies will be applicable, it might be of great help to create a community of users that fosters exchange of information about further possible uses. Pollock and Williams (2009) explained how a firm that developed a general-purpose enterprise-resource-planning (ERP) system for companies was able to successfully modify the business version of its software in a version ideal for universities by creating a community of users in universities who provided feedback.

To conclude then, the main challenge for market-for-ideas BMs is to render entrepreneurial ventures adopting this BM less dependent on third parties and less exposed to imitation. Moreover, this BM also requires searching actively for wider applications and users of the technology. This in turn requires frequent interactions with current and potential customers to get deeper insights and access to knowledge possessed by them. As discussed in more detail in the third section, proper organizational design can be of great help in overcoming the challenges posed by the market-for-ideas BM.

THE COMMUNITY COLLABORATION BUSINESS MODEL

As a reaction to the increase in development costs and competition, high-tech entrepreneurial ventures are opening up their innovation processes and increasingly using external knowledge produced by communities of users and developers. A prominent example of this trend is collaboration with the community producing OSS by entrepreneurial ventures operating in the software industry (Chesbrough and Appleyard, 2007). Despite its initiation as an ideological movement (Stallman, 1984), OSS has gained significant commercial importance in the software industry (Fitzgerald, 2006), shifting from a pure community model to a commercial milieu (Harison and Koski, 2010). The success of OSS products such as Linux, Apache web server, Sendmail, and Firefox has made OSS a market trend in the software industry (Von Hippel and Von Krogh, 2006). In 2013, more than 3.4 million developers contributed to 324,000 OSS projects hosted on Sourceforge.net.[6] A survey of 740 software industry executives undertaken in 2012 forecast that, in 2016, OSS-based solutions will dominate the majority of software markets.[7] Currently, many software entrepreneurial ventures have entered the market to profit from OSS (Gruber and Henkel, 2006), thus adopting a community collaboration BM based on the collaboration with the OSS community. The attractiveness of this BM has been fueled by the success of VA Linux and RedHat in their initial public offering (IPO), which led to a flow of capital to OSS entrepreneurial ventures (Moody, 2001; Weber, 2004; Aslett, 2009).

---

[6] Retrieved November 2014 at: <http://sourceforge.net/about>.
[7] Retrieved November 2014 at: <http://northbridge.com/2012-open-source-survey>.

Several studies have investigated why firms participate in the OSS and how they derive revenues from it (see, e.g., Behlendorf, 1999; Bonaccorsi, Giannangelli, and Rossi, 2006; Dahlander and Magnusson, 2005, 2008; Perr, Appleyard, and Sullivan, 2010 among many others). A community-collaboration BM has two main distinctive features: *collaboration with the OSS community* beyond firm boundaries and *a loose regime of intellectual property* protection, which fosters—instead of forbidding—access to information. OSS entrepreneurial ventures do not control the OSS community resources, which reside in the OSS community (Dahlander and Magnusson, 2008). This poses challenges, which OSS entrepreneurial ventures must address to achieve success. First, the OSS community is *open*: heterogeneous people with different skills and motives can join OSS projects (Von Krogh et al., 2012). Such heterogeneity is not (fully) observable from outside the community and influences the quality of produced codes (Colombo, Pica, and Rossi-Lamastra, 2013). Second, since there are no contractual ties and enforceable agreements between OSS entrepreneurial ventures and OSS developers, it is hard to control the OSS development process and its outcome. This is a major drawback for OSS entrepreneurial ventures, which must commit to clear a roadmap of high-quality software releases to make profits and attract external capital (O'Mahony and Bechky, 2008). Third, due to the leadership structure of OSS projects (O'Mahony and Ferrero, 2007; Dahlander and O'Mahony, 2011), relevant information about software development may be possessed by individuals who are not the leaders of the project and who OSS entrepreneurial ventures can hardly identify from the outside. Fourth, to collaborate efficiently with OSS developers, who often have a strong ideological orientation (Raymond, 2001), OSS entrepreneurial ventures must comply with the written and unwritten norms ruling the OSS community (Agerfalk and Fitzgerald, 2008). The ignorance of these norms creates conflicts with OSS developers, which hinder knowledge transfer (Dahlander and Magnusson, 2005).

In this framework, two different approaches for accessing and using the resources of the OSS community are possible. First, OSS entrepreneurial ventures can just use the OSS code freely available on the Web and modify it according to their customers' needs without any significant contribution to the OSS community. Despite being simple, this approach may create a negative image and also conflicts with OSS developers, who may perceive the venture as a free rider (Dahlander and Magnusson, 2005). Alternatively, OSS entrepreneurial ventures can play an active role in the OSS community by directly contributing to the development of OSS projects either by launching new OSS projects or by supporting existing projects (West and O'Mahony, 2008; Henkel, 2009). In this case, OSS entrepreneurial ventures pay their employees to write OSS code and documentation or to answer technical questions by OSS users (Lakhani and Von Hippel, 2003). This pro-active approach provides visibility and direct access to the development process and allows OSS entrepreneurial ventures to exert an influence on the project (O'Mahony and Bechkym, 2008). OSS entrepreneurial ventures with a proactive approach learn to identify high-quality pieces of OSS code to be integrated with their own solutions, gain specific knowledge about potential applications of the OSS code to their business, and can identify the most talented developers in the community to collaborate with (Dahlander and Wallin, 2006; Dahlander, 2007; Eilhard, 2008).

The loose IP protection makes revenue generation out of the OSS rather complicated, as OSS firms cannot directly sell OSS code. The literature on OSS has identified several models that OSS entrepreneurial ventures adopt to generate revenue from OSS (Perr, Appleyard, and Sullivan, 2010; Alexy and George, 2013). Perr, Appleyard, and Sullivan (2010) categorized OSS revenue-generation models in the major groups of *dual-licensing models* (Goldman and Gabriel, 2005), *proprietary extensions to OSS (hybrid models,* Bonaccorsi, Giannangeli, and Rossi, 2006; Casadesus-Masanell and Llanes, 2008) and *sales of complementary services or products*, such as professional services and consulting, support, subscription, and hardware devices (Gruber and Henkel, 2006).

In the dual-licensing model, OSS entrepreneurial ventures license two different versions of their software under different licenses (a *public licence* and a *commercial licence*) to different customer groups (e.g., individual users vs firms). Examples of OSS entrepreneurial ventures with this revenue generation model are MySQL and Sleepycat (Perr, Appleyard, and Sullivan, 2010; Goldman and Gabriel, 2005). In hybrid models, OSS entrepreneurial ventures make money by selling proprietary extensions for OSS core or alternatively by allowing OSS extensions to their proprietary code (Casadesus-Masanell and Llanes, 2008). The prominent examples of OSS entrepreneurial ventures with hybrid models are SugarCRM, Codeweavers, Zend, and Black Duck Software (Perr, Appleyard, and Sullivan, 2010). Finally, OSS entrepreneurial ventures can generate revenue by offering complementary services such as consulting, implementation, and training for customers that choose OSS solutions (Alexy and George, 2013). Among ventures offering complementary services, we can mention Red Hat, Compiere, JBoss, SpikeSource, and Mazu Networks (Perr, Appleyard, and Sullivan, 2010). Alternatively, OSS entrepreneurial ventures use OSS software in hardware products, which constitute their main sources of revenues. For example, OSS entrepreneurial ventures tailor the Linux operating system for devices such as mobile phones, game consoles, and machine controls (Gruber and Henkel, 2006). These revenue generation models are not mutually exclusive: OSS entrepreneurial ventures usually adopt more than one of them.[8] The success of each model requires careful attention to the design and management of collaborations with the OSS community and to IP rights, together with an in-depth understanding of the target market (Perr, Appleyard, and Sullivan, 2010). Again, we contend that entrepreneurial ventures' organizational design is crucial to this purpose.

---

[8] In addition, Bonaccorsi, Giannangeli, and Rossi (2006) have shown that OSS entrepreneurial ventures tend to mix both OSS and proprietary business models.

BMI and the Organizational Design of High-tech Entrepreneurial Ventures

THE ORGANIZATIONAL DESIGN OF HIGH-TECH ENTREPRENEURIAL VENTURES

Building on Colombo and Rossi-Lamastra (2013), in this section we illustrate the peculiarities of the organizational design of high-tech entrepreneurial ventures by focusing on two prominent dimensions: *structure* and *decision system*. In the next section, we explore the organizational design challenges posed by the adoption of the market-for-ideas BM and the community collaboration BM.

Structure is defined as the "sum of the total of the ways in which a firm divides its labor into distinct tasks and then achieves coordination among them" (Mintzberg, 1979: 2). In general, entrepreneurial ventures have a very simple structure (Stinchcomb, 1965). Hierarchy is flat and includes two layers: the top management team (TMT) and the non-executive employees (Baron, Hannan, and Burton, 1999). As firms grow, the two-layer hierarchies may evolve into a three-layer hierarchy through the creation of a middle-management layer (Colombo and Grilli, 2013).

The *decision system* determines who has the authority in the decision-making process. It specifies the members of organization who are responsible for decisions and the modes for taking these decisions (Keidel, 1995). Entrepreneurial ventures usually have a simple decision system (Colombo, Foss, and Rossi-Lamastra, 2012), with decision authority mainly concentrated in the hands of the members of the TMT.

The organizational design of high-tech entrepreneurial ventures is shaped by the exposure to high-velocity environments in which these firms operate (Bourgeois and Eisenhardt, 1988) and by the crucial role of highly skilled human capital in value creation (Unger et al., 2011). High-velocity environments require that the organizational structure and decision system be designed to achieve both *flexibility* and *efficiency* (Davis, Eisenhardt, and Bingham, 2009). Flexibility enhances the ability to capture new and unpredictable opportunities[9] (Weick, 1993), while efficiency favors the quick and efficient exploitation of these opportunities (Adler, Goldoftas, and Levine, 1999). As regards structure, formalization of roles and specialization of tasks are mandatory as they increase the speed and accuracy of decisions and execution through learning-by-doing (Colombo, Pica, and Rossi-Lamastra, 2013). Moreover, specialization allows organizational members to use their highly specific knowledge in decision making (Sine, Mitsuhashi, and Kirsch, 2006). As regards the decision system, selective decentralization of decisions is of crucial importance (Sine, Mitsuhashi, and Kirsch, 2006). Specifically, TMT members must delegate operative decisions while retaining authority on high-level strategic decisions (Bourgeois and Eisenhardt, 1988). Selective delegation positively affects organizational efficiency as it allows

---

[9] Developing a new product or service, entering a new market, etc.

TMT members to concentrate their time and effort on high-level strategic decisions (Colombo and Rossi-Lamastra, 2013).

Task specialization and selective decentralization of decisions have a close relationship with the depth of corporate hierarchy. By hiring a middle manager, thus creating a three-layer hierarchy, TMT members can delegate operative decisions to the middle manager and focus on strategic decisions. Colombo and Grilli (2013) show that the hiring of a middle manager is related to strength of competition and the uncertainty of the business environment in which high-tech entrepreneurial ventures operate. This is in line with Galbraith's (1974) argument: task specialization and organizational depth increase firms' capacity to process information.

Besides assuring both flexibility and efficiency, the organizational design of high-tech entrepreneurial ventures should serve the purpose of leveraging individual knowledge and transforming it into organizational knowledge (Foss, Husted, and Michailova, 2010). TMT members and key employees who master sophisticated technological knowledge play a vital role in sustaining high-tech entrepreneurial ventures' competitive advantage through innovation (McMullen and Shepherd, 2006). For instance, as high-tech entrepreneurial ventures usually lack resources to offer talented individuals an attractive salary, they can instead offer employees autonomy and challenging work to leverage their intrinsic motivations (Kemelgor and Meek, 2008).

THE ORGANIZATIONAL DESIGN CHALLENGES OF THE MARKET-FOR-IDEAS BM

It is reasonable to expect that the organizational design challenges faced by high-tech entrepreneurial ventures adopting a market-for-ideas BM differ from those of their peers that operate in the market for products. First, high-tech entrepreneurial ventures adopting a market-for-ideas BM are actually R&D labs. Despite the tight appropriability regime of the industries in which these firms usually operate, defending technologies from imitation is a major concern. In this regard, the granting of the *first patent* is a crucial milestone, although difficult to achieve. The limited resources of high-tech entrepreneurial ventures prevent these firms from obtaining and then effectively using patent protection (Acs and Audretsch, 1990). Thus, high-tech entrepreneurial ventures usually take time to get their first patent (if they ever succeed in obtaining it). Obtaining a patent involves significant application costs (e.g., filing and examination fees); and high-tech entrepreneurial ventures normally lack the resources to defend their patents in courts (Arundel, 2001).[10] Accordingly, in most cases, secrecy is the

---

[10] Resource scarcity also prevents high-tech entrepreneurial ventures from resorting to strategic appropriability mechanisms that are widely used by large, incumbent firms, such as quickly climbing the learning curve or reducing time to market (Levin et al., 1987). Obviously, the receipt of venture-capital funding relaxes the financial constraints plaguing high-tech entrepreneurial ventures, and thus significantly changes the scenario described here.

best protection mechanism for high-tech entrepreneurial ventures in the market for ideas. Therefore, in their pre-patenting phase, these firms must cope with significant *appropriability hazards*. To cope with these appropriability hazards, it is reasonable to expect that high-tech entrepreneurial ventures which adopt a market-for-ideas BM and rely mainly on secrecy prefer to avoid adding new functional competences to their TMT or hiring a middle manager so as to reduce the risks of technological linkage. When the need for new competences becomes compelling, these firms are likely to prefer to add to the TMT by taking on board another owner-manager instead of appointing a salaried top executive. Indeed, the financial investment that the new owner-manager makes in the high-tech entrepreneurial venture serves to strengthen her commitment not to disclose corporate secrets (Williamson, 1983). This level of commitment is lacking in the case of the appointment of a salaried manager, who invests only her human capital in the entrepreneurial venture without providing financial resources. Accordingly, the appointment of a salaried manager engenders the risk of opportunistic behaviors, which pave the way to detrimental technological leakages if the salaried executive leaves the firm because a competitor hires her or she founds her own entrepreneurial venture. In a similar vein, we posit that in the pre-patenting phase, high-tech entrepreneurial ventures would prefer to adopt more centralized decision systems. Indeed, centralization reduces the need for information exchanges among the firm's personnel, thus reducing the risk of detrimental technological leakages by the firm's executives and other staff.

Furthermore, we argue that high-tech entrepreneurial ventures in the market for ideas have a narrower set of decisions in comparison with firms that operate in the market for products. In most cases, owner-managers have to make just a few crucial decisions about technology and its licensing, thus being less likely to suffer from information overload. Consequently, we expect that high-tech entrepreneurial ventures adopting a market-for-ideas BM tend to centralize these few crucial decisions and are less compelled to increase the depth of their corporate hierarchy (see Colombo and Grilli, 2013 for a similar argument). Conversely, when high-tech entrepreneurial ventures operate in the market for products, complementary assets are fundamental for successfully developing the business (Teece, 1986; Gans and Stern, 2003). High-tech entrepreneurial ventures do not normally possess these complementary assets or the resources and competences to develop them. Thus, collaborations with external third parties possessing these assets are pivotal and urge high-tech entrepreneurial ventures to adopt a suitable organizational design. Indeed, numerous collaborations may cause information overload for TMT members (Simsek, 2009), while relevant knowledge may be dispersed across multiple sources. Adding new functional competences to the TMT, specializing TMT roles, or increasing the vertical depth of the organization may help to alleviate information overload and dispersion. For instance, high-tech entrepreneurial ventures might want to hire an alliance manager to whom they can delegate decisions regarding external collaborations with other firms or universities.

Third, since the core activity of entrepreneurial ventures adopting a market-for-ideas BM is focused on idea generation and technology development, the main assets of these firms are undoubtedly their highly skilled employees, who require a particular set of incentives. Innovative projects are associated with high uncertainty and task complexity, which make their outcome unpredictable, hard to quantify, and not immediately observable. Therefore, it is very difficult to link rewards to effort or performance. Having a flat organization may be of help as shorter organizational distance between TMT and researchers promotes better monitoring of employees (Zenger, 1994). More importantly, delegation of decision authority over technology-related domains to highly skilled employees may serve two main purposes. In line with the Hayekian principle of collocation of knowledge and decision rights, delegation allows highly skilled employees to better direct and conduct their knowledge-intensive work with a positive effect on performance,[11] Moreover, delegation boosts employees' intrinsic motivations (see, e.g., Bartling, Fehr, and Herz, 2013), thus serving as an effective incentive, along with salary (Gambardella, Panico, and Valentini, forthcoming).

THE ORGANIZATIONAL DESIGN CHALLENGES
OF THE COMMUNITY-COLLABORATION BM

As discussed earlier, OSS entrepreneurial ventures face severe challenges in insourcing valuable knowledge from the OSS community. Dealing with these challenges requires an appropriate organizational design.

Colombo, Pica, and Rossi-Lamastra (2013) have argued that the organizational practice of allowing firm programmers to contribute autonomously to OSS projects in which OSS entrepreneurial ventures do not contribute on their own behalf is highly beneficial. First, as noted earlier, highly skilled employees especially appreciate autonomy in their working environment (Finegold and Frenkel, 2006). Thus, granting autonomy to firm programmers boosts their intrinsic motivations, with a positive impact on job satisfaction and productivity (Foss, Husted, and Michailova, 2010). Second, the practice increases the reputation and visibility of OSS entrepreneurial ventures in the OSS community by showing respect and compliance with the OSS norms of reciprocity and knowledge sharing. Such a reputation makes OSS developers more likely to collaborate with these OSS entrepreneurial ventures (Osterloh and Rota, 2007). Finally, autonomous contribution by firm programmers to OSS projects helps OSS entrepreneurial ventures to identify

---

[11] Delegation implies the risk of *loss of control* (Aghion and Tirole, 1997). Accordingly, Gambardella, Panico, and Valentini (forthcoming) have shown that firms are more likely to delegate authority to knowledge-workers in projects that do not deal with a firm's core of business.

valuable OSS knowledge and to use it efficiently for their own ends (Colombo, Pica, and Rossi-Lamastra, 2013). Indeed, firm programmers usually have an information advantage over their corporate superiors with regard to collaboration with the OSS community. Indeed, they often play an insider role within OSS projects (Dahlander and Wallin, 2006), because participation in the OSS software development is part of their daily work or they contribute to OSS in their spare time. Thus, they possess specific knowledge of the OSS community. OSS entrepreneurial ventures can leverage this specific knowledge by granting their programmers autonomy and letting them act as gatekeepers between the firm and the OSS community (Chan and Husted, 2010).

Granting autonomy may also have a dark side. Firm programmers may behave opportunistically and choose to contribute to OSS projects that give them private benefits (e.g., OSS projects through which they can signal their ability on the job market: Lerner and Tirole, 2002; Von Krogh et al., 2012). Reasonably enough, employees adopting opportunistic behaviors run the risk of losing their autonomy or even their job (Baker, Gibbons, and Murohy, 1999). This of course limits their ability to follow their personal objectives, which are not aligned with those of their venture. Hence, opportunistic behaviors of programmers can reduce the return from granting autonomy. Powerful incentives—for example, linking programmers' salary to performance (Gambardella, Giarratana, and Panico, 2010)—prevent these behaviors. However, the adoption of these incentives is possible only when managers can closely monitor their employees. This happens for instance in small firms where employees can be directly observed by their superiors and there is mutual control among employees (Knez and Simester, 2001). In general, having a flat hierarchy favors monitoring and makes it is easier to align firms' objectives with those of their employees (Alonso and Matouschek, 2008). Accordingly, OSS entrepreneurial ventures intending to adopt the practice of allowing their programmers to contribute to OSS projects autonomously should carefully evaluate the benefits of having a flat hierarchy. Finally, the information advantage of firm programmers is likely to lead to task specialization, which, in turn, engenders learning-by-doing and gains from knowledge-related economies of scale (Argote and Epple Dargote, 1990). In other words, some employees specialize in insourcing knowledge from the OSS community.

More generally, the organizational design challenges faced by OSS entrepreneurial ventures depend on two major dimensions: the *scale and scope* of entrepreneurial ventures' OSS operations and firms' experience with the OSS community. Once a piece of software code is insourced from the OSS community, the firm must combine it with internally developed code to create ready-to-use software solutions. The gains from such knowledge integration activity crucially depend on the scale and scope of the OSS operations. Community-collaboration BMs are heterogeneous with regard to the importance of OSS for entrepreneurial ventures' systems of activity and revenue-generation model. While collaboration with the OSS community is pivotal for some OSS entrepreneurial ventures, other ventures relegate OSS to a more modest role. The larger the scale and scope of a firm's OSS operations, the larger the value to the firm of the knowledge that is insourced from the OSS community. Accordingly, we believe that choosing the appropriate organization design increases in importance as the OSS operations of an entrepreneurial venture become larger and broader. For instance, the benefits and the drawbacks of granting autonomy to firms' programmers will be more significant for firms that widely leverage the OSS community than for firms that have a more limited focus on OSS. In accordance with this argument, Colombo, Pica, and Rossi-Lamastra (2013) find that firms with higher OSS sales and a wider portfolio of OSS-based activities are more likely to authorize their programmers to contribute autonomously to OSS projects in which the firm does not contribute on its own behalf during working hours.

Finally, experience with the OSS community does matter. A firm that is a novice in collaborating with the OSS community must rely on the (few) employees who claim to possess individual knowledge of the OSS community (see Matusik and Heeley, 2005). Accordingly, task specialization is mandatory for novice firms as the (few) employees who are experienced in interactions with the OSS community should specialize in the gatekeeping task. It is also reasonable to expect that decision authority over interactions with the OSS community be delegated to these gatekeepers. As OSS entrepreneurial ventures gain experience in collaborating with the OSS community, more and more firms' programmers have contact with OSS users and developers in their daily working activities and so become knowledgeable of the OSS community. This results in a wider diffusion among employees of the ability to detect, screen, and insource high-quality knowledge from the OSS community. The information advantage of employees experienced in OSS over their corporate superiors and peers tends to vanish. Granting autonomy to employees experienced in OSS thus becomes progressively less beneficial.

Table 9.1 summarizes the organizational design of the various business models discussed here.

Table 9.1 BMI and organizational design

	Community Collaboration BM	Market-for-Ideas BM
Organizational structure (hierarchy)	✓ Flat organization	✓ Flat organization
Organizational structure (task specialization)	✓ Specialization in gatekeeping tasks by employees experienced in OSS	✓ Pre-patent: non-specialized TMT (founder managers) ✓ After patent: specialized TMT
Decision system	✓ Delegation of authority in both issues related to interaction with the OSS community	✓ Centralized in management domain ✓ Delegation of authority in technology domain

Concluding Remarks

This chapter focuses on the organizational design challenges of BMI, exploring these challenges by considering two prominent innovative business models increasingly adopted by high-tech entrepreneurial ventures: the market-for-ideas BM and the community collaboration BM. From this examination, we can conclude that entrepreneurial ventures should carefully design their structure and decision systems so as to master the complex system of activities and revenue generation model typical of these BMs and, in general, of BMI.

The chapter highlights interesting avenues for future research. First, research on the organizational design challenges of BMI is still in its infancy. Accordingly, this field of study would benefit greatly from further studies, offering insights to managers and entrepreneurs on how to structure their firms internally so as to unleash the full potential of BMI. Many aspects need attention. For instance, does BMI require firms to have a lower span of control as employees need to be closely monitored due to the complexity of their system of activities? Does BMI always require a flat hierarchy or does a more layered structure help to master the complexity of the revenue generation model? Which managerial practices are suitable for firms adopting BMI in order for them to attract and retain the talented employees who are the basis of the success of these firms? Second, research on the organizational-design challenges of BMI has largely adopted a descriptive and qualitative approach (see, e.g., Colombo, Pica, and Rossi-Lamastra, 2013 for an exception) and consequently it would benefit greatly from large-scale quantitative studies testing propositions and arguments derived from the literature. Third, the chapter considers OSS as a prominent example of community collaboration BM. However, new communities of users and developers are now emerging, which may pose different challenges to entrepreneurial ventures intending to leverage their knowledge. Social networks, developers, and firms producing apps, customers' groups active on the Internet, and crowdfunding platforms are relevant examples of communities whose knowledge can be leveraged by entrepreneurial ventures to build BMI. Finally, one may wonder how the BMIs examined in this chapter interact. What are the organizational design challenges faced by entrepreneurial ventures that develop and commercialize ideas generated by relying on the knowledge produced by community users and developers? Do the problems engendered by these two BMs overlap, or do positive externalities exist differently from one model to the other? For instance, if a firm does business by developing and commercializing a technology by leveraging community knowledge, it cannot count on a tight appropriability regime to protect its technology. The risks of technological leakages are thus more severe, but the firm can benefit from the wide diffusion of the community knowledge, which may in turn fuel the diffusion of its technology.

▧ REFERENCES

Acs, Z. J. and Audretsh, D. B. 1990. *Innovation and Small Firms*. Cambridge, MA: MIT Press.

Adler, P.S., Goldoftas, B., and Levine, D. I. 1999. "Flexibility Versus Efficiency? A Case Study of Model Changeovers in the Toyota Production System." *Organization Science*, 10 (1): pp. 43–68.

Aghion, P. and Tirole, J. 1997. "Formal and Real Authority in Organization." *Journal of Political Economy*, 105 (1): pp. 1–29.

Agerfalk, P. J. and Fitzgerald, B. 2008. "Outsourcing to an Unknown Workforce: Exploring Open Sourcing as a Global Sourcing Strategy." *MIS Quarterly*, 32 (2): pp. 385–409.

Alexy, O. and George, G. 2013. "Category Divergence, Straddling, and Currency: Open Innovation and the Legitimation of Illegitimate Categories." *Journal of Management Studies*, 50 (2): pp. 173–203.

Alonso, R. and Matouschek, N. 2008. "Optimal Delegation." *Review of Economic Studies*, 75 (1): pp. 259–293.

Ambos, T. C. and Birkinshaw, J. 2010. "How Do New Ventures Evolve? An Inductive Study of Archetype Changes in Science-based Ventures." *Organization Science*, 21 (6): pp. 1125–1140.

Amit, R. and Zott, C. 2001. "Value Creation in e-business." *Strategic Management Journal*, 22 (6–7): pp. 493–520.

Argote, L. and Epple, Dargote, L. 1990. "Learning-curves in Manufacturing." *Science*, 247 (4945): pp. 920–924.

Arundel, A. 2001. "The Relative Effectiveness of Patents and Secrecy for Appropriation." *Research Policy*, 30 (4), pp. 611–624.

Arora, A. and Gambardella, A. 1995. "The Division of Innovative Labor in Biotechnology." In N. Rosenberg, A.C. Gelijns, and H. Dawkins (eds), *Sources of Medical Technology Universities and Industry*. Washington, DC, The National Academies Press, pp. 188–206.

Arora, A. and Gambardella, A. 1998. "Evolution of Industry Structure in the Chemical Industry." In A. Arora, R. Landau, and N. Rosenberg (eds), *Chemicals and Long Term Economic Growth*. New York: John Wiley, pp. 379–414.

Arora, A. and Gambardella, A. 2010. "Ideas for Rent: An Overview of Markets for Technology." *Industrial and Corporate Change*, 19 (3): pp. 775–803.

Arora, A., Fosfuri, A., and Gambardella, A. 2001a. "Markets for Technology and their Implications for Corporate Strategy." *Industrial and Corporate Change*, 10 (1): pp. 419–451.

Arora, A., Fosfuri, A., and Gambardella, A. 2001b. *Markets for Technology*. Cambridge, MA: MIT Press.

Aslett, M. 2009. *Open to Investment:Venture Funding for Open Source 1997–2008*. New York: The 451 Group.

Baker, G., Gibbins, R., and Murohy, K. J. 1999. "Informal Authority in Organizations." *Journal of Law Economics & Organization*, 15 (1): pp. 56–73.

Baron, J. N., Hannan, M. T., and Burton, M. D. 1999. "Building the Iron Cage: Determinants of Managerial Intensity in the Early Years of Organizations." *American Sociological Review*, 64 (4): pp. 527–547.

Bartling, B., Fehr, E., and Herz, H. 2013. "The Intrinsic Value Of Decision Rights." CESifo Working Paper Series No. 4252, May 31.

Becker, S.W. and Gordon, G. 1966. "An Entrepreneurial Theory of Formal Organizations Part I: Patterns of Formal Organizations." *Administrative Science Quarterly*, 11 (3): pp. 315–344.

Behlendorf; B. 1999. "Open Source as a Business Strategy." In C. Dibona, S. Ockman, and M. Stone (eds), *Open-sources: Voices from the Open Source Revolution*. Sebastopol: O'Reilly, pp. 149–170.

Bonaccorsi, A., Giannangeli, S., and Rossi, C. 2006. "Entry Strategies Under Competing Standards: Hybrid Business Models in the Open Source Software Industry." *Management Science*, 52 (7): pp. 1085–1098.

Bourgeois, L. J. and Eisenhardt, K. M. 1988. "Strategic Decision-processes in High-Velocity Environments—4 Cases in the Microcomputer Industry." *Management Science*, 34 (7), pp. 816–835.

Casadesus-Masanell, R. and Enric Ricart, J. 2010. "From Strategy to Business Models and Onto Tactics." *Long Range Planning*, 43 (2–3): pp. 195–215.

Casadesus-Masanell., R. and Llanes, G. 2011. "Mixed Source." *Management Science*, 57 (7): pp. 1212–1230.

Casadesus-Masanell., R. and Zhu, F., 2013. "Business Model Innovation and Competitive Imitation: The Case of Sponsor-based Business Models." *Strategic Management Journal*, 34 (4): pp. 464–482.

Caves, R. E., Crookell, H., and Killing, J. P. 1983. "The Imperfect Market for Technology Licenses." *Oxford Bulletin of Economics and Statistics*, 45 (3): pp. 249–267.

Chan, J. and Husted, K. 2010. "Dual Allegiance and Knowledge Sharing in Open Source Software Firms." *Creativity and Innovation Management*, 19 (3): pp. 314–326.

Chesbrough, H. W. 2003. *Open Innovation: The New Imperative for Creating and Profiting from Technology*. Boston, MA: Harvard Business School Press.

Chesbrough, H. W. 2006. *Open Business Models: How to Thrive in the New Innovation Landscape*. Boston, MA: Harvard Business School Press.

Chesbrough, H. W. and Appleyard, M. M. 2007. Open Innovation and Strategy. *California Management Review*, 50(1): pp. 57–76.

Chesbrough, H. W. and Crowther, A. K. 2006. "Beyond High Tech: Early Adopters of Open Innovation in Other Industries." *R & D Management*, 36 (3): pp. 229–236.

Cockburn, I. M. and Macgarvie, M. J. 2011. "Entry and Patenting in the Software Industry." *Management Science*, 57 (5): pp. 915–933.

Colombo, M. G. and Delmastro, M. 2008. *The Economics of Organizational Design: Theoretical Insights and Empirical Evidence*. London: Palgrave Macmillan.

Colombo, M. G., Foss, N., and Rossi-Lamastra, C. 2012. "Organizational Designs for Absorptive Capacity: The Role of Task Specialization, Delegation of Decision Authority, and Knowledge Sharing Practices." Working paper. Retrieved November 2014 at: <http://druid8.sit.aau.dk/acc_papers/curfgqe9ldxs30e70fqjjs3npq0u.pdf>.

Colombo, M. G. and Grilli, L. 2013. "The Creation of a Middle-management Level by Entrepreneurial Ventures: Testing Economic Theories of Organizational Design." *Journal of Economics & Management Strategy*, 22 (2): pp. 390–422.

Colombo, M. G. and Rossi-Lamastra, 2013. "The Organizational Design Of High-Tech Start-Ups: State Of The Art And Directions For Future Research." In A. Grandori (ed.), *The Handbook of Economic Organization. Integrating Economic and Organization Theory*. Northampton: MA: Edward Elgar, pp. 400–415.

Colombo, M.G., Pica, E., and Rossi-Lamastra, C. 2013. "Authorising Employees to Collaborate with Communities During Working Hours: When is it Valuable for Firms?" *Long Range Planning*, 46 (3): pp. 236–257.

Dahlander, L. 2007, "Penguin in a New Suit: A Tale of How de novo Entrants Emerged to Harness Free and Open Source Software Communities", *Industrial and Corporate Change*, 16 (5): pp. 913–943.

Dahlander, L. and Magnusson, M. G. 2005. "Relationships Between Open Source Software Companies and Communities: Observations from Nordic Firms." *Research Policy*, 34 (4): pp. 481–493.

Dahlander, L. and Magnusson, M. G. 2008. "How Do Firms Make Use of Open Source Communities?" *Long Range Planning*, 41 (6): pp. 629–649.

Dahlander, L. and O'Mahony, S. 2011. "Progressing to the Center: Coordinating Project Work." *Organization Science*, 22 (4): pp. 961–979.

Dahlander, L. and Wallin, M. W. 2006. "A Man on the Inside: Unlocking Communities as Complementary Assets." *Research Policy*, 35 (8): pp. 1243–1259.

Davis, J. P., Eisenhardt, K. M., and Bingham, C. B. 2009. "Optimal Structure, Market Dynamism, and the Strategy of Simple Rules." *Administrative Science Quarterly*, 54 (3): pp. 413–452.

Dengan, S. A. 1998. "The Licensing Payoff from US R&D." *Journal of Licensing Executive Society International*, 3 (4): pp. 1–8.

Eilhard, J. 2008. "Firms on SourceForge." MPRA Paper No. 78092008.

Finegold, D. and Frenkel, S. 2006. "Managing People Where People Really Matter: The Management of Human Resources in Biotech Companies." *International Journal of Human Resource Management*, 17 (1): pp. 1–24.

Fitzgerald, B. 2006. "The Transformation of Open Source Software." *MIS Quarterly*, 30 (3): pp. 587–598.

Foss, N. J., Husted, K., and Michailova, S. 2010. "Governing Knowledge Sharing in Organizations: Levels of Analysis, Governance Mechanisms, and Research Directions." *Journal of Management Studies*, 47 (3): pp. 455–482.

Galbraith, J. H. 1974. "Organization Design: An Information Processing View." *Interfaces*, 4 (3): pp. 28–36.

Gambardella, A. and McGahan, A. M. 2010. "Business-model Innovation: General Purpose Technologies and Their Implications for Industry Structure." *Long Range Planning*, 43 (2–3): pp. 262–271.

Gambardella, A., Giarratana, M. S., and Panico, C. 2010. "How and When Should Companies Retain Their Human Capital? Contracts, Incentives and Human Resource Implications." *Industrial and Corporate Change*, 19 (1): pp. 1–24.

Gambardella, A., Panico, C., and Valentini, G. Forthcoming. "Strategic Incentives to Human Capital." *Strategic Management Journal*.

Gans, J. S. and Stern, S. 2003. "The Product Market and the Market for 'Ideas': Commercialization Strategies for Technology Entrepreneurs." *Research Policy*, 32 (2): pp. 333–350.

Giarratana, M. S. 2004. "The Birth of a New Industry: Entry by Start-ups and the Drivers of Firm Growth—The Case of Encryption Software." *Research Policy*, 33 (5): pp. 787–806.

Goldman, R. and Gabriel, R. P. 2005. *Innovation Happens Elsewhere*. San Francisco: Morgan Kaufmann, pp. 15–28.

Grindley, P. C. and Teece, D. J. 1997. "Managing Intellectual Capital: Licensing and Cross-licensing in Semiconductors and Electronics." *California Management Review*, 39 (2): pp. 8–43.

Gruber, M. and Henkel, J. 2006. "New Ventures Based on Open Innovation—An Empirical Analysis of Start-up Firms in Embedded Linux." *International Journal of Technology Management*, 33 (4): pp. 356–372.

Hall, B. H. and Ziedonis, R. H. 2001. "The Patent Paradox Revisited: An Empirical Study of Patenting in the US Semiconductor Industry, 1979–1995." *Rand Journal of Economics*, 32 (1): pp. 101–128.

Harison, E. and Koski, H. 2010. "Applying Open Innovation in Business Strategies: Evidence From Finnish Software Firms." *Research Policy*, 39 (3): pp. 351–359.

Henkel, J. 2009. "Champions of Revealing—The Role of Open Source Developers in Commercial Firms." *Industrial and Corporate Change*, 18 (3): pp. 435–471.

Keidel, R. W. 1995. *Seeing Organizational Patterns: A New Theory and Language Of Organizational Design*. San Francisco, CA: Berrett-Koelher Publisher.

Kemelgor, B. H. and Meek, W. R. 2008. "Employee Retention in Growth-oriented Entrepreneuerial Firms: An Exploratory Study." *Journal of Small Business Strategy*, 19 (1): pp. 74–86.

Knez, M. and Simester, D. 2001. "Firm-wide Incentives and Mutual Monitoring at Continental Airlines." *Journal of Labor Economics*, 19 (4): pp. 743–772.

Lakhani, K. R. and Von Hippel, E. 2003. "How Open Source Software Works: "Free" User-to-User Assistance." *Research Policy*, 32 (6): pp. 923–943.

Lamoreaux, N. R. and Sokoloff, K. L. 1996. "Long-term Change in the Organization of Inventive Activity." *Journal of Economic History*, 56 (2): pp. 494–495.

Lamoreaux, N. R. and Sokoloff, K. L. 1999. "Inventors, Firms, and the Market for Technology in the Late Nineteenth and Early Twentieth Centuries." NBER Historical Working Paper No. 98.

Lerner, J. and Tirole, J. 2002. "Some Simple Economics of Open Source." *Journal of Industrial Economics*, 50 (2): pp. 197–234.

Levin, R. C., Klevorick, A. K., Nelson, R. R., and Winter, S. G. 1987. "Appropriating the Returns from Industrial-research and Development." *Brookings Papers on Economic Activity*, (3): pp. 783–831.

Markides, C. 2008. *Game-changing Strategies: How to Create New Market Space in Established Industries by Breaking the Rules*. New York: Jossey-Bass.

Massa, L. and Tucci, C. L. 2014. "Business Model Innovation." In M. Dodgson, D. M. Gann, and N. Phillips (eds), *The Oxford Handbook of Innovation Management*, pp. 420–441. Oxford: Oxford University Press.

Matusik, S. F. and Heeley, M. B. 2005, "Absorptive Capacity in the Software Industry: Identifying Dimensions that Affect Knowledge and Knowledge Creation Activities." *Journal of Management*, 31 (4): pp. 549–572.

McMullen, J. S. and Shepherd, D. A. 2006. "Entrepreneurial Action and the Role of Uncertainty in the Theory of the Entrepreneur." *Academy of Management Review*, 31 (1): pp. 132–152.

Mintzberg, H. 1979. *The Structuring of Organizations: A Synthesis of the Research*. Englewood Cliffs, NJ: Prentice-Hall.

Moody, G. 2001. *Rebel Code—Inside Linux and the Open Source Revolution*. Cambridge, MA: Perseus Publishing.

O'Mahony, S. and Bechkym, B. A. 2008. "Boundary Organizations: Enabling Collaboration Among Unexpected Allies." *Administrative Science Quarterly*, 53 (3): pp. 422–459.

O'Mahony, S. and Ferraro, F. 2007. "The Emergence of Governance in an Open Source Community." *Academy of Management Journal*, 50 (5): pp. 1079–1106.

Osterloh, M. and Rota, S. 2007. "Open Source Software Development—Just Another Case of Collective Invention?" *Research Policy*, 36 (2): pp. 157–171.

Perr, J., Appleyard, M. M., and Sullivan, P. 2010. "Open for Business: Emerging Business Models in Open Source Software." *International Journal of Technology Management*, 52 (3–4): pp. 432–456.

Pollock, N. and Williams, R. 2009. *Software and Organisations: The Biography of the Enterprise-wide System or How SAP Conquered the World*. London and New York: Routledge.

Raymond, E. S. 2001. "A Brief Story of Hackerdrom." In E. S. Raymond (ed.), *The Cathedral and the Bazaar: Musings on Linux and Open Source by an Accidental Revolutionary*. Sebastopol, CA: O'Reilly & Associates.

Santos, J. F. P., Spector, B. A., and Van der Heyden, L. 2015. Chapter 3, this volume. "Toward a Theory of Business Model Change."

Sheehan, J., Martinez, C., and Guellec, D. 2004. Understanding Business Patenting And Licensing: Results Of A Survey. Patents, Innovation and Economic Performance–Proceedings of an OECD Conference, 4: pp. 89–110.

Simsek, Z. 2009. "Organizational Ambidexterity: Towards a Multilevel Understanding." *Journal of Management Studies*, 46 (4): pp. 597–624.

Sine, W. D., Mitsuhashi, H., and Kirsch, D. A. 2006. "Revisiting Burns And Stalker: Formal Structure and New Venture Performance in Emerging Economic Sectors." *Academy of Management Journal*, 49 (1): pp. 121–132.

Stallman, R. 1984–last update. "The GNU Manifesto." Retrieved November 2014 at: <http://www.gnu.org/gnu/manifesto.html>.

Stinchcombe, A. L. 1965. "Social Structure and Organizations." In J. G. March (ed.), *Handbook of Organizations*. New York, NY: Rand McNally, pp. 142–193.

Teece, D. J. 1986. "Profiting from Technological Innovation—Implications for Integration, Collaboration, Licensing and Public-Policy." *Research Policy*, 15 (6): pp. 285–305.

Teece, D. J. 2010. "Business Models, Business Strategy and Innovation." *Long Range Planning*, 43 (2–3): pp. 172–194.

Thoma, G. 2009. "Striving for a Large Market: Evidence from a General Purpose Technology in Action." *Industrial and Corporate Change*, 18 (1): pp. 107–138.

Trimi, S. and Berbegal-Mirabent, J. 2012. "Business Model Innovation in Entrepreneurship." *International Entrepreneurship and Management Journal*, 8(4): pp. 449–465.

Unger, J. M., Rauch, A., Frese, M., and Rosenbusch, N. 2011. "Human Capital and Entrepreneurial Success: A Meta-analytical Review." *Journal of Business Venturing*, 26 (3): pp. 341–358.

Van De Vrande, V., De Jong, J. P. J., Vanhaverbeke, W., and De Rochemont, M. 2009. "Open Innovation in SMEs: Trends, Motives and Management Challenges." *Technovation*, 29 (6–7): pp. 423–437.

Von Hippel, E. and Von Krogh, G. 2006. "Free Revealing and the Private-collective Model for Innovation Incentives." *R & D Management*, 36 (3): pp. 295–306.

Von Krogh, G., Haefliger, S., Spaeth, S., and Wallin, M. W. 2012. "Carrots and Rainbows: Motivation and Social Practice in Open Source Software Development." *MIS Quarterly*, 36 (2): pp. 649–676.

Weber, S. 2004. "*The Success of Open Source*." Cambridge, MA: Harvard University Press.

Weick, K. E. 1993. "The Collapse of Sensemaking in Organizations—the Mann Gulch Disaster." *Administrative Science Quarterly*, 38 (4): pp. 628–652.

West, J. and O'Mahony, S. 2008a. "The Role of Participation Architecture in Growing Sponsored Open Source Communities." *Industry and Innovation*, 15 (2): pp. 145–168.

West, J. and O'Mahony, S. 2008b. "The Role of Participation Architecture in Growing Sponsored Open Source Communities." *Industry and Innovation*, 15 (2): pp. 145–168.

Williamson, O. E. 1983. "Credible Commitments: Using Hostages to Support Exchange." *The American Economic Review*, 73 (4): pp. 519–540.

Zenger, T. R. 1994. "Explaining Organizational Diseconomies of Scale in Research-and-Development—Agency Problems and the Allocation of Engineering Talent, Ideas, and Effort by Firm Size." *Management Science*, 40 (6): pp. 708–729.

Zott, C. and Amit, R. 2007. "Business Model Design and the Performance of Entrepreneurial Firms." *Organization Science*, 18 (2): pp. 181–199.

Zott, C. and Amit, R. 2008. "The Fit Between Product Market Strategy and Business Model: Implications for Firm Performance." *Strategic Management Journal*, 29 (1): pp. 1–26.

Zott, C., Amit, R., and Massa, L. 2011. "The Business Model: Recent Developments and Future Research." *Journal of Management*, 37 (4): pp. 1019–1042.

Zuniga, M.P. and Guellec, D. 2008. *"Survey On Patent Licensing: Initial Results From Europe And Japan."* Paris: OECD.

10 Service-driven Business Model Innovation

Organizing the Shift from a Product-based to a Service-centric Business Model

DANIEL KINDSTRÖM AND
CHRISTIAN KOWALKOWSKI

Introduction

Firms in diverse industries have set out to transform their business models from product-based to service-centric ones. In the facilities management industry, firms like Johnson Controls and Siemens increasingly offer energy contracting with performance guarantees rather than focusing on equipment sales, and in the materials handling industry, firms like Toyota increasingly sell fixed-price rental plans rather than trucks and spare parts. The trend is driven by external factors, such as product commoditization, low-cost competition, and growing saturation on product markets (Spring and Araujo, 2013), as well as internal motivations, such as more stable revenues and opportunities for differentiation and stronger customer relationships (Eggert et al., 2014; Kowalkowski et al., 2012). In order to sustain growth and ensure competitive advantage, firms increasingly move from selling products to providing new value-adding services and customer solutions that better address customer needs. Such service-driven transformation goes beyond individual service initiatives; it is a large-scale change that involves reviewing the mission and strategies of the firm, and thus its overall business model (Kindström, 2010). In their identification of priorities for service research, Ostrom et al. (2010) highlight the need for research on business models for growth and expansion based on service. According to the CEO of Siemens, Europe's largest engineering group, in reference to innovative services, "You will see different business models evolving around this ... In terms of competitiveness, this is a key factor where you can differentiate yourself" (Schäfer and Milne, 2010).

Although there is no universal agreement on what constitutes a business model (Zott, Amit, and Massa, 2011), it generally includes elements such as market offering, organizational structure, processes, customer relationships, and value network (e.g., Chesbrough, 2007). Service-driven transformation, and other changes in the business model (for interesting examples, see, e.g., Rasmussen and Foss on the pharma industry (chapter 12), and Bogers, Sund, and Villarroel on the European postal industry (chapter 13), both in this volume), is frequently referred to as a business model innovation (e.g., Chesbrough, 2010; Amit and Zott, 2012). A case in point for a firm pursuing service-driven business model innovation is Xerox; the firm, teetering on the brink of bankruptcy in 2001, pursued a service transformation from selling office equipment to optimizing business process operations. Today, over 80 percent of total revenue is annuity-based revenue that includes contracted services, equipment maintenance, consumable supplies, and financing services. In this chapter, we define business model innovation as changes in the business model, resulting in a new-to-the-firm (that, of course, also may be new-to-the-industry) configuration of business model elements, opening opportunities for novel benefits for the firm, its customers, and/or other actors in the value network.

By analysing how market-leading firms organize when transforming their product-based business models to more service-centric ones, our objective is to identify key organizational issues in service-driven business model innovation. A better understanding of this fundamental shift is timely from both a theoretical and managerial point of view. Even if a firm can use its existing business model and innovation resources and capabilities to take advantage of current product-based opportunities, firms seldom understand how the resources and capabilities that underpin manufacturing extend to enable an increased focus on service and associated opportunities (Spring and Araujo, 2013; Ulaga and Reinartz, 2011). Prior studies have shown that product-based firms generally struggle to make this shift (cf. Fang, Palmatier, and Steenkamp, 2008; Gebauer, Fleisch, and Friedli, 2005; Ulaga and Reinartz, 2011). Therefore, firms must develop service-related resources and capabilities (den Hertog, Van der Aa, and de Jong, 2010; Martin and Horne, 1993) and reconfigure fundamental elements of their business models (Amit and Zott, 2012; Kindström, 2010).

In essence, firms need to think in terms of business model innovation in order to address the challenge of an increased focus on service, and they need to address not only the uniqueness or newness of the offering but other elements of the business model as well (Amara, Landry, and Doloreux, 2009; Bessant and Davies, 2007; Drejer, 2004). These challenges differ from those related to product-based business model innovation; aspects such as the delivery process and system, customer interfaces, and the value network (de Jong and Vermeulen, 2003; Stieglitz and Foss, chapter 6, this volume) become more pronounced. Business success in this changing setting consequently depends as much on various organizational rearrangements, such as a new structures and new incentive systems, as it does on the actual creation of new services (Oliva and Kallenberg, 2003). For example, successful firms tend to establish new central and local organizational units for service development, sales, and delivery as they amend their business model and expand their service business (Gebauer and Kowalkowski, 2012). Similarly, firms failing to capitalize on their service business may revert to their previous organizational structure (Gebauer and Kowalkowski, 2012). In addition, firms increasingly resort to value constellations with external actors for service provision (Kowalkowski, Witell, and Gustafsson, 2013). Furthermore, shifting the mindset and the organizational culture to that of providing service is also put forward as a challenge for many product firms (Gebauer and Friedli, 2005).

Method and Data

In this chapter a synthesizing research process is adopted (similar to that adopted by Storbacka et al., 2013), meaning that we use (synthesize) data from several previous research projects. Thus we did not collect new empirical data for this research; rather, our study relies on merging previously collected data into emerging themes. We draw on a multitude of case studies from the research projects and combine them for this research. When identifying and selecting firms, that is, cases, from the research projects to be included in this particular research a number of specific characteristics were used. The firms needed to: (1) extensively pursue activities related to services and service innovation, (2) strategically work with service infusion initiatives, and (3) openly grant access to key respondents at different hierarchical levels (including customers). Not all firms participating in the research projects were included. Brief information regarding the chosen firms can be found in Table 10.1.

The firms included represent industries such as avionics and defence, commercial vehicles, fluid handling, forklift trucks, industrial gas, industrial machinery, mining and construction equipment, roll bearings, and telecoms. Their customers include leading multinationals, as well as small and medium-sized firms.

More than 100 in-depth interviews were carried out in the included research projects with more than twenty workshops and focus group meetings being held (with multiple respondents from one or several firms) both to validate data and to present and discuss preliminary analyses. The interviews and workshops were carried out between 2004 and 2013. Respondents and workshop participants tended to be managers at different hierarchical positions, representing different organizational units, such as service

Table 10.1 The firms included in the synthesizing process

Firm	Core product business	Typical service offering*
AGA/Linde Gas	Industrial gases	Continuous supply of gas, inspection
ABB Robotics	Industrial robots	Maintenance and process services
Ericsson	Telecom products	Managed services, consulting, and optimization
Metso	Mining equipment	Process consulting and maintenance contracts
Saab	Aircrafts and related parts	Maintenance services
Sandvik Coromant	Tools for the metalworking industry	Engineering and training services
Toyota Material Handling Europe	Warehouse trucks	Long-term rental plans and maintenance contracts
Volvo Group	Commercial heavy vehicles	Maintenance contracts
Xylem	Industrial pumps	Monitoring and control, maintenance contracts

*Spare parts provision not included.

development, service delivery, sales, marketing, top management, product development, pricing, and key accounts.

This synthesizing research process adopted supported iterations between empirical data and theory, in an abductive process (Dubois and Gadde, 2002). This process should ensure a firm grounding in both empirical reality and managerial challenges, as well as providing in-depth considerations of the theoretical frameworks. The data analysis primarily adopted a pattern-matching logic where the authors first performed within-case analyses before merging them in cross-case analyses (Eisenhardt, 1989). In this analysis the business model framework functioned as a structuring tool.

Business Model Innovation and the Business Model

Business model innovation is a process where a firm introduces changes into its business model in order to realign it to fit a new competitive landscape. Technology becomes obsolete, customer demands change, and new value propositions emerge (see, e.g., Casadesus-Masanell and Ricart, 2010). These are all examples of occurrences that drive such changes. Furthermore, these changes might emanate from different (and new) actors and in different parts of the firm. As a consequence, firms need to change their business models. In this business model innovation process, as firms react to changes, they become, over time, more and more adept in matching their current environment. Through this process they become more stable and efficient but also run the risk of becoming rigid (Doz and Kosonen, 2010). Due to path-dependent behaviors, they also run the risk of becoming constrained in how they approach value creation (Bohnsacka, Pinkse, and Kolk, 2014). Thus, business model innovation needs to be an ongoing process and firms need to be strategically agile (Doz and Kosonen, 2010), develop dynamic capabilities (Teece, 2007), and reinvent themselves continuously.

A business model innovation can also disrupt an entire market, or industry, and the inherent business logic of that market or industry (see, e.g., Markides, chapter 7, this volume; Saebi, chapter 8, this volume). Typical examples of the potential disruptiveness of this process include the computer manufacturer Dell with its build-to-order business model that redefined the computer industry, and online bookseller Amazon.com's disintermediation model that not only redefined the book industry but also influenced how firms in general did business online.

Regardless of the scope of the changes, dynamic changes to the business model over time must be initiated for a firm to succeed (Teece, 2007). Unless established firms are able to innovate their business model there is an evident risk that they will be left behind as new actors take the lead with more innovative offerings, operational processes, or underlying business models (Bessant and Davies, 2007). Examples here are many but a good case in point is the Finnish mobile phone manufacturer Nokia, who has lost its seemingly insurmountable lead in the mobile phone market to new actors such as Apple and Samsung due to its inability to adjust to changes in, or shape, the competitive landscape.

The concept of the business model offers a useful analysis framework for understanding the firm and its component parts (Amit and Zott, 2001; Chesbrough and Rosenbloom, 2002). Although it is possible to identify a number of different conceptualizations, as well as more generic business models in what are sometimes called business model archetypes (Zott, Amit, and Massa, 2011), each firm has its own, unique model that recounts how it creates and captures value (sometimes called appropriation mechanisms). For a firm, adopting a more holistic business model approach can help it to sustain competitive advantages by reducing imitability, as competitors find it difficult to isolate and copy individual elements of an integrated business model (Porter, 1996). A business model that exhibits consistency across elements has greater potential to create long-term competitive advantage (Chesbrough, 2007). A successful service-driven business model innovation process indeed implies that firms address several elements of their business model and understand how they are interconnected (Galbraith, 2002; Neu and Brown, 2008; Kindström, 2010).

To conceptualize a business model, in this chapter, we begin with five fundamental business model elements, each linked to underlying resources and capabilities: offering, process, customer relationships, value network, and culture (cf., e.g., Chesbrough, 2007; Chesbrough and Rosenbloom, 2002). Given that many firms experience difficulties, such as not being able to communicate the value of services to customers and to get access to the needed resources when selling and delivering services in product-centric firms (Kindström and Kowalkowski, 2009; Ulaga and Reinartz, 2011), the process element is further divided into three distinct processes—development, sales, and delivery— each with specific organizational requirements. Culture is a "softer" business model element than the others, and it is generally not included in established conceptualizations of a business model. Yet it remains key to successful service initiatives and product-based firms frequently struggle with this intangible element when organizing the shift to a service-centric business model. Hence, putting culture as an explicit business model element is a means of highlighting its pivotal role as an important organizational factor in the shift.

The business model framework captures both internal and external elements, as well as the actual offering, and also addresses value creation and value capture (see, e.g., Baden-Fuller and Morgan, 2010; Teece, 2010). We derive, as mentioned earlier, the elements of the business model from previous literature (Chesbrough, 2007), but also link it to the analyses and insights gained from our studies of product-centric firms, and these elements are seen as generic and relevant to all firms.

Toward a Service-centric Business Model

For established firms with mature product-based business models, moving toward services is often a time-consuming and complex process since these firms often have an established business model that needs to be considered and that might be difficult to change (at least in the short term) in a radical fashion due to such things as path dependencies and organizational inertia (Kowalkowski et al., 2012; Bohnsacka, Pinkse, and Kolk, 2014). Smith, Binns, and Tushman (2010) refer to this as a complex business model that can be paradoxical in the sense that firms might need to address multiple strategies and business models, which are, in the words of Lewis (2000) "contradictory, yet interrelated" (in Smith, Binns, and Tushman, 2010: 450).

A resulting new business model can however very well be radically different from the old business model but, as said, the change process typically takes longer. Albeit simplified, a typical illustration of that process sees it as shifting gradually toward increased service content in an incremental movement on a continuum from one opposite—where services are considered as merely an add-on to a tangible good—toward the other opposite, where services form the very centre of the value proposition (Oliva and Kallenberg, 2003). Such a shift is typically referred to as service infusion or servitization (Baron, Warnaby, and Hunter-Jones, 2014).

Prior research has reported, variously, that understanding how to approach the development of new services constitutes a major hurdle in realigning a manufacturing firm's business model toward services (Martin and Horne, 1993); that a clear service development process and extensive knowledge of market conditions and customer needs will have a positive impact on the service business (Gebauer, Fleisch, and Friedli, 2005); that a more complete offering usually involves more service components, thus emphasizing the need to address service development; and that the reality—and thus the challenge—for many industrial companies is how to develop both products and services simultaneously. Other studies see developing a separate organizational unit to manage service offerings as a critical success factor for manufacturing firms intending to move toward a service-centric business model (see, e.g., Oliva and Kallenberg, 2003). However, isolating service operations and personnel from product-related activities may create obstacles to accessing the full range of intra-firm capabilities and resources needed to develop and market more advanced service offerings,[1] when it is vital to be able to integrate competences from different organizational units and cultivate intra-firm collaboration. Other studies highlight the importance of the ability of being able to include external actors in various collaborations to succeed (Agarwal and Selen, 2009).

Despite the opportunities inherent in a shift toward a service-centric business model, many firms are experiencing difficulties in realizing the promised benefits despite investing in service initiatives in various ways (Fang, Palmatier, and Steenkamp, 2008; Gebauer, Fleisch, and Friedl, 2005). Firms often end up focusing on redesigning one particular element of their business model while neglecting to realign the whole model to attain a configurational fit within its elements (Galbraith, 2002; Milgrom and Roberts, 1990). This has been referred to as the service paradox (Gebauer, Fleisch, and Friedl, 2005) and a profitability hurdle (Visnjic and Van Looy, 2013); many firms, often due to a strong product orientation and a focus on high-quality products, do not take a strategic perspective on the service business and often underestimate the difficulties in implementing a more service-centric business model. Instead, resources are allocated and investments made without a strategic congruence and intent throughout the firm. By taking a business model perspective and by acknowledging that a shift toward service needs aligning changes in many parts of the organization, we argue that firms vastly increase their chances of success and sustained profitability as well as achieving long-term competitive advantage.

THE ORGANIZATIONAL DIMENSION

As noted, the challenges of changing from a product-based to a more service-centric business model are often related to organizational factors. An inadequate organizational structure inhibits service initiatives; an appropriate structure facilitates it. Thus, an increased focus on services may require firms to change their organizational structure. For product-centric firms,

---

[1] Here, and in most research, a distinction is drawn between basic services, such as traditional repair and spare parts supply, and more advanced ones, such as full-service contracts and various availability- and performance-based solutions.

establishing separate service units within existing product units is generally seen as a first step in the service infusion process. However, it is rarely a long-term solution; despite equal formal authority, it is difficult for service divisions to achieve equal attention and commitment in a product-centric unit (Gebauer and Kowalkowski, 2012). A logical second step for many firms is thus the establishment of a distinct business unit with profit-and-loss accounting and responsibility for strategic service development (Oliva, Gebauer, and Brann, 2012). To pursue collaborative activities with customers and offer advanced services to a wide extent, firms such as Ericsson and Toyota Material Handling go even further and establish specific, customer-focused units that can be supported by a key-account-management approach (Gebauer and Kowalkowski, 2012). Such hybrid organizational approaches require close collaboration and linkages between product and service units (Neu and Brown, 2008), including shared understanding of customers and market conditions. Close collaboration between the service and product units also helps to clarify common approaches to address customer needs and prevents conflicts between the product and service businesses (Gebauer and Kowalkowski, 2012).

Another requirement is to find a structure and associated roles that provide a balance between exploitation (i.e., using existing capabilities efficiently) and exploration (i.e., creating new offerings and market spaces that stretch capabilities) (Lisboa, Skarmeas, and Lages, 2011; Day, 2007). Exploitation tends to be more vital for basic services, whereas exploration focuses on more advanced ones (Westerlund and Rajala, 2010); both are essential for extensive services (Kowalkowski, Kindström, and Brehmer, 2011a). Exploitation benefits from global integration, and exploration benefits from local responsiveness (Prahalad and Doz, 1988), especially when a firm provides services. For effective leveraging and sharing of technical and customer-specific knowledge and development and deployment of new services, firms must balance local and central forces and avoid either autonomous local units or rigid, centralized structures (Bartlett and Ghoshal, 2000). In turn, formal structures and various forms of informal structures are essential (Kowalkowski, Kindström, and Brehmer, 2011a). Overall, the role of the local organization is often more vital in a service-centric business model. For example, the role of local front-stage employees is more important for idea generation and customer inputs when innovating a service (Bitrain and Pedrosa, 1998). Gallouj and Weinstein (1997) in their research indicate that many service innovations do indeed emerge ad hoc, in iterative processes of trial and error close to the customer.

Service-driven Changes in the Business Model Elements—Empirical Findings

Drawing on marketing and management theory as well as the empirical analyses, this chapter, as outlined in Foss and Saebi in chapter 1 in this volume,

Business Model Elements

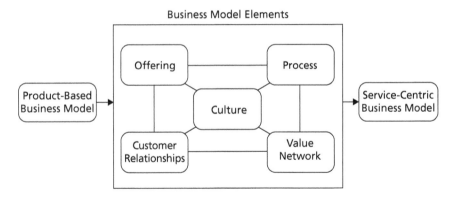

Figure 10.1 Shift to service-driven business model innovation

investigates organizational design aspects of business model innovation, such as focusing on how reward systems and other aspects of organizational structure and control (such as local vs. global) can be designed to support a service-centric business model. Also discussed are how the firm's often product-oriented organizational structures, capabilities, and culture can influence a firm's ability to innovate in relation to their new business models, and whether they need to change in order to do this. These important organizational aspects of business models and the innovation thereof have so far been missing from the literature (Foss and Saebi, chapter 1, this volume). The findings are structured in consonance with the five business model elements previously established; offering, processes, customer relationships, value network, and culture. All five elements have to be addressed in order to organize and manage the shift from a product-based to a service-centric business model, as illustrated in Figure 10.1.

OFFERING

The first business model element, the offering, is traditionally closely associated with service-related initiatives and especially the development of new service concepts. Services encompass a great diversity of offerings, from basic field services to extensive customer solutions that integrate a wide range of internal and third-party services and products.

For developing attractive offerings, an important organizational resource, which most product-centric firms possess, is an existing customer base. Customers do not go straight from being strangers to close partners (Johnson and Selnes, 2004), so an existing customer base, albeit only for product sales, is needed. Firms then can use this resource to become more service-centric by, for instance, shifting to more advanced services gradually. Another related key asset is the installed base of products, which product-centric firms can employ to systematically collect product usage and process data (Ulaga and Reinartz, 2011) and thus use as an important stepping stone in implementing a service-centric business model. The analyzed data can explicate each customer's process and identify new service opportunities. Particularly if the total installed base greatly exceeds the number of installations with a single customer, the firm can obtain a unique information advantage over pure service players and customers. New service concepts also increasingly rely on the development of information and communication technologies (ICT) (Gago and Rubalcaba, 2007). Bundling technology into the products must also address the systems and applications used for service provision. Therefore, ICT capabilities are required to exploit internal and external technological opportunities for new offerings. Yet a major challenge, particularly for heavily engineering-driven firms, is to avoid the temptation to put technology rather than the customer in the driver's seat when developing new offerings.

Because the requirements for different services in the firm's portfolio vary greatly, the firm must understand what services to offer, how to develop a coherent portfolio, and how extensive its service portfolio should be—what we refer to as offering portfolio management (cf. Eggert et al., 2014). Demand varies across markets, so managers must decide how standardized services should be. Another aspect is the issue of product–service integration: With a base in manufacturing and frequent bundling of services and products into more extensive offerings, firms should foster and employ strategic linkages between their services and products to achieve synergies for value creation through their offerings (Kowalkowski, 2011). Furthermore, as Dachs et al. (2013) empirically show, service innovation can trigger product innovation, and vice versa. Feedback from service operations is an important information source for product development (Goh and McMahon, 2009) and can enable the development of attractive new offerings.

Product usage and process data from the customers (existing customers and the installed base) are key inputs also when creating new revenue models, often an important part of implementing a service-centric business model, which then can become better aligned with the customer's value-creation processes, including availability-based and performance-based contracts. To succeed with such offerings, new revenue models are needed that enable the supplying firm to capture a fair share of the created value. Extensive knowledge of the technical system or subsystem of which the service is part is a related resource. This is referred to as service relatedness, that is, to what degree the service is related to the product, and is seen as contributing to increased firm value (Fang, Palmatier, and Steenkamp, 2008). The service often gets interlinked with other services, products, and subsystems that set the scope for what can be offered and how the firm can charge for it. Seamless offerings can provide the firm with increased flexibility regarding possible revenue models.

Pricing becomes important to determine how to charge for new services and possibly change the revenue model of existing services, such as moving from free to fee (Pauwels and Weiss, 2008; Witell and Löfgren, 2013). Many product-centric firms that traditionally gave away services for free to support their product sales struggle to start charging for them (Reinartz and Ulaga, 2008). Resistance may come not only from existing customers but also internally from sales companies. To alter revenue models (or lack thereof) or introduce new ones, firms also need a value-visualization capability. They can choose from various strategies and methods that might convince potential customers of the value-in-use and thus the benefits of the revenue model (Anderson, Kumar, and Narus, 2007; Kindström, Kowalkowski, and Nordin, 2012). Finally, a risk assessment and mitigation capability is required to manage the risks associated with service provision (Ulaga and Reinartz, 2011), particularly if the firm offers advanced services with availability- and performance-based revenue models or an extensive service portfolio with a diverse set of revenue models.

PROCESSES: DEVELOPMENT, SALES, AND DELIVERY

Development

Service development, as well as sales and delivery, are processes critical for the shift to a service-centric business model. To the extent that product-centric firms work systematically with services, it generally involves concept development, with several similarities with new product development (NPD). As one senior manager expressed it, "business development has always been synonymous with product development." Whereas NPD projects generally are heavy at the back, successful new service development (NSD) projects need to be heavy at the front; that is, firms need to ensure their rollout (Kindström and Kowalkowski, 2009). Many firms, including world-leading manufacturers, fail to commercialize their novel services due to their insufficient knowledge and skills, resources, and commitment in the sales and delivery phases. The risk of failure is particularly high if the firm blueprints complex NPD models without recognizing the differences between product and service development. The adoption of an NSD strategy also has substantial performance effects (Edvardsson et al., 2013). Firms such as the Volvo Group, therefore, develop distinct NSD processes and strategies, out of the recognition that rigid structures, processes, and routines—common to NPD projects—fail to account for the flexibility requirements for successful service development. In this sense, NSD models need a more flexible, iterative process, with extensive customer involvement (e.g., co-design methodologies), to ensure sufficient resources and competences for sales and delivery, as well as cross-functional and local–central involvement. Lead users for ideation, co-design, evaluation, and implementation and dedicated service development roles with necessary authority (service champions; Martin and Horne, 1993) are additional key organizational resources for successful NSD.

To take advantage of users and not just identify the "right" customers in NSD and pilot projects, the firm needs the capability and a complementary organizational structure to engage actively with them throughout all stages of the customer product and service lifecycles (Vandermerwe, 1994). An internal sensing capability refers to the ability to detect and support decentralized service initiatives (Kindström, Kowalkowski, and Sandberg, 2013). Whereas product development tends to be managed centrally and driven by technology, service development often takes place locally in interaction with key customers. Service innovation is rarely a planned NSD process; rather, services are frequently developed ad hoc (Gallouj and Weinstein, 1997; Kowalkowski et al., 2012). In multinational firms in particular, it can be difficult for central service managers to develop a comprehensive overview and understanding of local service activities and thus a decentralization of the authority for developing services is often necessary. Formalization and replication processes are therefore critical for formalizing, specifying, and standardizing services, as well as to take advantage of what Davies and Brady (2000) call economies of repetition, to deliver future services at lower costs and more effectively. The latter includes making professional expertise concrete and systematizing processes and methods (Jaakkola, 2011).

Sales

A major hurdle for product-centric firms to overcome is finding a way to sell their novel services. Edvardsson et al. (2013) determined that, of more than 500 NSD projects, the rate of new services introduced to the market and then withdrawn due to low sales was as high as 43 percent. Despite the common opinion that "what gets measured gets done," to the frustration of service managers, incentive systems and metrics are frequently still product-centric. Alignment between the incentive systems and the strategic service objectives of the firm is thus needed to promote service sales and change the behavior of a product-centric sales force (Reinartz and Ulaga, 2008; Shah et al., 2006). Other critical resources include customer involvement (customers must be willing to share insights to elaborate the value proposition) and inputs from the field service organization (e.g., new sales opportunities). Field technicians interact frequently with customers, and customers tend to trust them more (especially if they are located full-time on customer sites), which makes them a key resource for service sales (Ulaga and Reinartz, 2011). Developing coordination and integration mechanisms enabling cooperation between different organizational units during sales becomes an important activity. These mechanisms can be relatively simple, such as encouraging ride-alongs between sales and service roles, but can also be more advanced with cross-functional ICT systems as well as aligning incentive systems to consider cooperation. Back-office specialist support is another increasingly important organizational role, comprising not only traditional tools, such as customer relationship management systems, but also sophisticated support, such as SKF's Documented Solution Program.

For extensive service sales, particularly those combining products with services, we thus see that internal coordination is required (Gebauer and Kowalkowski, 2012). Coordination between the sales and field service organizations becomes essential, often leading to increased involvement of the service organization in the sales process. For example, to sell long-term rental plans, a Toyota service sales manager (service organization), a sales account manager (sales organization), and a project manager might need to work together. In addition, rental managers may work alongside their colleagues to ensure that the sales force has the necessary skills and is comfortable selling rental contracts. This can necessitate new skills geared toward team leading and group dynamics.

Many existing salespeople are unfamiliar with, and uncomfortable communicating the value of services (Kindström, Kowalkowski, and Nordin, 2012), and customers also find this type of value difficult to grasp and evaluate in advance. Additionally, traditional product salespeople often do not fit the competence profile required (Ulaga and Reinartz, 2011). As services (particularly complex ones) become more important, the salesperson needs to work more closely with the customer as a problem solver. In many cases, there might not be pre-defined solutions to the customer-specific problem. Although the service sales process is not necessarily more complex, it is generally longer. For large-scale services of strategic importance to customers, the sales process also requires interactions with decision makers at higher levels in the customer organization.

Delivery

A field service network is a prerequisite for successful service delivery. Services can be delivered through an internal arrangement, an external arrangement, or a through a combination of the two in a hybrid arrangement. For example, a firm might provide services in-house in one market and work with partners in another. It can also choose to provide some services in-house, particularly strategically important ones, and let partners provide services that are less important or that the firm lacks the resources to provide. Factors that determine the organizational arrangement can be classified as firm-, market-, or offering-specific (Kowalkowski, Kindström, and Witell, 2011b). If the firm understands the pros and cons of each arrangement, it can design an arrangement and delivery process that fits it. From a service point of view, *ceteris paribus*, an internal arrangement is preferable. Firms like Toyota Material Handling have deliberately internalized most of their service provision due to high service volumes and utilization rate, which makes internalization economically viable, and allows for better control and direct customer relationships on a day-to-day basis.

Recruiting and maintaining skilled technicians can prove challenging due to scarce human resources, particularly for remote locations such as mines in the Amazonas area or in the far northern parts of Scandinavia. An adaptable back-office infrastructure with clever ICT systems can enable not only more cost-efficient operations but also higher service quality, through better resource allocation and more accurate information sharing among the service staff. Customer involvement is another key resource; many services involve frequent (or continuous) interactions. Service delivery should be viewed as an ongoing customer–supplier relationship (Tuli, Kohli, and Bharadwaj, 2007), in which trust and commitment are key routes for receiving customer feedback throughout the delivery process.

Capacity utilization and prognostication can help address the challenges of demand fluctuation and service supply constraints, which are characteristic of many services (Lovelock, 1983). To smooth out the ups and downs of demand, firms can strive for long-term service-level arrangements, in which the supplier controls and schedules preventive maintenance. Many field services can, through this, be scheduled in advance, sometimes by up to a year. To maximize expertise skills, Metso, for example, assigns global specialist teams to provide knowledge-intensive services to mining customers worldwide.

CUSTOMER RELATIONSHIPS

The development of strong customer relationships on both firm and personal levels is often a key benefit of an internal service business and an important enabler for a service-centric business model. Because service innovation ought to be conducted from the perspective of the customers' value creation (Skålén et al., 2014), close relationships are a prerequisite. Consider the field service organization, where reps work together with customers. Although some firms opt for service provision mainly through external partners, "owning" the customer interface through an in-house service organization is a key asset for product-centric firms. Tuli, Kohli, and Bharadwaj (2007) highlight customer counselling and adaptiveness as key factors for successful customer solutions; we contend that these resources are vital for less complex services too. Customers' provision of information and guidance about their operations, policies, and political landscape helps the supplier provide better services, improve customer satisfaction, and increase relationship strength. Even if the supplier firm could offer competitive services with potentially high value-in-use, the customer's purchasing strategy, processes, and organizational structure might hinder the deal (Kowalkowski, 2011). An in-depth understanding of the buying center, the relationships of its members, and the internal political landscape is therefore needed.

Another prerequisite for many services is customer embeddedness, which refers to the firm's ability to develop close, long-term relationships. To increase embeddedness, firms must understand expressed and latent customer needs and be able to issue segment- and customer-specific value propositions

(Anderson and Narus, 1991; Storbacka et al., 2013). Firms such as Ericsson and Volvo, which have successfully established independent service units, have increased their customer focus by establishing customer-facing, front-end units (see also Davies, Brady, and Hobday, 2006). This organizational change can be described in matrix form: on the horizontal axis, companies distinguish between product and service business units, while the vertical axis describes different customer-focused business units (Gebauer and Kowalkowski, 2012). These units generally have strong resource flexibility for providing different types of products and services. One form of customer-focused unit is the traditional key-account-management (KAM) organization. For example, driven by the consolidation and centralization of its major customers, Toyota is experiencing a continuous increase in the number of key account-focused units, both nationally and regionally, as well as globally. The firm therefore finds it vital both to have a broad spectrum of services and financing alternatives available and to have the same service levels and terms and conditions regardless of local market. This is particularly important for multinational customers, such as Ikea. As a result, Toyota's customer-focused strategic business units have become more important and have greater internal leverage than only a decade ago.

VALUE NETWORK

A firm's resources include those it can exploit from other actors in its value network. Firms are embedded in networks of interconnected relationships that form a web of interactions, and this network extends far beyond the customer–supplier dyad. Within the network, firms deliberately work together in relationships with distinct structures that reflect intentionally created constellations of actors, referred to as value constellations, to mobilize value creation (Normann, 2001). For example, a distribution network or other types of value constellations can be powerful resources for firms that operate through dealers and service partners to mobilize value creation (Kowalkowski, Witell, and Gustafsson, 2013). In addition to providing service sales and delivery, it can offer critical information about customers, service operations, and the market. However, a disadvantage of an external arrangement regarding the service delivery structure is the lack of a direct customer interface, which offers a key resource for service innovation. Without a direct customer interface, it becomes difficult to develop the relationship and succeed with new services.

Other network-related resources that benefit service innovation are a specialist supplier base to access resources for innovation, such as software and hardware specialist skills, and influencer relationships to understand and influence a diverse range of actors, including business press and media, environmental groups, political and government agencies, unions, industry bodies, regulatory bodies, and financial and investor groups (Payne, Ballantyne, and Christopher, 2005).

Orchestration is an overarching capability, referring to an ability to manage and transform value constellations within the network, especially external actors that are central to service performance (cf. resource orchestration). It includes the ability to extend the resource base into new markets and services, incorporate complementary resources and co-specialization, and reconfigure roles, resources, locus of control, and power in the network (Kindström, Kowalkowski, and Sandberg, 2013). This is closely related to the notion of dynamic capabilities. The concept of dynamic capabilities views sustainable competitive advantage as the ability to create, extend, and modify valuable resources and capabilities over time (Helfat et al., 2007) and revolves around reconfiguring and changing an existing resource based in order to take advantage of new emerging opportunities (Teece, 2007). However, whereas dynamic capabilities depart in the recourse-based view of the firm, which (as the name indicates) is inherently firm-centric, orchestration refers to the mobilization of value creation through interactions and resource integration with other firms in the value network (Normann, 2001). Hence, we argue that the firm's value network, and its value constellations in particular, must be recognized as an extended resource base.

A critical issue when collaborating is that all actors perceive value creation and appropriation as equitable (Wagner, Eggert, and Lindemann, 2010); that is, costs and revenues—and other benefits and sacrifices, such as risk, responsibilities, and customer relationships—must be equitably divided when services are developed and launched. A prerequisite for such successful orchestration is understanding the level and extent of the partners' knowledge. Interestingly, we found that even world-class firms can lack fundamental service-related knowledge about their dealers and pure service partners. Firms might know their partners' strengths and weaknesses regarding the product business but lack fundamental views of their competence and commitment to new service initiatives. Success demands competence and commitment not only internally in local sales companies, but also among partners in the value network.

CULTURE

Moving from a product-centric to a service-centric business logic implies a cultural shift that has profound implications for the firm. Having a product-centric logic means that the focus is on selling as many products as possible and winning market shares on predefined product markets (Shah et al., 2006). Furthermore, the purpose of services is to protect the product business. Service-centric logic, on the other hand, focuses on supporting customers' value creation; what specific products and services are included in the offering is of secondary importance (Normann, 2001). Furthermore, fostering a service culture demands attitudes and perspective toward the long term, which can be challenging because a long-term view rarely matches short-term financial goals (Payne, Storbacka, and Frow, 2008).

To drive change and establish and foster a service culture, service leadership is required. Established, engineering-driven firms often are unwilling to change from their prevailing product-centric practices, norms, and values. Leadership is also needed to attract and retain key individuals working with service. Successful firms might be unable to change direction until they stand on a "burning product platform," as the telecoms firm Nokia exemplified in 2011. The root causes of such organizational inertia include lock-in to a specific set of fixed resources, organizational inflexibility, and reluctance to cannibalize existing (product) offerings (Lieberman and Montgomery, 1998). The latter is particularly problematic if firms offer availability-based and performance-based services where the revenue model is linked to customers' value creation. Such offerings generally create strong incentives to reduce the number of products sold and installed, and might even have a disruptive effect on the traditional core business. Strategic renewal then is required to reconfigure the resource base of the firm and acquire service innovation resources and capabilities (Kindström, Kowalkowski, and Sandberg, 2013). Service leadership must also address the issue of organizational inflexibility; across firms, it is a root cause of restrained service innovation.

Here top management have a crucial role to play in leading the way and establishing the importance of both services, but also regarding the change in culture. Several firms that experience success in shifting to services have established strategic goals for services, exemplified by Volvo aiming for a 50-percent share of their turnover coming from services (or soft products, to use their terminology). In our analyses we have also seen an increased focus on service also in external communications, such as annual reports where top management increasingly mention services and thus indirectly also promote a shift in cultural values.

Whereas large-scale cultural change requires time, some measures can prompt shorter-term effects. Firms can create internal awareness of the importance and potential of adding services. In product-centric firms, services often appear merely as add-ons to the core product offering or a necessary evil for future product sales (Robinson, Clarke-Hill, and Clarkson, 2002). Terms such as "aftermarket" (Cohen, Agrawal, and Agrawal, 2006), "after-sales service" (Porter, 1980), and "post-purchase marketing" (Burger and Cann 1995) reinforce the notion that services exist to support product sales. Replacing them with terms such as "service solutions" signals a shift in mindset. The signal can be reinforced by market communication, such as a CEO's annual statement that emphasizes services, and internal communications, such as corporate newsletters (Kowalkowski, 2011).

Service champions are also valuable, because they try to nurture and protect new services, from idea stage to launch. Our findings support Martin and Horne's (1993) argument that firms should let service champions stay and manage the service into the launch phase (sales and delivery). However, senior management and other key decision makers should also be champions for the move to a service-centric business model and define clear, measurable, service-related targets. The latter point refers to the need to develop a service-oriented incentive system to facilitate execution. Product–service balancing is a final challenge, specifically for product-centric firms. A constant challenge for the firms we reviewed was the need to balance assets related to products and services, to secure the interests of both product and service units, and thereby balance the interests of a product business and a people business (Kindström, Kowalkowski, and Sandberg, 2013). As firms increasingly offer advanced services, combining services and products, they find it necessary to add systemic characteristics and integration aspects. The tension between the two cultures is a constant challenge for product-centric firms—particularly those that choose to integrate products and services into customer solutions (Oliva, Gebauer, and Brann, 2012). It is especially evident in firms that have only recently begun to focus on their service business. The product business is a core activity for product-centric firms (and must be so), such that a product-oriented core of resources and capabilities (manufacturing, R&D activities) demand ongoing, parallel management of the product and service business (Kindström, Kowalkowski, and Sandberg, 2013).

Organizing the Shift to a Service-centric Business Model

Shifting a product-based business model to a service-centric business model requires changes in several areas. Earlier research has not explicitly explored the organizational dimension in this shift. In this section we summarize the key organizational factors identified in each business element as firms shift to a service-centric business model (see Table 10.2). We also outline key managerial actions linked to each of the factors.

ESTABLISHING THE STRATEGIC DIRECTION—A KEY FIRST STEP

Achieving alignment between the business model, strategy, and organizational changes is a dynamic, transformational process that is critical for all firms, including during the shift to service-centric business models (Davies, Brady, and Hobday, 2007). Service initiatives, particularly those in incumbent firms, tend to take time before they can make a major impact (Fang, Palmetier, and Steenkamp, 2008), and managers tend to underestimate the associated complexities. Thus firms must maintain a long-term orientation and create internal awareness and a "sense of urgency" strategically. In several firms, we identify a *business cycle paradox*; that is, in times of prosperity (e.g., before the 2008 financial crisis and its aftermath), the focus tends to be

Table 10.2 Summarizing key organizational factors and corresponding managerial actions as firms move toward a service-centric business model

Business Model Element	Key Organizational Factors	Key Managerial Actions
Offering	Exploration and exploitation	Balancing resources and KPIs to take advantage of both existing and future opportunities
	Local vs central units	Enabling local units to link with the customer, developing new services, and exploiting central units for standardization and industrialization
	Integration and socialization between local and central units	Establishing integrative mechanisms (e.g., liaison roles and ICT systems) and managing interaction
Development process	Specific NSD teams	Establishing separate roles and processes for services
	Feedback from local units and customers	Introducing systems and tools that connect local units and customers with central resources for development (e.g., mobile units)
Sales process	Coordination with product sales	Preventing a division between resources devoted to service and resources devoted to products
	Incentivization sales	Developing incentive systems that take service characteristics into account (such as indirect effects, lower volume/value ratio, repetitiveness, and the relationship aspect)
	Cross-functionality	Encouraging cross-functional cooperation and coordination between, e.g., sales and service delivery
Delivery process	Internal or external delivery	Deciding what strategically needs to be kept in-house and what needs to be sourced externally (e.g., competence-wise, relationship-wise, profitability-wise)
	Local units but also pooling of central resources (e.g., IT systems and global specialists)	Managing competence development (specialization) and the development of remote services (service automation)
Customer relationship	Lead user (and other key customers) involvement in NSD and other service initiatives	Identifying lead users and establishing relationships with these
	Relationships on different levels; form local, operational to central, senior executives	Identifying key relationships on various levels in the customer organization ("turn the pyramids") and training customer facing units to manage relationships on different levels
Value network	Dealer (as well as other partners) competence and commitment	Identifying key partners and initiating training programs; developing incentive systems that also encourage partners to actively embrace services
	Different partners on different markets	Managing a diversity of value constellation—may be very different on different markets
Culture	Having a service culture	Leading by example—establishing service roles, committing to service-related KPIs, setting strategic goals based on services
	Service logic thinking	Departing from the customers' business needs, not from the internal product resource base; making clear that services do not necessarily enhance product sales—they may also have negative effects
	Established relationships between product and service units (solutions, etc.)	Preventing silo mentality product units and service units and fostering collaboration

on how to capitalize on the core (product) offering, but during recessions, few resources are available to invest in services. The lack of long-term investments then fails to reduce vulnerability to future recessions (i.e., services are generally countercyclical); instead, the focus is on saving the product business.

Frequently, strategizing for services in product-centric firms appears to offer a well-defined, rational process. However, service initiatives may be emergent, reactive responses to new customer demands or other exogenous changes (i.e., network triggers, Spring and Araujo, 2013). The longer-term time horizon makes it difficult, if not impossible, for decision makers to understand all the strategic challenges ahead, because "successful service strategy involves continuous modifications, adaptability, the seizing of ad hoc innovation, a continuous recalibration of opportunities, and the management of intertwining goals" (Kowalkowski et al., 2012: 765).

Strategic decisions also set the foundation for future possible service activities. Therefore, the firm should define whether service infusion and a move to a service-centric business model implies a transition from products to services (i.e., outsourcing of manufacturing, such as pursued by IBM) or is a matter of expanding into service and broadening the range of offerings. The latter route generally appeared in the firms we analyzed; it implies the product business will remain the focus for most parts of the organization, at least in the short and medium term, which has consequences on the design of the business model. Furthermore, the primary purpose of the service might be to support and strengthen the traditional product business (i.e., a product-centric business logic) or develop a competitive service business on its own, the latter supporting a service culture and thus providing a much better breeding ground for service. Finally, firms can decide whether to provide service only for their own products or also provide extensive services on competitors' brands, which is more challenging but also can spur innovation.

BUSINESS MODEL INNOVATION—UNDERSTANDING THE PROCESS

A strategic realignment toward investments, both strategically and operationally, in service activities must be mirrored by changes throughout the business model, such that it becomes almost a merged business model innovation process. Successful change in one element depends on corresponding changes in and realignment of other elements. For example, to provide a new specialist service for process optimization, a firm might create a distinct organizational unit responsible for its delivery, as well as a new revenue model. New customer touch points and a new sales approach also might be required. Increased customer understanding is certainly needed, as is the ability to develop relationships with new members of the buying center. Furthermore, the service might increase the utilization of products installed and enable a reduction of the overall installed base of the customer, hence leading to decreased future sales of equipment and spare and wear parts.

In general, too much emphasis is placed on developing the new service concept, without providing sufficient clarity about other business model elements. Because the inadequate alignment of elements inhibits a strategic change toward services, these shortcomings can explain why so many new initiatives fail. We have seen many examples of such cases; despite the identified potential, firms are unable to commercialize new, innovative service concepts. Service infusion processes also differ among firms and over time, as may be reflected in the magnitude of change in the business model elements. A radical change is likely to include all elements of the business model; a more incremental change might imply a shorter and more focused change, limited to certain elements. The starting point also differs: A firm with an established, in-house service organization can exploit this resource and focus on elements other than the structure or delivery process. Another firm might have a strong service concept but lack necessary service processes, capabilities, and structures to sell and deliver it. Yet another firm might have strong customer relationships that it can harness to develop customized services, launched on the basis of its unique customer insights.

Managers can use business models, and a business model innovation perspective, to visualize how and when changes might occur, which should increase internal transparency, understanding, and awareness of service opportunities and necessary changes. It is important to understand the potential dependencies among elements; a change in one is likely to affect the others. Therefore, the initial step in service-based business model innovation is to determine the current situation and identify the target position, which presents the "big picture" and supports a discussion of what the business model should look like once the target position is reached. These insights give managers a better understanding of which major changes need to take place, in which elements, and in what sequence.

Future Research Directions

With the business model approach, we derive interesting avenues for research that start from a holistic perspective incorporating these new areas (see Baron, Warnaby, and Hunter-Jones, 2014). First, as changes occur in different business model elements, finding the evolutionary patterns by which these service-driven changes unfold over time promises great potential. Second, establishing appropriate starting points for each innovation pattern, depending on various contingencies, will be of great interest to practitioners. Third, furthering understanding of the consequences of employing a multidimensional perspective of service infusion and the effects, both positive and negative, can uncover important issues. The conceptual foundations of service infusion are becoming better researched, and a natural consequence is an expansion into assessments of the effects on profits, revenues, and costs due to an increased focus on service (this is seen, to some extent, in an increase of quantitative studies such as Visnjic and Van Looy, 2013 and Eggert et al., 2014). A related question is the development of decision support systems for top management struggling to get a handle on the process.

Finally, despite progress in recent years, we still note a lack of research centered on business model innovation processes. As we have discussed in this chapter, if taken far enough, investments in service infusion initiatives realign the business model altogether toward a more service-centric version. As firms infuse more services and embark on more service activities, they can approach the process from different starting points and in various sequences, depending on their particular contexts and goals. A knowledge gap in this area offers interesting opportunities: How should firms develop their business model innovation activities? Where should they focus their effort to achieve their goals?

■ REFERENCES

Agarwal, R. and Selen, W. 2009. "Dynamic Capability Building in Service Value Networks." *Decision Sciences*, 40 (3): pp. 431–475.
Amara, N., Landry, R., and Doloreux, D. 2009. "Patterns of Innovation in Knowledge-intensive Business Services." *Service Industries Journal*, 29 (4): pp. 407–430.
Amit, R. and Zott, C. 2001. "Value Creation in e-business." *Strategic Management Journal*, 22 (6): pp. 493–520.
Amit, R. and Zott, C. 2012. "Creating Value Through Business Model Innovation." *Sloan Management Review*, 53 (3): pp. 41–49.
Anderson, J. C. and Narus, J. A. 1991. "Partnering as a Focused Market Strategy." *California Management Review*, 33: pp. 95–113.
Anderson, J. C., Kumar, N., and Narus, J. A. 2007. *Value Merchants: Demonstrating and Documenting Superior Value in Business Markets*. Boston, MA: Harvard Business School Press.
Baden-Fuller, C. and Morgan, M. S. 2010. "Business Models as Models." *Long Range Planning*, 43: pp. 156–171.
Baron, S., Warnaby, G., and Hunter-Jones, P. 2014: "Service(s) Marketing Research: Developments and Directions." *International Journal of Management Reviews*, 16(2): 150–171.
Bartlett, C. A. and Ghoshal, S. 2000. *Transnational Management: Text, Cases, and Readings in Cross-border Management*. Third edition. Singapore: McGraw-Hill.
Bessant, J. and Davies, A. 2007. "Managing Service Innovation." In *Innovation in Services* (DTI Occasional Paper No. 9). London: Department of Trade and Industry.
Bitrain, G. and Pedrosa, L. 1998. "A Structured Product Development Perspective for Service Operations." *European Management Journal*, 16 (2): pp. 169–189.
Bohnsacka, R., Pinkse, J., and Kolk, A. 2014. "Business Models for Sustainable Technologies: Exploring Business Model Evolution in the Case of Electric Vehicles." *Research Policy*, 43 (2): pp. 284–300.

Bogers, M., Sund, K. J., and Villarroel, J. A. 2015. Chapter 13, this volume. "Organizational Aspects of Business Model Innovation: Examples from the Postal Industry."

Burger, P. C. and Cann, C. W. 1995. "Post-purchase Strategy: A Key to Successful Industrial Marketing and Customer Satisfaction. " *Industrial Marketing Management*, 24 (2): pp. 91–98.

Casadesus-Masanell, R. and Ricart, J. E. 2010. "From Strategy to Business Models and Tactics." *Long Range Planning*, 43(2): pp. 195–215.

Chesbrough, H. W. 2007. "Business Model Innovation: It's Not Just About Technology Anymore." *Strategy and Leadership*, 35 (6): pp. 12–17.

Chesbrough, H. W. 2010. "Business Model Innovation: Opportunities and Barriers." *Long Range Planning*, 43 (2–3): pp. 354–363.

Chesbrough, H. W. and Rosenbloom, R. S. 2002. "The Role of the Business Model in Capturing Value from Innovation: Evidence from Xerox Corporation's Technology Spin-off Companies." *Industrial and Corporate Change*, 11 (3): pp. 529–555.

Cohen, M. A., Agrawal, N., and Agrawal, V. 2006. "Winning in the Aftermarket" *Harvard Business Review*, 84 (5): pp. 129–138.

Dachs, B., Biege, S., Borowiecki, M., Lay, G., Jäger, A., and Schartiner, D. 2013. "Servitisation in European Manufacturing Industries: Empirical Evidence from a Large-scale Database." *Service Industries Journal*, 34 (1): pp. 5–23.

Davies, A., and Brady, T. 2000. "Organisational Capabilities and Learning in Complex Product Systems: Toward Repeatable Solutions." *Research Policy*, 29: pp. 931–953.

Davies, A., Brady, T., and Hobday, M. 2006. "Charting a Path Toward Integrated Solutions." *Sloan Management Review*, 47 (3): pp. 39–48.

Davies, A., Brady, T., and Hobday, M. 2007. "Organizing for Solutions: Systems Seller vs. Systems Integrator." *Industrial Marketing Management*, 36 (2): pp. 183–193.

Day, G. S. 2007. "Closing the Growth Gap: Balancing Big I and Small i Innovation." Working paper, Wharton School of the University of Pennsylvania, Philadelphia, PA.

De Jong, J. P. and Vermeulen, P. A. 2003. "Organizing Successful New Service Development: A Literature Review." *Management Decision*, 41 (9): pp. 844–858.

den Hertog, P., Van der Aa, W., and de Jong, M. W. 2010. "Capabilities for Managing Service Innovation: Towards a Conceptual Framework." *Journal of Service Management*, 21 (4): pp. 490–514.

Doz, Y. L. and Kosonen, M. (2010), "Embedding Strategic Agility." *Long Range Planning*, 43: pp. 370–382.

Drejer, I. 2004. "Identifying Innovation in Surveys of Services: A Schumpeterian Perspective." *Research Policy*, 33 (3): pp. 551–562.

Dubois, A. and Gadde, L. E. 2002. "Systematic Combining: An Abductive Approach to Case Research." *Journal of Business Research*, 55 (7): pp. 553–560.

Edvardsson, B., Meiren, T., Schäfer, A., and Witell, L. 2013. "Having a Strategy for New Service Development—Does it Really Matter?" *Journal of Service Management*, 24 (1): pp. 25–44.

Eggert, A., Hogreve, J., Ulaga, W., and Muenkhoff, E. 2014. "Revenue and Profit Implications of Industrial Service Strategies." *Journal of Service Research*, 17 (1): pp. 23–39.

Eisenhardt, K. M. 1989. "Building Theory from Case Study Research." *Academy of Management Review*, 14 (4): pp. 532–550.

Fang, E., Palmatier, R. W., and Steenkamp, J. 2008. "Effect of Service Transition Strategies on Firm Value." *Journal of Marketing*, 72 (5): pp. 1–14.

Foss, N. J. and T. Saebi. 2015. Chapter 1, this volume. "Business Models and Business Model Innovation: Bringing Organization into the Discussion."

Gago, D. and Rubalcaba, L. 2007. "Innovation and ICT in Service Firms: Towards a Multidimensional Approach for Impact Assessment." *Journal of Evolutionary Economics*, 17 (1): pp. 25–44.

Galbraith, J. R. 2002. "Organizing to Deliver Solutions." *Organizational Dynamics*, 31 (2): pp. 194–207.

Gallouj, F. and Weinstein, O. 1997. "Innovation in Services."*Research Policy*, 26 (4–5): pp. 537–556.

Gebauer, H., and Friedli, T. 2005. "Behavioral Implications of the Transition Process from Products to Services." *Journal of Business & Industrial Marketing*, 20 (2): pp. 70–78.

Gebauer, H. and Kowalkowski, C. 2012. "Customer-focused and Service-focused Orientation in Organizational Structures." *Journal of Business & Industrial Marketing*, 27 (7): pp. 527–537.

Gebauer, H., Fleisch, E., and Friedli, T. 2005. "Overcoming the Service Paradox in Manufacturing Companies." *European Management Journal*, 23 (1): pp. 14–26.

Goh, Y. M. and McMahon, C. 2009. "Improving Reuse of In-service Information Capture and Feedback." *Journal of Manufacturing Technology Management*, 20 (5): pp. 626–639.

Helfat, C. E., Finkelstein, S., Mitchell, W., Peteraf, M., Singh, H., Teece, D. J., Winter, S. G. 2007. *Dynamic Capabilities: Understanding Strategic Change in Organizations.* Malden, MA: Blackwell.

Jaakkola, E. 2011. "Unraveling the Practices of 'Productization' in Professional Service Firms." *Scandinavian Journal of Management*, 27 (2): pp. 221–230.

Johnson, M. D. and Selnes, F. 2004. "Customer Portfolio Management: Toward a Dynamic Theory of Exchange Relationships." *Journal of Marketing*, 68 (2): pp. 1–17.

Kindström, D. 2010. "Towards a Service-based Business Model—Key Aspects for Future Competitive Advantage." *European Management Journal*, 28 (6): pp. 479–490.

Kindström, D. and Kowalkowski, C. 2009. "Development of Industrial Service Offerings: A Process Framework." *Journal of Service Management*, 20 (2): pp. 156–172.

Kindström, D., Kowalkowski, C., and Nordin, F. 2012. "Visualizing the Value of Service-based Offerings—Empirical Findings from the Manufacturing Industry." *Journal of Business & Industrial Marketing*, 27 (7): pp. 538–546.

Kindström, D., Kowalkowski, C., and Sandberg, E. 2013. "Enabling Service Innovation: A Dynamic Capabilities Approach." *Journal Of Business Research*, 66 (8): pp. 1063–1073.

Kowalkowski, C. 2011. "The Service Function as a Holistic Management Concept." *Journal of Business & Industrial Marketing*, 26 (7): pp. 484–492.

Kowalkowski, C, Kindström, D., and Brehmer, P. O. 2011a. "Managing Industrial Service Offerings in Global Business Markets." *Journal of Business & Industrial Marketing*, 26 (3): pp. 181–192.

Kowalkowski, C., Kindström, D., and Witell, L. 2011b. "Internalisation or Externalisation? Examining Organisational Arrangements for Industrial Services." *Managing Service Quality*, 21 (4): pp. 373–391.

Kowalkowski, C., Kindström, D., Brashear Alejandro, T., Brege, S., and Biggemann, S. 2012. "Service Infusion as Agile Incrementalism in Action." *Journal of Business Research*, 65 (6): pp. 765–772.

Kowalkowski, C., Witell, L., and Gustafsson, A. 2013. "Any Way Goes: Identifying Value Constellations for Service Infusion in SMEs." *Industrial Marketing Management*, 42 (1): pp. 18–30.

Lewis, M. 2000. "Exploring Paradox: Toward a More Comprehensive Guide." *Academy of Management Review*, 25 (4): pp. 760–776.

Lieberman, M. B. and Montgomery, D. B. 1998. "First-mover Advantages." *Strategic Management Journal*, 9: pp. 41–58.

Lisboa, A., Skarmeas, D., and Lages, C. 2011. "Innovative Capabilities: Their Drivers and Effects." *Long Range Planning*, 43 (2–3): pp. 354–363.

Lovelock, C. 1983. "Classifying Services to Gain Strategic Marketing Insights." *Journal of Marketing*, Summer, 47: pp. 9–20.

Markides, C. 2015. Chapter 7, this volume. "How Established Firms Exploit Disruptive Business Model Innovation: Strategic and Organizational Challenges."

Martin, C. R. and Horne, D. A. 1993. "Services Innovation: Successful Versus Unsuccessful Firms." *International Journal of Service Industry Management*, 4 (1): pp. 49–65.

Milgrom, P. and Roberts, J. 1990. "The Economics of Modern Manufacturing: Technology, Strategy, and Organization." *The American Economic Review*, 80 (3): pp. 511–528.

Neu, W. and Brown, S. 2008. "Manufacturers Forming Successful Complex Business Services: Designing an Organization to Fit the Market." *International Journal of Service Industry Management*, 19 (2): pp. 232–251.

Normann, R. 2001. *Reframing Business—When the Map Changes the Landscape.* Chichester: John Wiley & Sons.

Oliva, R. and Kallenberg, R. 2003. "Managing the Transition from Products to Services." *International Journal of Service Industry Management*, 14 (2): pp. 160–172.

Oliva, R., Gebauer, H., and Brann, J. M. 2012. "Separate or Integrate? Assessing the Impact of Separation Between Product and Service Business on Service Performance in Manufacturing Firms." *Journal of Business-to-Business Marketing*, 19 (4): pp. 309–334.

Ostrom, A. L., Bitner, M. J., Brown, S. W., Burkhard, K. A., Goul, M., Smith-Daniels, V., Demirkan, H., and Rabinovich, E. 2010. "Moving Forward and Making a Difference: Research Priorities for the Science of Service." *Journal of Service Research*, 13 (1): pp. 4–36.

Pauwels, K. and Weiss, A. 2008. "Moving from Free to Fee: How Online Firms Market to Change Their Business Model Successfully." *Journal of Marketing*, 72 (3): pp. 14–31.

Payne, A. F., Ballantyne, D., and Christopher, M. 2005. "A Stakeholder Approach to Relationship Marketing Strategy." *European Journal of Marketing*, 39 (7/8): pp. 855–871.

Payne, A. F., Storbacka, K., and Frow, P. 2008. "Managing the Co-creation of Value." *Journal of the Academy of Marketing Science*, 36 (1): pp. 83–96.

Porter, M. E. 1980. *Competitive Strategy: Techniques for Analyzing Industries and Competitors.* New York: The Free Press.

Porter, M. E. 1996. "What is Strategy?" *Harvard Business Review*, 74 (6): pp. 61–78.

Prahalad, C. K. and Doz, Y. 1988. *The Multinational Mission: Balancing Local Demands and Global Vision.* New York: The Free Press.

Rasmussen, K. A. and Foss, N. J. 2015. Chapter 12, this volume. "Business Model Innovation in the Pharmaceutical Industry: The Supporting Role of Organizational Design."

Reinartz, W. and Ulaga, W. 2008. "How to Sell Services Profitably." *Harvard Business Review*, 86 (5): pp. 90–98.

Robinson, T., Clarke-Hill, C. M., and Clarkson, R. 2002. "Differentiation Through Service: A Perspective from the Commodity Chemicals Industry." *Service Industries Journal*, 32: pp. 149–166.

Saebi, T. 2015. Chapter 8, this volume. "Evolution, Adaption or Innovation? A Contingency Framework on Business Model Dynamics."

Schäfer, D. and Milne, R. 2010. "Siemens Seeks to Stay Ahead of Asian Rivals." *Financial Times*. Retrieved November 2014 at: <http://www.ft.com/cms/s/0/79a90f80-376c-11df-9176-00144feabdc0.html#axzz3JKXkeKsF>.

Shah, D., Rust, R. T., Parasuraman, A., Staelin, R., and Day, G. S. 2006. "The Path to Customer Centricity." *Journal of Service Research*, 9 (2): pp. 113–124.

Skålén, P., Gummerus, J., Von Koskull, C., and Magnusson, P. 2014. "Exploring Value Propositions and Service Innovation: A Service-dominant Logic Study." *Journal of the Academy of Marketing Science*, online, doi 10.1007/s11747-013-0365-2.

Smith, W. K., Binns, A., and Tushman, M. L. 2010. "Complex Business Models: Managing Strategic Paradoxes Simultaneously." *Long Range Planning*, 43: pp. 448–461.

Spring, M. and Araujo, L. 2013. "Beyond the Service Factory: Service Innovation in Manufacturing Supply Networks." *Industrial Marketing Management*, 42 (1): pp. 59–70.

Stieglitz, N. and Foss, N. 2015. Chapter 6, this volume. "Business Model Innovation: The Role of Leadership."

Storbacka, K., Windahl, C., Nenonen, S., and Salonen, A. 2013. "Solution Business Models: Transformation Along Four Continua." *Industrial Marketing Management*, 42 (5): pp. 705–716.

Teece, D. J. 2007. "Explicating Dynamic Capabilities: The Nature and Microfoundations of (Sustainable) Enterprise Performance." *Strategic Management Journal*, 28 (13): pp. 1319–1350.

Teece, D. J. 2010. "Business Models, Business Strategy and Innovation." *Long Range Planning*, 43: pp. 172–194.

Tuli, K. R., Kohli, A. K., and Bharadwaj, S. G. 2007. "Rethinking Customer Solutions: From Product Bundles to Relational Processes." *Journal of Marketing*, 71 (3): pp. 1–17.

Ulaga, W. and Reinartz, W. 2011. "Hybrid Offerings: How Manufacturing Firms Combine Goods and Services Successfully." *Journal of Marketing*, 75 (6): pp. 5–23.

Vandermerwe, S. 1994. "Quality in Services: The 'Softer' Side is 'Harder' (and Smarter)." *Long Range Planning*, 27 (2): pp. 45–56.

Visnjic I. and Van Looy B. 2013. "Servitization: Disentangling the Impact of Service Business Model Innovation on Manufacturing Firm Performance." *Journal of Operations Management*, 31 (4): pp. 169–180.

Wagner, S. M., Eggert, A., and Lindemann, E. 2010. "Creating and Appropriating Value in Collaborative Relationships." *Journal of Business Research*, 63: pp. 840–848.

Westerlund, M. and Rajala, R. 2010. "Learning and Innovation in Inter-organizational Network Collaboration." *Journal of Business & Industrial Marketing*, 25 (6): pp. 435–442.

Witell, L. and Löfgren, M. 2013. "From Service for Free to Service for Fee: Business Model Innovation in Manufacturing Firms." *Journal of Service Management*, 24 (5): pp. 520–533.

Zott, C., Amit, C., and Massa, L. 2011. "The Business Model: Recent Developments and Future Research." *Journal of Management*, 37 (4): pp. 1019–1042.

11 A Business Model Innovation by an Incumbent Late Mover

Containerization in Maersk Line

TORBEN PEDERSEN AND
HENRIK SORNN-FRIESE

Introduction

The "business model" construct has flourished in the management literature since the end of the 1990s, especially with the emergence of the Internet and the increased use of new models for e-commerce (Foss and Saebi, chapter 1 in this volume). The construct is typically applied as a useful lens for helping us to understand how firms might achieve advantages over competitors in the marketplace or as a formula describing how firms make money.

The business model lens generally promotes an outside-in perspective in which competitive advantages are gained from interactions among what firms do, the ways in which they carry out their activities, and how those activities create value for customers or other external stakeholders. As such, this lens may be seen as a response to the emphasis on internal resources—such as key knowledge and core competences—that accompanies the resource-based view (RBV). The RBV typically concentrates more on internal resources and capabilities than on how to organize and deliver value to customers. In contrast, the business model lens places the organization at the center, and focuses on the question of how to make money and on the underlying economic logic of how to create value for customers in each business.

The study of business models has been spurred by examples of firms that have achieved considerable success by changing the traditional formula for business in their respective industries. Prominent examples of disruptive business model innovations include those introduced by Southwest Airlines, easyJet, Ryanair, Dell Computer, E*Trade, and Amazon.com. None of these companies based their success on technological innovation. However, they have all been innovative in the organization of their activities, particularly with respect to how things are done and the delivery to customers.

In this chapter, we scrutinize a case—Maersk Line's entry into container-ized shipping—that, in some ways, runs counter to several of the conventional presumptions about the development of new business models. Maersk Line is the largest container liner company in the world. It can attribute at least some of its success to its business model innovations related to the contain-erization of shipping. However, Maersk Line was a late mover in container shipping. In addition, it was an incumbent, rather than an innovative entrant, and the decisions leading to the containerization of Maersk's liner business were incremental responses to emergent opportunities rather than the result of an overall strategy for business model innovation. As such, the case offers a good illustration of more common and mundane business model innovations than the spectacular innovations in which new entrants completely change the name of the game.

The shipping industry is particularly suitable for studies of business model innovations because changes in strategies often require huge investments in such elements as new vessels or port terminals. As a new vessel has a life span of approximately twenty-five years, container lines bet on future demand, technologies, and regulations when making these investments, even though future conditions are hard to predict. Therefore, the shipping industry encom-passes numerous competing business models, and has been characterized by experimentation with various business models, such as port-to-port trans-port versus door-to-door transport or alliances versus independent services. Containerization is a prime example of a complex business model innovation with transformative implications that reach far beyond the transportation of goods by sea. This study of the process of containerization in Maersk Line offers an opportunity to grasp the complexity of a systemic change in relation to strategic decision making and business model innovation at the firm level.

Prevailing Presumptions Regarding Business Model Innovation

The business model concept is appealing because it covers the interplay between internal organizational drivers, and it focuses on the creation and distribution of value. More specifically, it encompasses the value proposi-tion for the customer, the needed activities, and how the company profitably conducts these activities (Birkinshaw and Ansari, chapter 5 in this volume). However, while it may be possible to determine *ex post* when a firm has made a business model innovation by developing a new value proposition and reconfiguring the business system to correspond to that value proposition, it is difficult to identify what constitutes a business model innovation *ex ante*.

The notion of a "business model" is rather vague. Zott, Amit, and Massa (2011), who conduct a comprehensive study of the academic literature on business models, conclude that "scholars do not agree on what a business model is and that the literature is developing largely in silos." In fact, definitions of "business model" differ substantially in the literature, with varying emphasis on the elements that form a business model. Although definitions vary, Zott, Amit, and Massa (2011: 1038) identify four themes constituting a shared notion of "business model": (1) a *new unit of analysis*; (2) offering a *systemic perspective* on how to "do business"; (3) encompassing *boundary-spanning activities*; and (4) focusing on *value creation* and *value capture*.

In the extant literature, several presumptions flourish regarding the introduction of business model innovations (McGrath, 2010). One such presumption is that most business model innovations are introduced by new entrants, as they are able to spot new opportunities and market potential, while incumbents are trapped in the existing system and are unwilling to give up existing income streams until it is too late (Chesbrough, 2010; Santos, Spector, and Van der Heyden, chapter 3 in this volume). However, although established firms might be restricted by path dependencies and an unwillingness to run significant risks, there are cases of established firms developing new business models (Markides, 2000). The processes of changing the business model by established firms deserve greater scrutiny.

A related presumption is that the inventor or the first mover is the one that appropriates the benefits of the business innovation. However, this might not be the case when established firms are the innovators, as the advantages they derive from the development of the business model are more related to scale and networks than to speed and flexibility.

In addition, business model innovations are often conceptualized as deliberate strategic decisions based on planned analytical processes (McGrath, 2010). Contrary to this conceptualization, McGrath (2010) suggests that business model innovation is a discovery-driven process characterized by significant experimentation and learning. In this regard, business model innovations are similar to entrepreneurial activities in that they cannot be projected out of existing models and processes. Rather, they demand experimentation and learning about how things can be done differently. In many cases, it is nearly impossible to predict which design will be the most successful until the possibilities are unfolded and tested in the market. It is also important to note that business model experimentation occurs both within firms and across firms.

A sustainable business model innovation is rarely found immediately. Such innovations typically require progressive refinements to create internal consistency and/or to adapt to the environment. As Winter and Szulanski (2001: 731) argue: "The formula or business model, far from being a quantum of information that is revealed in a flash, is typically a complex set of interdependent routines that is discovered, adjusted, and fine-tuned by doing." Business model innovation does not occur smoothly. There is intense conflict between the existing business model and the potential new candidate. In other words, it is a "delicate balancing act" (Chesbrough 2010: 361).

In the following sections, we discuss Maersk Line's move into containerization. In particular, we relate the case to the assumption that business model innovations are conducted by fast-mover entrants that make a deliberate strategic decision to explore new opportunities. In this regard, we investigate the extent to which Maersk Line followed the assumed pattern of business model innovation.

Maersk Line and Containerization

Maersk Line's move into containerization highlights how an established company can introduce innovations to its otherwise profitable business model when it is under the impression that the model's sustainability may be undermined by fundamental changes in the competitive environment. This case study considers how Maersk Line's top management realized the need for business model change; how it decided to change the model; and how the constituent elements of the new model were identified, brought together, and embedded in the existing organization. As such the case is a prime example of a business model change as discussed by Santos, Spector, and Van der Heyden (chapter 3 in this volume).

We have relied extensively on secondary sources, such as news clips and articles in the leading maritime trade journals, consultancy reports, and the extensive literature on containerization. In addition, we interviewed the authors of *Creating Global Opportunities: Maersk Line in Containerization 1973–2013*, Chris J. Jephson and Henning Morgen, both of whom are employed by Maersk. Jephson and Morgen were very generous in sharing some of the material they had gathered while interviewing key former Maersk Line employees who had been at the forefront of Maersk Line's containerization. These employees had taken part in the company's decision to enter into container shipping and implement it throughout the organization.

CONTAINERIZATION AND THE EVOLUTION
OF THE LINER-SHIPPING INDUSTRY

Container liner shipping involves the movement of goods in standardized steel containers via fixed routes on a regular schedule. It relies on an increasingly global network of ports and terminals that allows for efficient shipping around the globe. The container trade lanes follow the patterns of world trade, and today the trade typically involves the transport of manufactured goods from production sites in Asia to consumers in Europe and North America and raw materials to points of production.

While several liner companies initially experimented with different models for consolidating break-bulk (i.e., non-unitized) cargo in secure, easy-to-move boxes, the real breakthrough in this regard came from the trucking industry. As such, containerization in the shipping industry required an outsider's perspective and, in that narrow sense, seems to have followed common paths in terms of sources of business model innovation (Chesbrough, 2010). However, we believe that the Maersk Line case shows that the dynamics may be more complex, and that incumbents can play an important role in industry renewal and, in fact, move timeously into new forms of business.

Containerization was mainly an organizational innovation that had enormous implications for delivery to customers and, eventually, for world trade. As Peter Drucker (2007: 26) writes:

> There was not much new technology involved in the idea of moving a truck body off its wheels and onto a cargo vessel. This "innovation", the container, did not grow out of technology at all but out of a new perception of a "cargo vessel" as a material handling device rather than a "ship" which meant that what really mattered was to make the time in port as short as possible. But this humdrum innovation roughly quadrupled the productivity of the ocean going freighter and probably saved shipping business. Without it, the tremendous expansion of world trade in the last sixty years—the fastest growth in any major economic activity ever recorded—could not possibly have taken place.

The containerization of maritime break-bulk transport took place in three phases (Broeze 2002; Van Ham and Rijsenbrij, 2012). It emerged from 1956 to the middle of the 1960s as a development in domestic trade in the United States. While such companies as Matson Navigation, Seatrain Lines, and the Alaska Steamship Company had experimented with unitized and palletized cargo even before the Second World War, the true pioneer was the trucking operator Malcom McLean, who invented the concept of "door-to-door transport of freight via ocean routes" (Hearth 1964: v). In January 1956, McLean purchased two shipping companies and thus obtained a fleet of cargo ships. In 1956, he successfully carried fifty-eight containers from Port Newark in New Jersey to the Port of Houston in Texas on the rebuilt oil tanker *Ideal-X*. Only a year later, he was running a full-scale containership operation along the US west coast and around Puerto Rico, carrying some 4,000 of his company's own containers. His greatest contribution was an entirely new technological model: "he was a 'systems builder.' He saw containerization whole, from unitized or cellular cargo to intermodal transport to seamless transfer from ship to truck to train" (Roland, Bolster, and Keyssar, 2008: 342). His grand idea was containerization as a system of intermodal transport.[1]

---

[1] Stopford (2009: 340) notes that with the advent of the container, the "components of the transport system needed to be developed into an integrated transport system to take advantage of the standardized unit and economies of scale. On the sea leg the investment was in purpose-built cellular containerships. On land it required investment in large numbers of road and rail vehicles capable of carrying containers efficiently. The third step was to build high-speed cargo handling facilities to transfer the container between one part of the transport system and another. Container terminals, inland distribution depots and container 'stuffing' facilities all played a part in this process."

Several shipping companies adopted containerization for domestic services around 1960, and a dominant design gradually emerged. That design included standards for container size and bolstering; and systems for the integration of sea and land transport, which included specialized ships, ports, and terminals, and hinterland transportation. The major entrepreneurs were located in the United States. In addition to Matson, Seatrain, Alaskan, and McLean's company, which was now named Sea-Land Service, Inc., they included Grace Line, White Pass & Yukon, and American President Lines (APL). In this phase, European containerization was largely confined to Irish shipping companies, where Bell Lines and, to some extent, the British and Irish Steam Packet Company (B + I Line), were committed to the concept. In Denmark, the United Steamship Company (DFDS) had experimented with unitized cargo systems as early as 1951, when it opened a container service to move beer and foodstuffs among Danish ports (Levinson 2006). In 1967, DFDS introduced ro/ro-container carriers on its Esbjerg–Grimsby line.

McLean's Sea-Land was certainly the most innovative and, for an extended period, the most successful container-shipping company. Rapid improvements in cranes, container designs, locking mechanisms, lifting gear, and ship architecture followed consecutively. Some came from McLean's own team, while others emerged from other companies, especially Matson and Seatrain, which were experimenting with containerization. All of these innovations were successfully integrated into Sea-Land's operations.

The second distinguishable phase of containerization was from 1966 until around 1970. Within this short period of time, containerization became the dominant mode of global liner shipping through its diffusion across the North Atlantic, the UK–Australia, and the transpacific US–Japan routes. Again, McLean was among the pioneers. On April 23, 1966, Sea-Land's container vessel *Fairland*, a converted C-2 cargo ship that had been used as a troopship by the US Army during the Second World War, departed New Jersey for Northern Europe with 236 containers on board. The trip was the first transatlantic voyage made by the company's new commercial line between New York and Northern Europe, which had been established, in part, to serve the US Army in Germany. McLean had prepared this voyage by developing an extensive network of liner agents all over Europe. McLean had also contracted with trucking and ferry companies to carry the containers and generate cargo for the homeward run (Broeze, 2002). Over the next few years, he extended his container liner services to Southeast Asia (serving the US Army in Vietnam), Japan, Hong Kong, Taiwan, and Singapore.

The success of Sea-Land's transatlantic container service spurred intense competition from established shipping lines (e.g., American Export-Isbrandtsen Lines, Moore-McCormack, United States Lines) as well as some newcomers (e.g., Seatrain).[2] Some long-established European liner-shipping

[2] American Export Isbrandtsen Lines was founded in 1964 by Jakob Isbrandtsen, the son of A. P. Møller's cousin Hans Isbrandtsen, as a merger between American Export Lines and Isbrandtsen

companies were also quick to enter transatlantic container shipping, although they entered through partnerships. McKinsey & Co. had predicted the adoption of this entry mode in a report delivered to the British Transport Docks Board in the same year that *Fairland* crossed the Atlantic Ocean (McKinsey and Co., 1966). While other US liner companies were focused on the US–Europe trade, the wealthy and powerful Matson chose to introduce container shipping into the Pacific trade. In the autumn of 1967, Matson launched the first fully containerized freight service between the US west coast and the Far East. The service was offered in close collaboration with the Japanese shipping company Nippon Yusen Kaisha (NYK). However, although NYK continued running containers across the Pacific Ocean, Matson chose to withdraw from this trade in 1970 in order to develop container services for his core California/Hawaii line. The Japanese government wanted Japanese liner-shipping companies to join in the containerization trend in the Pacific and at the end of 1966 forced the leading Japanese liner companies into container-shipping consortia.

From the late 1960s until the early 1970s, a number of aggressive newcomers entered in the Asian Pacific Rim and, later, in South America to challenge the domination of US, European, and Japanese container lines. Some were entirely new entrants, while others were active in the traditional liner business. Among the most prominent challengers were the Taiwanese companies Evergreen and Yangming, Singapore's Neptune Orient Lines (NOL), Malaysian International Shipping Corporation (MISC), the Hong Kong-based Overseas Orient Container Line (OOCL), the China Ocean Shipping Company (COSCO), Chile's Compañía Sud Americana de Vapores (CSAV), and Transportacion Maritima Mexicana (TMM). In the second half of the 1970s, the South Korean trio of Hanjin, Hyundai, and Cho Yang also entered the international container shipping market. In 1975, several of the companies listed here established the ACE Group, a primarily Asian shipping consortium, which entered the Europe–Far East trade in competition with the Trio Group and ScanDutch.[3]

The third development phase, which began in the early 1970s, brought the diffusion of containerization across all major trade routes. Maersk Line became a major influence in this stage, during which many new container routes were opened to connect Europe to the Far East, the Caribbean, and South Africa, and to connect Australia to the United States and East Asia. The new services were often controlled by international collaborative ventures. While the consortia of the 1970s generally operated in a single trade, the most influential alliances of the 1980s and 1990s were global in scope.

Steamship Company. The history of Isbrandtsen Steamship Company is closely related to the development of Maersk Line, as Isbrandtsen Steamship Company was a partner in the Isbrandtsen-Moller Company (Ismolco), which was instrumental in A. P. Møller's founding of Maersk Line.

[3] The ScanDutch consortium included the Danish EAC, the Norwegian Wilh. Wilhelmsen, the Swedish Svenska Ostasiatiska Kompaniet (Ostasiat), the Dutch Nedlloyd, and the French Messageries Maritimes. See Poulsen (2007) for a description of the consortium's history.

Hapag-Lloyd, NOL, NYK, and P&O formed the Grand Alliance in 1995, which offered services in the Europe–Asia and Asia–North America trades. APL, MISC, Mitsui-OSK, Nedlloyd, and OOCL responded by forming the short-lived Global Alliance, while Maersk and Sea-Land created a global alliance with vessel-sharing agreements covering the Europe–Asia, transatlantic, transpacific, and intra-Asian trades.

MAERSK LINE ENTERS INTO CONTAINER SHIPPING

When Maersk Line decided to enter into container shipping in 1973, containerization's third phase was well underway. The Maersk Group took delivery of its first containership (*Svendborg Mærsk*) in 1974, four semi-containerships in 1974 and 1975 ("M" class), and nine fast, single-screw fully cellular vessels in 1975 and 1976 ("A" class). From that point on, the group persistently developed its business as a reputable, highly reliable container-service provider. Within a short period of time, the company quickly caught up with its major competitors, and it became Scandinavia's and, later, the world's largest container-shipping company.

It is fascinating to compare Maersk Line's containerization process with that of its peer, EAC, which had entered into this business long before Maersk. EAC had been engaged in Europe–Far East liner shipping since its establishment in 1897, and it had gradually expanded its network to include Africa, Australia, and the US west coast. After some less successful experiments with various semi-containership designs in the late 1960s in which conventional cargo liners were furnished with some non-cellular container-carrying capacity, EAC took delivery of its first fully cellular containership in 1971. It immediately joined forces with foreign liner companies in various international consortia, such as Johnson Scan Star on the transatlantic route and ScanDutch on the Europe–Asia trade. EAC's initial collaborative strategy was successful, but its subsequent strategic move was an expensive failure that would eventually contribute to its complete exit from the shipping business in 1993. In 1976–77, EAC took delivery of seven liner replacement vessels (LRVs). These relatively small, highly energy-efficient ships had a capacity of 600 TEU each and the flexibility to transport various types of cargo. However, they were also slow, and they were insufficiently specialized to allow for the economies of scale that were so important in container shipping (Bjerrum, 1993; Lauring, 2008).

Maersk's background in liner shipping differed from that of EAC. While EAC worked as a conference member, operating its main liner network out of the Nordic home market, and was active in international joint ventures with like-minded ship owners, Maersk Line was more independent.[4] Furthermore,

---

[4] A liner-shipping conference is a system through which shipping companies collaborate on a particular traffic route. They do not necessarily pool resources, but they do agree how to divide the

Maersk Line had been established as a cross-trader (i.e., transporting cargo between foreign ports). This was particularly true for its transpacific service, which had been introduced as early as 1928 under the Maersk Line brand name, and for its Asia–Europe service, which was set up in 1968. In contrast to EAC, Maersk Line largely adopted a stand-alone strategy in which it ran its services single-handedly, initially however in cooperation with Japanese "K" Line.

When Maersk Line finally entered into container shipping, the shift was fast and comprehensive. In an early and rare interview with *Containerization International*, Maersk Line's Ib Kruse admitted that by waiting to enter into container shipping, Maersk Line had inevitably, but not deliberately, bene-fited from the other companies' experiences (Boyes, 1981).

Maersk Line's entry into container shipping with fully cellular ships hap-pened in two steps. The first involved investments in one big containership to be operated on the Europe–Asia run, and the second involved investments in nine containerships to be operated on the US–Far East line. Maersk Line was a member of the Far Eastern Freight Conference (FEFC), a multinational liner conference established in 1879 to regulate shipping in the Europe–Far East trade lanes. Throughout the late 1960s up and into the mid-1970s, the FEFC maintained a considerable degree of control over liner shipping on the Asia–Europe routes, but it faced increasing competition from external, outside-independent shipping lines (e.g., Evergreen and Yangming) and from the Trans-Siberian Railway, as well as considerable political pressure from the newly industrialized countries on the Pacific Rim (Gilman, 1983). It also observed the development of container shipping, in which some of its member consortia eventually took part.

Maersk Line was a small FEFC member and it decided to enter container shipping in partnership with "K" Line, which was also an FEFC member. The two companies agreed to each build a containership for a joint Europe–Asia service. In 1971, Maersk Line signed a contract with the Ishikawajima shipyard in Japan and two-and-a-half years later, in January 1974, took deliv-ery of its first containership, the 1,800 TEU *Svendborg Mærsk*. She would be the first ship to have the brand name "MAERSK LINE" painted on her hull (Jephson and Morgen, 2014). However, before the ship was delivered, "K" Line decided to terminate its cooperation with Maersk Line in order to join the ACE Group. Upon delivery, *Svendborg* was consequently chartered out to another container operator on a one-year contract.

In 1975 and 1976, Maersk Line took delivery of nine 1,200 TEU fast, cellu-lar containerships, which were the company's "A" class (all of the vessels were given names starting with the letter A; see Table 11.1 for an overview). The ships were for the company's transpacific line. With a total price exceeding

market among them. Therefore, it is essentially a collective monopoly. Although Maersk Line par-ticipated in established conferences, it remained somewhat on the sidelines and was highly exper-ienced as an independent company (Rasmussen, Rønne, and Johansen, 2000; Lauring, 2008).

Table 11.1 Maersk's owned container fleet (1974–84)

Service	Vessel (Built/Converted)	TEU	DWT	Speed Knots
Fully cellular containerships				
Flexible deployment	*Svendborg Mærsk/Dragør Mærsk* (1974)	1,800	32,153	27.0
USEC/USWC/Far East	*Adrian Mærsk* (1975)	1,400	31,000	26.0
New York, Philadelphia, Baltimore,	*Albert Mærsk* (1975)	1,400	31,000	26.0
Charleston, Long Beach, Oakland,	*Alva Mærsk* (1976)	1,400	31,000	26.0
Hong Kong (feeder to Manila and	*Anders Mærsk* (1976)	1,400	31,000	26.0
Kaohsiang), Singapore (feeder to	*Anna Mærsk* (1975)	1,400	31,000	26.0
Bangkok, Jakarta, Surabaya, Port	*Arild Mærsk* (1976)	1,400	31,000	26.0
Kelang, Penang and Belawan Deli),				
Hong Kong, Keelung, Kobe, Tokyo	*Arnold Mærsk* (1975)	1,400	31,000	26.0
(feeder to Busan). Feeder to ports	*Arthur Mærsk* (1976)	1,400	31,000	26.0
in People's Republic of China.	*Axel Mærsk* (1976)	1,400	31,000	26.0
US Gulf by minibridge.				
USGC/USEC/Mid-East/Med	*Charlotte Mærsk* (1968/1980)	1,200	24,100	21.0
Houston, New Orleans, Savannah,	*Chastine Mærsk* (1968/1980)	1,200	24,100	21.0
Baltimore, Philadelphia, New York,	*Christian Mærsk* (1968/1981)	1,200	24,100	21.0
Jeddah, Dubai, Dammam, Jubail,	*Clara Mærsk* (1968/1980)	1,200	24,100	21.0
Bahrain (feeder to Abu Dhabi,	*Clifford Mærsk* (1969/1980)	1,200	24,100	21.0
Kuwait, Umm Qasr), Minibridge US				
west coast				
Japan/Indonesia	*Cecilie Mærsk* (1967/1981)	1,200	24,100	21.0
Busan, Moji, Kobe, Nagoya,	*Cornelia Mærsk* (1967/1981)	1,200	24,100	21.0
Yokohama, Keelung, Hong Kong,				
Jakarta, Surabaya				
Europe/Far East	*Laura Mærsk* (1980)	2,100	31,700	24.5
Hamburg, Singapore, Hong Kong,	*Leise Mærsk* (1980)	2,100	31,700	24.5
Keelung, Busan, Kobe, Tokyo,	*Lexa Mærsk* (1981)	2,100	31,700	24.5
Hong Kong, Singapore, Antwerp,	*Lica Mærsk* (1981)	2,100	31,700	24.5
Rotterdam, Bremerhaven (feeders	*Leda Mærsk* (1981)	2,100	31,700	24.5
to Malaysia, Thailand, manila and	*Luna Mærsk* (1982)	2,100	31,700	24.5
Kaohsiang and range of Scandinavian	*Laust Mærsk* (1983)	2,100	31,700	24.5
ports)	*Louis Mærsk* (1984)	2,100	31,700	24.5
	Lars Mærsk (1984)	2,100	31,700	24.5
	Louis Mærsk (1984)	2,100	31,700	24.5
Far East feeder links	*Mærsk Pinto* (1971)	404	14,000	18.0
	Mærsk Mango (1978)	340	11,000	16.0
	Mærsk Tempo (1978)	340	11,000	16.0
	Mærsk Mondo (1969)	170	3,420	13.0
	Mærsk Rando (1969)	170	3,420	13.0
Semi-containerships/ro-ro ships				
Far East/Middle East	*Eleo Mærsk* (1979)	850	29,750	18.0
Busan, Moji, Kobe, Keelung, Hong	*Elisabeth Mærsk* (1980)	850	29,750	18.0
Kong, Karachi, Dammam, Kuwait,	*Emma Mærsk* (1979)	850	29,750	18.0
Umm Qasr, Bandar Khomeini, Dubai,	*Emilie Mærsk* (1980)	850	29,750	18.0
Karachi, Bombay	*Estella Mærsk* (1979)	850	29,750	18.0
	Evelyn Mærsk (1980)	850	29,750	18.0

(continued)

Table 11.1 (continued)

Service	Vessel (Built/Converted)	TEU	DWT	Speed Knots
Semi-containerships				
Far East/West Africa	*Marchen Mærsk* (1974)	500	21,150	20.0
Busan, Moji, Kobe, Yokohama,	*Margrethe Mærsk* (1975)	500	21,150	20.0
Nagoya, Shimizu, Keelung, Hong	*Mathilda Mærsk* (1975)	500	21,150	20.0
Kong, Freetown, Abidjan, Lagos,				
Lomé	*McKinney Mærsk* (1975)	500	21,150	20.0
Japan/Indonesia	*Trein Mærsk* (1962)	475	11,000	22.0
	Tobias Mærsk (1963)	475	11,000	22.0

USD 300 million, it was the largest investment in the company's history up to that point.

In the second stage, the company essentially did little more than follow its competitors' steps, but it took all of these steps at once. It invested in all of the technological elements necessary for success, including specialized cellular containerships, complex engines, large gantry cranes, railroad connections for landbridge and mini-bridge services, sophisticated containers, and chassis. After 1975, it quickly established a number of container terminals, some for the exclusive use of Maersk Line and some in cooperation with others. Feeder services were established for ports not directly visited by the big, ocean-going containerships.[5] The entry into containerization also provided new opportunities for related diversification, as evidenced by the establishment of Maersk Logistics in 1977, Maersk Container Industry in 1991, and APM Terminals in 2001.

Early on, Maersk Line assumed technological leadership with regard to ship design and equipment, and in its approach to ship conversion. The decision to construct the "A" class as turbine-driven, single-screwed containerships was a technological choice that would give Maersk Line a competitive edge (Bensen, Lambek, and Ørskov, 2004). Although the vessels were smaller than the size considered optimal for long-haul routes at the time, their high speed allowed for the establishment of a weekly service. The ships also contained a number of elements new to shipping, including IBM marine computer systems with collision-avoidance technology, satellite navigation, and optimum steering and course-plotting functions. Another novelty was found in the built-in facilities of the so-called "artificial tween-decks." The vessels were clearly state-of-the art floating assets.

The company continually introduced pioneering elements into its containerships and handling gear. Its post-Panamax containership *Regina*

---

[5] Feeder ships typically collect containers from smaller or difficult-to-approach ports, and transport them to central container terminals, where they are loaded onto bigger vessels for mainline transport. Landbridge and mini-bridge services handle movements among ports by road and/or rail.

Mærsk created uproar in the industry in 1996, and the introduction of the 15,200 TEU *Emma Mærsk* in 2006 had the same effect.[6] And in 2013, Maersk Line's introduction of the 18,000 TEU "Triple E" class (acronym: economy of scale, energy efficient, environmentally improved) containerships was an astonishing technological achievement. Not only were these the newest and largest containerships in the world, but they also encompassed several path-breaking design innovations that noticeably enhanced fuel efficiency.

The company's technological sophistication was also evident in its approach to conversion. Within the first three years of transpacific service, the nine "A" class vessels had become too small to cater to the rapidly growing market. However, instead of adding extra containerships to the fleet, the vessels were enlarged, or "jumboized." The alterations were meticulous, almost surgical, and with the flexible use of *Svendborg Mærsk* (renamed *Dragør Mærsk*) as a buffer, the alterations were largely carried out without disrupting the business. One by one, the ships were sent to Hitachi Zosen's Innoshima shipyard and cut in two. Within the timespan typical of a transpacific round-trip, each of the vessels was given a new container hold, bringing their capacity up to 1,400 TEU apiece. This gave Maersk Line the equivalent of an additional 1,350 TEU ship for less than USD 8.5 million (Gibney, 1984), which was about one-quarter of the price originally paid for each of the nine vessels, with no extra crew or engine costs.

While all of the US and many of the European container-shipping companies no longer exist, the bulk of the challengers that emerged in the late 1960s are now considered national champions in their home countries and are among the world's leading shipping companies today. In 1977, Maersk Line decided to focus even more on containerization (Gibney, 1984). The company ordered six new 850 TEU, 18 knot ro/ro containerships for its Far East–Middle East service, which were to be delivered by the Maersk Group's own shipyard in Odense in 1979 and 1980. This contract was soon followed by a contract for six 2,150 TEU, 24.5 knot containerships for delivery between 1980 and 1982. Around the same time, the company had five of its conventional liner vessels, the "C" class, jumboized and cellularized. By 1981, Maersk Line had become the world's third largest containership operator (Broeze, 2002; Donovan and Bonney, 2006; Levinson, 2006).

Throughout the international shipping crisis in the mid-1980s, which was the result of over-investments in the good years leading up to the OPEC I oil crisis and enforced by the subsequent economic turmoil and eventually OPEC II, Maersk Line focused on a forceful growth strategy within container shipping. New investments complemented its Asia–Europe and transatlantic services, which had been fully containerized by 1975, with a US west coast–Middle East service based on transhipments in Hong

---

[6] As the first containership capable of carrying more than 6,000 TEU containers, the *Regina Maersk* moved the technological frontier of naval architecture.

Kong. The company also invested in a major hub in Algeciras in southern Spain, which provided the foundation for the company's own feeder lines in the western Mediterranean and access to the west coast of Africa. Furthermore, it established a hub in Dubai, which served as the basis for services to the eastern coast of Africa (Fremont, 2007) and, moreover, extended its services further into the mainland, with major investments in land-based infrastructure in several countries. Therefore, throughout the 1980s, Maersk was spanning the globe with an extensive hub-and-spoke container network.

THE DECISION PROCESS LEADING UP TO THE CONTAINERIZATION OF MAERSK LINE

Those in charge of the Maersk Group had carefully watched the early movers, and then replicated their effective moves and circumnavigated pitfalls. However, there was one element that Maersk Line did not seek to replicate— focusing on established intercontinental routes. Maersk Line had an ingrained customer base in the transpacific trade and it was also well situated in Far Eastern ports. Therefore, its containerization decisions focused on penetrating even further into Asia. This focus covered such countries as Thailand, Indonesia, and the Philippines, which were developing quickly in tandem with the general relocation of manufacturing production from the high-cost west to the low-cost east.

The "A" class vessels were put into service one after another from September 1975 to mid-1976, and a sophisticated transpacific container liner network was gradually established. Uniquely, in an era characterized by an oil crisis and a focus on fuel efficiency, "Maersk Line decided to stuck with fast ships and the concept of faster transit times" (Boyes, 1981: 13). The ships' itineraries were formidable, with ports of call on both US coasts (New York, Philadelphia, Baltimore, Charleston, Los Angeles/Long Beach, and San Francisco/Oakland), and in Japan (Kobe and Tokyo), Manila, Hong Kong, Singapore, Malaysia, and Indonesia, all of which were serviced on a nine-week turnaround schedule. To assist the nine mainline vessels, the company established an important network of smaller cellular ships. These ships supported the transpacific routes and provided feeder services among the ports of Kelang, Penang, and Belawan Deli, thereby allowing Maersk Line to offer weekly, fully containerized services to and from Malaysia and Sumatra. The semi-containerships that Maersk Line had been operating in the Pacific since 1974 were redeployed to its Far East–West Africa service (the four "M" class vessels) and to the company's extensive conventional liner services (chartered-in vessels).

Table 11.1 provides an overview of Maersk Line's container fleet for the first ten years as well as the routes served.

Major investments in ports were key to creating an efficient, customer-focused network in the Pacific. *Fairplay*'s Michael Grey (1975) described Maersk Line's initial terminal investments. In Newark, New Jersey, the company entered into an exclusive contract for use of a 46-acre area on Berth 51 in the Elizabeth Channel with a parking area for 1,100 40-foot chassis and a 150,000 square foot covered shed. In Baltimore, Maryland, it secured a parking area and an exclusive gate for the delivery and reception of containers. In Charleston, South Carolina, it obtained a preferential berth at the Columbus Street Terminal. In Los Angeles, the company secured a seven-acre yard with its own delivery and reception gates, while in Oakland, California, it gained access to a 12-acre area, and special facilities for the delivery of heavy loads by rail. In Japan, Maersk Line was slotted in for weekly service at the new Port Island Terminal Number 9 in Kobe, and the company became the main user of the new Ohi Terminal Number 3 in Tokyo. In Singapore, Maersk Line utilized the 60-acre common-user terminal held by the Port of Singapore Authority (PSA), where it provided considerable numbers of its own conveyers and chassis to prevent bottlenecks in peak periods. In Hong Kong, Modern Terminals Ltd invested heavily in a new berth to accommodate the Maersk vessels. By January 1976, Modern Terminals had become the largest container terminal in Hong Kong, with nearly 3,000 feet of quay, four quay cranes, and a 62-acre back-up area. Maersk Line held a 9-percent ownership share in the facilities (Boyes, 1981).

In Malaysia and Indonesia, Maersk Line had to basically develop ports to accommodate its enhanced feeder operations. In a recent, non-published interview with Jephson and Morgen (September 2012), former Maersk Line executive Flemming Jacobs described the challenge:[7]

> We had to create the foundation. We could not just go in and then ... you know, tie up alongside a container terminal facility ... We had to create it. We had to go to Jakarta. Had they seen a container before? Yes. Had they seen a container yard where, you know, containers are standing like this in all different corners? We had to go and find—well—Jakarta and Belawan Deli on Sumatra. We had to ... clear land to create an off-dock terminal because you would never be able to handle having anything in the port. You had to get the container off and get it away from the port. The port would sink if you came there with 50 containers.

Maersk Line introduced a series of business model innovations that would allow it to optimize its liner network with the goal of running a scheduled service with containers arriving on time. The nine-week turnaround schedule allowed Maersk Line to operate a weekly service in the Pacific with numerous mainline port calls. This was a major change in the competitive landscape

---

[7] Flemming Jacobs held many positions in the Maersk Group from 1960 to 1999, most of which were related to Maersk Lines' container shipping activities. He later became President and CEO of American President Lines (APL) and CEO of Neptune Orient Lines (NOL).

and demonstrated that "the lordly days when the containership consortia kept their ports of call to a minimum" were over (Grey 1975: 7). Maersk Line's Ib Kruse summarized the company's successful move into containerization with the notion of "good service" (Boyes 1981: 14). This concept accurately described the company's business model, which was configured around the following items:

- *Rigorous adherence to a timetable*: The ships departed at a specific hour on specific days. Arrivals were promised at specific hours on specific days—and those promises were kept. This "airline-scheduling philosophy" was a Maersk specialty of which the company was immensely proud (Boyes, 1981: 14). It was promoted in radio spots with the slogan, "You can set your watch by Maersk" (Jephson and Morgen, 2014: 75). Sticking to the timetable and living up to customer expectations was considered key, even if it meant that the company would periodically earn less money. For example, when congestion in the Panama Canal resulted in delays in the late 1970s, Maersk Line chose to add a tenth ship to its transpacific service—the company's 1,800 TEU *Dragør Mærsk* (the former *Svendborg Mærsk*). Although this was an expensive measure in a business with extremely tight profit margins, it was seen as necessary to maintain the schedule (Boyes, 1981).
- *Flexible vessels*: All of Maersk Line's containerships were built with artificial tween-decks (ATD), which allowed the company to accommodate non-containerized freight—cargo of non-standard shapes and sizes, especially oversized and heavy machinery loads.

The focus on operating according to a fixed timetable was a major commercial decision. None of the containerized competitors were geared for such operations. For years, Sea-Land had focused on its US–Vietnam service, which mainly carried containers for the US Army during the Vietnam War. This service had proven very profitable, and had been expanded into a full liner service in which the ships continued from southern Vietnam to Okinawa, Japan, and then transported merchandise from Japan to the United States. Sea-Land could not operate the line as a scheduled service because it was completely dependent on the military.

BUSINESS MODEL EXPERIMENTATION AND COMPANY TRANSITION

The Maersk Group will celebrate its 110th anniversary in 2014, an event that is not uncommon among the Danish shipping companies. The longevity of leading Danish shipping companies is notable when compared with the lifespans of companies in other traditional maritime nations (Sornn-Friese, Poulsen, and Iversen, 2012). However, Maersk's history is particularly remarkable. Whereas other Danish shipping companies have experienced, and eventually overcome, several serious crises, the Maersk Group has essentially experienced constant growth throughout its existence. Its growth path has been characterized by an entrepreneurial spirit that has taken the company into an array of activities, usually with great success. Over time, the company has proven itself inherently capable of adapting to changing circumstances and exploiting new opportunities.

The company's dynamic capability may be partly explained by the entrepreneurial talent of the Møller family, which has steered the company since 1904. The passing of the control of the Maersk Group from generation to generation is not unique in international shipping. Individuals have strongly influenced the development of this industry (Svendsen, 1981), which is rich with examples of uncompromising entrepreneurs. Anyone wishing to be a ship owner must have a special combination of self-confidence and optimism "to sell ships when they're making money, buy them when they're losing money, build brand new ones just when the world has too many—and a breathtaking amount of one's own capital at risk in a business that is inherently perilous" (LaRocco, 2012: x). More striking, however, is the fact that family ownership and control have always been prominent in shipping, and are often emphasized as important explanations for the longevity and growth dynamics of shipping firms, whether in tramp shipping (Harlaftis and Theotokas, 2004; Theotokas, 2007; Theotokas and Harlaftis, 2009) or in liner shipping (et al., 2013). The direct involvement of the Møller family in all matters of the group's management and development, and the generally conservative business values to which A. P. Møller and Mærsk Mc-Kinney Møller adhered, have been key to the company's success and underscored all major decisions. These values are clearly expressed in the family credo: "No loss should hit us which can be avoided with constant care" (Hornby, 1988).

Mærsk Mc-Kinney Møller considered the possibilities for containerization early on, but he was deliberately and naturally cautious. He postponed the decision to enter this trade for roughly eight years. On a business trip to the United States in 1965, he visited a Sea-Land containership that was docked in port. He eagerly inspected the ship, after which he told his personal assistant that he was not convinced and that the time was not right to start building containerships (Bensen, Lambek, and Ørskov, 2004). Containerization was not an issue to be taken lightly. First, unprecedentedly high investments were necessary to enter the business. Second, containerization was not restricted to the maritime sector. Rather, it required major land-based investments and broader logistical competencies. Third, the productivity of the new containerships was so vastly superior that the main question became how the frequency of sailings in any given service could be maintained with only a fraction of the departures to which exporters and importers had become accustomed (Broeze, 2002).

In 1968, Mærsk Mc-Kinney Møller turned to McKinsey & Company for advice and assigned them the task of analysing the Maersk Group's business potential and recommending improvements. The general assessment for Maersk Line was that its liner operations worked better than those of its competitors. However, McKinsey stressed that the main challenge for Maersk Line was to protect its US–Far East Line in light of the containerization threat (Jephson and Morgen, 2014). When following up on the report, Mærsk Mc-Kinney Møller brought an investigative team together in the company's liner department to scrutinize the arguments for and against containerization of the Maersk Line. In a presentation made to management in August 1970, the liner department spoke against containerization, stating that Maersk Line "alone should not invest in container ships, nor transform the existing tonnage to container ships, but continue to operate the semi-conventional ships in this trade" (quoted from Jephson and Morgen, 2014: 51).

The reception of the McKinsey report must be understood in the context of developments in the main Southeast Asian markets served by Maersk Line at the time. The company's key ports in Thailand, Indonesia, and Malaysia simply could not handle container shipping. Containers were nevertheless already a fact of life, and Maersk Line's sales staff had to accept that some customers considered a unit load to be a container rather than a pallet. This meant that Maersk Line was increasingly moving containers on ships designed to carry a very different type of load. At about the same time, Maersk Line was in serious negotiations with "K" Line regarding the establishment of a joint container liner service on the Asia–Europe route (see the earlier discussion). In addition to that venture, Maersk Line ordered four semi-containerships for its Far East–West Africa line to be delivered in 1974 and 1975.

Mærsk Mc-Kinney Møller again considered the container question. In August 1972, he had formed a "crash committee" to work keenly on the container question. The committee was steered from the Copenhagen headquarters and included the managing directors of Maersk Line's main offices in the US, Japan, Thailand, and Indonesia. Contrary to most other international shipping companies, Maersk Line had already established a structure with its own branches in the most strategically important countries.[8]

The committee was assigned the task of investigating opportunities and risks, benchmarking and learning from competitors, and preparing a base for entering into container shipping. The operation of a container business was believed to be very different from conventional liner shipping. Therefore, the crash committee was kept separate from the Copenhagen-based liner department. The committee eventually spoke in favor of entering into container shipping. The decisive moment came during a meeting in late January 1973. The committee, together with colleagues from the liner department

---

[8] Hornby (1988) states that the Maersk Group's desire to establish its own organization abroad stemmed from its experiences during the Second World War. The war had highlighted the group's vulnerability in times of war and occupation. A. P. Møller and Mærsk Mc-Kinney Møller wanted to establish a structure that would allow them to manage their ships from abroad if Denmark were to ever be occupied again.

and the technical organization led by Ib Kruse, presented its final proposal to Mærsk Mc-Kinney Møller, his partner and cousin, Georg E. R. Andersen, and Rodney Leach of McKinsey & Company. The unanimous conclusion of the crash committee was given:

> The U.S./Far East liner trade is dominated by continuing growth and the rapid adoption of containerization, which will increase demand for an integrated, intermodal, door-to-door service. This is an entirely new concept in methods of transportation in which ocean shipping is only a part. Maersk Line has responded to these trends by adapting existing vessels to carry containers—a development that has been well received by our customers and improved our profitability. However, these adaptations are largely a "stop-gap", or interim, step.
>
> (Quoted from Jephson and Morgen, 2014: 64.)

A. P. Moller's strong international organization, which had been built up in the post-war years to match the company's considerably growing liner business, proved an important prerequisite for the company's success in container shipping. Not only were the Maersk Line branches in the United States, Japan, Thailand, and Indonesia heavily involved in the decision to enter into container shipping, but they were also important building blocks in the containerization of Maersk Line's markets.

When Maersk Line finally entered into container shipping, its geographically dispersed organization allowed it to standardize its services, while ensuring a regional focus. As its services expanded, Maersk Line continued establishing offices in its major markets. The group's annual reports indicated that Maersk Line started to prepare for containerization on the US–Far East run in 1974 by establishing fully owned organizations in Hong Kong, Singapore, and Malaysia. In 1975, the New York-based Moller Steamship Co. established offices in Philadelphia, Baltimore, New Orleans, Dallas, and Houston. In 1979, the company's conventional Europe–Far East liner service, which had been established in 1966, was containerized, and Maersk Line opened new offices in Holland, Belgium, and Germany.

THE CONTAINER ORGANIZATION IN COPENHAGEN

In 1971, a section named "Container Administration" was added to the Liner Department's organizational chart. Four people were hired for this new section to work primarily with customer relations. In 1972, three people were hired for a section in the Liner Department's Cargo Operation Unit, which was also named "Container Administration." Thus, a total of seven people were employed in container shipping operations in 1972, out of the ninety-eight people employed in the Liner Department.

In 1972, the Stanford Research Institute stated in a report written for Maersk Line that the transition into container shipping would force Maersk Line to consider extensive organizational and operational changes. The crash committee had also stressed the importance of developing new skills to meet the unique requirements of door-to-door container services. As a result, Maersk Container Line was established as a separate department in 1973. This name was only used internally—externally, the brand remained Maersk Line (Jephson and Morgen, 2014). The new organization was headed by the former Head of Technical Organization in A. P. Moller, Ib Kruse. It was very different from the company's traditional liner department, which continued to run its successful business based on palletized units and occasional containers on conventional break-bulk ships.

Implications for the Business Model Literature

The conditions for business model innovations vary from industry to industry. The more dynamic industries will typically facilitate more business model innovations than those industries characterized by more stable technologies. The shipping industry belongs to the latter group, as it is highly capital intensive and generally conservative. As such, shipping is far from the dynamic and fast-moving industries that generate most of the popular examples of business model innovations. However, business model innovations do take place in shipping, as illustrated by the Maersk Line case.

Although containerization has been accompanied by some technological developments, our study of Maersk Line suggests that the core of containerization is organizational in nature. The main challenge for liner-shipping companies was to change the perception of shipping from a goal in itself to a means to the goal of transporting cargo from door-to-door. This change in perception had immense implications, as it required the optimization of the whole system of cargo handling, not just the elements related to sea transport. The business model lens is particularly useful for understanding the competitive dynamics, as containerization brought a fundamental change in the formula for making money (from the transport of pallets from port to port to the transport of containers from door to door).

According to the literature, business model innovations consist of three elements: the value proposition for customers, the needed activities, and the profits gained from engaging in these activities (Birkinshaw and Ansari, chapter 5 in this volume). Containerization entailed standardization, which paved the way for cheaper, better, and more reliable transportation of goods from door to door. However, the bottlenecks in containerization were the change of the mindset in shipping and the development of new vessels and ports with the necessary infrastructure, such as large cranes and sufficient space for storing containers.

The Maersk Line case provides numerous insights into business model innovations in terms of the decision process, timing, and the actors involved. The case challenges some of the presumptions in the business model literature.

As such, it highlights several areas of business model innovation that deserve more scrutiny. First, as a business model innovation, containerization did not happen quickly. Rather, the development of standards and the assembly of the system's elements took decades. Furthermore, containerization was not the result of a single company's innovation, but rather the outcome of the common effort of many actors in shipping and surrounding industries. In that sense, as a business model innovation, containerization was very different from the commonly mentioned examples of Apple, Google.com, and Ryanair. In fact, a single company could hardly make all of the required investments and adaptions needed for the business model innovation of containerization. However, the social implications of this innovation are probably greater than those associated with any other business model innovation, as it has helped to pave the way for globalization and increased trade across continents.

Second, although Maersk Line was very late into containerization—much later than many of its competitors—it undertook adoption forcefully and with substantial investments. This enabled it to not only catch up in a few years but also to take the innovation further than its competitors by, for example, building larger vessels and bigger, more modern port facilities and maintaining tight control of these. As a late mover, Maersk Line was able to take advantage of the standards that had already emerged and many of the experiences of its competitors. In that sense, Maersk Line was able to take the best from its competitors' experiences and scale its operations to a new level. This peculiar feature of the competitive dynamics of business model innovation around containerization corroborates the more general observation that late movers focused on the organizational set-up and the exploitation of commercial capabilities (e.g., operating routines for creating products, managing the sales and distribution channels, providing customer service, maintaining reputation and brand recognition, and participating in the development of industry standards and practices) tend to outperform first movers that focus on technological capabilities (Lee, 2009). In this regard, the Maersk Line case enhances our general understanding of how late movers may participate in growing the market (see also Markides and Geroski, 2004).

Third, although a new entrant—McLean's Sea-Land company—conducted much of the initial containerization experiments, it was the incumbent Maersk Line that took the concept to a higher level and reaped the benefits of this development. Notably, Sea-Land was acquired by Maersk Line in 1999 after years of partnership. Although Sea-Land initially recognized the opportunities of containerization, Maersk Line was better able to exploit them by using its network to scale and optimize the innovation.

Fourth, at the organizational level, Maersk Line experimented by setting up a new department in Maersk Line focused on containerization. This department was established alongside the traditional liner department in 1973. This new department could advocate for the interests of the new business model of containerization, while other units in Maersk Line were advocating for the old business model. In this sense, Maersk Line was experimenting with the organizational set-up in what might be characterized as a discovery process (as highlighted by McGrath, 2010) and thereby providing an organizational platform for the business model change (as highlighted by Santos, Spector, and Van der Heyden, chapter 3 in this volume). The new container department encompassed different competencies, relationships, and mindset than the traditional liner department and as such formed an organizational anchor for the innovation of the business model.

Fifth, containerization in Maersk Line was never an offensive strategic decision designed to be a game changer. Rather, the decision process was characterized by a conservative stance of waiting to enter until it could no longer be deferred. Different views on the need for containerization were evident, as Maersk Line's exposure to the new development varied. For a time, Maersk Line tried to bridge the old pallet system and the new container system by, for example, developing vessels that could handle both types of cargo. The view of top management was that a move into containerization should be based on a unanimous decision. Therefore, the move was backed by all of the important actors and subsidiaries in Maersk Line from the outset. As such, the decision process was summarized by Mærsk Mc-Kinney Møller at the inauguration of Pier 51 in Newark in 1975: "… it was a question of one big step or none at all" (Jephson and Morgen, 2014: 76).

■ REFERENCES

Bensen, P. S., Lambek, B., and Ørskov, S. 2004. *Mærsk. Manden og magten.* Copenhagen: JP/Politikens Forlagshus A/S.

Birkinshaw, J. and Ansari, S. 2015. Chapter 5, this volume. "Understanding Management Models: Going Beyond 'What' and 'Why' to 'How' Work Gets Done in Organizations."

Bjerrum, C. A. 1993. *ØK i uvejr: Da ØKs aktiekapital forsvandt i Stillehavet.* Copenhagen: Børsen.

Boyes, J. R. C. 1981. "Maersk Lets Its Mask Slip … But Only Just." *Containerization International*, January: pp. 12–18.

Broeze, F. 2002. *Globalization of the Oceans: Containerisation from the 1950s to the Present. Research in Maritime History No. 23.* St. John's, Newfoundland: International Maritime Economic History Association.

Chesbrough, H. W. 2010. "Business Model Innovation: Opportunities and Barriers." *Long Range Planning*, 43: pp. 354–363.

Donovan, A. and Bonney, J. 2006. *"The Box That Changed the World." Fifty Years of Container Shipping—An Illustrated History.* East Windsor, New Jersey: Commonwealth Business Media.

Drucker, P. 2007. *Innovation and Entrepreneurship: Practice and Principles.* Burlington, MA: Butterworth-Heinemann.

Foss, N. and Saebi, T. 2015. Chapter 1, this volume. "Business Models and Business Model Innovation: Bringing Organization into the Discussion."

Fremont, A. 2007. "Global Maritime Networks. The Case of Maersk." *Journal of Transport Geography*, 15: pp. 431–442.

Gibney, R. F. 1984. *Container Lines: The Strategy Game.* London: Lloyd's of London Press Ltd.

Gilman, S. 1983. *The Competitive Dynamics of Container Shipping*. Hants, UK: Gower Publishing Company Ltd.

Grey, M. 1975. "Maersk Begins Its Trans-Pacific Container Challenge." *Fairplay International Shipping Weekly*, October, 2: pp. 7–9.

Harlaftis, G. and Theotokas, I. 2004. "European Family Firms in International Business: British and Greek Tramp-shipping Firms." *Business History*, 46(2): pp. 219–255.

Hearth, J. 1964. "Sea-land. Portrait of a 'Shipping' Company." *Fairplay Cargo Handling Supplement*, October 1, 1964: pp. vi–xxi.

Hornby, O. 1988. *"With Constant Care … "*. *A. P. Møller: Shipowner 1876–1965*. Copenhagen: H. Schultz Information.

Jephson, C. and Morgen, H. 2014. *Creating Global Opportunities: Maersk Line in Containerization 1973–2013*. Cambridge: Cambridge University Press.

Jones, O., Ghobadian, O., O'Regan, N., and Antcliff, V. 2013. "Dynamic Capabilities in a Sixth-generation Family Firm: Entrepreneurship and the Bibby Line." *Business History*, 55(6): pp. 910–941.

LaRocco, L. A. 2012. *Dynasties of the Sea. The Shipowners and Financiers Who Expanded the Era of Free Trade*. Stamford, Connecticut: Marine Money, Inc.

Lauring, K. 2008. *Containertrafik gennem 50 år—Container Traffic for 50 Years*. Elsinore: Handels-og Søfartsmuseet.

Lee, G. K. 2009. "Understanding the Timing of 'Fast-second' Entry and the Relevance of Capabilities in Invention vs. Commercialization." *Research Policy*, 38: pp. 86–95.

Levinson, M. 2006. *The Box: How the Shipping Container Made the World Smaller and the World Economy Bigger*. Princeton, NJ: Princeton University Press.

Markides, C. C. 2000. *All the Right Moves*. Cambridge, MA: Harvard Business Press.

Markides, C. C. and Geroski, P. 2004. *Fast Second: How Smart Companies Bypass Radical Innovation to Enter and Dominate New Markets*. San Francisco, CA: John Wiley & Sons.

McGrath, R. G. 2010. "Business Models: A Discovery Driven Approach." *Long Range Planning*, 43: pp. 247–261.

McKinsey and Company, Inc. 1966. *Containerization: Its Trends, Significance and Implications*. London: British Transport Docks Board.

Poulsen, R. T. 2007. "Liner Shipping and Technological Innovation: Ostasiat and the Container Revolution, 1963–75." *Scandinavian Economic History Review*, 55(2): pp. 83–100.

Rasmussen, F. A., Rønne, B. V., and Johansen, H. C. 2000. "Damp og diesel." *Dansk Søfarts Historie*, vol. 6: 1920–1960. Copenhagen: Gyldendal.

Roland, A., Bolster, W. J., and Keyssar, A. 2008. *The Way of the Ship: America's Maritime History Reenvisioned, 1600–2000*. Hoboken, NJ: John Wiley & Sons.

Santos, J. F. P., Spector, B., and Van der Heyden, L. 2015. Chapter 3, this volume. "Towards a Theory of Business Model Change."

Sornn-Friese, H., Poulsen, R. T., and Iversen, M. J. 2012. "'Knowing the Ropes': Capability Reconfiguration and Restructuring of the Danish Shipping Industry." In S. Tenold, M. J. Iversen and E. Lange (eds), *Global Shipping in Small Nations. Nordic Experiences After 1960*. London: Palgrave Macmillan, pp. 61–99.

Stopford, M. 2009. *Maritime Economics*. Third edition. New York: Routledge.

Svendsen, A. S. 1981. "The Role of the Entrepreneur in the Shipping Industry." *Maritime Policy and Management*, 8(3): pp. 137–140.

Theotokas, I. 2007. "On Top of World Shipping: Greek Shipping Companies' Organization and Management." *Research in Transportation Economics (Maritime Transport: The Greek Paradigm)*, 21: pp. 63–93.

Theotokas, I. and Harlaftis, G. 2009. *Leadership in World Shipping. Greek Family Firms in International Business.* London: Palgrave Macmillan.

Van Ham, H. and Rijsenbrij, J. 2012. *Development of Containerization. Success Through Vision, Drive and Technology.* Amsterdam: IOS Press BV.

Winter, S. G. and Szulanski, G. 2001. "Replication as a Strategy." *Organization Science*, 12 (6): pp. 730–743.

Zott, C., Amit, R., and Massa, L. 2011. "The Business Model: Recent Developments and Future Research." *Journal of Management*, 37: pp. 1019–1042.

12 Business Model Innovation in the Pharmaceutical Industry

The Supporting Role of Organizational Design

KLEMENT A. RASMUSSEN
AND NICOLAI J. FOSS

Introduction

The pharmaceutical industry assumes a major economic role in a number of countries (e.g., the United States, Germany, and Denmark) in terms of its share of overall value-added, R&D inputs, exports, and innovativeness. The industry also captures general interest because of its role as the key originator of medical innovation in the world, and has, partly for this reason, for a long time been heavily regulated. The pharmaceutical industry has captured scholarly interest because of, for example, the highly "closed" innovation model, pricing policies, and dynamics of the boundaries of the firm that have characterized this industry (e.g., Bianchi et al., 2011; Danzon, 2006; Pisano, 1991). Thus, the last decades have witnessed major merger and acquisition activity, and substantial alliance activity, for example, with biotechnology firms. Much of this activity may be seen as attempts to patch a business model—namely, the "blockbuster model" based on high-volume, high-margin sales of drugs for common conditions and driven by mainly internal and very substantial R&D inputs, as well as scale economies in R&D, production, marketing, and sales (Gilbert, Henske, and Singh, 2003)—that, some argue, is "becoming extinct" (Mattke, Klautzer, and Mengistu, 2012: 1). This prediction is based on an argument that technological opportunities in the pharmaceutical industry are declining, development costs are soaring, copy products are proliferating, and regulatory pressures that threaten margins are building up.

The strength and relative weight of these ongoing changes are subject to substantial debate. We argue that these changes, some of which are external to the industry (e.g., regulatory pressure) and some internal (e.g., declining R&D productivity), drive the ongoing experimentation with business models that can be observed in the industry. Much of this experimentation takes the form of introducing a service dimension as an integral part of the emerging business models, a dynamic that has been building up over the last decade. Business models are often taken to denote the firm's core logic for creating and capturing value by specifying the firm's fundamental value proposition(s), the markets and market segments it addresses, the structure of the value chain which is required for realizing the relevant value proposition, and the mechanisms of value capture that the firm deploys. We describe the reconfigurations of three companies, partly relying on the framework of Santos, Spector, and Van der Heyden (chapter 3 in this volume).

We show how these reconfigurations are embedded in, and related to changes in, organizational designs. Indeed, the managerial challenges of business model innovation are to a large extent organizational challenges that involve the redesign of organizational structure and control. We describe various changes in the organizational design of three selected players in the industry, discuss how these are related to the deep-seated changes the industry is witnessing, and discuss the managerial challenges of implementing organizational designs that fit the emerging business models in the industry, particularly those that shift the value-proposition toward a service-based one.

We begin with a presentation of the industry context—particularly the drivers that prompt the ongoing experimentation with business models; briefly discussing our data sources and the method of diverse cases; discussing the forms that the actual experimentation takes; and end by discussing the challenges of choosing organizational design that can embed the changing business models faced by pharmaceutical firms.

Drivers of Business Model Innovation in the Pharmaceutical Industry

The extant literature does not point to any unique drivers of business model innovation (or, business model "learning," "evolution," "modification," "reconfiguration," or "renewal"; cf. Demil and Lecocq, 2010; Doz and Kosonen, 2010; Dunford, Palmer, and Benveniste, 2010; Teece, 2010). Rather, it generically points to forces such as globalization, deregulation, technological advances, and changing preferences as drivers. Clearly, the ensemble of forces that drive business model innovation differs across industries. In the context of the pharmaceutical industry, we argue that the particularly important drivers are mounting payer pressures, regulatory changes, and, more controversially, declining technological opportunity.

THE PAYMENT CHALLENGE

What is referred to by industry insiders as the "payment challenge" refers to a host of structural changes in the costs of health care and the willingness and ability of governments and insurance companies to pay for treatments that jointly put margins in the industry under strong pressure, a tendency that has been exacerbated by the emphasis on fiscal austerity since the onset of the financial crisis of 2008. Data from the OECD (2010) suggest that health care spending per capita in OECD countries has risen by over 70 percent in real terms since the early 1990s. This increased spending can be partly attributed to deep-seated demographic, epidemiological, and economic changes. By 2020, there will be more than 7.6 billion people in the world, with 719 million (9.4 percent) being over 65—the segment of the population that consumes most medicine per capita. Furthermore, the size of this segment will double relative to its size in the year 2000 (Hunter, 2011). In the developed countries, life expectancy has increased by, on average two years for every decade since the early 1990s. However, Hunter (2011: 1818) noted, this "has not been matched by a concomitant increase in health, leading to an actual increase in the economic burden."

The World Health Organization (WHO) (2002) found that if chronic conditions are not adequately prevented and/or managed, they may become the most expensive problems faced by health care systems. Current health care systems are mainly designed to treat acute problems related to illnesses (i.e., diagnosing, testing, relieving symptoms, and developing cure). While these tasks are important for acute and episodic health problems, a remarkable discrepancy emerges when adopting this model for the management of chronic conditions. Substantial evidence suggests that patients with chronic conditions are usually undertreated in emerging countries due to limited access to medicine (WHO, 2003), while in developed countries the problem is that they do not comply to prescribed treatment regimens. In particular, medical *noncompliance* has been identified as a major issue of public health, which in turn imposes a considerable financial burden upon modern health-care systems (Donovan, 1995; Weinman and Petrie, 1997). WHO studies show that 50 percent of people with a chronic condition are non-compliant (WHO, 2003). This has been estimated to cost $177 billion annually in the United States (approximately a quarter of total annual pharmaceutical revenues) (IMS, 2008) and account for 78 percent of health care spending (Bodenheimer and Fernandez, 2005). For patients, non-compliance is directly related to poorer health outcomes (Loden and Schooler, 2000) and increased health care costs (Kane and Shaya, 2008).

Against this backdrop, pharmaceutical companies face surging demands from payers, who, in their efforts to control soaring health care costs, are increasingly requiring that pharmaceutical companies demonstrate that their products provide therapeutic or cost advantages over competitors' products and non-pharmaceutical treatment options.

REGULATORY CHANGE

Changes in the regulatory environment have also led to the introduction of additional demanding hurdles that a new drug must clear prior to market launch. Following the well-publicized market withdrawals of high-profile pharmaceutical products such as rofecoxib (Vioxx, Merck), cerivastatin (Baycol, Bayer), troglitazone (Rezulin, Warner-Lambert) and cisapride (Propulsid, Janssen Pharmaceutica), the US Food and Drug Administration (FDA) and its counterparts in other major markets have put more focus on pre-approval safety evaluations and increased their reliance on post-approval systems to monitor product safety and use (Munos, 2009). For example, with the ratification of the Food and Drug Administration Amendments Act of 2007[1] in the United States, the FDA was granted new authority to require submission of risk evaluation, mitigation strategies, and application for regulatory approval, and to demand post-market clinical studies on approved products if safety issues arise. Under such circumstances, they would be able to mandate changes to a drug's approved labeling, and to impose new distribution and use restrictions on marketed drugs (Kaitin, 2010). Globally, regulators also collaborate more closely, so when a product is rejected in one market, it is more likely to be rejected in others. In 2010, for instance, The European Medicines Agency (EMA) pulled the diabetes drug Avandia, while the FDA imposed severe restrictions on its use, and the two agencies exchanged notes before reaching a final decision.[2]

DECLINING TECHNOLOGICAL OPPORTUNITY IN THE PHARMACEUTICAL INDUSTRY

In spite of steadily increasing levels of investments in R&D over the past two decades, the pharmaceutical industry has not been able to avoid a continuous decline in the number of new molecular entities (NMEs) that enter clinical development and subsequent market entry (Light and Lexchin, 2012). To illustrate, in 2002 the FDA only approved seventeen NMEs for sale in the United States, that is, only a small fraction of the fifteen-year high of fifty-six approved NMEs in 1996 and the lowest since 1983 (Cockburn, 2004). The United States is by no means alone. Thus, worldwide statistics suggest that the annual number of new active substances approved in major markets declined by fifty during the 1990s, while private-sector R&D expenditures tripled.[3] These numbers have prompted concerns from industry leaders,

[1] FDA Amendments Act. Pub. L. No. 110-85, 121 Stat. 823.
[2] Sten Stovall, "Europe's Drug Regulator Says Innovation Must Pick Up." *The Wall Street Journal*, December 15, 2010.
[3] EFPIA member companies spent $47 billion in 2002. European Federation of Pharmaceutical Industries and Associations. 2003. "The Pharmaceutical Industry in Figures, 2003 update." Brussels: EFPIA.

observers, and policy makers, with some declaring an innovation crisis within pharmaceutical research.

Some scholars argue that these concerns are almost surely exaggerated: The so-called innovation crisis rests on the decline in NMEs, since the sharp peak in 1996 that resulted from the rapid backlog reduction of applications after the FDA deployed the augmented staff hired under the Prescription Drug User Fee Act of 1992 to reduce approval times (Scherer, 2007). This decline ended in 2006, when approvals of NMEs reverted to their long-term mean of between fifteen and twenty-five a year.[4] On the basis of FDA records, Munos (2009) showed that pharmaceutical companies " ... have delivered innovation at a constant rate for almost 60 years," and new biologicals[5] have followed a similar pattern "in which approvals fluctuate around a constant, low level." According to Hopkins et al. (2007), not even the revolution of biotechnology changed the rate of approval of NMEs, though it influenced strategies for drug development.[6]

Thus, whether there is a crisis or not is a much more complex question than the absolute number of NMEs brought to market. More important is the number of NMEs that represent an actual therapeutic advance. Although innovation is often measured in terms of NMEs as a stand-in for therapeutically superior new medicines by the industry and its analysts, most have only provided trivial clinical advantages over existing treatments (Light and Lexchin, 2012). This is not a new phenomenon; the dominance of drugs without major therapeutic gains can be traced back to the "golden age" of pharmaceutical innovation. Covering the period from 1974 to 1994, the industry's Barral report on all internationally marketed NMEs concluded that only 11 percent were therapeutically and pharmacologically innovative (Barral, 1996). Since the mid-1990s independent reviews have reached roughly the same conclusion that approximately 85–90 percent of NMEs provide minor or no clinical advantages for patients (see, e.g., Angell, 2005; Luijn, Van Gribnau, and Leufkens, 2010).

---

[4] US Food and Drug Administration. 2011. New Molecular Entity Approvals for 2010." Silver Spring: FDA, 2011. Retrieved November 2014 at: <http://www.fda.gov/downloads/drugs/developmentapprovalprocess/howdrugsaredevelopedandapproved/drugandbiologicapprovalreports/UCM242695.pdf>.

[5] A "biologic" is manufactured in a living system such as a microorganism, or plant or animal cells. Most biologics are very large, complex molecules or mixtures of molecules. Many biologics are produced using recombinant DNA technology. A drug is typically manufactured through chemical synthesis, which means that it is made by combining specific chemical ingredients in an ordered process. <http://www.bio.org/articles/how-do-drugs-and-biologics-differ>.

[6] Such accounts obviously raise the issue of why there has been an escalating discussion of declining technological opportunities and a crisis to medical innovation. Adamini et al. (2009) suggest that telling stories about the "innovation crisis" to politicians and the press is a rent-seeking plot: It helps to attract a range of government protections from the "generic" competition.

EMPOWERING END USERS AND HEALTH CARE PROFESSIONALS

Historically, patients have played an essentially passive role in health delivery. In most cultures, the physician has been the sole decision maker with regard to diagnosis and the optimal treatment regimen; after all, they have had much more training and possess more medical knowledge than patients. Further, in markets where patients have enjoyed health insurance, insurers have not only insulated patients from financial shocks but also from the prices of various treatments which are essential for creating optimal resource allocation in efficient markets. Patients have followed obligingly, while experts have made decisions that could, quite literally, have life-or-death consequences for them.

Prompted by the recent advances in internet and communication technologies (ICTs), transparency is expected to increase, in turn likely empowering patients and changing the practice of health care into a patient-centric model with patients having more "on-demand" access to information. Social media networks—from PatientsLikeMe to Sermo and Medscape Physician Connect— are making data on outcomes and efficacy more transparent and freeing it from the control of corporate giants. New mobile technologies and apps enable patients to take a more active role in managing their own health care. For example, in diabetes, where effective disease management requires a coordinated and holistic approach, new apps assist patients in not only managing their blood glucose but also other aspects of their health, such as diet and exercise. The range of apps is by no means limited to diabetes. For example, these include apps that aid patients in keeping track of vaccination schedules (i.e., Novartis' VaxTrak), control their hemophilia A Factor VIII infusions (i.e., Bayer's Factor Track), and map cancer clinical trials within 150 miles (i.e., GSK's Cancer Trials).

With the new ICTs, health care professionals can potentially access patient records from any given location. For example, physicians' access to patient history files, the newest pharmaceutical data, laboratory results, insurance information, and medical resources would be more effectively used by ICTs, and in turn, improve the quality of patient care (Istepanian, Jovanov, and Zhang, 2004). Further, the data that can be mined from such systems can be used to compare efficacy between different treatments. Kaiser Healthcare and Intermountain Health, have already been doing this for a while, and new entrants in the personal health record (PHR) business such as Google Health and Microsoft HealthVault could take "value mining" to an entirely new level. These trends are likely to result in more empowered and better-informed patients, which in turn means that physicians spend less time in explaining rudimentary facts about diseases, and rather set aside time to discuss more complex treatment aspects and listen to each patient.[7]

---

[7] Kaplan et al. (1996) found that patients that engaged with the physician in a "participatory decision-making style" had improved health outcomes and were more satisfied. The study also showed that physicians with this kind of decision-making style were 30% less likely to have patient

Data and Data Analysis

SMALL-N RESEARCH DESIGNS

In the following we adopt a small-N research design to explore the organizational challenges that companies in the pharmaceutical industry face when seeking to innovate their business models. Such designs are often criticized on the ground that they are vulnerable to sample bias and, hence, problems of external validity (Bryman, 1988; King, 1994). However, most scholars agree that when there are fundamental gaps in the understanding of a phenomenon concerning which variables matter and how, explorative research based on small-N samples is warranted (Eisenhardt, 1989; Westney and Van Maanen, 2011). Moreover, as Dyer and Wilkins (1991: 617) explain, if executed well, case studies can be "extremely powerful" when "authors have described general phenomenon so well that others have little difficulty seeing the same phenomenon in their own experience and research." Thus, "good stories" are successful in terms of identifying generative mechanisms that other researchers can recognize in the cases they investigate (Hedström, 2005). This study is basically an attempt to identify the operation of such mechanisms in the context of the pharmaceutical industry.

We specifically draw on a diverse-case method of selection, with the primary objective of achieving maximum variation along relevant dimensions (while homogenizing other dimensions). In line with the diverse-case approach, the selection of specific pharmaceutical companies was based on the study's aims, that is, seeking a balanced sample of companies in which issues and processes related to the organizational dimensions of business model innovation can be compared, while at the same time keeping variability reasonably high. We selected the following three companies for the sample, namely *Novo Nordisk A/S*, which pursues a "traditionalist" strategy; *LEO Pharma A/S*, which pursues a "simultaneous" approach, explicitly balancing different business models; and *UCB Pharma*, which is transitioning toward a service-oriented model. Our interviews and general industry knowledge indicates that these three firms can be taken to be representative of different kinds of experimentation with business models in the pharmaceutical industry.

---

defection. In a different study based on patients with hypertension and breast cancer, they found that communication between patients and physicians affected the health status of patients. Notably, consultations where patients had engaged in prior information gathering, more information sharing between the patient and the physician, and more expression of emotion were all related to improved health outcomes (Kaplan et al., 1996).

DATA COLLECTION AND ANALYSIS

The data for this study were collected from three overlapping sources, namely in-depth, semi-structured interviews, documents, and observation studies. These sources were triangulated to maintain the integrity of the analysis (Miles and Huberman, 1994; Silverman, 2006). We relied on Lincoln and Guba's (1985) guidelines for "purposeful sampling" and initially interviewed top managers about how they change the organizational design of their firms in order to facilitate and encourage business model innovation. Next a "snowball" technique was adopted, asking each top manager for his or her recommendations as to who could best explain the processes of interests. Prior research (see, e.g., Daft and Weick, 1984; Isabella, 1990) and the study's research objective, suggested that sampling should begin with top managers because they typically play a key role in ventures that represent new strategic directions and resource configurations for the firm. As active participants in championing a new business model, these managers represent key informants (Kumar, Stern, and Anderson, 1993) who have overall insight into the company's core capabilities, organizational structures, resource allocation, strategies, etc., and are therefore in a unique position to recommend additional key and role informants at all levels within the organization.

In total, thirty in-depth interviews were carried out.[8] All interviews started with open questions about the company's overall strategy and recent experience. As the interviews progressed, the questions gradually became more structured, delving into organizational design issues in the relevant firms, and the specific challenges they faced on the organizational side with respect to business model innovation. In addition, non-participant observations were made by one of the authors of the chapter, who, in the interest of full disclosure, is working as an industrial PhD researcher in one of the interviewed companies (i.e., LEO Pharma). Finally, we examined relevant documents, such as internal powerpoint presentations, annual company reports, and consulting reports. The documents not only supplied additional information, but also allowed us to control for memory bias by comparing interview statements with the collected document data (Miller, Cardinal, and Glick, 1997). Our discussion of the drivers of business model innovation in the industry is mainly based on documents.

To analyze the data, we adopted Yin's (2003) "pattern-matching" method of analysis. In this approach the empirical patterns of the case (and the embedded cases) are compared with those of theory. To facilitate discerning patterns in the data, the interviews were transcribed. Following triangulation with documents, this procedure allowed for the derivation across the interviews

---

[8] Specifically, the interviews were distributed as follows over the three firms: UCB Pharma: fifteen interviews in total, ranging from Executive Vice President to manager level; LEO Pharma A/S: thirteen interviews in total, ranging from Executive Vice President to manager level; Novo Nordisk A/S: two interviews in total, ranging from Corporate Vice President to manager level.

of patterns relating to how the relevant firms were changing their organization to facilitate business model innovation. In order to further strengthen validity, respondent validation was also applied (Silverman, 2006).

Business Models Changes in the Pharmaceutical Industry

DYNAMICS OF BUSINESS MODELS

Established pharmaceutical companies have reacted to the above drivers in terms of more or less radical changes to their basic value propositions, the organization of their value chains, internal organization, key resources, and revenue models. Santos, Spector, and Van der Heyden (chapter 3 in this volume) explain how firms can reconfigure their existing business models by either (1) "reactivating," that is, altering the set of elemental activities that the firm offers to its customers (e.g., offering a hot meal on flights); (2) "repartitioning," that is, altering the boundaries of the firm by moving activities and the organizational units that perform activities (e.g., outsourcing); (3) "relocating," that is, altering the (physical, cultural, and institutional) location of units currently performing activities (e.g., off-shoring); and (4) "relinking," that is, altering the linkages between the organizational units that perform these activities (e.g., an arms-length relation with a supplier becomes an alliance). This classification provides a highly convenient way to think about business model innovation, as such innovations may be understood as more or less radical changes in elements (1) to (4), either in only one of them (modular business model innovation) or in most or all of them (architectural business model innovation) (cf. Stieglitz and Foss, chapter 6 in this volume). We rely on the Santos, Spector, and Van der Heyden classification in the following.

The pharmaceutical industry demonstrates various ongoing adjustments of or experimenting with existing business models ranging from changes that only involve one or few of the above reconfigurations, for example, an increase in the number of alliances with biotechnology firms (i.e., (2) above), to more radical changes that involve most of the reconfigurations noted and which are clearly in the nature of distinct business model innovation. The data suggest a meaningful distinction between an incremental and modular "traditionalist approach" (here exemplified by Novo Nordisk A/S), an architectural but also relatively incremental "service-oriented approach" (UCB Pharma), and the in-between "simultaneous approach" (LEO Pharma A/S). We fully acknowledge that this taxonomy is neither fully exhaustive (there may be other business model and associated business model innovations), nor fully exclusive (the three business models may be partly overlapping for certain companies). Indeed, one of them, namely the simultaneous, arguably represents an unstable form. Nevertheless, the three approaches represent useful ideal types that adequately represent many of the important players.

THE TRADITIONALIST APPROACH: LEVERAGING EXTANT CAPABILITIES

Companies that pursue this model are not necessarily traditionalists in the sense that they stick to the block buster model. Rather, they are traditionalist in the sense that they seek to leverage all of the traditional capabilities of pharmaceutical companies to a more or less incremental change of the basic business proposition. Thus, some traditionalists leverage existing capabilities in the context of "targeted medicine," that is, targeting drugs toward well-defined populations where "pharmacogenomics" suggests that the relevant drugs have maximum beneficial impact. Most traditionalists continue the classic "one-size-fits-all" approach, that is, they target drugs to a mass market rather than a smaller target population. Many traditionalists are changing firm boundaries, both upstream and downstream. Thus, they engage in partnerships across the entire lifecycle of a drug, from pre-competitive collaboration related to elucidating targets all the way to commercialization. They build more and deeper ties to universities to identify new treatments. Such a strategy may be complemented by buying smaller innovative firms and/or engaging in licensing agreements in order to get the production of the relevant drug in-house.

This incremental approach to business model innovation may be exemplified by the case of Novo Nordisk A/S (Novo Nordisk). The origins of Novo Nordisk started with the two small Danish companies Nordisk Insulinlaboratorium and Novo Terapeutisk Laboratorium, founded in 1923 and 1925, respectively. Today, Novo Nordisk is a global health care company with nearly a century of innovation and leadership in diabetes care; it also has strong positions within haemophilia care, growth hormone therapy, and hormone replacement therapy. The company is headquartered in Denmark, employs approximately 36,300 employees in seventy-five countries, and markets its products in more than 180 countries. In the following we briefly describe recent changes to the Novo Nordisk business model, relying on the Santos, Spector, and Van der Heyden (chapter 3, this volume) classification of business model changes.

Reactivating

In 2007, Novo Nordisk discontinued its small molecule business to focus on biopharmaceutical research and its protein-based pharmaceuticals. "Our core competences lie within therapeutic proteins, and it is within this area we can make the greatest difference in terms of patient outcomes and company growth," said

Mads Krogsgaard Thomsen, Chief Science Officer of Novo Nordisk. In 2011, Novo Nordisk launched a bottom-of-the-pyramid business model in Kenya, a country in which 250,000 people are in need of insulin, but where 80,000 of those in need have an annual income of between only USD 1,500 and 3,000. To make insulin more affordable and accessible to this segment, the new model has lowered price-markups in the supply chain to the extent that insulin can be obtained at 20 cents daily, equivalent to a third of the previous price.[9]

Relinking

The DAWN™ study was initiated by Novo Nordisk in a partnership with the International Diabetes Federation and an international advisory panel of leading diabetes experts and patient advocates in 2001. The study was undertaken in response to the fact that despite the availability of effective therapies, less than half of individuals with diabetes were achieving adequate glycaemic control. The partnering organizations and experts recognized that new global as well as national knowledge was sorely needed. This required taking a 360-degree view to explore the barriers inhibiting more effective delivery of diabetes care and continuous support to those in need. During that time there were no equivalent global studies stressing the importance of non-medical attitudinal and psychological aspects of diabetes management in multiple countries.

Relocating

As a part of Novo Nordisk's R&D internationalization strategy, the company established an R&D center in Beijing as a wholly owned subsidiary in 2001. They considered the centre to be a bridge between the scientific communities in Europe and China, and being located in the Chinese market, it solidified an important milestone for their future competitive position. Another reason for its location was to provide support to existing activities and to ensure the goodwill of the Chinese government in the future.

THE SERVICE-ORIENTED BUSINESS MODEL

The full-blown service-based business model involves several radical reconfigurations relative to the traditional pharmaceutical business model. Companies that belong to this category aim to expand the value proposition offered to customers by providing, notably, patient support services. To implement the new value proposition(s), new business models are developed which include the identification and development of new capabilities and/or redeployment of capabilities in new ways. In addition, these companies also look for new external partners that can help generate new ideas and facilitate access to the end users.

---

[9] Like many other pharmaceutical companies, Novo Nordisk is offering a patient support program, though only in its US market. Their so-called Cornerstone4care™ patient assistance program is specifically targeted at patients that have household income below the federal poverty level.

Union Chimique Belge (UCB) illustrates these reconfigurations. UCB was founded in 1928 and headquartered in Brussels, Belgium. UCB is a patient-centric global biopharmaceutical leader (notably in epilepsy) focusing on severe diseases in two therapeutic areas, namely the central nervous system and immunology.[10] Here are the main elements of the company's reconfigurations toward a patient-centric business model:

Reactivating

In recent years, UCB has added a range of different (online-and offline-based) patient support programs (e.g., Crohn's and Me™, Parkinson's Well-being Map™, etc.) to assist patients in better understanding their condition, and to guide them to better cope and manage their disease. As the Head of HR in Europe explains: "Typically physicians are only looking at the physical symptoms related to a disease. For example, in epilepsy, physicians are primarily concerned with the number of seizures per week. But the patient demands more; s/he is not just a seizure machine—s/he is a human being. So together with patients we developed an online multi-dimensional well-being map addressing concerns such as quality of life, stigma and sexual activity—things that physicians tend to neglect." It should also be mentioned that all the patient support programs are provided free of charge with equal access for all patients.

Relinking

Over the past five years, UCB has increasingly been active in seeking new partnerships with various stakeholders in the industry, notably with health care payers. Recently, the National Institute for Health and Care Excellence (NICE) reversed a previous decision and has accepted certolizumab pegol (Cimizia®) for the treatment of Rheumatoid Arthritis after UCB offered a risk-sharing agreement with the Department of Health in the United Kingdom. Specifically, UCB agreed to provide the first twelve weeks of Cimizia® (ten pre-loaded 200-mg syringes) free of charge to all patients beginning treatment. Initially, Cimizia® did not receive reimbursement[11] because it was determined that it did not achieve a significant degree of cost-effectiveness. Even more radically, UCB has initiated partnerships with non-traditional stakeholders such as IBM and PatientsLikeMe.

Repartitioning

Traditionally, UCB's market research was primarily performed in-house. However, the ability to gain access to and collect information and data about patients plays an increasingly important role: First, it is instrumental

---

[10]   The company had revenues of €3.4 billion in 2012, operations in approximately forty countries worldwide, 9,000 employees, and is listed on the Euronext Brussels Stock Exchange.

[11]   Reimbursement can be regarded as a "passive" payment system: the insurer/payer covers a fixed percentage of price as set by industry or regulator, thereby limiting out-of-pocket expenses for patients.

to develop and deliver patient-centered solutions; and second, payers are increasingly demanding patient-reported outcomes during their reimbursement. However, as explained by the Vice President and Head of Europe HR: "While data-mining is clearly important, it is not really within our core competencies, companies such as IBM and PatientsLikeMe are better suited for those tasks which is why we have partnered with them. Rather, based on our strong disease understanding it is up to us make sense of all the data and subsequently convert it into solutions for patients."

THE SIMULTANEOUS APPROACH: AMBIDEXTROUS BUSINESS MODEL INNOVATION

This approach constitutes a middle ground between the two extremes (i.e., the traditionalist and the full-blown service model). Companies pursuing the simultaneous approach maintain their incumbent business model, while at the same time pursuing business model innovation, a kind of "ambidextrous" approach (Markides, 2013). From a managerial perspective this involves the challenge that adding a new business model necessitates different and potentially incompatible value-chain activities and supporting organizational designs from the ones that the company has in place for its incumbent model. LEO Pharma A/S (LEO) illustrates the simultaneous approach.

LEO is a stand-alone, research-based pharmaceutical company founded in 1908 in Denmark. The firm develops, manufactures, and markets pharmaceutical drugs to dermatologic and thrombotic patients in more than 100 countries globally.[12] In late 2011, LEO began development of its first real patient support service, namely QualityCare™. In 2012, COLUMBUS was launched as a company-wide project explicitly aimed at business model experimentation; 29 pilot projects ("pilots") were set up in a number of subsidiaries.

Reactivating

In 2013, LEO became a service provider by adding QualityCare™ (an online platform) to its incumbent business model. Currently, QualityCare™ consists of two global frameworks, one for psoriasis and one for actinic keratosis. Through the combination of a customized web page, SMSs, emails, and nurse calls, patients enrolling into QualityCare™ receive information and support about their condition. The aim is to improve the overall treatment outcomes by improving the experience patients receive. One of the COLUMBUS pilots also attempts to improve customer experience by providing a direct-to-patient delivery model. Through an alliance with the Dutch Thuis Apoteek, LEO

---

[12] LEO Pharma has its own sales forces in fifty-nine countries and employs more than 3,900 employees worldwide, with an annual turnover of approximately €1,072 billion Euro. The company headquarters are in Denmark. The company is wholly owned by the private and independent LEO Foundation.

products are delivered directly to patients' households, who, in turn experience greater convenience.

Relinking

Although LEO had an in-house digital department, they used market transactions with respect to QualityCare™. First, LEO lacked the technical capabilities to develop such a platform. Second, due to legal ramifications, LEO had to have a third-party vendor that could collect and store the individual patient data. For that reason, LEO initiated a long-term partnership with Vertic, a strategic digital agency specialized in advanced digital solutions, in 2011.

Repartitioning

While in the past, most strategic thinking with respect to innovation occurred in LEO's headquarters, COLUMBUS is an attempt to move innovation closer to the market. Hence, each pilot is led by a business model innovation or patient engagement manager from the respective subsidiary or region rather than someone from headquarters. Relatedly, to co-develop with patients, LEO initiated the "Psoriasis Frontiers" project in collaboration with the National Psoriasis Foundation (patient organization) in the United States. In particular, a survey is distributed to the members of the patient organization and based on the survey responses LEO selects participants for a full-day workshop. The aim is to identify specific lead users (i.e., creative individuals with strong needs). During the workshop, LEO provides the lead users with an opportunity to express their ideas and concerns related to their life as a psoriatic patient. These workshops have already been fruitful. Following the first three workshops, two concrete projects have started in new product development based on user-generated ideas.

Organizational Challenges of Business Model Innovation in the Pharmaceutical Industry

While there is a general understanding among business model scholars that business models need to be aligned with the firm's overall corporate strategy and organization (Casadesus-Masanell and Ricart, 2010), little business model research has investigated how firms can realign their existing organizational design to facilitate business model innovation and what are the organizational design ramifications of such innovation. We argue that the changing business models in the pharmaceutical industry call for important changes in the organizational design of these firms. Traditionally, firms in the industry have been organized along strictly functional lines, so that each stage in the value chain from initial idea conception to eventual (and much later) marketing of a drug is associated with a distinct organizational unit. This is an organizational design that is geared to facilitate an emphasis on scale and throughput in the production of products. However, changing value propositions toward a higher service-content and restructuring value chains toward more partnerships with external parties call for different, typically more project-based organizations with new roles, task structures, key performance indicators (KPIs), and so on. Overall, the changing business models in the industry call for organizational structures that lie closer to the matrix form than to the functional form.

INTERNAL ORGANIZATION

In an early paper, O'Reilly and Tushman (2004) explicitly linked business model innovation and organizational design. They argued that firms tend to structure business model innovation in one of four basic ways, depending on how radical the business model innovation is: (1) In the *functional design* structure, business model innovation activities are completely integrated into the regular organizational and management structure; (2) the *cross-functional team* still operates within the established organization but outside the existing management hierarchy; (3) *the unsupported team* is a new unit set up outside the established organization and management hierarchy; and (4) in *ambidextrous organizations*, efforts are organized as structurally independent units, each having its own processes, structures, and cultures, yet integrated into the existing top management hierarchy.

In general, all three companies have moved away from purely functionally oriented structures toward more project-based organizations. UCB's introduction of its "patient solution teams"—so called in order to stress that the aim is to provide solutions that go beyond the drug—provides an example. Being team-based, the new organization facilitates the speedy integration of different bodies of knowledge (in particular, UCB wanted to promote the integration of marketing and R&D) so that complex patient needs can be addressed in potentially novel ways. The solution teams were headed by a Vice President and allowed to self-organize. As a result, twelve autonomous units were set up, each with their own processes to fulfill their new patient missions—resembling the organizational flexibility and entrepreneurial spirit embodied in the design of the ambidextrous organization.

Novo Nordisk also seeks a stronger alignment of R&D with marketing. However, the internal organization differs in several respects from the ambidextrous organization of UCB. Novo Nordisk is more focused on exploiting its existing capabilities in developing and commercializing new drugs, rather than developing new services that address more diverse patient needs. This is in line with the traditional value proposition, and for that reason the functional design structure suffices for Novo Nordisk. That is, when new projects are initiated, they often go through the same sequence of stages and are assessed using existing criteria. Although employees may work cross-functionally in such projects, they do so only for a limited period and they still have to carry out their given functional tasks. Overall, Novo Nordisk's approach to its business model is one that emphasizes changing the model in a highly incremental manner by fine-tuning existing elements of the model and the underlying activities, such as sales, market access, disease understanding, and lifecycle management.

In contrast, LEO has yet to implement a formal organization that exhibits an integrated approach to drug development, but a version of (Cooper, 1990) the stage-gate model is currently being developed to mitigate this issue (interview with Director of Scientific Affairs, LEO). Much like UCB, LEO strives to be a solution provider, with products and services co-developed and fitted individually for customers. A new department, Global Patient Engagement (GPE), supports this strategic reorientation. GPE is tasked with extending the incumbent business model to include a service dimension, and in general act as an active and credible integrator of business model innovation activities across the organization. To some extent, this resonates with the unsupported team structure in the sense that GPE performs a range of new value-chain activities (e.g., the development and implementation of an Internet-based patient support service) that lie outside the scope of the established organization. In addition, because of its explorative purpose, GPE has more autonomy than existing departments. Of the three cases we studied for the research in this chapter, LEO is the only company that has a dedicated department with an explicit focus on business model innovation. A reason may be that LEO's incumbent model is less successful relative to the other companies in terms of profitability, hence the more explicit focus on business model innovation.

CHANGING TASK ENVIRONMENTS: COORDINATION REQUIREMENTS AND RESOURCE NEEDS

Business model innovation usually involves addressing new task environments. Turbulent environments tend to force companies to make substantial changes to their internal task structures (Tushman, 1979). Nevertheless, despite the significant changes in the industry, Novo Nordisk has only made minor changes (e.g., the greater integration between R&D and marketing) to their internal task structure (relative to LEO and UCB). Indeed, because Novo Nordisk fundamentally sticks to its existing business model, its activities involve routine tasks that are managed through supervisory control, reliance on formalization, and centralized communication, as opposed to UCB's autonomous patient solution teams. Rather, Novo Nordisk augments its business model by strengthening the company's already strong capabilities within their key functional areas.

LEO's decision to extend its current value proposition to also include services has resulted in a range of non-routine tasks. For example, the development and subsequent launch of QualityCare™ in the subsidiaries were not a routine task. As the Director of Global Patient Engagement explained: "Initially, we very much influenced and limited by our product-centric routines and constantly insisted on applying the same strict processes, principles and tactics that pharmaceuticals go through." In addition, initially QualityCare™ was not included in LEO's short- and mid-term business plans, which made it difficult to get the proper prioritization and resource commitments from the subsidiaries. As a senior manager in Global Patient Engagement explained: "Basically, some [subsidiaries] did not make any kind of market preparation prior to launch, in a sense, they expected that corporate headquarters would just implement the service." As this suggests, the simultaneous approach to business model innovation in LEO has given rise to substantial coordination issues.

Although UCB's incumbent business model had been quite successful in recent years, top management felt that UCB should be more proactive to changes in the external environment; hence, the introduction of the patient solution team structure. An interesting aspect of this structure is that an explicit logic of complementarity was present in the development of the teams. As a Senior Vice President noted: "Market access will play a pivotal role due to the health transaction technology assessments. Companies need to get ready for innovation—not only from product and regulatory approval perspective but also how they get their products reimbursed." This implied that over the course of six months a significant part of the organization was structured around twelve patient solution teams that consisted of people from the most crucial functions such as market access, R&D, regulatory affairs, etc. in an attempt to ultimately speed up the time to market and (perhaps more importantly) address emerging needs from patients, payers, and physicians. Overall, even though this was a radically different way of structuring (e.g., new tasks, reporting lines, goals, and relations among people), UCB was able to limit coordination costs by "getting the complementarities right."

NEW HUMAN CAPITAL PORTFOLIOS

Business model innovation often entails building new assets or combining existing ones in new ways. This may involve specific investments and individual and organizational learning processes.[13] It may also entail building new human resource portfolios by means of hiring and training.

LEO is actively looking for new competences: "To prepare for the more systemic nature of the industry, we search for individuals with hybrid profiles—preferably with knowledge in science, strategy, economics and marketing as well as experience from the fast-moving consumer industry and services" (Senior Director). Furthermore, the establishment of GPE has created two

---

[13] As Winter (2000: 984) states: " … to create a significant new capability, an organization must typically make a set of specific and highly complementary investments in tangible assets, in process development, and in the establishment of relationships that cross the boundaries of the organizational unit in which the process is deemed to reside."

new types of job positions, namely, the roles of business model innovation and patient engagement manager. Initially, these positions were only found in GPE, but lately there has been a steady increase in patient engagement and business model innovation managers at the regional and subsidiary level.

Similarly to LEO, UCB is looking for generalists with capabilities of working cross-functionally and with a taste for the web, social media, and customer relationship management, because of the importance of this to connecting to patients. Further, devices and diagnostics play an integral part in UCB's mission to become a patient solution provider; hence people with skills in these areas are also desired. Perhaps more importantly, UCB is aggressively recruiting for candidates that are savvy in the payer negotiation dimension (interview with the UCB Vice President and HR of Europe).

Novo Nordisk (perhaps to a larger degree) has taken several steps to upgrade their human capital, including the so-called STAR and graduate programs. The former is targeted at PhDs and Post Docs, whereas the latter is intended for Masters students. Both programs are very structured and designed to provide talents with firm-specific competencies.

Market access was highlighted several times during the interviews. In contrast to the other marketing functions, market access functions are typically staffed with several people holding PhD degrees or equivalent qualifications. As argued by Eichler et al. (2010), while getting regulatory approval is still important, it is of little use to industry and patients when a drug is not reimbursed, since access to high-priced drugs will likely be precluded for most patients.

ORGANIZATIONAL PRACTICES

Business model innovation usually involves bringing new tasks inside the company, raising new coordination requirements that in turn demand new organizational practices that can address these requirements. UCB has made significant changes to their underlying organizational practices. Thus, decision rights have been delegated to the Vice Presidents, allowing them to create their own teams (by pulling in people from across the organization) and pursuing projects without interference from the executive committee. This reallocation of decision rights was made explicitly to address the new challenge of creating and delivering patient-centered solutions, namely to move decisions to where the relevant knowledge and information reside (interview with Senior Vice President and President of Europe region, UCB).

However, to further strengthen the new value proposition and structure, UCB introduced a set of other complementing practices. First, the ability to source and process relevant patient data and then convert it into an insight (i.e., a useful and meaningful piece of digested information) that can be incorporated into new services, products, and activities required that UCB increased their internal communication (particularly along the lateral dimension) by installing Lync (an instant messaging service) and recently UCB Plaza (a new intranet platform). Second, to compensate for the lack of human capital that can work with patient solutions in a cross-domain context, the HR department regularly conducts organizational reviews. Based on these, they rotate talents to other positions within the company, where they can have a more significant business impact.

In contrast, LEO has placed less emphasis on developing and diffusing organizational practices that reflect its new strategic orientation. Similarly to UCB's Plaza, LEO has introduced an intranet platform ("Pulse") with the aim of improving internal knowledge sharing. That goal has proven difficult, however, partly because LEO has yet to develop a culture that leverages intranet communication software. Rather, internal knowledge sharing is primarily sought by means of informal communication and meetings. As an additional knowledge sharing practice, LEO's GPE has arranged a variety of global workshops for employees involved in business model innovation. These have been quite useful in exploiting synergies among the business model pilots. In addition, GPE recently introduced the "Elite project" concept to refine some of the more promising business model pilots and in general speed up the pilot phase. Such projects received their own coach from top management and received longer visits from GPE (wherein expert knowledge about business model innovation reside). In conjunction with the launch of QualityCare™, GPE developed a launch excellence tool for the subsidiaries—reflecting the (generic) steps and challenges associated with the implementation of an Internet-based platform.

Not surprisingly, Novo Nordisk has not introduced any new organizational practice to accommodate business model innovation, since the company refines rather than innovates its existing business model. Novo Nordisk probably has the strongest institutionalized practices as reflected in the codification of these practices in the so-called "Novo Nordisk Way": " … We do have a very strong and unique culture. The key objective was hence not to change anything radically; on the contrary, there was a strong wish to reinforce the existing business principles and values." The "Novo Nordisk Way" is based on/encompasses essentially ten statements describing the core practices of Novo Nordisk.[14] To ensure the widespread use and adherence to these guiding practices, Novo Nordisk conducts so-called "value audits." Senior employees are selected as "facilitators" and they travel the organization to interview employees, managers, and internal stakeholders of the units, looking into documents and local business practices. Based on that, an assessment is conducted assessing the degree to which the unit operates its business

---

[14] The ten Novo Nordisk commandments are as follows: "1) We create value by having a patient centred business approach. 2) We set ambitious goals and strive for excellence. 3) We are accountable for our financial, environmental and social performance. 4) We provide information to the benefit of our stakeholders. 5) We build and maintain good relations with our key stakeholders. 6) We treat everyone with respect. 7) We focus on personal performance development. 8) We have a healthy and engaging working environment. 9) We optimize the way we work and strive for simplicity. 10) We never compromise on quality and business ethics." Retrieved November 2014 at: <http://www.novonordisk.com/about_us/novo_nordisk_way/nnway_essentials.asp;>.

in accordance with "Novo Nordisk Way," areas for improvement are high-lighted, and best practices that can potentially be shared across the organization are identified (interview with Corporate Vice President, Novo Nordisk).

PERFORMANCE MEASUREMENT SYSTEMS

The implementation of a business model innovation requires alignment between organizational elements. Performance measurement systems play a pivotal role in this regard because they help to formulate, communicate, and implement business model innovation across the organization. Specifically, they are used to control and influence behavior in the organization and guide the strategic reorientation process (Wouters, 2009).

Overall, none of the companies seem to have completely abandoned the performance management systems traditionally associated with pharmaceutical companies. Hence, measurement related to, for example, sales, time to market, and physician visits are still prevalent in each company. Since the majority of revenues still come from traditional drug sales, this is hardly surprising. Nevertheless, LEO has incorporated a few new KPIs into their existing systems. These are used to keep project leaders accountable. For example, GPE tracks the stages of all business model pilots, including the number of pilots in preparation, progress, on hold/discontinued, and implemented into daily business. Furthermore, the QualityCare™ platform has a number of inbuilt KPIs, such as customer satisfaction linked to the various services it provides and number of enrolled patients. In addition, the platform also tracks the quality of life through the dermatology life quality index (DLQI).[15] Finally, GPE also measures the number of failed business model pilots vs successful pilots and the diffusion of successful pilots to other subsidiaries.

Although Novo Nordisk sticks to existing KPIs, new strategic company goals have been set up to stress the importance of new markets (especially developing countries). For example, to support their bottom-of-the-pyramid strategy, two new indicators measure: (1) the number of least developed countries where Novo Nordisk operates, and (2) the number of least developed countries which have chosen to buy insulin under the best possible pricing scheme. Whereas the former is a proxy of access to essential medicines, the latter addresses the affordability of essential medicines. A number of indicators have also been set up to emphasize the importance of the "Novo Nordisk Way" (interview with Corporate Vice President, Novo Nordisk). The first measures the average of respondents' answers as to whether social and environmental issues are important for the future of the

---

[15] The DLQI was developed in 1994 and it was the first dermatologically specific quality-of-life instrument. It is a simple 10-question validated questionnaire that has been used in over 40 different skin conditions in over 80 countries and is available in over 90 languages. Retrieved November 2014 at: <http://www.dermatology.org.uk/quality/dlqi/quality-dlqi.html>.

company. The second measures the average of respondents' answers as to whether their manager's behavior is consistent with Novo Nordisk values, and the third, the percentage of fulfillment of action points planned arising from "value audits" of the "Novo Nordisk Way" of management and values.

In contrast to LEO and Novo Nordisk, top management in UCB is more skeptical about furnishing their new internal organization with a range of new KPIs. As a Senior Vice President put it: "During the inception of the patient solution teams, we discussed the appropriateness of new KPIs. However, the conclusion was that KPIs tend to become a tick box exercise without adding much value." Relatedly, it would not make sense to impose very rigid KPIs, as they could interfere with the autonomous nature of the teams. Rather, teams that actually succeed in fulfilling a specific patient mission through the process of translating patient insights into a final solution are considered to be a proper indication of solid performance (interview with Vice President and HR of Europe, UCB). Nevertheless, to ensure that resources were congruent with the new business model, subsidiaries had to submit regular reports about their budget allocation. The target explicitly stated that at least 30 percent of the budget must be allocated to non-traditional marketing activities.

DRIVERS AND FACILITATORS OF ORGANIZATIONAL CHANGES

There is general agreement among scholars and practitioners that change processes are complex and challenging for organizations engaged in such initiatives. Change drivers, including culture, vision, leadership, and communication have been argued to facilitate the organizational change process (Whelan-Berry, Gordon, and Hinings, 2003). In all three companies, several of the key informants noted that the external environment had changed substantially in the past decade and this, as such, partly explains the surge in business model innovation activity. Similarly, leadership, and notably the appointment of a new CEO, appeared to prompt organizational change in all three cases.

Novo Nordisk was one of the first companies in the industry to address patient-centricity. Following his appointment as CEO of Novo Nordisk in 2000, Lars Rebien initiated a number of important changes.[16] Traditionally, the physician had been the customer, but Novo Nordisk decided that the user of their products should be the primary customer. A program was initiated that made it mandatory for all Novo employees to meet a diabetic patient. In 2007, Novo Nordisk discontinued its small-molecule business in an effort to focus on biopharmaceutical research and its protein-based pharmaceuticals. "Our core competences lie within therapeutic proteins, and it is within this area we can make the greatest difference in terms of patient outcomes and company growth," said Mads Krogsgaard Thomsen, Chief Scientific Officer

---

[16] Prior to his appointment, he had led the divestment of Novo Nordisk's enzyme business (today Novozymes A/S).

of Novo Nordisk. Ever since its emergence in 2001, "The Novo Nordisk Way" has been instrumental in facilitating Novo Nordisk's strategic direction. As a Corporate Vice President at Novo Nordisk explained: "Only today I used it as an argument to why we [his team] should not dedicate time and resources to a specific project."

In 2003, Roch Doliveux joined UCB and was appointed CEO in 2005. This initiated a period of many far-reaching change initiatives. Like Lars Rebien, Roch Doliveux was also a strong believer in patient-centricity. As noted by the Vice President of New Patient Solutions and Alliance and Portfolio Management, UCB: "Roch was the first person to start bringing patients to our management meetings." A new vision was conceived, making patient-centricity center stage. In 2006, UCB turned into a biopharmaceutical company by acquiring Schwarz Pharma, the largest acquisition in UCB's history. In 2009, UCB made 2,400 of its employees redundant—almost 20 percent of its total workforce. This was the so-called SHAPE project, intended to focus on its core assets (notably within central nervous system), redeploy resources, advance R&D, and simplify its organization. In 2010, UCB replaced One UCB with Shared UCB, an initiative aimed at changing the identity of the company, promoting values such as diversity, connectivity, and co-creation.

In 2011, senior management assembled the "New Journey board", consisting of the eight most talented individuals from across the organization. Their role was two-fold: first, they had a year to explore the dynamics of the industry and what it may look like in 2020, and more importantly, what the implications of this were for UCB. Second, they served as change agents, promoting the new values. These initiatives were part of a greater plan, namely to prepare the company for a fundamental structural change, which was the birth of the patient solution teams in 2012. As the Vice President and HR of Europe, UCB argued: "It is likely that sub-cultures will emerge in very autonomous units such as the patient solution teams, which in turn may stifle knowledge sharing among them. We believed that these initiatives would be able to counterbalance some of the issues derived from such a new structure."

In 2008, Gitte Pugholm Aabo took over as CEO in LEO. A new vision was enacted to focus efforts on dermatology. This was followed by a new growth strategy, called "Going for Gold." This implied change for the hitherto conservative company. In 2009, LEO acquired Peplin Inc. for USD 287.5 million. Although this was a small acquisition relative to other acquisitions in the industry, it was the largest in company history. "Going for Gold" followed the bandwagon by stating that LEO should become a patient-centric company. To implement that change, the "Growing LEO leaders program" was launched in late 2011, aimed at infusing 450 leaders with new values and concepts (e.g., agility, active learning, and business models) to help reshape the organizational culture into a truly global, patient-centric enterprise. Shortly after, GPE was created with the purpose of developing new patient support services and to prepare the ground for business model innovation.

While all three companies seemed to adopt similar change drivers (e.g., leadership, vision, and culture) in their efforts to prompt and facilitate changes or adjustments of their business models, the nature and number of facilitators differ widely. For example, while some of Novo Nordisk and UCB's initiatives (such as "The Novo Nordisk Way" and "Shared UCB") have been implemented across the whole organization, LEO's leadership program was solely directed at 450 individuals. Perhaps not surprisingly given the subsequent changes to UCB's internal organization, UCB has adopted more facilitating drivers relative to the other companies.

MISFIT IN CHANGING BUSINESS MODELS IN THE PHARMACEUTICAL INDUSTRY?

As is evident from the previous sections, a number of different change facilitators (ranging from new structures to new organizational identity) have been implemented to support the various types of business model innovation. However, as Zenger (2002: 80) notes, managers often " ... overlay new measures on existing, functionally-oriented structures; they implement new structures without new performance measures and without new pay systems; they implement new pay systems, but fail to restructure or develop new performance measures."

Although UCB made the most fundamental changes to its business model and underlying organization, they were not able to achieve perfect internal fit among choices with respect to activities, organization structure, and practices. As the Vice President and HR of Europe, UCB notes: "Typically we experience an after shock after such a fundamental change; some people do not fit the new model; others are not happy with their new tasks and responsibilities; and some of the interfaces are not perfectly aligned. Nevertheless, when we change things in UCB we do it fast. The price we pay for that is that we do not achieve perfection the first time." For example, the increased delegation in the patient solution teams was not accompanied by new incentives or performance measures to reflect the peculiarities of their new tasks.

Similarly, though to a larger degree, LEO experienced a number of internal fit inconsistencies. Although there has been a surge in the number of business model innovation managers, these managers have a dual role in the sense that they still have to carry out activities associated with the incumbent model; and since they are still formally held accountable for short-term sales targets, some of them tend to give less priority to their business model pilots. This issue is further exacerbated by the fact that, while COLUMBUS is regarded as a key priority, it has yet to be incorporated into the company's annual business plan (interview with Senior Business Model Innovation Manager, GPE). Similarly to UCB, LEO has not made any efforts to change its current incentive system. "I strongly believe incentives could play an important role in changing certain behaviors in the organization. However, it is a very delicate matter and should be used with caution," said the Director of GPE, LEO. In contrast to UCB and Novo Nordisk, most of LEO's business model innovation facilitators are not formalized or institutionalized across the organization, implying that some subsidiaries put more effort and resources into business model innovation than others. Not surprisingly, these are typically the ones that have most informal interaction with GPE. Relatedly, a recent survey among employees affiliated with COLUMBUS showed that business model innovation has not been sufficiently implemented in LEO.

Given Novo Nordisk's more incremental approach to business model innovation, they have not suffered the same degree of internal inconsistencies compared to LEO and UCB. Although changes have been made to its incumbent model, these have not significantly violated the internal fit among existing activities, policies, capabilities, etc. Rather, these changes aimed at creating a tighter fit to further exploit the success of its incumbent model. However, once Novo Nordisk's incumbent model starts negating value it might be increasingly difficult to facilitate change due to the tight coupling. As Levinthal (1997: 936) asserts: "Incumbent firms may have difficulty navigating a changing environment not only because the changes in the environment negate the value of the organization's assets, but also because a tightly coupled organization may have difficulty adapting to such changes."

Conclusion

We have argued that a number of deep-seated drivers rooted mainly in internationalization, regulatory forces, payer pressure, increased competition from generics producers, and changing technological opportunities are shaking up the pharmaceutical industry, a tendency that has been visible for more than a decade (cf. Gilbert, Henske, and Singh, 2003). The result is a decline in the importance of the traditional blockbuster business model, and an ongoing quest to discover the new model(s) that may yield sustained levels of high appropriable value creation.

This chapter has identified three ideal types that exhibit different degrees of business model innovation, primarily with respect to changing value propositions toward a higher service-content and restructuring value chains toward new activities and external partnerships. This was done in an attempt to examine the organizational design choices accompanied by such models as well as some of the liabilities of such choices. In particular, the focus has been on changes in the internal organization and its underlying task structure. A main finding was the move toward organizational structures that lie closer to the matrix form than to the functional form. UCB's "patient solution teams" was the most extreme case—providing the organizational flexibility and entrepreneurial spirit embodied in the design of the ambidextrous organization. In contrast, Novo Nordisk is more concerned with exploiting existing capabilities to drive the traditional value proposition, and for that reason relies on the functional design structure. In between, we find LEO who has dedicated a new department (GPE) to the task of increasing the service-content and experimenting with new business models—resembling the unsupported team structure in the sense that GPE performs a range of new value-chain activities in parallel with the existing business.

The call for new structures was partly driven by the changing task environment, particularly in the cases of LEO and UCB, which expanded their value propositions toward services. The development and launch of LEO's patient support service QualityCare™ involved a number of non-routine tasks, which gave rise to coordination issues between the new value-chain activities and the existing product-centric routines. UCB was able to mitigate these issues by swiftly structuring a significant part of the organization around the "patient solution teams" and thereby limiting coordination costs by "getting the complementarities right." Unlike the other companies, Novo Nordisk did not encounter any notable coordination issues because they fundamentally stuck to their incumbent business model.

Relatedly, the different types of business model innovation and their accompanying organizational structures were followed by adjustment and/ or renewal in other areas. A recurring theme was need for new human capital to either augment the incumbent model or drive more radical business model experimentation. To address the new non-routine tasks, a number of organizational practices were installed (such as reallocation of decision rights, lateral communication, and workshops) to help with the new coordination requirements. Similarly, new performance measurement systems and KPIs were also set up to support (though to varying degrees) the firms' new strategic reorientations.

A number of drivers prompted the desire or need for change and facilitated the subsequent implementation of the firms' new business models. In particular, the appointment of a new CEO appeared to spark organizational change in all three cases. This was followed by new visions and strategies in the companies to drive the change. Perhaps more importantly, a range of different initiatives (e.g., "Shared UCB," "The Novo Nordisk Way," and "Growing LEO Leaders") were initiated in the three firms to implement change across the organization (though to a larger degree in UCB and Novo Nordisk). Of the three companies, UCB adopted more facilitating drivers than the other companies, which is not surprising given the fundamental change to its internal organization.

The three ideal types also gave rise to an increasing misfit between the traditional organization and the emerging organization dictated by the new models. Another main finding was the problem with internal fit inconsistencies, namely that managers overlay, or introduce new practices and measures in parallel with existing functionally oriented structures (cf. Zenger, 2002). This was evident in all three cases, though to a much lesser degree in Novo Nordisk. For example, while UCB made the most far-reaching changes to its business model and organization, they more or less kept the traditional incentives and performance measures intact—not reflecting the peculiarities of their new service-based model. Selecting a new business model is complex already, but when one considers all the elements of organization required to implement a new model, the problem becomes mindbogglingly complicated. However, if pharmaceutical companies are to succeed in innovating their incumbent models (especially in cases of radical change), the organizational context should be changed in accordance with the new business model in order to realize complementarities and limit coordination costs.

Despite the small size of our sample, we believe that the three ideal types are, at least to some extent, generalizable to other pharmaceutical companies. Companies such as Janssen Pharmaceuticals, Eli Lilly, Abbott, Pfizer, and many more have expanded their value propositions to include different patient support services. GlaxoSmithKline (GSK) restructured its R&D administrative system with the introduction of Centers of Excellence in Drug Discovery (CEDD). As with UCB's patient solution teams, "each CEDD had its own leader and management team, and possessed most of the functions required to move a molecule from discovery to proof of concept" (Pisano, 2012: 6). Several companies (e.g., Sanofi, GSK, and Pfizer) are also exploiting existing capabilities with respect to rare diseases. This is because these so-called orphan drugs tend to enjoy premium prices, reduced marketing costs, increased reimbursement, longer exclusivity, small clinical trials, and fast-track approval procedures.

■ REFERENCES

Adamini, S., Maarse, H., Versluis, E., and Light, D. W. 2009. "Policy Making on Data Exclusivity in the European Union: From Industrial Interests to Legal Realities." *Journal of Health Politics, Policy and Law*, 34 (6): pp. 979–1010.

Angell, M. 2005. *The Truth About the Drug Companies: How They Deceive Us and What to Do about It*. Rev. and updated. New York: Random House Trade Paperbacks.

Barral, É. P. 1996. *20 Years of Pharmaceutical Research Results Throughout the World (1975–94)*. Paris: Rhône-Poulenc Rorer Foundation.

Bianchi, M., Cavaliere, A., Chiaroni, D., Frattini, F., and Chiesa, V. 2011. "Organisational Modes for Open Innovation in the Bio-pharmaceutical Industry: An Exploratory Analysis." *Technovation*, 31 (1): pp. 22–33.

Bodenheimer, T. and Fernandez, A. 2005. "High and Rising Health Care Costs. Part 4: Can Costs Be Controlled While Preserving Quality?" *Annals of Internal Medicine* July, 5, 143 (1): pp. 26–31. Retrieved November 2014 <http://www.ncbi.nlm.nih.gov/pubmed/15998752>.

Bryman, A. 1988. *Quantity and Quality in Social Research*. London; Boston, MA: Unwin Hyman.

Casadesus-Masanell, R. and Ricart, J. E. 2010. "From Strategy to Business Models and onto Tactics." *Long Range Planning*, 43 (2–3): pp. 195–215.

Cockburn, L. M. 2004. "The Changing Structure of the Pharmaceutical Industry." *Health Affairs,* 23 (1): pp. 10–22.

Cooper, R. G. 1990. "Stage-gate Systems: A New Tool for Managing New Products." *Business Horizons,* 33 (3): pp. 44–54.

Daft, R. L. and Weick, K. E. 1984. "Toward a Model of Organizations as Interpretation Systems." *Academy of Management Review,* 9 (2): pp. 284–295.

Danzon, P. M. 2006. "Economics of the Pharmaceutical Industry." *The National Bureau of Economic Research.* Retrieved November 2014 at: <http://www.nber. org/reporter/fall06/danzon.html>.

Demil, B. and Lecocq, X. 2010. "Business Model Evolution: In Search of Dynamic Consistency." *Long Range Planning,* 43 (2–3): pp. 227–246.

Donovan, J. L.1995. "Patient Decision Making: The Missing Ingredient in Compliance Research." *International Journal of Technology Assessment in Health Care,* 11 (3): pp. 443–455.

Doz, Y. L. and Kosonen, M. 2010. "Embedding Strategic Agility: A Leadership Agenda for Accelerating Business Model Renewal." *Long Range Planning,* 43 (2–3): pp. 370–382.

Dunford, R., Palmer, I., and Benveniste, J. 2010. "Business Model Replication for Early and Rapid Internationalisation: The ING Direct Experience." *Long Range Planning,* 43 (5–6): pp. 655–674.

Dyer, G. W. and Wilkins, A. L. 1991. "Better Stories, Not Better Constructs, to Generate Better Theory: A Rejoinder to Eisenhardt." *Academy of Management Review,* 16 (3): pp. 613–619.

Eichler, H.-G., Bloechl-Daum, B., Abadie, E., et al. 2010. "Relative Efficacy of Drugs: An Emerging Issue Between Regulatory Agencies and Third-party Payers." *Nature Reviews Drug Discovery,* 9 (4): pp. 277–291.

Eisenhardt, K. M. 1989. "Building Theories from Case Study Research." *Academy of Management Review,* 14 (4): pp. 532–550.

European Federation of Pharmaceutical Industries and Associations. 2003. "The Pharmaceutical Industry in Figures, 2003 Update." Brussels: EFPIA.

Gilbert, J., Henske, P., and Singh, A. 2003. "Rebuilding Big Pharma's Business Model." *Vivo,* 21 (10): pp. 73–80.

Hedström, P. 2005. *Dissecting the Social: On the Principles of Analytical Sociology.* Cambridge, UK; New York: Cambridge University Press.

Hopkins, M. M., Martin, P. A., Nightingale, P., Kraft, A., and Mahdi, S. 2007. "The Myth of the Biotech Revolution: An Assessment of Technological, Clinical and Organisational Change." *Research Policy,* 36 (4): pp. 566–589.

Hunter, J. 2011. "Challenges for Pharmaceutical Industry: New Partnerships for Sustainable Human Health." *Philosophical Transactions of the Royal Society A,* 369: pp. 1817–1825.

IMS. 2008. *IMS Special Strategy Supplement: Revising the Primary Care Market.* IMS Health.

Isabella, L. A. 1990. "Evolving Interpretations as a Change Unfolds: How Managers Construe Key Organizational Events." *Academy of Management Journal,* 33 (1): pp.7–41.

Istepanian, R. S. H., Jovanov, E., and Zhang, Y. T. 2004. "Guest Editorial Introduction to the Special Section on M-Health: Beyond Seamless Mobility and Global Wireless Health-Care Connectivity." *IEEE Transactions on Information Technology in Biomedicine,* 8 (4): pp. 405–414.

Kaitin, K. L. 2010. "Deconstructing the Drug Development Process: The New Face of Innovation." *Clinical Pharmacology & Therapeutics*, 87: 356–361.

Kane, S. and Shaya, F. 2008. "Medication Non-adherence is Associated with Increased Medical Health Care Costs." *Digestive Diseases and Sciences*, 53 (4): pp. 1020–1024.

Kaplan, S. H., Greenfield, S., Gandek, B., Rogers, W. H., and Ware, J. E., Jr 1996. "Characteristics of Physicians with Participatory Decision-making Styles." *Annals of Internal Medicine*, 124 (5): pp. 497–504.

King, G. 1994. *Designing Social Inquiry: Scientific Inference in Qualitative Research*. Princeton, NJ: Princeton University Press.

Kumar, N., Stern, L. W., and Anderson, J. C. 1993. "Conducting Interorganizational Research Using Key Informants." *Academy of Management Journal*, 36 (6): pp. 1633–1651.

Levinthal, D. A. 1997. "Adaptation on Rugged Landscapes." *Management Science*, 43 (7): pp. 934–950.

Light, D. W. and Lexchin, J. R. 2012. "Pharmaceutical Research and Development: What Do We Get for All That Money?" *BMJ*, 1012; 345; e4348.

Lincoln, Y. S. 1985. *Naturalistic Inquiry*. Beverly Hills, CA: Sage Publications.

Loden, D. J. and Schooler, C. 2000. "Patient Compliance." *Pharmaceutical Executive*, 20 (7): pp. 88.

Luijn, J. C. F., Van Gribnau, W. J., and Leufkens, H. G. M. 2010. "Superior Efficacy of New Medicines?" *European Journal of Clinical Pharmacology*, 66 (5): pp. 445–448.

Mattke, S., Klautzer, L., and Mengistu, T. 2012. "Medicines as a Service: A New Commercial Model for Big Pharma in the Postblockbuster World." Retrieved November 2014 at: <http://www.rand.org/pubs/occasional_papers/OP381.html>.

Miles, M. B., and Huberman, A. M. 1994. "Qualitative Data Analysis: An ExpandedSourcebook." Sage Publications. Retrieved November 2014 at: <http://www.google.com/books?hl=da&lr=&id=U4lU_-wJ5QEC&oi=fnd&pg=PR12&dq=Miles+%26+Huberman,+1994&ots=kC_E-GUVXO&sig=3RzAWRZ0BDVvok2x3zFVcCvW_3o>.

Miller, C. C., Cardinal, L. B., and Glick, W. H. 1997. "Retrospective Reports In Organizational Research: A Reexamination Of Recent Evidence." *Academy of Management Journal*, 40 (1): pp. 189–204.

Munos, B. 2009. "Lessons from 60 Years of Pharmaceutical Innovation." *Nature Reviews Drug Discovery*, 8 (12): pp. 959–968.

O'Reilly, C. A. and Tushman, M. L. 2004. "The Ambidextrous Organization." *Harvard Business Review*, 82 (4): pp. 74–83.

Pisano, G. P. 1991. "The Governance of Innovation: Vertical Integration and Collaborative Arrangements in the Biotechnology Industry." *Research Policy*, 20 (3): pp. 237–249.

Pisano, G. P. 2012. "Creating an R&D Strategy." Harvard Business School Working Paper, No. 12.

Santos, J.F.P., Spector, B., and Van der Heyden, L. 2015. Chapter 3, this volume. "Toward a Theory of Business Model Change."

Scherer, F. M. 2007. "Pharmaceutical Innovation." SSRN Scholarly Paper, ID 902395. Rochester, NY: Social Science Research Network. Retrieved November 2014 at: <http://papers.ssrn.com/abstract=902395>.

Silverman, D. 2006. *Interpreting Qualitative Data: Methods for Analyzing Talk, Text, and Interaction*. Third edition. London; Thousand Oaks, CA: Sage Publications.

Stovall, S. 2010. "Europe's Drug Relator Says Innovation Must Pick Up." *The Wall Street Journal*, December 15, 2010.

Teece, D. J. 2010. "Business Models, Business Strategy and Innovation." *Long Range Planning*, 43 (2–3): pp. 172–194.

Tushman, M. L. 1979. "Work Characteristics and Subunit Communication Structure: A Contingency Analysis." *Administrative Science Quarterly*, 24 (1): pp. 82–98.

US Food and Drug Administration. 2011. "New Molecular Entity Approvals for 2010." Silver Spring, FDA. Retrieved November 2014 at: <http://www.fda.gov/downloads/drugs/developmentapprovalprocess/howdrugsaredevelopedandapproved/drogandbiologicalapprovalreports/UCM242695.pdf>.

Weinman, J. and Petrie, K. J. 1997. "Illness Perceptions: A New Paradigm for Psychosomatics?" *Journal of Psychosomatic Research*, 42 (2): pp.113–116.

Westney, D. E. and Van Maanen, J. 2011. "The Casual Ethnography of the Executive Suite." *Journal of International Business Studies*, 42 (5): pp. 602–607.

Whelan-Berry, K. S., Gordon, J. R., and Hinings, C. R. 2003. "The Relative Effect of Change Drivers in Large-scale Organizational Change: An Empirical Study." *Research in Organizational Change and Development*, 14: pp. 99–146.

WHO. 2002. "Integrating Prevention into Health Care." Fact Sheet No. 172.

WHO Media Centre. 2003. "Adherence to Long-term Therapies: Evidence for Action."

Winter, S. G. 2000. "The Satisficing Principle in Capability Learning." Strategic Management Journal, Special Issue, 21 (10–11): pp. 981–996.

Wouters, M. 2009. "A Developmental Approach to Performance Measures—Results from a Longitudinal Case Study." *European Management Journal*, 27 (1): pp. 64–78.

Yin, R. K. 2003. *Case Study Research: Design and Methods*, vol. 5. Thousand Oaks, CA: Sage Publications.

Zenger, T. R. 2002. "Crafting Internal Hybrids: Complementarities, Common Change Initiatives, and the Team-based Organization." *International Journal of the Economics of Business*, 9 (1): pp. 79–95.

13 The Organizational Dimension of Business Model Exploration

Evidence from the European Postal Industry

MARCEL BOGERS, KRISTIAN J. SUND, AND JUAN ANDREI VILLARROEL

Introduction

In this chapter, we explore the organizational challenges that affect incumbent organizations in mature industries, when they react to disruptive changes in their environment by searching for new business models—the logic by which organizations create and capture value. In particular, we will present evidence from the European postal industry, which has undergone fundamental changes that challenged national postal operators' traditional business model of physical mail collection, sorting, and delivery. The empirical base of this case is primarily drawn from a set of interviews with the three managers who were responsible for business model innovation in the Danish, Portuguese, and Swiss postal operators. These national postal operators have found it necessary to react to the disruptive changes in the industry by reinventing the fundamental logic of how they create and capture value, mainly by venturing into the digital world.

The literature on business models shows that a multitude of understandings and definitions of the concept exist (e.g., Foss and Saebi, chapter 1 in this volume; Osterwalder, Pigneur, and Tucci, 2005; Zott, Amit, and Massa, 2011). There appears to be a general consensus that a business model explains the logic with which an organization creates, delivers, and captures value (e.g., Chesbrough and Rosenbloom, 2002; Osterwalder and Pigneur, 2010; Teece, 2010). Furthermore, the business model includes linkages between activities, or between the organizational units that perform certain activities, as well as with external stakeholders in the firm's attempt to create, deliver, and capture value (Santos, Spector, and Van der Heyden, chapter 3 in this volume; Stieglitz and Foss, 2009; Zott, Amit, and Massa, 2011). In the words of George and Bock (2011: 99), "a business model is the design of organizational structures to enact a commercial opportunity." Business model innovation thus implies a new way to organize business (Casadesus-Masanell and Zhu, 2013). Some organizational themes surrounding this type of innovation have been discussed in the literature, such as organizational barriers to business model innovation, but most aspects of "organizing" and of organizational design have been largely ignored so far (Foss and Saebi, chapter 1 in this volume).

Building on this observation, and on the above conceptualization of business model innovation, this chapter will explore the organizational aspects of business model innovation in a specific industry. Our particular objective then is to describe the organizational aspects of business model innovation in the European postal industry by exploring how incumbent postal operators dealt with some of the major changes that affected their organizations. Within the case of the European postal industry, the Danish, Portuguese, and Swiss postal operators are particularly useful cases because they do not compete directly with each other; they represent geographic areas of Europe that, in our opinion, have somewhat distinctive national cultures; and they all needed to develop new services, capabilities, and structures, in order to adapt to industry changes. We will not claim perfect representativeness in our sample, but at least a significant degree of independence and diversity.

A key finding is the possibility of distinguishing between two stages of business model innovation, namely business model *exploration* and business model *exploitation*. We deliberately use similar labels for these two stages to those used by March (1991) to describe two different types of organizational learning, to hint at the fact that these types of learning may be associated with the two stages of business model innovation. We posit that each of the stages could engender particular sets of organizational challenges, while our chapter specifically focuses on business model exploration and the relevant organizational challenges that have led to a large degree of organizational experimentation in the case studies here. We find a number of dynamic tensions between the core business and the new innovative business models with cognition, the struggle for resources, and capabilities to be among the most relevant challenges for these firms.

The European Postal Industry: A Shifting Business Landscape

The European postal industry has been undergoing a rapid transformation over the past two decades. Among the main drivers of this transformation is the growth of the Internet, which has resulted in digital substitution for many applications of letter mail. At the same time, e-commerce has resulted in substantial growth in the parcel delivery business. Other drivers have been the gradual liberalization of the industry by national governments and the European Union alike, as well as moves toward privatization in some countries. Figure 13.1 illustrates some of the effects of this transformation in terms of (1) a move from physical to digital mail processing, (2) a move from private mail items toward mainly business mail items, and (3) a move from monopoly positions toward increased competition.

National postal operators have responded in a variety of different ways to these changes. For example, some have diversified their national business, whilst others have internationalized their activities (Dietl and Jaag, 2011). Where before these operators held national monopolies and cooperated in cross-border activities, they now compete much more directly with each other.

Today, the industry continues to face the challenges of digital substitution, with gradually declining physical mail volumes in all European countries (Figure 13.2). The recent global economic downturn has only accentuated this decline, and although some economies in Europe have partially recovered

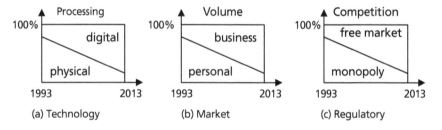

Figure 13.1 Changing landscape exerting pressure on the postal industry

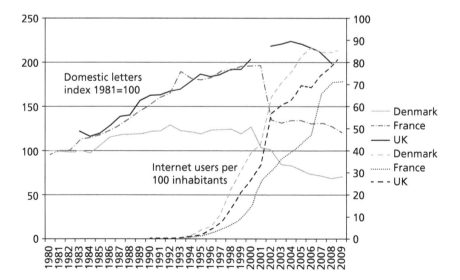

Figure 13.2 Growth in physical mail items and Internet users

economically, there is no reason to believe that mail volumes, in particular for private addressed mail, will ever recover in any significant way. Having said this, some areas, such as direct mail (essentially advertisement mail) and hybrid mail[1] may still hold potential for postal operators. Direct mail is an integral part of the media mix, and electronic commerce has contributed to a healthy development in the traffic of parcels. Increases in global trade have also benefitted all areas of logistics, a business in which many posts are active. Finally, competition and digitization in financial services, along with the growth in world trade, have strengthened those postal operators active in banking, finance, and insurance (Sund, 2011).

In response to the changes in the business environment, important strategic choices have been or are being made by individual postal operators. Most have by now thoroughly modernized their operations, and downsized their workforce in order to remain profitable despite the sharp decline in volumes (Brannström and Lindeborg, 2011). Just as importantly, postal operators are maintaining their grip on the letter market. There will presumably always be some level of need for the physical exchange of documents, and postal operators are in a good position to provide this service at a lower cost than competitors due to economies of scale, in addition to being able to offer hybrid solutions. Furthermore, many postal operators have experienced positive growth in the traffic of parcels. Others have diversified into other business areas, such as finance, logistics, or mobile telecommunications (Sund, 2011). Finally, there are those that have started experimenting with entirely new business models, which is also the focus of this chapter.

Reinventing the Post: Business Model Innovation in the Danish, Portuguese, and Swiss Postal Operators

CASE BACKGROUND

Similarly to many other national postal operators, the Danish, Portuguese, and Swiss posts have all attempted to create new business models over the past decade or so. During the summer of 2012, we conducted interviews with the three managers directly responsible for the business units involved in these efforts, all of whom have been in their positions during all or most of the period during which these changes took place. The interviews were semi-structured,

---

[1] Hybrid mail refers to new service offerings by post, where a digital file is turned into a mail item, or a mail item into a digital file—on the one hand, allowing business customers to outsource the printing of documents to be mailed, and on the other hand, allowing all customers to have their mail items scanned.

and aimed to explore the organizational themes surrounding their attempts at change. Triangulation was achieved through the use of written sources of secondary data, such as industry and yearly reports. In order to ensure construct validity, we used a general structure of questions and framework to investigate and subsequently analyze the different themes related to how they dealt with some of the major changes that affected their organizations. The initial interview guideline consisted of the following categories of questions: example(s) of business model innovation (successfully implemented); business model components (extant, novel); relation to existing sources of revenue (substitute, complement); relation to the organization's activities (core, peripheral); and impact in relation to key capabilities (enhancing, destroying).

The interviews were recorded and transcribed, and the authors independently analyzed the content of transcriptions and listened to the recordings, in order to characterize and classify the themes. We then compared and discussed the themes in order to arrive at a common interpretation. This thematic analysis was theory-led, in the sense that we did not aim to create new labels for the identified themes, but rather to identify relevant labels within the extant organizational theory literature. To support our analysis, we constructed a resource–activity–revenue value-structure comparison from the examples of business model innovations (cf. Figure 13.3 and Table 13.1). We compared each finding across cases as an analytic technique. We thus built on the general principles of grounded theory to construct categories of findings by developing categories of information (open coding), interconnecting the

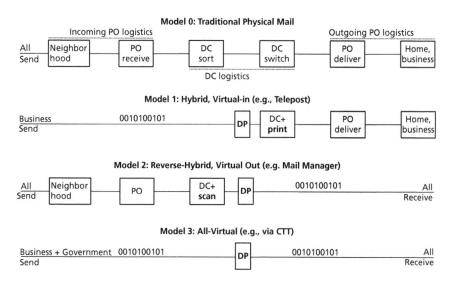

Figure 13.3 Three business model innovations and new organization configurations

Notes: DP = digital processing; PO = Post Office; DC = distribution center;
All = personal mail + business + government. Examples drawn from the Portuguese postal operator CTT.

Table 13.1 Three business model innovations and new value structure

	Business Model			
	Model 0	Model 1	Model 2	Model 3
	Traditional mail (baseline)	Hybrid virtual-in (e.g., Telepost)	Reverse hybrid virtual-out (e.g., Mail Manager)	All-virtual (e.g., Via CTT)
Description	Offers all customers (personal mail, business, government) the universal ability to communicate with one another via physical correspondence	Offers businesses a cost-efficient and eco-friendly alternative for sending mass correspondence that is printed at the delivery location	Offers personal mail customers a flexible and eco-friendly alternative for receiving correspondence that is scanned at the sending location	Offers businesses and government a secure online communications mechanism to exchange real-time correspondence that is spam-free
Organizational Resources				
Existing				
Incoming PO logistics	Y			
Outgoing PO logistics	Y	Y		
DC logistics	Y	Y	Y	
New				
Physical-to-digital conversion			Y	
Digital-to-physical conversion		Y		
Digital processing		Y	Y	Y
Cost Structure				
Transportation				
Neighborhood–PO	Y		Y	
PO–DC	Y		Y	
DC–DC	Y		O	
DC–PO	Y	Y	O	
PO–destination	Y	Y	O	

Sorting			
Inbound	Y	Y	
Outbound	Y	Y	O
Switching			
All-physical	Y		O
Physical-to-digital conversion		Y	Y
Digital-to-physical conversion		Y	
Storage			
Physical	Y	Y	Y
Digital	Y	Y	Y
Customer Segments			
Personal correspondence	Y	Y	Y
Business correspondence	Y	Y	Y
Government correspondence	Y		Y
Value Proposition			
Communication	Y	Y	Y
Real-timeliness (instant delivery)			Y
Cost-efficient (scale/scope)	Y	Y	Y
Flexibility (anytime/anywhere)	Y		Y
Ecological (environment friendly)	Y	Y	Y
Revenue Streams			
Mailing services	Y	Y	Y
Scanning services		Y	Y
Printing services		Y	
Cloud services			Y

Notes: DC = distribution center; PO = Post Office; O = optional; Y = applies; [blank] = does not apply. Linked to Portugal's CTT examples in Figure 13.1.

categories (selective coding), and building a story that connects the categories (axial coding), upon which the final findings are based (Dougherty, 2002; Strauss and Corbin, 1990). As such, the construction of categories—identified key organizational issues—can be seen as an iterative process that establishes common meaning across multiple observations (Locke, 2001).

The postal story is particularly salient as a context within which to explore the organizational themes that surround business model innovation. The Danish, Portuguese, and Swiss postal operators are all organizations with histories stretching back centuries. In fact, the Portuguese Post Office was already established in the 1520s, the Danish Post Office in its original form dates back to 1624, and the Swiss Post Office to 1675. As government agencies, all three, for many years, pursued a business model originally advocated by Sir Rowland Hill, a nineteenth-century teacher, inventor, and social reformer. In 1837, Rowland Hill edited a pamphlet with his plan for a "Post office reform." The two main points were the reduced and uniform postage (the penny post), and payment by the sender instead of the recipient. The price of a stamp was to be uniform irrespective of distance sent within the nation's geographical boundaries. This is essentially the cornerstone of the business model that was used for both mail and parcels relatively unaltered until now.

For most of the twentieth century the three postal operators studied here experienced steady development in the traffic of letter mail, relatively highly correlated with general economic growth. Simply put, more industrial and service sector output led to more pieces of mail traveling through the postal system (Ansón et al., 2006). The same was true for the telecommunications sector, which at the time was the twin sibling of the postal sector. The 1990s saw the first major signs of change for the three operators studied. The telecommunications arms of the three companies were all divested, liberalized, and privatized. The Portuguese Post Office (CTT) was incorporated in 1991, and the Danish Post Office in 1995, in an effort to prepare for liberalization and privatization following a similar model as the telecommunications industry. The Swiss Post Office followed in 1998. The expectation was that the postal operators should become profitable in preparation for a later possible sale by government, which pushed the postal operators to seek opportunities for diversification and to improve efficiency. Investments in automation became important. It was during the late 1990s that all three postal operators started exploring alternative business models. The focus appears to have been on models that embraced the observed explosion in mobile and Internet technologies, as a way to secure future business growth. In the words of one of the interviewed postal managers:

> There is a shift of paradigm … we have not only to reinvent our traditional business, because we can no longer come to you offering solutions and services only for the physical part of the business, we have to reinvent ourselves, we have to create new services, new sources of revenue and so on.

In our analysis of the case of the European postal industry, based on the three postal operators, we start by discussion of the general distinction between business model *exploration* and *exploitation*. Following this we examine the dynamic tensions that develop between old and new business models, which we suggest leads to a great degree of experimentation and subsequent trial-and-error learning in organizational design. We find that the tensions revolve around issues of cognitive barriers, due to the strong dominant logic of the core business, issues of capability substitution, issues of struggle for resources, and issues of product substitution.

THE EXPLORATORY ORIGINS OF BUSINESS MODEL INNOVATION

Much of the business model innovation literature builds on an underlying assumption that such innovation starts with an idea or technology, around which a business model is then created (Chesbrough, 2010). This idea may be generated by an entrepreneur (Gruber, MacMillan, and Thompson, 2008), by an organization (Mitchell and Coles, 2003), or through collaborative efforts between organizations (Chesbrough, 2003). A novel business model may thus accompany an existing or new product or service, aiming for example to fully realize the new product's commercial value (Zott, Amit, and Massa, 2011), or may be aimed at creating or capturing value from an existing value network (Amit and Zott, 2001; Hamel, 2000). The common view therefore appears to suggest that at least some of the key elements comprised in the description of the business model, such as product, production process, sources of supply or market, are already known or pre-exist as the actual business model is generated. At least one ingredient in the new business model recipe is known at the start of the process of business model innovation.

Our interviews suggest significantly more uncertainty during the initial stages of business model innovation than is suggested in this literature. During initial stages of innovation, very little, if anything, was known or understood by the three postal operators regarding future business models. All three decided to explore opportunities in the digital space (examples of actual innovations that resulted from this exploration can be found in Table 13.1 and Figure 13.3), but the efforts at business model innovation in this context appear largely to have been driven by necessity, not by vision. Furthermore, there was no roadmap or initial idea that launched the process. In the words of one manager: "We need to modify our business without necessarily exactly knowing how to earn money in the future." The three postal operators all initiated their process of new business model exploration around the turn of the century, but without a clear picture of what the end products or services would be, who the users would be, what production would look like, or how to create or extract value. In a sense, *all* elements of the future business model appear to have been unknown at the beginning. This uncertainty seems to have continued for years after the initial explorations, which showed in the discussion of the innovations introduced more recently. One interviewee commented that "we don't exactly know how it will look in ten years from now." This also implied that, in line with Chesbrough (2010), the incumbent operators needed to engage in a process of experimentation (Thomke, 2003) and effectuation (Sarasvathy, 2008). We therefore suggest that there are two distinct stages of business model innovation: a more uncertain exploration stage, which precedes the later exploitation stage, during which at least one ingredient of the business model recipe has been determined.

TENSIONS BETWEEN THE OLD AND NEW BUSINESS MODEL

Our interviews suggest that business model innovation fosters particular organizational challenges. One such challenge is linked to missing future revenue estimates in the early stages of exploration. The exploratory efforts require an investment in time and resources for an outcome that is not just uncertain, but in the early stages entirely unknown. To illustrate how business model innovation affects the organization, Table 13.1 and Figure 13.3 contain some examples of new business models developed by the Portuguese Post Office. Consider the business model innovations depicted in Table 13.1, by contrasting each to the established baseline model. Each new business model builds on important organizational resources of the original (traditional) model. With the original model already being strained by the tensions of the business environment, the expanded workload placed on some of the existing resources (distribution centers in our example) only makes the strain more acute. As such, the existing organization and its constituency may not perceive any benefits from this use of resources to enable unproven models to emerge. This is a particular challenge when the general strategic focus in the core business is on optimization, cost cutting, and the downsizing of the workforce.

One manager told us: "it is not a big revenue generating business for the company, and that's the weak part in knowing that the company is switching from the physical to the digital." Another comment unveiled the importance of shielding the exploratory efforts from the rest of the organization during this early stage: "We really managed to make sure that from the top … these organizations were protected. You need to have ownership by the CEO, otherwise this is destroyed extremely quickly." The stories of these three post offices confirm the particular challenge to business model innovation pointed out by Christensen (1997), whereby established technologies may be given more resources since they appear more profitable, at least in the short term. However, all three postal operators were able to effectively overcome this barrier. As one manager stated: "We quite successfully managed to convince the internal management that, for the moment, revenue streams shall not be the most important KPI [key performance indicator]."

The tensions between the existing business model and the new one may persist beyond the strict exploration stage and into the exploitation stage of

business model innovation. The tension becomes one between the exploitation of existing core activities and the refinement and establishment of
the new business models. Where Amit and Zott (2001) discussed conflicts
between traditional and new configurations of firm assets in general, we
found in the postal cases that this type of tension is due to several specific
factors.

First, there is the type of creative destruction that leads to old capabilities
diminishing in importance as new capabilities are being created. For these
postal operators, the new capabilities developed in the business unit responsible for new business models within, for example, IT, had the potential to
replace existing capabilities in the core business:

> We could have the mandate to being responsible really for [the development
> of digital services] for all divisions ... but if we did that we destroyed
> probably something very successful, something existing. The acceptance
> [by the organization] would be probably moderate ... if we took away their
> responsibility for developing their services (Postal Manager, illustrating this
> conflict between new and old capabilities).

Figure 13.1 conceptually explains this process of creative destruction of
capabilities facing the postal organizations.

Second, there is the potential for products and services using the new business model to compete directly with those using the old business model:

> There are three kinds of services probably ... There are services which help to
> even stimulate demand for existing business. They are of course those who
> have the least resistance among the managers who are responsible for [the] core
> business and traditional business ... The second group, they are indifferent ...
> these kinds of services neither substitute for the existing services, nor do
> they generate additional demand ... the third category is then going into the
> substitution (Postal Manager, illustrating the competition between new and
> old business models).

Figure 13.2 empirically illustrates how the volume of personal letter mail-
ing has been falling since the beginning of this century, as the volume of
digital communications increased.

Third, there is the internal negotiation or even struggle for scarce organizational resources:

> In different stages ... over the ten years, sometimes we felt we needed more
> resources to keep up the pace to make something new ... I think one of the
> big challenges for us ... is access to IT resources. That has perhaps been the
> biggest barrier: that we are competing and working to get access to the same
> IT resources within the company (Postal Manager, illustrating the struggle for
> scarce organizational resources).

Table 13.1, in the section entitled Organizational Resources, comparatively
shows, on the one hand, how some of the *existing* inbound/outbound logistics
resources are shared by new and old models, and, on the other hand, how *new*
digital-processing resources are needed to enable the new models to operate.

ORGANIZATIONAL COGNITION

A particular set of organizational issues are linked to the cognitive activities of sense making, sense giving, and even organizational learning, that naturally accompany the process of business model innovation. Chesbrough and Rosenbloom (2002) argue that the success of established business models may influence the information flow that gets routed into or filtered out of decision making about business model designs. Thus, the dominant logic of the existing business model directs the way executives perceive new ideas for business models (Bettis and Prahalad, 1995; Chesbrough, 2010). In the case of the postal organizations examined in this chapter, there was evidence of the importance of the dominant logic as a cognitive barrier (Nonaka, 1994). As one manager stated:

> [The] more I work at the post, the more I am attached to [a] conclusion. It is that we have to make an effort to think outside the box they put us in when I started working for this corporation. Because they format our mind: "the business of the post is this" and so on. And at a certain time you realize that I am thinking the way those guys want me to think."

We would argue that business model innovation must *de facto* involve an element of sense making, as the people involved in creating the new business model must frame or re-frame what they conceive of as their recipe for business, and thus create a new shared meaning (Weick, 1995). One manager stated that "we need to change our minds, how we do business and how we develop our business." Once it has emerged, the new shared meaning (the business model) must be communicated more widely across the organization and a particular focus emerging from our interviews seems to be this need to "change minds" within the wider organization, through sense-giving activities. Such sense-giving activities include internal communication. Creating a shared meaning is an effective way to overcome the tensions discussed earlier, including changing the dominant logic (Chesbrough, 2010). In the words of one manager:

> Whenever we launch these projects there is also a lot of internal communication. So we are very careful when announcing this new solution, what are the benefits. When [a particular product] was conceived ... designed and developed ... there were also a lot of actions to explain internally what [the product] was about ... so that people could understand.

ORGANIZATIONAL DESIGN

The organizational design accompanying new business models is one critical aspect that was emphasized by our interviewees. As one manager stated: "When we started this, ten years ago, we discussed in detail how it would be organized." A key element expressed by all three organizations was that the new business models had to co-exist and grow alongside the stagnating traditional business model that has nevertheless continued to provide the organizations with the lion's share of its revenues and profits. Key decisions needed to be made regarding where to position the new business models in the organizational structure, but also in the power structure, as alluded to earlier in this chapter. Ensuring sufficient power in the struggle for scarce organizational resources is one concern; another is ensuring that a more innovative and creative culture is allowed to exist in relation to the new business model. Such decisions have all been made on the basis of some degree of trial and error, and, in general, experimentation seems to have been an important capability in establishing the details, particularly relating to organizational design, of the new business models (Sosna, Trevinyo-Rodríguez, and Velamuri, 2010). In the words of one interviewee: "We are constantly learning and also modifying the way in which we organize ourselves." In the case of all three organizations a new business unit was created to house the new business models being explored, effectively shielding the innovation process from the rest of the organization, even from top management. One manager stated:

> We needed to keep this a bit separate from the ordinary business. Not too separate. We decided to go for, to make a separate company, but we saw that there would be some extra cost, extra handling, extra management, if we do that. So we decided to establish a business unit. That was one way of handling a kind of small new-biz idea and small new-biz organization, but still keep it within the company. But in some extent able to give them some free room and some free space to innovate, to sell, to operate and so on.

In the case of new business models that have nothing to do with the core business, the tensions between the new and old businesses are likely to be low and the core business will have little interest. As one interviewee stated: "We develop e-health and e-government systems, and there the acceptance from the other divisions is of course extremely high, because they don't see themselves in that business." However, as previously discussed (see Figure 13.3 and Table 13.1), some innovations may be seen as either complementary to the core business (see Table 13.1: model 1 and model 2), or potential substitutes for it (see Table 13.1: model 3), and it was essential to establish some degree of cooperation with the core business (see Figure 13.3: model 1 and model 2). For other projects the new business unit might even offer its services directly to the core business, to help them solve problems of their own.

Deciding where exactly to house the new business unit thus appears to have been a critical and difficult decision for all three organziations. One of them openly stated that the "unit has moved a bit around over the years." For some time they were part of one business owned by the operator that was perceived to have complementary capabilities, but the issue of organizational power became a problem: "We were part of their organization … because we actually wanted to kind of merge some of our product … but then we discovered that this company ... was not as visible and doesn't have the power the postal operator has. So we went back to the postal operator." When the new business unit aims to directly sell their services to other divisions the positioning is likewise of great importance. Another interviewee illustrated this: "We will probably try ... to position it directly reporting to the CEO ... and one of the organizational problems or difficulties is that because it is embedded today in one of our divisions, some other divisions may claim independent responsibility ... to choose a developer or a consultancy from where they [want]."

Cultural differences between the new and old business units do not appear to have received much attention in the business model innovation literature. In our interviews organizational culture appeared to be an important element of organizational design, accompanying, to some extent, the cognitive issues previously discussed. Part of the problem lies with differences in the competences needed in the new business unit, which are more often than not completely different to those needed in the traditional business model. We discuss this in more detail later. Another part of the problem is simply the need for a more creative workforce in the new business unit. This comes back to the need to "give them some space ... to innovate." One interviewee went a step further in telling us that it "is clearly an advantage if people are a little bit remote from the head office. The head office has an existing way of doing business ... you develop much more successfully if you give these people space and distance from the core."

Although the discussion above seems to suggest a need to separate the new business unit from the core, our respondents also suggested that there were efforts at socializing members of the new business unit. In one case, for example, the operator had launched a business by acquiring a small technology start-up, and ultimately populated this start-up with a mix of people that included the original founders. "The second group [of employees] comes from the head office, being integrated into this new incubator, and the third group [are] recruits from outside ... [it] is a quite good mix of people who were formally a part of [the] founding team and of the head office."

In terms of designing and positioning the innovative business unit, the picture that emerges is one of a dynamic tension between positioning the unit sufficiently close to the top management for there to be strong support and protection from the top, but also sufficiently far from the top management to maintain a separate identity and culture. It is this tension that has most likely led to the high degree of organizational experimentation in the case of the Danish, Portuguese, and Swiss postal operators.

SOURCING AND BUILDING NEW ORGANIZATIONAL CAPABILITIES

Any discussion of the organizational dimensions of business model innovation needs to acknowledge the importance of resources and capabilities. Four issues in particular were picked up in our study: (1) the question of how to create and grow the new capabilities necessary to explore (and exploit) new business models, and in particular the choice of sourcing the capabilities through organic creation versus external acquisition; (2) what subsequent production competences have the potential to become core and thus need to be internally developed; (3) the question of complementarity between capabilities of the new and the core businesses; and (4) questions related to open innovation, and in particular the role of customers in shaping the business model innovations.

In all three postal organizations studied here, strategic acquisitions appear to have played a key role in building rapidly the capabilities necessary to create business model innovations. Speed was a key to success. One interviewee stated that an acquisition gave the organization the potential to establish key capabilities with one quick investment, rather than having to slowly develop these capabilities. Another described how "we needed competences we didn't have ... we need the skills from people who have competences from the IT side of the business world. They need to have a feeling about data, output management, and different kind of services, software, and also to some extent integration into existing businesses." This particular organization, on one occasion, made a strategic acquisition in the form of a 50/50 joint venture with a consortium of potential future customers, as a way to not only secure the necessary production capabilities but also at the same time to gain the access to and commitment of a number of large customers (commercial banks in this particular case). However, all three postal operators appear to have been very aware of the need to protect their ideas. One manager told us: "at a certain point we decided to develop something on our own ... nowadays we are not using any third party solutions." Another explained how in the case of a particular new service there was an initial joint venture, from which the postal operator ultimately withdrew, in order to develop its own solution. In this case, the solution was seen as complementary to the core business and the indication seems to have been that this solution was therefore important to control entirely in-house.

An important consideration when acquiring new capabilities was the potential for complementarity with existing capabilities. One postal operator considered this complementarity when making a particular strategic acquisition where "they had already traveled miles along the roadmap, but they had no sales [and] marketing capabilities and also no network. They were not able to really access their target groups. But they had the technology and they had the brains." Another obvious example of complementarity is how all three postal operators have attempted to leverage the established postal brand when approaching new customers. One interviewee told us that "it would have been impossible for postal operators to set up this operation if all society, and corporations that in most cases compete against each other, did not trust [the post office]." Another referred to an important mix between "old credibility and new competences," and stated that the post office was now in a position to "help you no matter where you go, physical or digital or other ways." He further stated how "we discussed the other day that it is still incredible that we can call up ... most companies ... and be able to establish a meeting on the board of directors' level."

The potential of open innovation approaches, in particular those that involve the end user, have been described at length in the recent literature (Bogers, Afuah, and Bastian, 2010; Huff, Moeslein, and Reichwald, 2013). The postal organizations examined here have all experimented to some degree with involving the customer; in particular there has been close contact with the government as a large customer for whom new services can be developed. However, one manager expressed some degree of disappointment at the current level of general customer involvement, stating that

> "We could ... be better in taking the customer inside of our innovation project. The customer is still kind of outside of our innovation process ... we have been very good ... to try to assess what kind of commercial value we see in this product. And some of the reason, product features are coming even from the government from this kind of tenders, where they have some kind of specification of needs, we could see that could bring value not only to the government, but as a general service offer to the market."

The degree of sharing of capabilities openly with customers has thus been very limited in the cases of these postal operators. Further organizational challenges to effectively addressing business model innovation would include not only how internal capabilities enable such linkages to customers but also how they enable effective integration and efficient value capture, in line with the overall business model (Chesbrough and Bogers, 2014; West and Bogers, 2014).

Discussion and Conclusion

Business model innovation is gaining momentum as a field of academic inquiry, and in practice as a purported source of competitive advantage in a changing world. As the core of this book advocates, the literature on innovation and strategic management requires an expanded framework to explain how competitive advantage can be effectively derived from business model innovation. In particular, changes in the external environment—be they (1) of a technological nature, (2) linked to changes in the regulatory environment, or (3) linked to changing market needs, or any combination thereof—that make the organizational resources held by the firm obsolete, go beyond the successful incumbent firm's ability to accumulate valuable protected assets and achieve unique positioning in its industry. In the context of incumbent firms, the organizational dimension of business model innovation takes center stage, where timely managerial responsiveness and the ability to renew the firm's competences to deal with such changes is paramount to the firm's survival.

Through the postal service industry case study presented in this chapter, we have described how a number of different organizational themes played an important role in the business model explorations (and likely subsequent exploitation) of these organizations. We focused our discussion on the themes that appear to have led to experimentation in organizational design. Our findings point to several areas of particular interest. Besides being important areas for future research, these findings also highlight points of concern for managers dealing with the organizational challenges of business model innovation in practice.

The evolving dynamics of resource-, product-, and capability-related tensions between the stagnating core and the developing business models appear in our case study to shape elements of the organizational design in the new business units. The particular design elements that are thus identified in our study, which deserve further validation and examination, can be defined as: (1) organizational structure in terms of reporting relationship to the core business; (2) power relations to existing product divisions; (3) the degree of decentralization of decision making; (4) the degree of vertical integration; and (5) the degree of separation and protection of the sub-culture of the new business unit. We cannot from our small study discuss design optimality as such, but we certainly have evidence of experimentation and trial-and-error learning in organizational design. We also have a suggestion that the two stages of business model exploration and business model exploitation may somehow have influenced the degree of experimentation. In other words, the higher uncertainty in the very early stage of business model innovation may have led to greater experimentation than has been the case more recently in these cases. Alternatively, the two stages may have required distinctive organizational designs, which remains a subject of future inquiry.

While our findings are based on long-established firms in a single industry, we expect similar processes and patterns to occur in other industries that go through a disruptive change that challenges the underlying assumptions of the incumbents' business model. More generally, any organization that goes through a process of business model exploration and experimentation will be faced with significant organizational barriers that need to be overcome in the face of business model innovation. As such, we believe that many of our findings are generalizable to other industries and settings, although future research will have to determine what the external organizational conditions and processes are for business model innovation, including exploration and exploitation, for various organization types, industries, and other contextually different situations.

■ REFERENCES

Amit, R. and Zott, C. 2001. "Value Creation in e-Business." *Strategic Management Journal*, 22 (6–7): pp. 493–520.

Ansón, J., Cuadra, R., Linhares, A., Ronderos, G., and Toledano, J. 2006. "First Steps Towards New Postal Economics Models for Developing Countries: Learning from the Latin American Experience." In M. A. Crew and P. R. Kleindorfer (eds), *Liberalization of the Postal and Delivery Sector*. Cheltenham (UK): Edward Elgar, pp. 217–236.

Bettis, R. A. and Prahalad, C. K. 1995. "The Dominant Logic: Retrospective and Extension." *Strategic Management Journal*, 16 (1): pp. 5–14.

Bogers, M., Afuah, A., and Bastian, B. 2010. "Users as Innovators: A Review, Critique, and Future Research Directions." *Journal of Management*, 36 (4): pp. 857–875.

Brannström, P. and Lindeborg, P. 2011. "The Journey for Future Success—PostNord, Meddelande." In D. Osborn and K. J. Sund (eds), *The Future is in the Post Vol II: Perspectives on Transformation in the Postal Industry*. Faringdon: Libri Publishing, pp. 23–28.

Casadesus-Masanell, R. and Zhu F. 2013. "Business Model Innovation and Competitive Imitation: the Case of Sponsor-based Business Models." *Strategic Management Journal*, 34: pp. 464–482.

Chesbrough, H. W. 2003. *Open Innovation: The New Imperative for Creating and Profiting from Technology*. Boston, MA: Harvard Business School Press.

Chesbrough, H. W. 2010. "Business Model Innovation: Opportunities and Barriers." *Long Range Planning*, 43 (2–3): pp. 354–363.

Chesbrough, H. W. and Bogers, M. 2014. "Explicating Open Innovation: Clarifying an Emerging Paradigm for Understanding Innovation." In H. W. Chesbrough, W. Vanhaverbeke, and J. West (eds), *New Frontiers in Open Innovation*. Oxford: Oxford University Press, pp. 3–28.

Chesbrough, H. W. and Rosenbloom, R. S. 2002. "The Role of the Business Model in Capturing Value from Innovation: Evidence from Xerox Corporation's Technology Spin-Off Companies." *Industrial and Corporate Change*, 11 (3): pp. 529–555.

Christensen, C. M. 1997. *The Innovator's Dilemma: When New Technologies Cause Great Firms to Fail*. Boston, MA: Harvard Business School Press.

Dietl, H. and Jaag, C. 2011. "Postal and Regulatory Reform in Intermodal Competition." In D. Osborn and K. J. Sund (eds), *The Future is in the Post Vol II: Perspectives on Transformation in the Postal Industry*. Faringdon: Libri Publishing, pp. 49–55.

Dougherty, D. 2002. "Building Grounded Theory: Some Principles and Practices." In Joel A. C. Baum (ed.), *The Blackwell Companion to Organizations*. Oxford: Blackwell, pp. 849–866.

Foss, N. J. and Saebi, T. 2015. Chapter 1, this volume. "Business Models and Business Model Innovation: Bringing Organization into the Discussion."

George, G. and Bock, A. J. 2011. "The Business Model in Practice and Its Implications for Entrepreneurship Research." *Entrepreneurship Theory and Practice*, 35 (1): pp. 83–111.

Gruber, M., MacMillan, I. C., and Thompson, J. D. 2008. "Look Before You Leap: Market Opportunity Identification in Emerging Technology Firms." *Management Science*, 54 (9): pp. 1652–1665.

Hamel, G. 2000. *Leading the Revolution*. Boston, MA: Harvard Business School Press.

Huff, A., Moeslein, K., and Reichwald, R., eds. 2013. *Leading Open Innovation*. Boston, MA: MIT Press.

Locke, K. 2001. *Grounded Theory in Management Research*. Thousand Oaks, CA: Sage Publications.

March, J. G. 1991. "Exploration and Exploitation in Organizational Learning." *Organization Science*, 2 (1): pp. 71–87.

Mitchell, D. and Coles, C. 2003. "The Ultimate Competitive Advantage of Continuing Business Model Innovation." *Journal of Business Strategy*, 24 (5): pp. 15–21.

Nonaka, I. (1994). "A Dynamic Theory of Organizational Knowledge Creation." *Organization Science*, 5 (1): pp. 14–37.

Osterwalder, A. and Pigneur, Y. 2010. *Business Model Generation: A Handbook for Visionaries, Game Changers, and Challengers*. Hoboken, NJ: Wiley.

Osterwalder, A., Pigneur, Y., and Tucci, C. L. 2005. "Clarifying Business Models: Origins, Present, and Future of the Concept." *Communications of the Association for Information Systems*, 16: pp. 1–25.

Santos, J. F. P., Spector, B., and Van der Heyden, L. 2015. Chapter 3, this volume. "Toward a Theory of Business Model Change."

Sarasvathy, S. D. 2008. *Effectuation: Elements of Entrepreneurial Expertise*. Cheltenham, UK: Edward Elgar.

Sosna, M., Trevinyo-Rodríguez, R. N., and Velamuri, S. R. 2010. "Business Model Innovation Through Trial-and-Error Learning: The Naturhouse Case." *Long Range Planning*, 43 (2): pp. 383–407.

Stieglitz, N. and Foss, N. J. 2009. "Opportunities and New Business Models: Transaction Cost and Property Rights Perspectives on Entrepreneurship." In J. A. Nickerson and B. S. Silverman (eds), *Economic Institutions of Strategy (Advances in Strategic Management)*, Vol. 26. Thousand Oaks, CA: Sage Publications, pp. 67–96.

Strauss, A. and Corbin, J. 1990. *Basics of Qualitative Research: Grounded Theory Procedures and Techniques*. Newbury Park, CA: Sage Publications.

Sund, K. J. 2011. "Transformation and Diversification in the Context of Regulated Industries: The Case of Poste Italiane and PosteMobile." *International Journal of Management Education*, 9 (4): pp. 77–85.

Teece, D. J. 2010. "Business Models, Business Strategy and Innovation." *Long Range Planning*, 43 (2): pp. 172–194.

Thomke, S. H. 2003. *Experimentation Matters: Unlocking the Potential of New Technologies for Innovation*. Boston, MA: Harvard Business School Press.

Weick, K. E. 1995. *Sensemaking in Organizations*. Thousand Oaks, CA: Sage Publications.

West, J. and Bogers, M. 2014. "Leveraging External Sources of Innovation: A Review of Research on Open Innovation." *Journal of Product Innovation Management*, 31 (4): pp. 814–831.

Zott, C., Amit, R., and Massa, L. 2011. "The Business Model: Recent Developments and Future Research." *Journal of Management*, 37 (4): pp. 1019–1042.

■ INDEX